China and the Founding of the United States

China and the Founding of the United States

The Influence of Traditional Chinese Civilization

Dave Xueliang Wang

LEXINGTON BOOKS
Lanham • Boulder • New York • London

Published by Lexington Books
An imprint of The Rowman & Littlefield Publishing Group, Inc.
4501 Forbes Boulevard, Suite 200, Lanham, Maryland 20706
www.rowman.com

86-90 Paul Street, London EC2A 4NE

Copyright © 2021 by The Rowman & Littlefield Publishing Group, Inc.

All rights reserved. No part of this book may be reproduced in any form or by any electronic or mechanical means, including information storage and retrieval systems, without written permission from the publisher, except by a reviewer who may quote passages in a review.

British Library Cataloguing in Publication Information Available

Library of Congress Cataloging-in-Publication Data

Names: Wang, Dave Xueliang, author.
Title: China and the founding of the United States : the influence of traditional Chinese civilization / by Dave Xueliang Wang.
Other titles: Influence of traditional Chinese civilization
Description: Lanham : Lexington Books, [2021] | Includes bibliographical references and index. | Summary: "This book examines the influence of China on the founding of the United States. The author analyzes how the Founding Fathers recognized China's distinct approaches to agriculture, architecture, and philosophy and drew from them as they sought to establish a political identity and heritage for the United States"—Provided by publisher.
Identifiers: LCCN 2021032397 (print) | LCCN 2021032398 (ebook) | ISBN 9781793644350 (cloth) | ISBN 9781793644374 (paperback) | ISBN 9781793644367 (ebook)
Subjects: LCSH: United States—Civilization—Chinese influences. | United States—Civilization—18th century. | United States—History—1783-1815. | Constitutional history—United States. | United States—Relations—China. | China—Relations—United States. | China—History—Qing dynasty, 1644-1912.
Classification: LCC E163 .W36 2021 (print) | LCC E163 (ebook) | DDC 303.48/27305109033—dc23
LC record available at https://lccn.loc.gov/2021032397
LC ebook record available at https://lccn.loc.gov/2021032398

*For my parents Yuxian Gong and Cai Wang,
my parents-in-law Xianrong Li and Guozhu Gu
For Ping, Amy, and Dan with all my love*

Contents

List of Figures	ix
List of Tables	xi
Foreword	xiii
Acknowledgments	xv
Introduction	1
1 Ideas from the East: The Founders Used Chinese Wisdom to Build a Flourishing Society	13
2 Technologies from the East: How the Founders Leveraged Chinese Technologies in the North American Colonies	47
3 Plants from the East: The Founders' Efforts to Transplant Chinese Plants to North America	89
4 The Influence of Chinese Material Culture on Early U.S. History	103
5 Trade with the East: The Founders' Efforts to Open China Trade	121
6 Confucianism in the Making of U.S. Democracy	143
7 The Founders' Legacy	229
Epilogue	233
Bibliography	237
Index	257
About the Author	265

List of Figures

Figure 1.1	"From The Morals of Confucius," Pennsylvania Gazette, Published by Benjamin Franklin in 1737	35
Figure 2.1	A Scene of the Grand Canal of China in the Eighteenth Century	50
Figure 2.2	Allen Well, the Only Relics of Franklin's Great Wall	57
Figure 2.3	Chinese Pavilion in William Chambers's *Designs of Chinese Buildings, Furniture, Dresses, Machines and Utensils*, Published in London in 1757	66
Figure 2.4	Thomas Jefferson's Drawing of a Typical Pavilion the Albemarle Academy in 1814	67
Figure 2.5	Silk Production in China in the Eighteenth Century	71
Figure 3.1	George Washington's Handwriting in His Diaries	96
Figure 4.1	Franklin's Chinaware in the Franklin Museum	110
Figure 5.1	Thomas Jefferson's Handwriting, Jefferson to Albert Gallatin, August 15, 1808	126
Figure 6.1	Benjamin Franklin's Theory Chart	157
Figure 6.2	Franklin and His Friends at the Constitutional Convention	165
Figure 6.3	Chinese Civil Service Examination in 1590	175

List of Tables

Table 3.1 List of Chinese Plants That John Ellis Recommended Should Be Brought into North America   90

Table 4.1 American Ships and Exports of Tea at Guangzhou (Canton) 1785–1800 (in Pounds)   108

Foreword

The creation of the United States in the late eighteenth century was a bold experiment with new ideas that would change the course of history forever. Such ideas as power residing in the hands of the people, representative government, freedom of religion, and the peaceful transition of power were a direct challenge to a European world largely dominated by autocratic governments that withheld many of these rights from their own citizenry.

The American Founding Fathers, however, did not develop their novel ideas of government out of thin air. Quite the contrary. They had been educated and profoundly influenced by certain Western schools of thought as expounded by the European Enlightenment. For example, the Founders were very open to the concepts of popular rule and responsibility of the government to the service of the people. One of the most important of these political philosophers was the Englishman John Locke (1632–1704). Locke developed his important Social Contract Theory in his *Two Treatises on Government (1689 and 1690)*. Locke's ideas strongly opposed the divine right of kings in favor of a form of government based on the consent of the governed as long as the latter agreed to forfeit certain liberties in exchange for basic rights to life, liberty, and property.

Several leaders of the Enlightenment such as Locke and Voltaire studied Chinese philosophy broadly and became greatly fascinated with the ideas of Confucius. They held various Confucian governing principles in high regard. Locke, for instance, recognized the Confucian notion of the right of rebellion if a government failed to protect its subjects' natural rights. The people had the right to revolt and establish a new ruling class.

Several of America's Founding Fathers learned about Chinese culture and philosophy through their studies of the European Enlightenment. It is through such studies that Chinese cultural and even technological influence played a key role in the creation of the United States. Chinese culture began to play an important role when some of the US founders began looking for resources and ideas that could be implemented when building a new nation. Chinese ideas and techniques were varied. Several Founding Fathers sought guidance from Chinese philosophy in their efforts to cultivate personal virtue and to educate younger generations as to how to be virtuous. The Founders also adopted some Chinese inventions and technologies to facilitate the social and economic development of the new nation.

Dr. Dave Xueliang Wang analyzes the scope of Chinese cultural and technological influence on what would become the United States even before this country was born. Dr. Wang clearly demonstrates how such American leaders as Benjamin Franklin and Thomas Jefferson were deeply influenced by Chinese philosophical ideals and technology. Traditional histories of the United States give the impression that our Founders were uniformly influenced by European Enlightenment thinkers while not shedding any light on Chinese contributions. Dr. Wang's book offers up a whole new avenue to understand the complex thinking process that led to the creation of the United States. Chinese ideas filtered through the Enlightenment had a key role in developing our American heritage.

I am especially impressed with Dr. Wang's in-depth examination of how the Founders introduced Confucian ideas of government in their creation of a new political institution in the United States.

Dr. Daniel A. Metraux
Professor Emeritus of Asian Studies
Mary Baldwin University
Staunton, Virginia
October 2020

Acknowledgments

Over twenty years ago, as a doctoral candidate at the University of Arizona, I fortuitously came across a volume of *The Papers of George Washington* as I was preparing reading materials for one of my undergraduate courses. When I flipped through the anthology, I was struck by one of Washington's journal entries from July 1785, in which he described sowing Chinese flowers in his estate at Mount Vernon. This seemingly innocuous reference piqued my curiosity: how and why were these Chinese flowers in the American colonies on the other side of the world and was it possible that other aspects of Chinese culture had found their way overseas as well?

These questions sparked a decades-long academic journey on how the U.S. Founding Fathers were influenced by Chinese culture. After more research, I discovered that Washington had supported opening trading channels with China and was fond of Chinese porcelain; that Benjamin Franklin had promoted Confucian moral philosophies on numerous occasions; and that the Founding Fathers had drawn from Chinese civilization in many other ways as they crafted their new nation. I drafted an initial textbook based on the Founders' papers for my undergraduate students with the support of my academic advisors, Professors Michael Schaller, Jing-shen Tao, and Brian McKnight.

I want to begin by thanking Professors Schaller, Tao, and McKnight for their interest, support, and encouragement as I began my academic journey. I would also like to thank the late Dr. Wilton Dillon, Senior Scholar Emeritus of the Smithsonian Institute, for his wonderful mentorship over the years. I wish to convey my heartfelt appreciation for Dr. Mark Skousen, a direct descendant of Benjamin Franklin and the Benjamin Franklin Chair of Management of Grantham University, for his support and feedback.

Many others deserve special recognition and gratitude for their thoughtful and critical feedback over the years. They include Dr. Walter Isaacson, the former Chairman and CEO of CNN News Group, the president of the ASPEN institute, and the author of bestsellers including *Benjamin Franklin, an American Life*; Dr. Phanindra Chakrabarti; Dr. Claude-Anne Lopez; Dr. Hwa-Wei Lee; Dr. David L. Sills; Dr. Richard Stichler; Dr. Eleanor Munro; Dr. Don Munro; Dr. Seymour S. Block, and Dr. Bernadette Li.

I also wish to express my appreciation for Dr. Daniel Metraux, Dr. Lucien Ellington, Dr. Page Talbott, Dr. Bayasakh Jamsran, Dr. Penelope Corfield, Dr. Ka Sing Chua, and Mr. Jeffrey Bingham Mead for helping bring my papers to readers. I would also like to express my appreciation to the following individuals for the support over the years: Dr. Daniele Fiorentino; Dr. Guisy De Sio; Professor Ralph Robert Bauer; Professor John Ruff; Professor Tokubumi Shibata; Professor Shu-Ping lee; Professor Xiping Zhang; Professor Jiaquan Liu; Professor Jizhi Wang, Professor Yan Liang; Dr. Wenzhao Tao; Dr. Yongqian Guan; and Dr. Guiqi Ji.

Furthermore, I wish to thank Roy Goodman, Former Librarian & Curator of Manuscripts Library & Museum of the American Philosophical Society, Joe Dillulo, Reference Librarian, Library & Museum, American Philosophical Society, Bruce Kirby, Reference Librarian, Manuscript Division, Library of Congress, and Charles Greifenstein, Associate Librarian & Curator of Manuscripts Library & Museum of the American Philosophical Society, Susannah Carroll, Assistant Director of Collections & Curatorial, the Franklin Institute, and Karie Diethorn, Chief Curator, Independence National Historical Park, National Park Service, U.S. Department of the Interior, for their help in providing original manuscripts and documents. I would also like to extend my gratitude to *The Virginia Review of Asian Studies*, *Education about Asia* and *Journal of Asian Studies* for publishing several of my articles in their journals over the years.

I finally wish to thank several editors from the Lexington Books, including Ms. Kasey Beduhn, Alexandra Rallo, and especially Acquisitions Editor Eric Kuntzman and Mikayla Mislak. Their help was vital for the publication of this book.

ILLUSTRATION ACKNOWLEDGEMENT

Grateful acknowledgement is made to the following for use of the images that appear in this book: Manuscripts Library & Museum of the American Philosophical Society (Figures 1.1), Wikimedia Commons (Figure 2.1), *William Chambers' Designs of Chinese Buildings, Furniture, Dresses, Machines and Utensils* (Figure 2.3), Albert and Shirley Small

Special Collections Library, University of Virginia (Figure 2.4), New York Public Library Collection (2.5), Manuscript Division, Library of Congress, Washington, DC. (Figures 3.1), The Franklin Institute, Philadelphia (4.1), Thomas Jefferson Papers at the Library of Congress, Manuscript Division (Figure 5.1), The Library of Congress (Figure 6.2), and, Peking Palace Museum Wikimedia Commons (Figure 6.3).

Introduction

The mere thought of Chinese cultural influence on the founding of the United States is unimaginable to some. Misperceptions—colored by potent, biased assumptions in the West—are partially responsible.

This book presents evidence—based on investigation and analysis—that the founders of the United States were influenced by many positive elements derived from their study of classical Chinese culture. Indeed, those same cultural and technological influences on what emerged as an independent, forward-thinking nation started even before the formal Declaration of Independence on July 4, 1776.

Although China was geographically far removed from direct contact with the British Empire's North American colonies, the newly independent, fledgling American republic's relationship with China started with trade in 1784 via the voyage of the *Empress of China*.

Chinese civilization was the object of intrigue, curiosity, and admiration by Europeans and Americans alike, carried over by Jesuits' articles and translations of Chinese classics and conveyed via the stories of traders and explorers. Influences varied. They ranged in the areas of agriculture, architecture, Confucian-based moral and political philosophies, and more as foundations for the new American nation evolved.

Recognized as one of the world's most stable and successful classical civilizations, China offered many lessons and precedents that were distinct from the founders' European heritage. To some of the founders, China presented a model for the young nation. They welcomed positive elements from Chinese civilization while integrating those same elements into an authentic, distinctly American culture that in turn had been inspired by the winds of change propelled by the best of the Age of Enlightenment that had emerged in Europe.

In pre-independence America, the founders introduced elements of Chinese agriculture practice to the North American colonies, facilitating advances in social and economic development. Chinese-inspired agriculture and industrial technologies bolstered the colonial economies, resulting in prosperity for the Americans. Personal letters and other records indicate that Benjamin Franklin obtained seedlings of select Chinese plants. Washington and Jefferson experimented with Chinese flowers in their personal gardens.

Franklin—America's most famous original scientist and philosopher—expressed great interest in Chinese industrial technologies, such as milling, heating, shipbuilding, and papermaking. He and fellow statesman Benjamin Rush promoted silk-making (or sericulture) in North America. Almost simultaneously, Thomas Jefferson was influenced by classical elements of Chinese architecture where it took form at Monticello.

George Washington, Alexander Hamilton, and Gouverneur Morris were inspired through published literature by explorers on the Grand Canal of China. Later, these same Chinese technological innovations would influence the construction of the Erie Canal and spur the development of New York City.

America's Founding Fathers modeled efforts toward the self-cultivation of personal virtue. In turn, younger generations of Americans had free access to published works where traditions associated with Confucian philosophy were articulated. The founders frequently drew from Confucian philosophies, embracing a new political framework for the young nation. Many prominent colonists—Benjamin Franklin, Thomas Jefferson, John Adams, Thomas Paine, John Bartram, and Jedidiah Morse, among others—demonstrated their respect for Confucian moral philosophy, incorporating its principles into American culture.

Chinese culture became important when some of the U.S. founders looked for resources that could be mobilized in their efforts to build a new nation after declaring independence from Great Britain. Chinese contributions to early America were varied. In their efforts to cultivate personal virtue and to educate the younger generations to be virtuous, several Founding Fathers sought guidance from Confucian philosophy. The founders also adopted Chinese inventions to facilitate the social and economic development of colonies and introduced elements of Chinese agriculture to North America.

The timing of China's impact on America's founders is particularly significant. Why did such American notables as Benjamin Franklin, Thomas Jefferson, George Washington, and John Adams focus their attention and insatiable curiosity on China? As one of the most stable, and certainly the most long-lived civilization in the world, to the architects of the new, independent American nation China was the subject of intrigue and admiration. Charles Thomson, known as the "Samuel Adams of Philadelphia" and a close associate of Franklin's, mirrored his mentor's feelings in recognizing the connection between China's success as a society and its large population: *"Could we be so fortunate as to introduce the industry of the Chinese, their arts of living and improvements in husbandry, as well as their native plants, America might be in time become as populous as China, which is allowed to contain more inhabitants than any other country, of the same extent, in the world."*[1]

When the storm clouds of revolution started to gather momentum, Franklin astutely promoted his theory of social progress by combining Confucian political ideas with the Western tradition of social progress. Franklin and other statesmen would later apply this theory to craft the U.S. Constitution, thus solidifying the foundations of the nation's political infrastructure. Chinese civilization provided an opportunity to fuse its social and political frameworks with notions of the European Enlightenment, supporting the Founding Fathers' efforts to create a uniquely American tradition. These same founders sought to establish a political identity that was distinct from European aristocratic traditions.

Washington observed that Europe *"has a set of primary interests"* that *"have none or a very remote relation"* with the United States, and as a result, the new nation should *"pursue a different course."* Jefferson also admired the *"desirability of Chinese isolation,"* and recommended that there should be in *"place an ocean of fire between the new nation and Europe."*

Facing British trade sanctions after the Revolutionary War, U.S. political leaders initiated efforts to build direct economic connections with China. Robert Morris and George Washington were directly involved in the opening of trade with China with support from other American founders. One important reason behind Thomas Jefferson's quest for westward expansion through the acquisition of the Louisiana Purchase in 1803 was the search for a shortcut to China, and late in his presidency, he communicated the desirability of creating something like a U.S.-China policy.

IDEAS FROM THE EAST

During the colonial era, the founders realized the value of Chinese civilization and applied certain Chinese ideas to improve social and economic life in the colonies. In the wake of the victory of the revolution, some main founders even looked to China as a guide for their new nation. They regarded China's long agrarian tradition as a rich resource from which the newborn United States could learn valuable lessons. Chinese ideas, particularly Confucian moral philosophy, inspired the founders. Chinese ideas that the founders believed to be of great value to North America included certain practices of the Chinese imperial government, the social mobility based on meritocracy, and gentry spirits of community services.

Franklin probably read *The Morals of Confucius* as early as his 1724–1726 stay in London. From his autobiography, it appears that—partially influenced by Confucius—Franklin focused on the cultivation of personal virtue as early as 1726. Confucius designed the path for virtuous perfection—from oneself to one's family, to the state, and then to the whole empire. In 1737, Franklin introduced this notion to American colonists. Franklin agreed with Confucius that a man should not only cultivate personal virtues but also disseminate them to others—including political leaders. In a 1749 letter to George Whitefield, one of the most influential of all colonial American clergy, Franklin advocated that knowledge of Confucian ideas could even foster social tranquility.

Confucius yearned to see people, especially rulers, adopt better morals and more compassion. For him, virtue was the foundation of a good and flourishing empire. Confucius asserted that rulers should behave appropriately in court and at home because they would certainly be imitated. During the Revolutionary War, Franklin worked hard to promote this important principle. After the American victory, some veterans wanted permanent recognition for their triumph through formation of an order of hereditary knights. Franklin raised objections to this idea by using Confucius's principle of social promotion.

Confucius maintained that law and punishment were the minimum requirements for order, but social harmony can only be achieved by virtuous behavior. In his enormously influential *Poor Richard's Almanack*, most of Franklin's advice for readers stresses virtues such as hard work, frugality, and attention to family.

Jefferson, concerned about his reputation and honor, was highly conscious of his behavior and positively regarded the well-loved and respected Chinese Prince Wu, featured in The Great Learning—one of the canons of Confucianism—as an exemplary role model for other leaders. Thomas Paine wrote that Confucius, like Christ, was a great moral teacher. Paine reiterated this point in an article he wrote a decade later for *The Prospect*, a New York magazine. As a book of morals there are several parts of the New Testament that are good, but they are no other than what had been preached in the East several hundred years before Christ was born. Confucius, the Chinese philosopher, who lived 500 years before the time of Christ, says, "acknowledge thy benefits by the turn of benefits, but never revenge injuries."[2]

Dr. Benjamin Rush, an ardent patriot, in a 1798 essay on education in the new republic, asserted that "the only foundation for a useful education in a republic is to be laid in Religion. Without this there can be no virtue, and without virtue there can be no liberty, and liberty is the object and life of all republican governments." Having expressed his veneration for Confucianism that "reveals the attributes of the Deity," Rush declared that he would rather see the opinions of Confucius "inculcated upon our youth, than see them grow up wholly devoid of a system of religious principles."[3] John Adams, in a letter to Thomas Jefferson, criticized the English theologian and natural philosopher Joseph Priestley for ignoring Confucius in his writing.

James Madison, father of the U.S. Constitution, hung a portrait of Confucius at his home. It was probably not a historical coincidence that Confucian moral ideals were respected in an era when some U.S. leaders sought to liberate American culture from what they viewed as failed European ideologies.

CHINESE TECHNOLOGY

Chinese innovations in areas such as heating technology, silk production, porcelain ware, manufacturing, navigation, canal construction, and even regarding the construction of the Great Wall of China found their way to North America via Europe. The founders realized this information could be used to promote social and economic development. In 1763, Benjamin Franklin, in an effort to promote the creation of a colonial silk industry, sent prominent American academic and Congregationalist minister Ezra Stiles copies of Chinese prints illustrating silk production. Scarce energy resources also stimulated Franklin to examine Chinese technology. By the 1740s, the growing colonial population resulted in noticeable diminishment of forests, which supplied fuel. The heating of houses was growing more expensive. Wood utilization was inefficient, and much of the heat—83 percent, Franklin estimated in many cases—was lost up chimneys. Franklin carefully studied the Chinese technology of heating their houses in the cold winters. Franklin in part used these principles to invent the Pennsylvania Fireplace, which was later improved upon and became the famous Franklin Stove. Better heating technology made the cold winter less harsh and induced more colonists to move to the North—which later contributed greatly to its development as a manufacturing center. Franklin also carefully studied Chinese ship construction and publicized the Chinese practice of watertight compartment construction.

During the French and Indian War, 1754–1763, Franklin introduced the notion of a defensive wall—similar to the Great Wall of China—into public debate. He maintained that building an American Great Wall was the most efficient way to protect the thirteen colonies. Franklin again raised the notion of the Great Wall during the Revolutionary War.

A few Chinese technological innovations were also used to advance certain economic goals prior to American independence. Some colonial leaders, for example, viewed porcelain manufacturing as essential to national economic self-reliance. Chinese porcelain, like tea, had been a major colonial import. Benjamin Rush was among the first who advocated building a porcelain factory in North America with the intent of overcoming American dependence on British imports.

Gouverneur Morris, prominent founder of the republic, studied China's Grand Canal. With his encouragement, the New Yorkers built the Erie Canal, connecting New York to the Midwest. The canal played a role in New York City's rise, triggered an explosion in canal building, facilitated economic growth, and linked the Northeast with the Great Lakes region.

The colonists' pursuit of domestic Chinese porcelain ware became a powerful call for patriotic support of American economic independence. Franklin, in London when Rush was promoting colonial porcelain production, echoed this sentiment in a letter to his wife: "I am pleased to find so good progress made in the China Manufactory. I wish it Success most heartily."[4] The American China Manufactory in Philadelphia became noted for its quality, and more importantly, succeeded in cultivating patriotism as it challenged Britain's monopoly of the product and indirectly contributed to the struggle for independence.

Explicit examples of Chinese architectural influences are present in one of America's most historic buildings. Jefferson developed a new type of architecture by incorporating certain Chinese designs into his famous neoclassical-style home, Monticello. Jefferson used Chinese lattice in many buildings, including Barboursville, the Orange County, Virginia home he designed. Jefferson also planned to build a Chinese pavilion when he remodeled Monticello in the last decade of the eighteenth century.

THE FOUNDERS AND CHINESE PLANTS

"The greatest service which can be rendered any country is, to add a useful plant to its [agri]culture, especially a bread grain" (Thomas Jefferson). Agriculture was the major component of the American colonial economy and employed 90 percent of the workforce. As the founders searched for foreign plants to improve agriculture, China was considered a rich source of possible valued additions. Some colonists realized that many valuable trees, unknown in Europe, grew in the northern provinces of China and could be transplanted. Numerous plants were brought into North America. For instance, paper mulberry was introduced in 1754.

In 1765, Franklin encountered Chinese soybeans in England and sent the soybeans to John Bartram, a famous colonial botanist. In 1772, Franklin also sent Chinese rhubarb seeds and Chinese tallow trees to North America.

Tallow trees, which were highly useful in the manufacturing of candles, soap, cooking oil, and herbal remedies, spread widely throughout the South. George Washington, owner of Mount Vernon plantation, had a lifetime preoccupation with agriculture. Washington worked hard to plant Chinese flowers and recorded his experiments in detail in his diary, suggesting how much he valued his effort.

THE FOUNDERS AND CHINA MARITIME TRADE

The *Empress of China*, the first American international commercial ship launched after national independence, left New York for Canton, China, on February 22, 1784. About a month after the *Empress of China* departed, Washington told Jefferson that "from trade our citizen will not be restrained."[5] Washington's words had significant meaning for the fledgling United States. The successful sailing of the *Empress of China* symbolized not only the hope of trade itself but also made a statement to the world—the United States is now an independent nation.

Efforts to build direct commercial relations with China began during a critical period following the American Revolution. The new national government, operating under the Articles of Confederation (1781–1789), was grappling with the consolidation of thirteen independent states while the economy and nation's finances were on the brink of chaos. With traditional trading partners now closed to the fledgling nation, new ones had to be cultivated—or otherwise, political independence might well have proven to be a barren victory.

France, Holland, and other European countries were willing to export goods to the United States but not purchase American products—which attracted some Americans to cast their gaze toward China. Superintendent of Finance Robert Morris took the lead in arranging the *Empress of China* venture by personally financing much of the voyage. Washington also contributed to the effort by recommending Samuel Shaw (1754–1794) to be the ship's supercargo—the officer in charge of the critical task of sales and purchases of cargo.

As soon as the *Empress of China* returned to New York, American founder Richard Henry Lee wrote to Thomas Jefferson, Samuel Adams, and James Madison about the event. In his letter to Jefferson, Lee stated that the enterprise of America is well marked by the successful voyage made by a ship from New York to Canton, China. Later, Lee informed Samuel Adams that the success of the sail was "a proof of American enterprise, and will probably mortify, as much as it will injure our old oppressor, the British."[6]

Encouraged by the profit of the *Empress of China*'s maiden voyage, Lee planned to open up the Potomac River and the James River to build ports for the China trade on each of them. Secretary of the Treasury Alexander Hamilton also closely followed the U.S.-China trade. He requested that Thomas Randall, the American vice-consul at Canton, provide him with specific information on the trade. Randall, who had served as the "joint supercargo" of the *Empress of China*, sent very detailed reports to Hamilton.

After this first successful commercial American voyage to China, Washington became even more interested in U.S.-China trade. He attempted to collect as much related information as possible. On July 6, 1789, President Washington ordered his subordinates to provide a list of American ships that traded in China. As president, Washington continued to understand the significance of the flourishing China trade. In a letter to the Marquis de Lafayette, Washington wrote that profits to individuals who were engaged in the China trade were "so considerable as to induce more persons to engage in it continually."

Thomas Jefferson had substantial interest in U.S.-China trade. While serving as American representative in France in 1785, Jefferson obtained a complete report concerning the *Empress of China*. As Washington's secretary of state, Jefferson suggested exploration to find a shorter trade route to East Asia. Later, shortly after the Louisiana Purchase, President Jefferson sent the famed explorers Louis and Clark west in hopes of finding a quicker route to China. During Jefferson's administration (1801–1809), U.S.-China trade reached new heights, with the number of involved American ships having increased from two in 1785 to forty-two in 1806. U.S.-foreign trade was severely limited in the brief period after President Jefferson signed the 1807 Embargo Act, supposedly prohibiting all American exports, in his attempt to keep the United States out of the war between Great Britain and France. Even though only eight American ships sailed to China between 1808 and the first months of 1809, Jefferson realized China's significance to the new nation and viewed strengthening U.S.-China trade as a strategy to coerce European countries to recognize American interests.

In 1808, and with Jefferson's permission, New York-based merchant John Jacob Astor succeeded in sailing one of his vessels to China despite the current trade embargo. Jefferson firmly believed that Astor's deed provided the United States with an opportunity to open a fresh start of favorable relations between the two nations.

Jefferson's pronouncement remained fundamental in American dealings with China long into the future. At least one authority on U.S.-East Asian relations acclaimed the statement as "the nearest to an official opinion on American policy."[7]

The American success that began with the *Empress of China* was not only profitable but also contributed to the new nation's international economic and political ascendancy. Fueled by political support and entrepreneurs' responses to a huge domestic demand for Chinese products, U.S.-China trade grew rapidly. By 1795, only a little over a decade after the *Empress of China* voyage, the United States had already passed all European rivals except Great Britain in the volume of its China trade. Port cities like Salem, New York, and Boston benefited significantly from the China trade, earning investment funds for new industry. Factory towns sprang up, and Americans began to experiment with the techniques of mass production. The United States began to lay the groundwork that eventually contributed to post–Civil War industrialization.

China trade helped to change the U.S. political map, moving much of American power from Virginia to New York City and New England. In the early 1790s, in part because of China profits and newly affluent business concerns, Hamilton had the power to establish a stronger financial role for the federal government. This strengthened New York and New England commercial and financial elites and weakened the previously powerful great Virginia planters.

The China trade was a joint effort by the Founding Fathers. Robert Morris financed the first American commercial ship to China; George Washington helped choose the business manager; Richard Henry Lee and Rufus King supported the first attempt to build an economic relationship with China; and Thomas Jefferson used successful American trade with China as an opportunity to move toward establishing a distinct American national identity in China that was clearly separate from the United Kingdom.

CONFUCIANISM IN THE MAKING OF U.S. DEMOCRACY

In the Founding and the Early Republic eras, when the founders were contemplating how to inaugurate and initiate the new nation, they discovered the value of Confucianism and adopted some of Confucian social and political principles to help to build a democratic system. After the victory of the American Revolution, the founders took Confucian ideas and used them to build new political institutions. The Confucian merit-based approach was implemented to transform the infant American civil service system. Through drawing positive elements from Confucian educational principles, Thomas Jefferson revolutionized the American educational system.

The founders' efforts to embrace some positive Confucian moral, social, and political concepts were part of a broader ideological shift that replaced the historic Western emphasis on birthright with systems of merit-based succession. Their efforts contributed to the emergence of a "[distinct] American character with new sets of values," one that was further removed from its European roots and was prepared to craft its own national identity.

THE FOUNDERS' LEGACY

Chinese cultural influence reached North America and influenced the American founders. Chinese agricultural, philosophical, and architectural beliefs and practices affected the United States in both material and nonmaterial ways. The timing of China's impact is particularly significant given that it occurred in the formative period of American independence.

Why did such American notables as Franklin, Jefferson, and Washington pay close attention to China? China, as one of the most stable, and certainly the most long-lived civilization in the world, could provide the architects of the new nation with valuable models to draw upon. Charles Thomson, known as the "Samuel Adams of Philadelphia" and a close associate of Franklin, mirrored his mentor's feelings in recognizing the connection between China's success as a society and its large population:

> Could we be so fortunate as to introduce the industry of the Chinese, their arts of living and improvements in husbandry, as well as their native plants, America might be in time become as populous as China, which is allowed to contain more inhabitants than any other country, of the same extent, in the world.[8]

Although significantly influenced by Europe in many ways, the American founders did not want to blindly follow in Europe's footsteps. Washington articulated the desirability of at least some American isolation from Europe in his 1796 farewell address, telling the American people and their leaders,

> Europe has a set of primary interests which to us have none or a very remote relation. Hence she must be engaged in frequent controversies, the causes of which are essentially foreign to our concerns. Hence, therefore, it must be unwise in us to implicate ourselves by artificial ties in the ordinary vicissitudes of her politics, or the ordinary combinations and collisions of her friendships or enmities. Our detached and distant situation invites and enables us to pursue a different course.[9]

Jefferson also echoed Washington in expressing the "desirability of Chinese isolation and of the need to place an ocean of fire between us and the old world."[10] In realizing this goal, the founders needed a new resource outside of Europe, such as China, which they could use for their efforts.

The use of positive elements from Chinese civilization in building the newly independent nation helped create a special pattern for integration of elements from other cultures into American culture. Today, as has been the case in the nineteenth, twentieth, and now the twenty-first centuries with China learning from the United States, Americans of all ethnic backgrounds consume intellectual and technological innovations. Today, Americans have accepted acupuncture, martial arts, tai chi, and meditation. This cross-cultural interaction started with the founders of this great nation.

NOTES

1. Jonathan Goldstein, *Philadelphia and the China Trade, 1982–1846: Commercial, Cultural, and Attitudinal Effects* (University Park: Pennsylvania State University Press, 1978), 10.
2. Thomas Paine, "Of the Old and New Testament," *The Prospect*, March 31, 1804. See also *Complete Writings*, vol. 2, ed. Philip S. Foner (New York: Garden City Press, 1945), 805.
3. Benjamin Rush, "Of the Mode of Education Proper in a Republic, 1798," in *The Selected Writings of Benjamin Rush*, ed. Dagobert D. Runes (New York: Philosophical Library, 1947). http://press-pubs.uchicago.edu/founders/documents/v1ch18s30.html.
4. Philadelphia Museum of Art Exhibition, Colonial Philadelphia Porcelain: The Art of Bonnin and Morris, March 8–June 1, 2008.
5. Letter from George Washington to Thomas Jefferson, March 29, 1784, The Library of Virginia, http://www.lva.virginia.gov/lib-edu/education/psd/nation/gwtj.htm.
6. *The Letters of Richard Henry Lee*, vol. 2, Richard Henry Lee, National Society of the Colonial Dames of America (New York: Macmillan, 1914), 360.
7. Tyler Dennett, *Americans in Eastern Asia: A Critical Study of the Policy of the United States with Reference to China, Japan and Korea in the 19th Century* (New York: Macmillan, 1922), 77.
8. Jonathan Goldstein, *Philadelphia and the China Trade, 1982–1846: Commercial, Cultural, and Attitudinal Effects* (University Park: Pennsylvania State University Press, 1978), 10.
9. George Washington, "Farewell Address, 19 September 1796," Founders Online, National Archives, https://founders.archives.gov/documents/Washington/05-20-02-0440-0002. Original source: *The Papers of George Washington*, Presidential Series ed. David R. Hoth and William M. Ferraro, vol. 20, *1 April–21 September 1796* (Charlottesville: University of Virginia Press, 2019), 703–722.
10. Robert W. Tucker and David C. Hendrickson, *Empire of Liberty: The Statecraft of Thomas Jefferson* (New York: Oxford University Press, 1990), 246.

Chapter 1

Ideas from the East

The Founders Used Chinese Wisdom to Build a Flourishing Society

During America's colonial period, a handful of eminent colonists—who would later emerge as the new nation's founders—observed the enduring value of Chinese civilization. They embraced certain Chinese ideas intended to improve social and economic life in the newly independent United States. Some prominent founders went even further by looking to China as a guide for the new nation. They regarded China's centuries of prolonged agrarian tradition as a rich resource that the United States could emulate.

Below I will start with a general survey about China's image and Chinese civilization in the colonial and early republic periods. Then I will focus on how Chinese ideas—particularly Confucian moral philosophy—inspired some of the founders. I will discuss Chinese ideas that the founders believed to be of great value to North America, such as certain practices of the Chinese imperial government, the social mobility based on meritocracy, and gentry's spirit of community services. I will also examine Benjamin Franklin's moral cultivation and his relationships with Confucian moral philosophy. Finally, I will discuss the inspiration that Jefferson received from Confucian classics. Readers will have a basic understanding of the founders' efforts to draw positive elements from Chinese civilization.

CHINA'S IMAGE AND CHINESE CIVILIZATION IN COLONIAL AND EARLY REPUBLIC PERIODS

After the American victory in the Revolutionary War, when the founders were pondering the direction in which the fledgling United States would head, some, including John Adams (1735–1826), Thomas Jefferson (1743–1826), and James Madison (1751–1836), expressed their penchant for

Chinese tradition. John Adams recommended to the president of Congress that the United States should follow China's example, saying that the British "System of Colonies in distant regions for the Purpose of Monopolies, was at an end."[1] It was time for Americans to

> turn their attention, to give exertion to their own internal powers like the police of China, cultivate their waste lands, improve agriculture, encourage manufactures, abolish Corporations: as all the remnants of Barbarism, shall be removed, the powers of the Community will create those surpluses which will become the Source, and open the channells of commerce.[2]

Predictably, Thomas Jefferson, whose vision was of an agricultural-based prosperous nation, shared Adams's vision that the United States should follow the Chinese model. In 1785, he told Gijsbert Karel Count van Hogendorp (1762–1834),

> You ask what I think on the expediency of encouraging our states to be commercial? Were I to indulge my own theory, I should wish them to practice neither commerce nor navigation, but to stand with respect to Europe precisely on the footing of China. We should thus avoid wars, and all our citizens would be husbandmen.[3]

James Madison professed that "civilization is never seen without agriculture: nor has agriculture ever prevailed, where the civilized arts did not make their appearance."[4] Naturally, he regarded China highly because he fully understood there was "a much higher state of agriculture in China than in many other countries far more advanced in the improvements of civilized life."[5]

The founders were not the only influential political figures who articulated their positive attitudes toward China. William Jarvis (1770–1859), an American diplomat, financier, and philanthropist, regarded China as a nation of compassion in the world. He declared to Thomas Jefferson,

> So far as my little reading extends, China is the only Country where so benevolent a place in all its parts, has ever been, even partially attempted; and if Confucius was the author, the comparative happy state of China, with the rest of Asia, does as much honor to his Philosophical Wisdom as to the goodness of his intentions.[6]

Philip Mazzei (1730–1816), a close friend of Jefferson, told Adams on September 27, 1785,

> I am old, & have no children; but the honest part of the inhabitants of this Globe are my brethren, Posterity my children; & was I to go & spend the remainder

of my days in China, I would with pleasure, & in compliance with what I think my duty, contribute all my exertions to the forming of an asylum for Mankind from oppression.[7]

Augustus B. Woodward (1774–1827), the first chief justice of the Michigan Territory, told James Madison that Chinese are "virtuous, orderly, pacific, and benevolent people";[8] Woodward stated that the United States had "the favorable impressions" in China.[9] He then told Madison that because of "many features of resemblance in the physical and moral character of the two countries, the Americans will be more favored in China than the European nations." He then told Madison that neither nation "had ambition to conquer other nations. Both countries prohibited an aristocratic system." The two nations owned "a countless population." In the future, the United States and China would "become objects of reciprocal interest to each other." In this scenario, the United States should start "an establishment of American youth for the purpose of learning their language."[10] He speculated that the Chinese government "may allow some of their distinguished youth to visit our country for a similar purpose." Because of the friendship between the two nations, the Chinese government "might be extended so far as to assign" the Americans "a peculiar port for their particular commerce, distinct from the nations of Europe."[11] Woodward recommended that the United States should initiate "A prompt and rapid intercourse with China." Furthermore, "Our existing commerce too requires that our government should be introduced to the attention of that nation."[12]

The founders' positive image in China was fully reflected in a widely used textbook authored by Jedidiah Morse. In the textbook, Morse stated, "China is so happily situated, and produces such a variety of materials for manufactures, that it may be said to be the native land of industry; and which is exercised with vast art and neatness."[13]

The founders' and other prominent political figures' affirmative attitudes toward and admiration of China were not something that appeared suddenly. They had deep roots in the colonial era. Those favorable opinions on China reflected the influence of Chinese culture in colonial North America. During the founding of the United States, China was not unknown to the North American colonies. Knowledge about China "was almost as widespread and as readily available there as in Europe." During the eighteenth century, only two Chinese literary works of importance were translated into Western languages; "both were available in North America."[14] Chinese cultural impact on the colonists was well documented in the founders' papers, including their journals, correspondence with other figures, and publications.

As a society established by European colonists, the influence from Europe was unavoidable. However, the colonists also made efforts to learn about

China before the "China Fever," generated by the famous voyage of the *Empress of China*, the first American commercial ship that reached China in 1784. There was no direct contact between China and North America before then. All Chinese products were brought to North America through Europe. Americans' knowledge about China was also derived largely from European literary sources. Ever since the seventeenth century, the reports of European missionaries in China had been "so filled with admiration that European intellectuals were seized with a mania for things Chinese."[15] Chinese philosophical "impact on Western philosophy was of far greater and more lasting significance."[16] Confucian concepts and knowledge entered European culture, and thus "became emblematic for the image of Chinese culture, its government and bureaucratic administration, its moral rules."[17] The intellectuals were "particularly impressed with Confucian ideas regarding government."[18]

The admiration of Chinese culture had become a characteristic of the Age of Enlightenment in Europe.[19] Some prominent European thinkers turned to Confucian philosophy for theory to support their arguments in their debates on moral, political, or religious issues. Francois-Marie Arouet, a French Enlightenment writer known by his pen name Voltaire (1694–1778), used Confucian philosophy to criticize the French monarchy and church system. Europe's "admiration for things Chinese" reached a climax in Voltaire's *Essai sur les mœurs et l'esprit des nations* (*An Essay on Universal History, the Manners, and Spirit of Nations*, 1756). Voltaire stated that Confucius's morality "is as pure, as severe, and at the same time as human as that of Epictetus."[20] He stated that Confucius (551–479 BC) was "an anticipation of the philosophies of the eighteenth century."[21] For Voltaire, "The happiest and most respectable time ever on the earth" was that Confucian ideas were followed.[22] He claimed that Confucius "as a legislator, never wished to deceive men. Has anyone since devised better rules of conduct."[23]

Gottfried Wilhelm Leibniz (1646–1716), a prominent German philosopher, extolled "the virtue of the Confucian system." He told Europeans that the Chinese missionary should be sent to Europe "to teach us the aims and practice of natural theology."[24] Influence of Leibniz on his contemporaries and upon his successors "was just as important in the field of Chinese studies as it was in general philosophy and mathematics."[25] Christian Wolff (1679–1754), a most leading philosopher between Leibiniz and Kant, extolled the merits of Chinese moral philosophy. He claimed that the Chinese should be commended "for developing a rational natural morality, in no way dependent upon religion or revealed truth, in which duty and virtue were exalted."[26] In England, Sir William Temple admired Confucius as "the most learned, wise and virtuous of all the Chinese." He termed Confucius "a true patriot of his country and a lover of mankind." Temple then concluded, "No people are better governed nor with greater felicity than the Chinese."[27] John Locke's (1632–1704) belief "that government is the province of gentlemen with learning" came from "Confucian attitude toward government service."[28] In eighteenth-century English politics, the "Confucian notion that moral merit exemplified in learning should be a qualification for government office" had become an important idea.[29]

The French economic school of physiocracy, known for its admiration of Chinese culture, was another example of Chinese influence. Most ideas of physiocracy "bore an amazing resemblance to those found in Confucian political and economic philosophy."[30] For example, like Confucius, the physiocrats maintained that an enlightened government "must operate in conformity with certain economic and social laws—natural order." The state should give special encouragement to agriculture, and on the other hand, should not aid the "sterile process of manufacturing and commerce by offering them tariff protection or permitting the creation of great private monopolies, for this, in their opinion, would interfere with the natural process of distribution and violate the Natural Order."[31] François Quesnay (1694–1774), the leader of the Physiocratic School, was known for his love of Chinese civilization and was called the "European Confucius."[32] In his book *Le Despotisme de la Chine*, written in 1767, Quesnay explains his view and support of Chinese politics and society.

Concurrently with the Enlightenment, some prominent colonists recognized that Chinese culture and traditions could offer tremendous value for the socioeconomic development of the North American colonies. Discussion on China appeared in such favorite English periodicals as the *Monthly Review* and the *Gentleman's Magazine*.[33] In August 1775, just before the eve of independence, Thomas Paine (1737–1809), author of *Common Sense*, showed his great "interests in China."[34]

Paine regarded China as a source of inspiration and innovation.[35] He pronounced his interest in China through periodicals such as *Pennsylvania Magazine*. Other influential authors of the period, including James Logan (1674–1751), a statesman and scholar, and John Bartram (1699–1777), a colonial scientist and scholar, made similar efforts to study and introduce Chinese culture to the colonists. Benjamin Franklin (1706–1790) told his fellow colonists that China had been a civilized nation.[36] He published some essays about China in the *Pennsylvania Magazine*.[37]

Certain aspects of Chinese economic theory and the legal system also impressed the colonists. As early as 1774, Franklin showed his interest in a Chinese emperor's economic principle. Still other colonists showed great interest in the Chinese legal system. A writer told his readers that China's laws were "maintained with such strict impartiality, that the guilty seldom escape punishment or the injured fail to obtain prompt justice."[38]

Arthur Lee (1740–1792), an American diplomat during the Revolutionary War, exchanged his opinions on China with Franklin in 1777. Both "agreed on their admiration for the Chinese government."[39] Lee told Franklin,

If an envoy were sent to the Emperor to inform him that being a young people, desirous of adopting the wisdom of his Government, and therefore wishing to have his code of Laws, it might induce him to give it, as they would not appear, as other Nations had generally appeared, in a state to alarm the fears and excite the jealousies of that cautious Government.

Franklin agreed upon his view and expressed "the same opinion."[40]

Like Europe, Confucius and his works were discussed in North America. As early as 1733, James Logan acquired a copy of the first European printing of Confucius's philosophy (Confucius Sinanum Philosophus, Sive Scientia Sinensis Latine Exposita. Paris: Apud Danielem Horthmels, 1687).[41] This book includes *Tsa Hsueh* (Great Learning, in modern days it is *Daxue* in Chinese phonic system). It was translated by Sicilian Jesuit Fray Intorcetta and was the first printing in Europe.[42] Logan told Josiah Martin (1699–1778), that he was gratified with the book, and he even stated that he wished he could get "Confucius' own sentiment, or the true sense delivered to us."[43]

The Physiocratic School had strong influence on the founders, including Benjamin Franklin, Thomas Jefferson, and James Madison. While in France, Franklin and Jefferson "spent significant time in the salons of France socializing with the Physiocrats."[44] Jefferson held an extensive collection of physiocratic works, and Franklin also owned copies of important physiocratic writings.[45] For Jefferson, husbandry should stay the primary vocation of people. This is "to the benefit of a democratic United States" and Jefferson habitually made his claim in his writings as well as in letters to Pierre-Samuel du Pont de Nemours (1739–1817).[46]

During the American colonial and postcolonial periods, the people in North America experienced a dramatic social and political transformation. As former subjects of Great Britain they were transformed into citizens of an independent nation. American fascination with Chinese civilization continued. Positive elements from Chinese civilization exposed the colonists-turned-American citizens to a new culture far different from their own traditions. After independence, the founders, when unfolding their plan for a new nation, took inspiration from China and worked to include some of the best components of Chinese civilization into their endeavors to shape a new American culture.

CONFUCIAN MORAL PHILOSOPHY IN THE COLONIAL AND FEDERAL PERIODS

Confucius and his works had been well known by the first half of the eighteenth century in colonial North America. James Logan obtained for his personal library a copy of the first European printing of Confucian philosophy in 1733. In May 1788, an article carried in the *Columbian Magazine* introduced its readers to Confucius's filial piety.[47] In its September 1793 issue, the influential *New Hampshire Magazine* published "an outstanding tribute to Confucius and Chinese religion."[48] A writer, using Confucius Disciple as his pen name, wrote "a concise History of Confucius, a famous Chinese philosopher," in which he demonstrated his belief that Confucius was "a Character so truly virtuous."[49]

For Jedidiah Morse (1761–1826), the well-known author of a textbook, Confucius was "the Solon and Socrates of China."[50] Morse cited *Daxue* (Great Learning), the new French translation, and *Zhongyong* (the Doctrine of the Mean), two of the four classics of Confucian philosophy. Morse praised the two works as "the most excellent precepts of wisdom and virtue, expressed with the greatest eloquence, elegance and precision." In his word, Confucius "is very striking, and which far exceeds, in clearness, the prophecy of Socrates."[51]

The same volume contains the translation of two books of great antiquity, the one entitled *Tahio*, or the Grand Science; The other *Tsong|y ng*, or the exact middle way, with a preface and notes. These two pieces of morality contain the most excellent precepts of wisdom and virtue, expressed with the greatest eloquence, elegance, and precision.[52] Morse called that Confucian "virtue shall fill the universe—shall vivify all things, and shall rise to the *Tier* or Supreme Deity. What a noble course is opening to our view! What new laws and obligations!"[53]

John Bartram, America's preeminent botanist and a friend of Benjamin Franklin, showed his interest in the personality of Confucius.[54] He published a biography of Confucius, called *Life and Character of The Chinese Philosopher Confucius: Autograph Manuscript*.[55] Bartram's biography of Confucius was from his reading notes of *The Morals of Confucius*, which had been recently acquired by the Library Company of Philadelphia.[56] Possibly inspired by this book, Bartram delivered a message in Meeting for Worship about the parallels between the lives and teachings of Confucius and Jesus, and his estimation that they were comparably great men.[57] Confucius, to Bartram, was "the most learned man that this or any other nations ever blessed with."[58] He wrote, "The whole doctrine of this great philosopher tended to restore human nature to its original dignity and the first lustre, purity which has received from heaven, & which had been sullied and corrupted with ignorance."[59] Confucius was "the original ultimate end of all things, that he is one supreme holy, supreme intelligent and invisible."[60]

In the years preceding independence, several prominent Americans, most notably Benjamin Franklin, disseminated Confucian ideas and "raised the sense of morality among workmen."[61] Other founders, such as Thomas Jefferson, Thomas Paine, Benjamin Rush (1745/6–1813), John Adams, and James Madison also expressed their favor of Confucian moral philosophy.

Jefferson, concerned about his reputation and honor, was highly conscious of his behavior and regarded the well-loved and respected Chinese Prince Wu, featured in *The Great Learning* (one of the canons of Confucianism), as an exemplary role model for other leaders. In his 1794 essay, "The Age of Reason," Thomas Paine, the famous polemicist of republicanism, wrote that Confucius, like Christ, was a great moral teacher. Paine reiterated this point in an article he wrote a decade later for *The Prospect*, a New York magazine: "As a book of morals there are several parts of *the New Testament* that are good, but they are no other than what had been preached in the East world several hundred years before Christ was born."[62] Paine continued, "Confucius, the Chinese philosopher . . . says, 'acknowledge thy benefits by the turn of benefits, but never revenge injuries.'"[63]

Dr. Benjamin Rush, an ardent patriot, in a 1798 essay on education in the new republic, asserted that "the only foundation for a useful education in a republic is to be laid in Religion. Without this there can be no virtue, and without virtue there can be no liberty, and liberty is the object and life of all republican governments."[64] Having expressed his veneration for Confucianism that "reveals the attributes of the Deity," Rush declared that he would rather see the opinions of Confucius "inculcated upon our youth, than see them grow up wholly devoid of a system of religious principles."[65] John Adams, in a letter to Thomas Jefferson, criticized the English theologian and natural philosopher Joseph Priestley (1733–1804) for ignoring Confucius in his writing, even though Adams thought Christ the greater moral teacher: "Priestley ought to have given us a sketch of the religion and morals of Zoroaster, of Sanchuniathon, of Confucius, and all the founders of religions before Christ, whose superiority would, from such a comparison, have appeared the more transcendent."[66]

James Madison, father of the U.S. Constitution, even hung a portrait of Confucius at his home. It was probably not a coincidence that Confucian moral ideals were respected in an era when some U.S. leaders sought to liberate American culture from what they viewed as failed European ideologies. In 1809, Punqua Wingchong, a Chinese businessman who visited the United States, sent Madison a box of Confucius's works.[67]

By piecing together the above information of the favorable attitudes of notable figures, we will have a basic understanding of how Confucianism made its way to North America. The evidence also provides us a window through which we can perceive the influence of Confucianism in the colonial, federal, and early republic periods.

CHINESE MANAGEMENT OF STATE AFFAIRS INFLUENCED FRANKLIN AND JEFFERSON

The founders and other political figures expressed their disappointment in Great Britain's management of colonial affairs. Franklin expressed to Joseph Galloway (1731–1803), an American politician, his disappointment at British Parliament and told Galloway "the general Corruption and Servility of Parliament is now so generally seen and known to all the Nation, that it is no longer respected as it used to be."[68] Franklin then listed some misconduct, including that Parliament's censures "are no more regarded than Popes Bulls." He afterward assumed that Parliament had been "despis'd for its Venality, and abominated for its Injustice."[69]

Facing this situation, Franklin turned his eyes to the East. Only three years prior to the formal Declaration of Independence, Franklin labored to create an improved and more efficient system of management. In 1773, Franklin voiced that he was deeply impressed by the effectiveness of the statistics system of the Chinese Imperial Court. He recorded in detail how local officials collected economic information and reported to the imperial court. From his letter to Thomas Percival (1740–1804), an English physician and ethicist, one can tell that Franklin was impressed at the fact that the Chinese provincial authority held accurate information on the population and the "Quantities of Provision produc'd."[70] The provincial authority then reported this information to China's imperial court. Then, the imperial ministers "can thence foresee a Scarcity likely to happen in any Province, and from what Province it can best be supply'd in good time."[71] He then made a detailed record of how the local officials had obtained farmers' household information: "each House is furnish'd with a little Board to be hung without the Door during a certain time each Year, on which Board, is marked certain Words, against which the Inhabitant is to mark Number or Quantity."[72]

According to Franklin, the age of sixteen was the entry into adulthood. Individuals sixteen years and under were counted as children. Those above the age were counted as adults. He expressed his admiration for the system's effectiveness. Due to the statistics system, officials would get information on a household "without giving the least Trouble to the Family."[73]

Franklin also explored other Chinese management methods, such as the salary of a handcraft master and a medical doctor's income from visiting his patients. He wrote in his journal in 1762,

> Silversmith and his Apprentice earn 6s. 3d. in 22 Days. Their Provisions allow'd cost 3d. per Day. Physicians Pay, for a Visit of 4 Miles, in a Chair receives One Mace 4 Candrins. Note the 4 Candrins is for Chair hire. The Mace is 7½d. Sterling 10. Candrins is a Mace.[74]

Under the influence of European physiocratic thought, Thomas Jefferson was interested in borrowing China's land tax system. In 1810, Pierre-Samuel du Pont de Nemours (1739–1817), a French American writer, economist, publisher, and government official, wrote a letter in which he introduced to Jefferson the Chinese tax system. He reported to Jefferson, "the Chinese understood that the difference between the cost of farming and the productivity of the land would make a tithe of the same rate on all crops extremely unjust and ruinous to land of a middling quality."[75] They comprehended that "deserting the farming of the latter would remove a great portion of the means of subsistence from their populous nation." Therefore, the Chinese "established twenty different proportions for the collection of the land tax based on the superior or inferior quality of the land, which tax is nevertheless taken as a tithe on the total crop."[76]

Du Pont respected the Chinese system. He called it "a great improvement on the general system of the tithe."[77] He then advised Jefferson that the Chinese system "was not entirely unknown in France."[78] In France, "the different classes had not been clearly differentiated at all."[79] He stated to Jefferson, "On the contrary, in China the classification of the land tax was the result of enlightenment acquired through experience, and it was calculated with sufficient care, according to wise administrative views."[80]

Jefferson read the letter "with great pleasure."[81] He supported du Pont's proposal for "drastic alterations to the American system of taxation as the United States." Jefferson adored the Chinese land tax system so much that he "dispatched his only copy to President James Madison" merely six days after he received the letter. He requested Madison to share the letter with Secretary of the Treasury Albert Gallatin (1761–1849) before returning it.[82]

MERITOCRACY: THE CHINESE SYSTEM OF SOCIAL PROMOTION

In the aftermath of the American Revolution, some sought to establish a hereditary aristocracy. Their aim was to distinguish themselves and their descendants, consequently organizing the Society of Cincinnatus.[83] In April 1783, General Henry Knox (1750–1806), Washington's closest friend, drafted a plan for the Society of Cincinnati, to which "the retired officers of the Continental army might belong."[84] The society's membership "was defined in hereditary terms, passing exclusively to the eldest male descendant in the next generation."[85] The society continued to gain popularity in the years following the Revolution, with many of its members carrying roles in the federal and state governments. Franklin and other Founding Fathers were alarmed at the potential creation of a hereditary elite reminiscent of European aristocracy. Franklin endorsed China's civil service system, an ancient method of merit-based social promotion that rewarded those with talent and education, as an alternative to the Society of Cincinnatus.

Franklin was among the society's earliest critics. Franklin had been aware of the Society of Cincinnati since at least mid-December 1783, when Pierre-Charles L'Enfant (1754–1825), a French American military engineer, arrived in Paris to deliver George Washington's letters and began launching a French branch of the society. John Jay and Jefferson expressed their opposition to the society.[86] In March 1784, Lafayette informed George Washington that "Most of the Americans Here are indecently Violent Against our Association. . . . Doctor Franklin Said little. But Jay, Adams, and all the others warmly Blame the Army."[87]

Unlike his fellow founders, Franklin did not convey his opposition to the society in public. Instead, Franklin wrote a letter to "show that Cincinnati's attempt to transplant the customs of European nobility to an American setting exposed the fundamental absurdity of all such distinctions and practices."[88] He did not send his letter to any national leaders in the United States. In early March, he sent his letter to the Abbé Morellet (1727–1819), a French economist, to translate into French. After translation, Abbé Morellet told him not to make it public. Franklin decided that the piece would not be made public during his lifetime.[89] In 1790, several months after Franklin passed away, Morellet's partial translation of the letter was published in Paris.[90] In 1817 Franklin's letter was made public in Franklin's writings by William Temple Franklin (1760–1823).[91] Historical records show that in July 1784, Franklin had relayed his letter to French Revolutionary writer Honoré Gabriel Riqueti, comte de Mirabeau, his associate in France. Mirabeau used Franklin's opposition to the Cincinnati society in his first signed work: *Considerations sur l'ordre de Cincinnatus.*[92]

Franklin articulated concerns about the apparent creation of a noble order. Franklin drew on Chinese examples to fight against this idea. In his letter to Sarah Bache, his only daughter, Franklin stated that in China a person was promoted because of "his Learning, his Wisdom, or his Valour, but not because of his ancestors."[93] If a man was "promoted by the Emperor to the Rank of Mandarin," it was "due to the Mandarin himself; on this Supposition, that it must have been owing to the Education, Instruction, and good Example afforded him by his Parents that he was rendered capable of Serving the Publick."[94] Franklin enunciated that the United States should follow China's system of promotion, for the system "is therefore useful to the State as it encourages Parents to give their Children a good and virtuous Education."[95] In the meantime, Franklin believed that the European style of *"descending Honour,"*—allowing promotion on ancestors' achievements—

is not only groundless and absurd, but often hurtful to that Posterity, since it is apt to make them proud, disdaining to be employed in useful arts, and thence falling into Poverty and all the Meannesses, Servility and Wretchedness attending it.[96]

One account for Franklin's addressing this letter to his daughter was that he wanted to "cloak[ed] what was intended to be a public essay in a fictional veneer of privacy."[97] It is reasonable to understand that the reason Franklin held his letter from the public until his death was his concern about his fellow founders' reputation.

Franklin rejected Europe's tradition of claiming that power based on aristocracy was a source of greater social equality. He liked to present himself as a plain, uncomplicated person, unblemished by European aristocratic luxury.[98] For Franklin, China's system of social promotion offered an opportunity for all Americans with talent and education, replacing the European system of inequality based upon feudalist birthright and divine right. By recommending that Americans should adopt Chinese methods for social promotion, Franklin introduced the notion of meritocracy. However, Franklin didn't use the word "meritocracy" because the term was created in 1958,[99] 174 years after Franklin voiced his opposition to the European system of feudalistic aristocracy—and 157 years after Jefferson decided to make meritocracy the official system for the United States.

Confucianism led to the creation of the concept of government-based standardized examinations throughout China. According to Confucius, governing authority should be based on merit, and not inherited status. The public service positions should be given to those who passed the imperial examinations. The Han dynasty (206 BC–220 AD), which established Confucianism as its official philosophy, installed the meritocracy as its governmental system to select officials in the second century BC. The Han dynasty began choosing public service officials based on civil service exams—a first in world history.[100] During the Enlightenment (1715–1789), the idea of meritocracy reached Europe and some enlightened intellectuals realized that meritocracy, as a system, should replace the traditional noble blood system of Europe.[101]

For Benjamin Franklin, meritocracy—the Chinese way of advancement—was preferable to a feudal aristocracy or caste system. Its legitimacy was based upon appeals to formal equality and fairness. We will discuss this idea and its influence on the founders in later chapters.

John Adams also agreed with the Chinese way of social promotion. He and Jefferson also "strongly opposed the Society of Cincinnati."[102] Adams told Alexander Bryan Johnson (1786–1867), an American philosopher and banker, "Everybody knows that nobility in China ascends when a Man is ennobled, he ennobles all his Ancestors but none of his Posterity."[103] He told

Johnson that he believed the Chinese way of social promotion was "a wise institution" and he alleged that the system was "much wiser than to ennoble a long list of puppies, and Butterflies to all future ages."[104]

LEADING THROUGH VIRTUE VERSUS LAW

Confucius upheld that the masses should be led by leaders who governed through their virtue rather than through their laws. He believed that if a government rested its rule entirely on laws, its people would try to escape punishment and have no sense of shame. Therefore, he reasoned that if the people were led by virtue, they would possess a sense of shame and follow their leaders through their own will.[105]

Founders such as Franklin, Paine, and Adams espoused the importance of moral leadership. Franklin specifically advised Americans on the importance of virtue. In 1778, two years after American colonists declared their independence, Franklin emphasized the significance of morality. He pointed out the necessity of governing with morality, especially for the leaders of the United States. He told fellow Americans that laws were not enough for the new nation. He used his experiences to advice Americans on the importance of virtues. Franklin raised the question, "What can laws do without morals?" He clearly expressed that he believed that without morals, human society "will in a course of minutes become corrupt like those of other and older Bushes, and consequently as wretched."[106]

Paine believed that Confucian morals were necessary for politicians in their political debate. He raised Confucius's principles during his political polemic with the federalists. To support his argument against the federalists, Paine quoted Confucian moral principles to criticize their moral faults. He told these federalists to follow Confucian teachings so they could be worthy to argue with "I recommend to them the observance of a commandment" regulated by Confucius, "that existed before either Christian or Jew existed." He then listed Confucius's principles:

> Thou shalt make a covenant with thy senses, With thine eye, that it beholds no evil. With thine ear, that it hear no evil. With thy tongue, that it speak no evil. With thy hands that they commit no evils.[107]

A GENTLEMAN SHOULD SERVE THE COMMUNITY

Alexis de Tocqueville (1805–1859) was legendarily struck by the American way of joining to help the community. This communal tradition of the United

States was promoted by the founders. Confucian moral philosophy helped the founders nurture a tradition of community service. Confucius pointed out that a person should "love his neighbor as himself, to conquer and submit his passions unto reason, to do nothing, say nothing, nor think nothing contrary to it."[108] The process of personal cultivation was for Confucius simultaneously a process of community creation.[109]

Confucius taught rulers to be virtuous. He formulated a series of ethical principles for leaders of the state. Therefore, an especially important part of Confucianism is personal cultivation. Confucius desired leaders to be gentlemen who should always claim moral leadership to exercise proper influences to put society in good order.[110] Following Confucian moral principles, in traditional Chinese society gentlemen of good virtue always served the community with their talents and resources. They "devoted attention to local welfare institutions," such as educational promotion. They "printed their rhymed quotations for effective communications to the less educated as rhymes were easy for them to learn."[111]

Benjamin Franklin provides an example of all the characteristics of a Confucian gentleman. Franklin accumulated wealth in his middle age. He gradually retired from business. Although Franklin was an excellent and successful businessman, he retired "from active business at forty-two and spent forty-two years more in the service of the public."[112] He "remade himself" as "a public-spirited gentleman."[113] He donated his time and energy to public affairs and welfare. From the 1730s to the 1740s Franklin helped to establish some cultural and philanthropic institutions. These include the Library Company, the American Philosophical Society, the Public Academy of Philadelphia (the University of Pennsylvania), and a network of volunteer fire companies. In his popular weekly newspaper, *Pennsylvania Gazette*, Franklin often published some rhymed quotations for his readers. Most impressively, in 1737, he published Confucius's moral works in the same newspaper.

Benjamin Franklin's contribution to America's tradition of voluntary community service has become a valuable legacy. His hard work had helped produce the phenomenon noted by Alexis de Tocqueville in 1830 that Americans were very good at "subordinating their individualism to voluntary groups of one type or another."[114]

The Founding Fathers were resolved in drawing wisdom from Chinese civilization. I should point out here that I am not aiming to ignore the influence that the founders received from the leading intellectuals in the European Enlightenment. The founders were not content with or limited to Europe as their only sources for inspiration for their cause in North America. In fact, I have discerned that the founders were not satisfied with the Chinese ideas transmitted by the European intellectuals. The founders, such as Franklin, Jefferson, Adams, and Paine, turned their attention to original Chinese classics. Franklin quoted from Chinese sources directly in his fight against the traditional system of aristocracy in Europe. Jefferson included the Chinese poem from Confucian classics in his own personal journal. Paine cited Confucius's teaching directly in his political essays.

THOMAS JEFFERSON AND CONFUCIAN CLASSICS

Many intellectuals in nineteenth-century America created personal scrapbooks to archive poems and newspaper articles in personal anthologies. Thomas Jefferson was one such intellectual. Sometime between 1801 and 1809, Jefferson saved an ancient Chinese poem from *The Book of Odes*, which Confucius had edited. Jefferson's love of this poem provides a window through which to investigate his efforts to learn from Chinese civilization.[115]

Sometime from 1801 to 1809 Jefferson included in the section of his scrapbook titled Poems of the Nations[116] an ancient Chinese poem from *The Book of Odes*.[117] What had he wanted to learn from the poem?

Below is Jefferson's clipping of the poem:

> A Very Ancient Chinese Ode
> Translated by John Collegins seq
> Quoted in the *To Hio*[118] of Confuciues
> (from a manuscript presented in the Bodleian Library)[119]
> The following ode has been translated into Latin by Sir William Jones,[120] who informs us in his Treatise on the second classic book of the Chinese, that the Ode is taken from 1st Vol. of the Shi King.[121] "It is a panegyrick (says he) on Vucan. Prince of Guey, in the Province of Honang, who died near a century old, 756 years before the birth of Christ. The Chinese poets might have been contemporary with Homer and Hesiod, or at least must have written the Ode before the Iliad and Odyssey were carried into Greece by Lycurgus."

> SEE! how the silvery river glides,
> And leaves' the fields bespangled sides!
> Hear how the whispering breeze proceeds!
> Harmonious through the verdant reeds!
> Observe our prince thus lovely shine!
> In him the meek-ey'd virtues join!
> Just as a patient carver will, Hard ivory model by his skill,
> So his example has impress'd Benevolence in every b[re]ast;
> Nice hands to the rich gems, behold,
> Impart the gloss of burnish'd gold:
> Thus he, in manners, goodly great,

Refines the people of his state. True lenity,
how heavenly fair!
We see it while it threatens,—spare!
What beauties in its open face!
In its deportment—what a grace!
Observe our prince thus lovely shine!
In him the meek-ey'd virtues join!
His mem'ry of eternal prime,
Like truth, defies the power of time![122]

The poem pays tribute to Prince Wu from the State of Wei, who was loved, respected, and remembered by the people of his state.[123] Confucius (551–479 BC) highly praised Prince Wu, described in the poem, when he quoted this poem in his famous book, *The Great Learning*, to provide a standard to inspire other princes and leaders of various states to follow.[124] Confucius said,

> In the Book of Ode, "Ah! The former kings are not forgotten." Future princes deem worthy what they deemed worthy, and love what they loved. The common people delighted in what they delighted them and are benefited by their beneficial arrangements. It is on this account that the former kings, after they have quitted the world, are not forgotten.[125]

It is safe to say that Jefferson's choice to place this poem in his scrapbook reflects his contemplation of his position in American history. It further demonstrates his purpose to follow Prince Wu and be a great leader who would be remembered positively by American people. He wanted to be "in manners goodly great, Refine the people of the state." Therefore, "His mem'ry of eternal prime, Like truth, defies the power of time!"

The first section of his scrapbook, "Poems of Nation," constitutes something of a commentary in verse on Jefferson's presidency and his political philosophy.[126] Jefferson used his scrapbook to dramatize the "victory" of his own position over those of his critics. Jeffersonian scholars will undoubtedly discover other such examples of literary-political ventriloquism in this collection.[127] If the "Poems of Nation" reveal Jefferson as a political apologist,[128]

> Jefferson viewed his legacy as intertwined with the success of the republican experiment. Believing that he had a political, moral, and personal stake in how the history of the American Revolution and its aftermath would be conveyed to future generations, Jefferson collected documents, books, newspapers, and other materials so that later historians could construct an appropriate version of the American revolutionary history.[129]

Most of the prominent leaders of the revolutionary generation recognized that they were making history. They took care to preserve their correspondence and edit their memoirs with an eye for posterity's judgment.[130] The Founding Fathers knew they were writing for posterity, and so "they purposely down played their own achievements and, by extension, their own missteps."[131] Realizing his papers were well worth preserving, Washington had hired a secretary and copyists to make sure "his correspondence was boxed in sturdy trunks and shipped to safety during the Revolution." He "even planned to build a small library at Mount Vernon."[132]

In the election of 1800, Jefferson was elected to be the third president. Benjamin Franklin and George Washington (1732–1799) were now dead. John Adams had moved far away from the political center of Washington, DC, and was spending his retired life in rural Massachusetts. The younger generation of the American Revolution, including Alexander Hamilton (1755–1804), Aaron Burr (1756–1836), John Marshall (1755–1835), James Madison, John Randolph (1772–1833), James Monroe (1758–1831), and Thomas Jefferson "moved into the last act of the American Revolution, the one that would disclose the character of the society brought into begin in 1776."[133]

That younger generation of the American Revolution expressed its own points of view on the positions of the Founding Fathers' generation. When federalists asked the House to praise Washington and his farewell address, Andrew Jackson (1767–1845) expressed his opposition. Other Republicans were willing to honor Washington for the Revolution and Constitutional Convention, but not for his presidency. Raising glasses in Philadelphia, they cried, "George Washington—down to the year 1787. And no further!"[134]

When he left the office in 1809, Jefferson was already thinking about the fifth and final volume of John Marshall's *Life of George Washington*, which was published in 1807.[135] Volume V was the portion that dealt with Washington's last decade, when two distinct political parties formed. Jefferson was worrying about the book. "How could he simply rely on posterity—on unnamed future biographers—to use his papers to his best advantage, and consign Federalism, like monarchism, to the dust heap?"[136] Jefferson wanted Joel Barlow (1754–1812) to return to Washington, DC, and told him that he had "cut out a piece of work" for Barlow. Jefferson told Barlow "to write the history of the United States, from the close of the War downwards."[137] Jefferson told Barlow that he would "open all the public archives" for him. Jefferson asked him to stay in Washington, DC, because a great deal of knowledge was not available in paper form, only from "verbal communications."[138]

Jefferson began to rebuild White House etiquette after he became the president of the United States. He separated himself from the "rags of royalty,"[139] and turned to modesty—of person, place, and ceremony—as an important feature of his administration. The federalists idealized a president who was shielded by a remote dignitary. Hamilton had "advised Washington to be accessible only to department heads, foreign ministers, and U.S. senators."[140] Jefferson banished this protocol. With the White House doors thrown open, the capital residents "could commemorate the day with the author of the Declaration of Independence."[141]

Jefferson was serious about preserving his legacy. His inclusion of the ancient Chinese poem in his scrapbook shows that Jefferson regarded Prince Wu as his example to encourage himself to be a leader loved by the future American people. His love of the poem served clearly as the indicator of demonstrating that he would like the historical Jefferson to be another Prince Wu, as a great leader of the people, praised and remembered by all the posterity of the United States.

BENJAMIN FRANKLIN AND CONFUCIAN MORAL CULTIVATION

Franklin probably read *The Morals of Confucius* as early as his 1724–1726 stay in London. From his autobiography it appears that, partially influenced by Confucius, Franklin focused on the cultivation of personal virtue as early as 1726. Confucius designed the path for virtuous perfection—from oneself to one's family, to the state, and then to the whole empire. In 1737, Franklin introduced this notion to the colonists when he published some excerpts adopted from *The Morals of Confucius* in his *Pennsylvania Gazette*:

> This is what Confucius proposed to the princes, to instruct them how to rectify and polish first their own reason, and afterwards the reason and person of all their subjects. But to make the greater impression, after having gradually descended from the wise conduct of the whole empire, to the perfection of the understanding, he re-ascends, by the same degrees, from the illuminated understanding to the happy state of the whole empire.[142]

Franklin agreed with Confucius that a man should not only cultivate personal virtues but also disseminate them to others—including political leaders. In a 1749 letter to George Whitefield, one of the most influential of all colonial-era clergy, Franklin advocated that knowledge of Confucian ideas could even foster social tranquility. "The mode [Confucius's mode of teaching moral principles] has a wonderful influence on mankind."[143]

Confucius yearned to see people, especially rulers, adopt better morals and more compassion. For him, virtue was the foundation of a good and flourishing empire. Confucius asserted that rulers should behave appropriately in court and at home because they would certainly be imitated. During the Revolutionary War, Franklin worked hard to promote this important principle.

Confucius maintained that law and punishment were the minimum requirements for order, but social harmony can only be achieved by virtuous behavior. In his enormously influential *Poor Richard's Almanack*, most of Franklin's advice for readers stresses virtues such as hard work, frugality, and attention to family.

Franklin presented to his readers the content of Confucius's moral philosophy. He told his readers that Confucian moral philosophy "treats of three considerable things":

1. Of what we ought to do to cultivate our Minds, and regulate our Manner,
2. Of the Method by which it is necessary to instruct and guide others, and
3. Of the Care everyone ought to have to tend to the Sovereign Good, to adhere thereunto, and, I may say to repose himself therein.[144]

Franklin's publication of Confucius's work reflected his own efforts at using Confucian teachings to purify his morals and help fellow colonists enhance their virtue. Franklin argued that Confucian moral philosophy was "the gate through which it is necessary to pass to arrive at the sublimest wisdom and most perfect."[145]

Franklin made great efforts to apply the philosophy to the practice of elevating his own virtue. Recent scholarship has found that Franklin published Confucius's teachings due to the fact that Confucian thinking related to Franklin's "efforts to establish a personal code of behavior."[146] Through his autobiography, Franklin related to us a vivid story of how trained virtue could change a person's life. He used his own personal experience from a poor family background to "a State of Affluence and some Degree of Reputation in the World" to demonstrate the significance of moral cultivation. He wrote down his valuable experience so his descendants "may like to know, as they may find some of them suitable to their own Situations, and therefore fit to be imitated."[147]

Franklin treasured his own success and tried to pass on his personal experience to the younger generation. What did he want to pass on? One of the main concepts that he wanted to let his reader understand was how he tried to use Confucius's moral philosophy to improve his virtue. Through his autobiography, Franklin emphasized that his moral virtue was extremely important to his success, both socially and economically. From reading his autobiography, we have learned that Franklin accomplished this virtue throughout his life. Franklin said that he wanted to live "without committing any fault at any time." Therefore, he designed "the bold and arduous project of arriving at moral perfection." He made his determination to "conquer all that either Natural Inclination, Custom, or Company might lead me into."[148]

Confucius maintained that an individual's moral perfection was the ultimate value of one's life and of society.[149] In his autobiography, Franklin provided us with a vivid description on how he tried to arrive "at moral Perfection."[150] He listed in his autobiography the thirteen virtues he thought to be the most important elements that contributed to his rise from a lower-class petty printer to a world-famous individual. The thirteen virtues clearly played an important role in Franklin's drive for moral perfection; they include (1) temperance; (2) silence; (3) order; (4) resolution; (5) frugality; (6) industry; (7) sincerity; (8) justice; (9) moderation; (10) cleanliness; (11) tranquility; (12) chastity; and (13) humility.[151]

In total, there are actually fourteen virtues. The one virtue not listed among the thirteen that Franklin sought to cultivate was charity, love of one's fellow man—the one virtue that in Professor Edmund Morgan's words was the "great principle" of Franklin's life. Morgan explained this curious omission: "by exhibiting it conspicuously in his own life while making no pretension to it, he was perhaps affirming to himself the superiority of a 'moral perfection' that has nothing to do with Christianity."[152] One does not have to be a scholar specializing in Confucianism to tell that all Franklin's fourteen values are the most important contents of Confucius's moral philosophy.

The following paragraph might provide readers the references for influences on Franklin's mind when he made his list for moral advancement.

> That moreover Virtue is an Ornament which embellishes, as I may say, the whole Person of Him that possesses it, his Interior and Exterior; that to the Mind it communicates inexpressible Beauties and Perfections; that as to the Body, it there produces very sensible Delights; that is affords a certain Physiognomy, certain Transports, certain ways which infinitely please; and as it is the Property of Virtue to becalm the Heart, and keep Peace there, so this inward Tranquility and secret Joy do produce a certain Serenity in the Countenance, a certain Joy, and Air of Goodness, Kindness and Reason, which attracts the Heart and Esteem of the Whole World.[153]

Franklin listed temperance as the first of the thirteen virtues. For him,

> "Temperance first, as it tends to procure that Coolness and Clearness of Head, which is so necessary where constant Vigilance was to be kept up, and Guard maintained against the unremitting Attraction of Ancient Habits, and the force of perpetual temptation."[154]

It is fair to say that Franklin had decided to control his feelings in accordance with the Confucian moral philosophy. We read the following paragraph from *The Morals of Confucius* carried in his *Pennsylvania Gazette* in 1737:

[Confucius's moral principle] concludes, that the principle of Business of a Man is to rectify his Mind, and so well to rule his Heart, that his Passions might always be calm; and if it happen that they be excited, he ought to be mov'd no further than is necessary, in a word, that he may regulate them according to right Reason. For as for instance, adds he, if we suffer ourselves to be transported with excessive Anger, that is to say, if we fall into a rage without any cause, or more than we ought when we have Reason, we may conclude, that our mind had not the Rectitude it ought to have. If we condemn and mortally hate a person, by reason of certain Defects that we observe in him, and render not Justice to his good and excellent Qualities, if endowed therewith, if we permit ourselves to be troubled by a too great Fear; if we abandon our selves to an immoderate Joy, or to an excessive Sorrow, it cannot be said that our Mind is in the State wherein it ought to be, that it has its rectitude and uprightness.[155]

Through the comparison of Franklin's thirteen virtues with Aristotle's list of virtues discussed in his *Ethics*, we will find Franklin's resistance to aristocracy. Franklin did not include courage, ambition, generosity, magnificence, magnanimity, friendliness, and wit. Professor Harvey C. Mansfield identified that these are aristocratic virtues. They are virtues that are "out of the ordinary."[156] Franklin replaced Aristotle's generosity with Confucian frugality.[157]

This is a very controversial conclusion. Some scholars have considered the above virtues to be from the New England Puritan tradition.[158] It is a well-proven fact that Franklin was "no Puritan."[159] Franklin's virtues "had proponents well beyond the realm of Calvinism." Professor James Campbell has also realized that "it seems much more valuable to emphasize Franklin's connections with other practical-minded moral thinkers for whom, unlike the Puritans, a social and naturalistic conception of human well-being was the central interest."[160] Social and naturalistic conception of human well-being is one of Confucianism's most important concepts.

It shouldn't surprise us when we learn through reading Franklin's autobiography that he gave "strict attention to each of the Virtues successfully."[161] In "From the *Morals of Confucius*," Franklin had advised himself and his readers.

He [Confucius-author] says we know the End to which must attain, it is necessary to determine, and incessantly to make towards the End, by walking in the Ways which lead thereunto, by daily confirming in his mind resolution fixt on for the attaining it, and by establishing it so well that nothing may in the least shake of it. When you have thus fixt your mind in this great Design, give up yourself, adds he, to Meditation: Reason upon all things upon yourself: Endeavour to have some clear Ideas thereof; Consider definitely what prevent itself to you. Pass, without prejudice, solid judgment thereon; Examine everything, and weigh everything with Care. After Examination and Reasonings you may easily arrive at the End where you must fix, at the End where you ought resolutely to stand, viz, at perfect conformity of all your Action, with what Reason suggests.[162]

Confucius said, "that the perfect Man always keeps a just Mean, whatever he undertakes" and "he continually watches over himself, over his thoughts, over the most secret motions of his Heart, always to square himself according to this just mean."[163] Franklin told his readers he checked his own behavior on "each day of the Week," making sure he followed exactly his thirteen good virtues.[164]

Confucius taught,

if as a Son, he is Obedient to his Father; if in quality of the Eldest Son, he is courteous to his younger Brethren, and lives peacefully with them; if, as the youngest, he as a respect and esteem for the eldest.[165]

Let us look at what Franklin did to his elder brother—who treated Franklin in a way a brother should not toward his younger brother.

When this elder brother, James, found that Franklin would leave him, he took some arduous, painful actions. He went around town and told "every master" not give his brother work. As a result, Franklin couldn't get "employment in any other printing-house of the town." In this situation, Franklin found no way out and decided, "I then thought of going to New York."[166]

In comparison, Franklin treated his brother in a different manner. In his autobiography, Franklin told his readers that he returned to Boston after ten years of successful business in Philadelphia. He visited his brother in Newport on his way. He put his former differences with his brother behind and had a "very cordial and affectionate" meeting with his brother. James, who was in poor health, hoped that Franklin could bring up his ten-year-old son and train him to be a printer. After his brother passed away, Franklin brought his son home, sent him to receive an education for several years and "took him into the Office" after that. Franklin let his brother's wife carry on the printing business, and when his nephew grew up, he "assisted him with an Assortment of new Types, those of his Father being in a Manner worn out."[167]

Once he accumulated wealth, Franklin gradually retired from business. He entrusted his press to a junior partner. He "remade himself" as "a public-spirited gentleman."[168] This action demonstrated that Franklin was not a "prototype of the American Capitalist." Had he possessed the soul of a true capitalist, he would have devoted the time he saved from printing to making money in other businesses.[169]

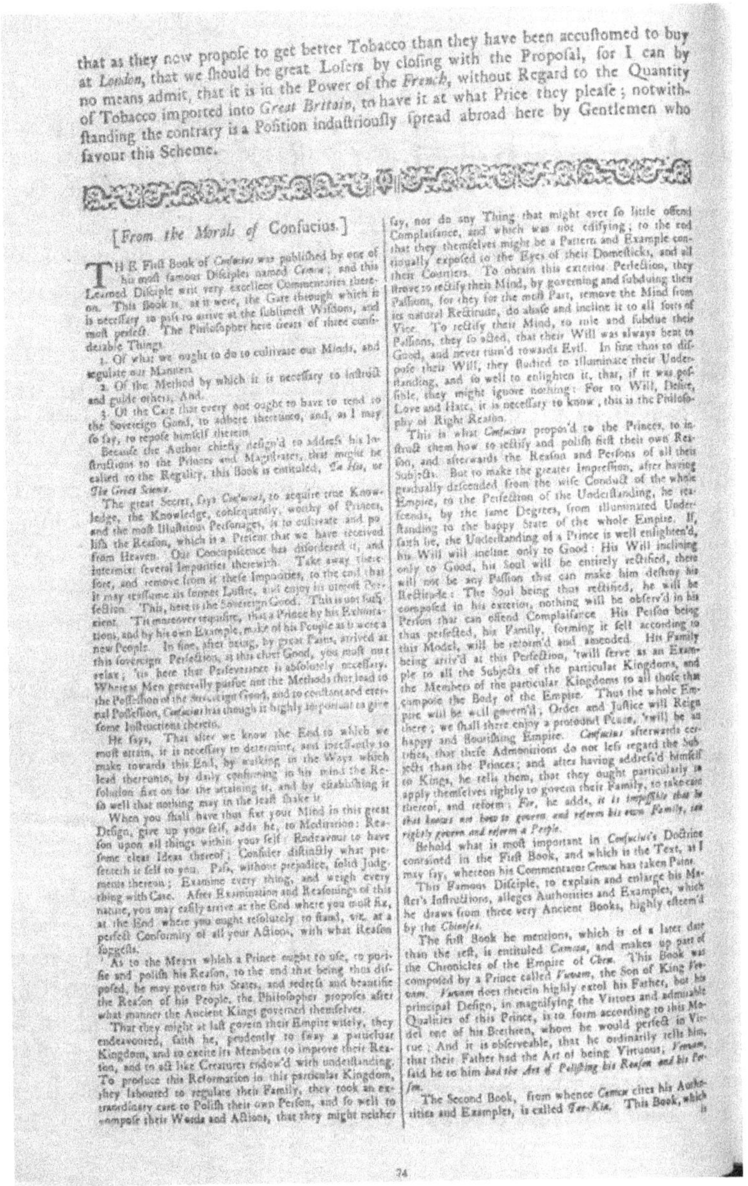

that as they now propose to get better Tobacco than they have been accustomed to buy at *London*, that we should be great Losers by closing with the Proposal, for I can by no means admit, that it is in the Power of the *French*, without Regard to the Quantity of Tobacco imported into *Great Britain*, to have it at what Price they please; notwithstanding the contrary is a Position industriously spread abroad here by Gentlemen who favour this Scheme.

[*From the Morals of* Confucius.]

Figure 1.1 "From The Morals of Confucius," Pennsylvania Gazette, Published by Benjamin Franklin in 1737. *Source*: Manuscripts Library & Museum of the American Philosophical Society.

What did Franklin do next? As noted above, he donated his time and energy to public affairs and welfare.[170]

A person with a basic knowledge of Confucianism will find that Franklin's behavior demonstrated that he was a typical Confucian gentleman. In traditional Chinese society, as already indicated, Confucian gentlemen "always claimed moral leadership to exercise proper influences was necessary to put the country in good order."[171] They "devoted attention to local welfare institutions," such as promoting education.[172] They "printed their rhymed quotations for effective communications to the less educated as rhymes were easy for them to learn."[173]

If we imagine Franklin living in China during his lifetime, we could imagine him receiving an award from the Chinese imperial government. He was a "filial" son to his parents and a "filial" younger brother to his elder brothers.[174] Confucian moral philosophy had a tremendous influence on Benjamin Franklin's virtue development. Franklin admitted that "in the various enumerations of the moral virtues I had met with in my reading, I found the catalogue more or less numerous, as different writers included more or fewer ideas under the same name."[175]

Franklin did not mention the name of Confucius. We know that Franklin learned of Confucius through European sources. Europeans' attitudes toward Confucianism certainly influenced Franklin. By the last three decades of the eighteenth century, about the time when Franklin wrote his autobiography, the Jesuits, the main carriers of Chinese civilization to Europe, became "thoroughly discredited." Since then, the esteem for China had declined in Europe.[176] This may explain the reason that Franklin did not mention Confucius's name among the "numerous" persons who had influenced his virtue growth.

Through careful examination, we have learned that although China was physically remote to North America—as either a British colony or a newly independent nation—China and its civilization loomed large in the minds of the Founding Fathers. They were influenced by numerous aspects of Chinese ideas, ranging from Confucian moral philosophy to the system of social promotion. As one of the most stable and successful civilizations at the time, China offered various lessons and precedents that were distinct from the founders' European heritage (figure 1.1).

NOTES

1. "To the President of Congress, No. 49, 19 April 1780," Founders Online, National Archives, https://founders.archives.gov/documents/Adams/06-09-02-0115-0002. Original source: *The Adams Papers, Papers of John Adams*, ed. Gregg L. Lint

and Richard Alan Ryerson, vol. 9, *March 1780–July 1780* (Cambridge, MA: Harvard University Press, 1996), 164–96.

2. Ibid.

3. "From Thomas Jefferson to G. K. van Hogendorp, 13 October 1785," Founders Online, National Archives, https://founders.archives.gov/documents/Jefferson/01-08-02-0497. Original source: *The Papers of Thomas Jefferson*, ed. Julian P. Boyd, vol. 8, *25 February–31 October 1785* (Princeton: Princeton University Press, 1953), 631–34.

4. "Address to the Agricultural Society of Albemarle, 12 May 1818," Founders Online, National Archives, https://founders.archives.gov/documents/Madison/04-01-02-0244. Original source: *The Papers of James Madison, Retirement Series*, ed. David B. Mattern, J. C. A. Stagg, Mary Parke Johnson, and Anne Mandeville Colony, vol. 1, *March 4, 1817–January 31, 1820* (Charlottesville: University Press of Virginia, 2009), 260–85.

5. Ibid.

6. "To Thomas Jefferson from William Jarvis, 18 February 1809," Founders Online, National Archives, https://founders.archives.gov/documents/Jefferson/99-01-02-9828.

7. "To John Adams from Philip Mazzei, 27 September 1785," Founders Online, National Archives, https://founders.archives.gov/documents/Adams/06-17-02-0253. Original source: *The Adams Papers, Papers of John Adams*, ed. Gregg L. Lint, C. James Taylor, Sara Georgini, Hobson Woodward, Sara B. Sikes, Amanda A. Mathews, and Sara Martin, vol. 17, *April–November 1785* (Cambridge, MA: Harvard University Press, 2014), 479–83.

8. "To James Madison from Augustus B. Woodward, 12 June 1809," Founders Online, National Archives, https://founders.archives.gov/documents/Madison/03-01-02-0266. Original source: *The Papers of James Madison, Presidential Series*, ed. Robert A. Rutland, Thomas A. Mason, Robert J. Brugger, Susannah H. Jones, Jeanne K. Sisson, and Fredrika J. Teute, vol. 1, *1 March–30 September 1809* (Charlottesville: University Press of Virginia, 1984), 244–47.

9. Ibid.

10. Ibid.

11. Ibid.

12. Ibid.

13. Jedidiah Morse, *The American universal geography, or A view of the present state of all the empires, kingdoms, states, and republics in the known world, and of the United States of America in particular. In two parts ... The whole comprehending a complete and improved system of modern geography. Calculated for Americans: Illustrated with maps of the countries described.* Published according to act of Congress; Part I [-II]. p. 421. Printed at Boston, by Isaiah Thomas and Ebenezer T. Andrews. Sold at their bookstore, Faust's Statue, no. 45, Newbury Street; by said Thomas, in Worcester; by Berry, Rogers and Berry, in Newyork; by H. and P. Rice, in Philadelphia; and by W. P. Young, in Charleston., MDCCXCIII. [1793]

14. A. Owen Aldridge, *The Dragon and the Eagle: The Presence of China in the American Enlightenment* (Detroit: Wayne State University Press, 1993), 21.

15. Peter Gay, *Great Ages of Man: A History of the World's Cultures—Age of Enlightenment* (New York: Time-Life Books, 1966), 61.

16. Ibid.

17. Paolo Santangelo, "Confucius in the 18th Century Italy: A Case of 'Complex Cross-Cultural Reflection'" (paper presented at the Conference held in Venice International University, September 19, 2015), https://www.academia.edu/27262975/Confucius_in_the_18th_century_Italy_a_case_of_complex_intermediate_cross_cultural_reflection_.

18. Arnold H. Rowbotham, "The Impact of Confucianism on Seventeenth Century Europe," *Far Eastern Quarterly* 4, no. 3 (May 1945): 229.

19. A. T. Steele, *The American People and China* (New York, Toronto, and London: McGraw-Hill, 1966), 7.

20. Voltaire, *Essai sur les mœurs*, Tome I (Paris: Classiques Garnier, 1990), 220.

21. M. S. Anderson, *Europe in the Eighteenth Century 1713–1789* (London and New York: Pearson Education, 2016), 308.

22. Voltaire, *Essai sur les mœurs*, 220.

23. Voltaire, *The Philosophical Dictionary*, selected and trans. H. I. Woolf (New York: Knopf, 1924). See also Allan G. Grapard, "Voltaire and East Asia—A Few Reflections on the Nature of Humanism," in *Cahiers d'Extrême-Asie*, vol. 1, 1985, 60.

24. Rowbotham, "Impact of Confucianism on Seventeenth Century Europe," 233.

25. Donald F. Lach, "Leibniz and China," *Journal of the History of Ideas* 6, no. 4 (1945): 453.

26. Walter W. Davis, "China, the Confucian Ideal, and the European Age of Enlightenment," *Journal of the History of Ideas* 44, no. 4 (October–December 1983): 536.

27. William Temple, "Essay on Heroic Virtue," *The Works of Sir Wm. Temple*, vol. III (London, 1814), 342. See also Rowbotham, "Impact of Confucianism on Seventeenth Century Europe," 236.

28. Edmund Leites, "Confucianism in Eighteenth Century England: Natural Morality and Social Reform," *Philosophy East and West* 28, no. 2, Sonological Torque (April 1978):147.

29. Ibid., 153.

30. Derk Bodde, "Chinese Ideas in the West," in *China: A Teaching Workbook*, Asia for Educators, Columbia University, 2005, http://projects.mcah.columbia.edu/nanxuntu/html/state/ideas.pdf.

31. Ibid.

32. Murray N. Rothbard, *Economic Thought Before Adam Smith: An Austrian Perspective on the History of Economic Thought*, vol. I, CreateSpace Independent Publishing Platform (January 1, 2006), 366.

33. Louis B. Wright, "'The Gentleman's Library' in Early Virginia: The Literary Interests of the First Carters," *Huntington Library Quarterly* 1, no. 1 (1937): 55; Lawrence C. Wroth, *An American Bookshelf, 1755* (Philadelphia: University of Pennsylvania Press, 1934), 24, 35, 97; Carl Bridenbaugh, "The Press and the Book in Eighteenth Century Philadelphia," *Pennsylvania Magazine of History and Biography* LXV, no. 1 (1941): 1–30.

34. Ibid.

35. As for Benjamin Franklin's fondness for Chinese civilization, see Dave Wang, "Benjamin Franklin and China: Franklin's Efforts to Draw Positive Elements from Chinese Civilization during the Early the formative Age of the United States," *Historical Review: A Biennial Journal of History and Archaeology* XIII (2005): 1–22; "Exploring Benjamin Franklin's Moral Life," *Franklin Gazette* 17, no. 1 (Spring 2007): 4–5; "Benjamin Franklin and the Great Wall of China," *Franklin Gazette* 18, no. 1 (Spring 2008): 5–7; and "The US Founders and China: The Origins of Chinese Cultural Influence on the United States," *Education about Asia* 16, no. 2 (2011): 5–11.

36. "The Morals of Chess [before 28 June 1779]," Founders Online, National Archives, https://founders.archives.gov/documents/Franklin/01-29-02-0608. Original source: *The Papers of Benjamin Franklin*, ed. Barbara B. Oberg, vol. 29, *March 1 through June 30, 1779* (New Haven and London: Yale University Press, 1992), 750–57.

37. Paine was the editor of the magazine. The works, composed based on the three works written by some seamen who had been to China, including *A Voyage to China and the East Indies*, *A Voyage to Suratte*, and *Account of the Chinese Husbandry*, were "published as a unit in Swedish in 1757." They were translated into German in 1765 and into English in 1771.

38. Kenneth Latourette, *The History of Early Relations between the United States and China, 1784–1844* (New Haven: Yale University Press, 1917), 369.

39. "The Committee for Foreign Affairs to the American Commissioners, May 2, 1777," Founders Online, National Archives, https://founders.archives.gov/documents/Franklin/01-24-02-0010. Original source: *The Papers of Benjamin Franklin*, ed. William B. Willcox, vol. 24, *May 1 through September 30, 1777* (New Haven and London: Yale University Press, 1984), 12–16.

40. Ibid.

41. Edwin Wolf, *James Logan, 1674–1751: Bookman Extraordinary, An exhibition of books and manuscripts from the library of James Logan, supplemented by his writings and documents relating to the history of the Bibliotheca Loganiana. In honor of the visit to Philadelphia of the seventh International Congress of Bibliophiles* (Philadelphia: The Library Company of Philadelphia, 1971), 41.

42. Ibid.

43. Ibid.

44. Marianne Johnson, "'More Native than French': American Physiocrats and Their Political Economy," *History of Economic Ideas* 10, no. 1 (2002): 16.

45. Ibid., 17.

46. Ibid.

47. The *Columbian Magazine* (also known as the *Columbian Magazine or Monthly Miscellany*) was a monthly American literary magazine, published in Philadelphia from 1786 to 1792. May 1788, 2, 257–63.

48. Aldridge, *Dragon and the Eagle*, 35.

49. *New Hampshire Magazine*, September 2, 1793, 199–203.

50. Morse, *American Universal Geography*, 426.

51. Ibid., 424.
52. Ibid.
53. Ibid.
54. See https://www.publishersweekly.com/978-0-679-43045-2.
55. The manuscript is in Morgan Library and Museum in New York City.
56. A file in the online version of the Kouroo Contexture, http://www.kouroo.in fo/kouroo/thumbnails/B/WilliamBartram.
57. Ibid.
58. John Bartram, *Life and Character of the Chinese Philosopher Confucius: Autograph Manuscript*, Pierpont Morgan Library Department of Literary and Historical Manuscripts, Morgan Library and Museum.
59. Ibid.
60. Ibid.
61. Kishichi Watanabe, "The Business Ideology of Benjamin Franklin and Japanese Values of the 18th Century," *Business and Economic History* 17 (1988): 81.
62. Thomas Paine, "Of the Old and New Testament," *The Prospect*, March 31, 1804. See also *Complete Writings*, ed. Philip S. Foner, vol. 2 (New York: Garden City Press, 1945), 805.
63. Ibid.
64. Benjamin Rush, "Of the Mode of Education Proper in a Republic, 1798," in *The Selected Writings of Benjamin Rush*, ed. Dagobert D. Runes (New York: Philosophical Library, 1947), http://press-pubs.uchicago.edu/founders/ documents/v1ch18s30.html.
65. Ibid.
66. John Adams, "To Thomas Jefferson," *The Works of John Adams*, vol. 10, *Letters 1811–1825*, Indexes.
67. "To James Madison from Punqua Wingchong, 5 February 1809," Founders Online, National Archives, https://founders.archives.gov/documents/Madison/99-01-02-3982.
68. Benjamin Franklin, to Joseph Galloway, ALS: Yale University Library, London, April 20, 1771, vol. 18, https://franklinpapers.org/framedVolumes.jsp.
69. Ibid.
70. See http://www.thornber.net/cheshire/ideasmen/percival.html.
71. Franklin to Galloway.
72. Ibid.
73. Benjamin Franklin, "Franklin to Percival," ALS (draft): American Philosophical Society; copy; National Library of Scotland, in William Willcox ed., *The Papers of Benjamin Franklin*, vol. 20 (New Haven and London: Yale University Press, 1979), 442–43. See also John Bigelow, ed., *The Complete Works of Benjamin Franklin*, vol. IV (New York and London: G. P. Putnam's Sons, 1887), 421–22.
74. "Notes on Reading an Account of Travel in China, [1762?]," Founders Online, National Archives, https://founders.archives.gov/documents/Franklin/01-10-02-0098. Original source: *The Papers of Benjamin Franklin*, ed. Leonard W. Labaree,

vol. 10, *January 1, 1762 through December 31, 1763* (New Haven and London: Yale University Press, 1959), 182–83.

75. "Pierre Samuel Du Pont de Nemours to Thomas Jefferson, [ca. 28 July 1810]," Founders Online, National Archives, https://founders.archives.gov/documents/Jefferson/03-02-02-0471. Original source: *The Papers of Thomas Jefferson*, Retirement Series, ed. J. Jefferson Looney, vol. 2, *16 November 1809 to 11 August 1810* (Princeton: Princeton University Press, 2005), 569–656.

76. Ibid.
77. Ibid.
78. Ibid.
79. Ibid.
80. Ibid.
81. Ibid.
82. Ibid.
83. See http://www.hereditary.us/cin_history.htm.
84. Isaac Asimov, *The Birth of the United States, 1763–1816* (Boston: Houghton Mifflin, 1974), 128.
85. Joseph J. Ellis, *His Excellency: George Washington* (New York: Alfred A. Knopf, 2004), 158.
86. "From Benjamin Franklin to Sarah Bache, 26 January 1784," Founders Online, National Archives, https://founders.archives.gov/documents/Franklin/01-41-02-0327. Original source: *The Papers of Benjamin Franklin*, ed. Ellen R. Cohn, vol. 41, *September 16, 1783, through February 29, 1784* (New Haven and London: Yale University Press, 2014), 503–11.
87. Ibid.
88. Ibid.
89. Ibid.
90. Ibid.
91. Ibid.
92. Carl Van Doren, *Benjamin Franklin* (New York: Viking, 1938), 709–10.
93. Benjamin Franklin to Sarah Bache (unpublished) Passy, January 26, 1784, in *The Papers of Benjamin Franklin*, ed. Yale University, http://www.franklinpapers.org/franklin/framedVolumes.jsp; See also Mark Skousen, ed., *The Completed Autobiography by Benjamin Franklin* (Washington DC: Regnery, 2006), 311–12.
94. Ibid.
95. Ibid.
96. Ibid.
97. "From Benjamin Franklin to Sarah Bache, 26 January 1784."
98. D. H. Meyer, "The Uniqueness of the American Enlightenment," *American Quarterly* 28, no. 2, *Special Issue: An American Enlightenment* (Summer 1976): 173.
99. Michael Dunlop Young, *The Rise of the Meritocracy* (New York: Thames and Hudson, 1958).
100. Wilson Casey, *Firsts: Origins of Everyday Things That Changed the World* (New York: Penguin, 2009).

101. Bill Schwarz, *The Expansion of England: Race, Ethnicity, and Cultural History* (New York: Routledge, 1996), 229.

102. David McCullough, *John Adams* (New York and London: Simon & Schuster, 2001), 377.

103. "From John Adams to Alexander Bryan Johnson, 21 January 1823," Founders Online, National Archives, https://founders.archives.gov/documents/Adams/99-03-02-4231.

104. Ibid.

105. 朱熹,论语集注, vol. 1, 8; 杨伯峻,论语译注, 15; and 吴国珍,论语:平解·英译, 16–18.

106. Benjamin Franklin to Madame Brillon, "The Ephemera," Founders Online, National Archives, https://founders.archives.gov/documents/Franklin/01-27-02-0408. See also 朱熹,论语集注, volume 12, 94; 杨伯峻,论语译注, 174.

107. Thomas Paine, *The Political Works of Thomas Paine*, 2 vols. (Oxford: Oxford University Press, 1864), 15. Paine quoted from Confucius's following teaching maxims to Yan Yuan, one of his well-known students: "Look not at what is contrary to propriety; listen not to what is contrary to propriety; speak not what is contrary to propriety; make no movement which is contrary to propriety." (Section 12 of the Analects), http://wengu.tartarie.com/wg/wengu.php?no=294&l=Lunyu. See also 杨伯峻,论语译注, 174.

108. *The Morals of Confucius: A Chinese Philosopher, Who Flourished above Five Hundred Years before the Coming of our LORD and Saviour JESUS CHRIST. Being One of the Choicest Pieces of that Nation*, 2nd. ed. (London: Printed for T. Horne, at the South Entrance into the Royal Exchange, Cornhill, 1691), 22.

109. Michael Collins, "China's Confucius and Western Democracy," *Contemporary Review* 290, no. 1689 (Summer 2008): 161.

110. 朱熹,论语集注, vol. 1, 7; 杨伯峻,论语译注, 14.

111. James T. C. Liu, *China Turning Inward: Intellectual-Political Changes in the Early Twelfth Century* (Cambridge, MA: Harvard University Press, 2003), 39.

112. Carl Van Doren, "Meeting Doctor Franklin," in *Benjamin Franklin and The American Character: Problems in American Civilization*, ed. Charles L. Sanford (Boston: D. C. Heath, 1955), 32.

113. Alan Taylor, "For the Benefit of Mr. Kite," *New Republic* 224, no. 12 (March 19, 2001): 40.

114. Francis Fukuyama, "Confucianism and Democracy," access provided by the University of Arizona, http://www.u.arizona.edu/~zshipley/pol437/docs/fukuyama_1995.pdf.

115. Colin Wells, review of *Thomas Jefferson's Scrapbooks: Poems of Nation, Family, and Romantic Love Collected by America's Third President*, by Jonathan Gross, *Early American Literature*, 42, no. 3 (November 2007): 626.

116. Jonathan Gross, *Thomas Jefferson's Scrapbooks: Poems of Nation, Family, and Romantic Love Collected by America's Third President* (Hanover, NH: Steerforth Press, 2006), 337.

117. 诗经*Shijing, Classics of Poetry*, is the earliest collection of Chinese poems, including 305 poems, some were written as early as 1000 BC. It is one of the Five

Classics edited by Confucius, canonized in the Han dynasty (206 BC–220 AD). The five classics include *Classics of Changes, Classic of Poetry, Classic of Rites, Classic of History and Spring and Autumn Annals. Shijing* has been translated as *The Classics of Poetry, The Book of Songs* or *The Book of Odes*.

118. It is the ancient translation of *The Great Learning*.

119. Bodleian Library, the main research library of the University of Oxford, was established in 1602.

120. Sir William Jones (1746–1794) was an English scholar and the founder of the Asiatic Society.

121. An old written form of *Shijing* in Chinese phoenix.

122. Gross, *Thomas Jefferson's Scrapbooks*, 163. This poem is titled "The Odes of Wei" (Prince of Wu of the Wei State). It is in the section of the Airs of the States in *The Book of Ode*. 子曰:「於止,知其所止,可以人而不如鳥乎!」

詩云:「穆穆文王,於緝熙敬止,」為人君,止於仁;為人臣,止於敬;為人子,止於孝;為人父,止於慈;與國人交,止於信.詩云:「瞻彼淇澳,菉竹猗猗.有斐君子,如切如磋,如琢如磨.瑟兮僩兮,赫兮喧兮.有斐君子,終不可諠兮!」如切如磋者,道學也;如琢如磨者,自脩也;瑟兮僩兮者,恂慄也;赫兮喧兮者,威儀也;有斐君子,終不可諠兮者,道盛德至善,民之不能忘也.

詩云:「於戲前王不忘!」君子賢其賢而親其親,小人樂其樂而利其利,此以沒世不忘也.右傳之三章.釋止於至善.

子曰:「聽訟,吾猶人也,必也使無訟乎!」無情者不得盡其辭.大畏民志,此謂知本.右傳之四章.釋本末.

In the *Book of Poetry*, it is said, "Look at that winding course of the Ch'i, with the green bamboos so luxuriant! Here is our elegant and accomplished prince! As we cut and then file; as we chisel and then grind: so has he cultivated himself. How grave is he and dignified! How majestic and distinguished! Our elegant and accomplished prince never can be forgotten." That expression—"As we cut and then file," the work of learning. "As we chisel and then grind," indicates that of self-culture. "How grave is he and dignified!" indicates the feeling of cautious reverence. "How commanding and distinguished! Indicates an awe-inspiring deportment. Our elegant and accomplished prince never can be forgotten," indicates how, when virtue is complete and excellence extreme, the people cannot forget them.

In the *Book of Poetry*, it is said, "Ah! The former kings are not forgotten." Future princes deem worthy what they deemed worthy, and love what they loved. The common people delight in what delighted them and are benefited by their beneficial arrangements. It is on this account that the former kings, after they have quitted the world, are not forgotten. See *The Great Learning of Confucius* translated by James Legge (1893).

It is available at http://www.sacred-texts.com/cfu/conf2.htm.

123. The *Book of Poetry* says: "O how unforgettable the former sovereigns were!" Those in superior positions showed reverence to the virtuous people and affection to their kinsfolk, so that in inferior positions enjoyed their pleasure and benefited from their beneficial ruling, and that is why they will never be forgotten. See 吴国珍, 孟子·大学·中庸: 平解·英译, 528.

124. *Great Learning* is one of the four books, including *The Doctrine of the Mean*, *The Analects*, and *The Mencius*. They were edited by Confucius. See 吴国珍,孟子·大学·中庸:平解·英译, 527–29.

125. Confucius, *The Great Learning*, trans. James Legge, 1893, http://www.sacred-texts.com/cfu/conf2.htm.

126. Wells, "Thomas Jefferson's Scrapbooks," 626.

127. Ibid.

128. Ibid.

129. Gene Allen Smith, "Thomas Jefferson: Reputation and Legacy," *Journal of American History* 94, no. 1 (June 2007): 260–61.

130. Ellis, *His Excellency: George Washington*, 151.

131. Joshua Zeitz, "Joseph Ellis Explains Just How Revolutionary the Revolution Was," *American Heritage* 58, no. 3 (Winter 2008): 62.

132. Ralph K. Andrist, ed., *The Founding Fathers: George Washington—A Biography in His Own Words*, vol. 1 (New York: Newsweek Book Division, 1972), 6.

133. Joyce Appleby, *Thomas Jefferson* (New York: Times Books—Henry Holt and Company, 2003), 28.

134. Michael Beschloss, *Presidential Courage: Brave Leaders and How They Changed America 1789–1989* (New York: Simon & Schuster, 2007), 31.

135. Andrew Burstein, *Jefferson's Secrets: Death and Design at Monticello* (New York: Basic Books, 2005), 212.

136. Ibid., 211.

137. Ibid.

138. Ibid., 215.

139. Appleby, *Thomas Jefferson*, 46.

140. Ibid.

141. Ibid.

142. *Morals of Confucius*, 55.

143. Benjamin Franklin, "To George Whitefield" (Philadelphia, July 6, 1749). Reprinted from *The Evangelical Magazine*, XI (1803), 27–28; also, AL (fragment) American Philosophical Society, http://www.franklinpapers.org/franklin/framedVolumes.jsp.

144. Benjamin Franklin, "From the *Morals of Confucius*," *Pennsylvania Gazette*, February 28 to March 7, 1738, 74.

145. Ibid.

146. Aldridge, *Dragon and the Eagle*, 26.

147. Louis P. Masur, ed., *The Autobiography of Benjamin Franklin with Related Documents*, 2nd ed. (Boston and New York: Bedford/St. Martin's, 2003), 27.

148. Ibid., 94.

149. Wang Yuechun, *Discover the Orient* [Faxian Dongfang] (Beijing: Beijing Library Press, 2003), 108.

150. Benjamin Franklin, *The Autobiography of Benjamin Franklin*, ed. Leonard W. Labaree, Ralph L. Ketcham, Helen C. Boatfield, and Hellene H. Fineman (New Haven: Yale University Press, 2003), 148.

151. Ibid., 95–96.

152. Jay Tolson, "The Many Faces of Benjamin Franklin," *U.S. News & World Report* 134, no. 22 (June 23, 2003): 37.
153. *Morals of Confucius*, 51–52.
154. Franklin, *Autobiography*, 150.
155. Franklin, "From the *Morals of Confucius*," 81.
156. Harvey C. Mansfield, "Liberty and Virtue in the American Founding," in *Never a Matter of Indifference: Sustaining Virtue in a Free Republic*, ed. Peter Berkowitz (Stanford: Hoover Institution Press, 2003), 14.
157. Frugality is well-known Confucian virtue. "He who will not economize will have to agonize" is a quotation from the *Analects* by Confucius.
158. Numerous authors have labeled Franklin's virtues as the values from Puritan tradition. In the following I just list some main authors' names and their works; interested reader can find and read them to know more about their argument. Paul Anderson and Max Harold Fisch, *Philosophy in America: From the Puritan to James* (New York, Appleton Century, 1939); Henry Steele Commager, *The American Mind: An Interpretation of American Thought and Character Since the 1880's* (New Haven: Yale University Press, 1950); David Levine, "The Autobiography of Benjamin Franklin: The Puritan Experimenter in Life and Art," *Yale Review* 53, no. 2 (December 1963); Perry Miller, "Benjamin Franklin, Jonathan Edwards," in *Major Writers of America* (New York: Harcourt, Brace and World, 1962); Stow Persons, *American Minds: A History of Ideas* (New York: Henry Holt, 1958); Larzer Ziff, *Puritanism in America: New Culture in a New World* (New York: Viking, 1973).
159. James Campbell, *Recovering Benjamin Franklin: An Exploration of a Life of Science and Service* (Chicago and La Salle, IL: Open Court, 1999), 166.
160. Ibid., 174.
161. Franklin, *Autobiography*, 151.
162. Franklin, "From the *Morals of Confucius*," 74.
163. *Morals of Confucius*, 66.
164. Masur, *Autobiography of Benjamin Franklin*, 97.
165. *Morals of Confucius*, 58.
166. Masur, *Autobiography of Benjamin Franklin*, 95.
167. Ibid.
168. Taylor, "For the Benefit of Mr. Kite," 40.
169. Ibid.
170. Ibid.
171. Liu, *China Turning Inward*, 39.
172. Ibid., 138.
173. Ibid., 140.
174. Franklin had the following sentence inscribed in his parents' marble stone monument: "Their youngest son, in filial regard to their memory, Places this stone." See Masur, *Autobiography of Benjamin Franklin*, 35–36.
175. Masur, *Autobiography of Benjamin Franklin*, 95.
176. Herrlee Glessner Creel, *Confucius: The Man and the Myth* (New York: John Day Company, 1949), 263. Creel (1905–1994) was a "highly regarded authority on Confucianism." See *New York Times*, June 4, 1994.

Chapter 2

Technologies from the East

How the Founders Leveraged Chinese Technologies in the North American Colonies

The American Founding Fathers leveraged Chinese technologies. They wanted to create a better quality of life and to move the newly independent republic forward. Benjamin Franklin, George Washington, Thomas Jefferson, Benjamin Rush, Alexander Hamilton, and Gouverneur Morris, among others, regarded China as a resource for both knowledge and inspiration. While fighting for independence from British rule, the founders used Chinese inventions to develop innovative technologies. Immediately after the Revolutionary War's conclusion, they used the example of the Great Wall of China as a model for maintaining national independence. In the following pages, I will first present the founders' efforts to make use of various Chinese technologies. Then I will provide several examples of the impact that Chinese technology had on the early history of the United States, including Benjamin Franklin, George Washington, and the Great Wall of China, Thomas Jefferson and Chinese architectural designs, Benjamin Franklin's efforts to promote sericulture in North America, and Franklin and Chinese heating technology and medical theories. Finally, I will survey Franklin's exertions to study Chinese navigation and papermaking technologies.

THE FOUNDING FATHERS AND CHINESE TECHNOLOGY

The Founding Fathers drew inspiration from Chinese innovations. Facing the task of developing a new and flourishing society for American colonies, they paid particular attention to what they could benefit from—such as Chinese agricultural and technological innovations. Charles Thomas

(1729–1826), secretary of the Continental Congress and later the U.S. Congress, emphasized the sophistication of Chinese industry, such as advancing the arts of living and improving in husbandry and native plants.[1] The American Philosophical Society, founded in 1768, told the American people if they could "introduce the industry of the Chinese, their arts of living and improvements in husbandry, America might become in time as populous as China."[2]

Chinese inventions in areas such as heating technology, silk production, porcelain ware, manufacturing, navigation, canal construction, and even the construction of the Great Wall found their way to North America via Europe. The founders understood this information could be used to promote social and economic development.

Benjamin Franklin was eager to borrow valuable and practical technologies from China. His interests were wide-ranging, from the creation of everyday goods to the intricacies of commerce. In 1763, Franklin sent prominent American academic and Congregationalist minister Ezra Stiles copies of Chinese prints illustrating silk production to promote the creation of a colonial silk industry. Franklin was interested in Chinese painted candles; he tried to analyze "of what are they made." In addition, Franklin recorded solar eclipses in China and the gifts of the emperor to his subjects. He wrote down the following notes in 1762:

Oct. 17. 1762 between 5 and 6 PM. an Eclipse of the Sun
Nov. 12. 1761 A total Eclipse of the Moon near Canton, between 6 and 10 aClock PM
Nov 2. 1762 An Eclipse of the Moon at 4 in the Morning. Fees paid on a Gift from the King of £200 amounted to £23 5s. 6d.[3]

To develop American commerce, Franklin also studied the technology used to preserve Chinese tea during transport to North America. The tea that was shipped from China to Europe, then to America, was well-preserved, dry, and crisp, although it "comes all the way by sea in the damp hold of a ship." Franklin reasoned that this technology could be used to preserve grains. He told Peter Franklin, "by this method, grain, meal, &c. if well dry'd before 'tis put up, may be kept for ages sound and good."[4] Scarce energy resources also led Franklin to examine Chinese ship construction, prompting him to publicize the Chinese development of watertight compartment technology. Franklin also explored Chinese windmills. He said that it was a "pleasure to see the Contrivance of horizontal Wind mills become generally useful" and "that almost every Farmer may execute without the help of any Workman, and which, or something like it, I have had an imperfect Account of as used in China."[5]

Finally, Franklin turned his attention to Chinese food. In 1770, he was animated upon learning about Chinese Doufu (bean curd). He sent to John Bartram (1699–1777) "some Chinese Garavances, with Father Navaretta's account of the universal use of a cheese made of them, in China." Franklin attempted to discover what "the Tau-fu is made of." He shared the information with Bartram, "that some runnings of salt (I suppose runnet) is put into water when the meal is in it, to turn it to curds."[6] He even wanted to understand the base ingredient for Chinese vinegar, Liche, asking "What is it?"[7]

Thomas Jefferson employed Chinese technological practices to develop his own clock. A letter from Jefferson to Benjamin Franklin Bache (1769–1798) in 1794 revealed that Jefferson made use of the Chinese gong from Benjamin Franklin "as the bell for a chateau clock."[8] Jefferson used the Chinese gong for "calling people together." Margaret Bayard Smith (1778–1844), an American author and political commentator in the Early Republic of the United States, visited Jefferson at his home and recalled that she saw the Chinese gongs in Monticello. She reminisced, "I cannot tell, except it is on account of its newness and originality. Another was placed in a tree on the lawn, to summon the workmen to their meals."[9]

Innovations in Chinese technology for trade infrastructure and agriculture, the founders observed, could be utilized. In 1777, Alexander Hamilton had understood the function of the Chinese Grand Canal, reporting that "There is an immense canal in China 1000 Miles long which traverses the whole Chinese empire from Canton to Pekin.[10] George Washington also thought to build a canal in the Cheat River (figure 2.1).[11]

After survey of the river, he surmised that a canal of fifteen miles long should be constructed "from the Dunkers bottom, along the river."[12]

In order to open a gateway to the West (specifically, the Ohio Valley) for settlement and trade, Washington created the Shenandoah & Potomac Navigation Company—one of the first stockholder companies in the United States. Washington's goal was to construct a canal on the Virginia side of the Potomac so that shallow, pole-driven vessels could bypass the Great Falls.[13] In 1762, Thomas Johnson, an early and active promoter of commercial navigation on the upper Potomac, became a manager of the navigation company and began correspondence with Washington on the feasibility of opening a canal above the great falls of the Potomac River.[14]

John Ledyard (1751–1789), an American explorer and adventurer who visited China with Captain Cook's third voyage to the Pacific, noticed that the Chinese were very eager for furs and were willing to pay a great deal for them. Under his encouragement, American traders looked for furs in the Northwest, bought them from the Indians, and shipped them to China. Washington's letter to David Stuart evidenced that Washington adored the idea of bringing furs from the Ohio Valley and sending them to China.[15]

Figure 2.1 A Scene of the Grand Canal of China in the Eighteenth Century. This picture, Junks on the Canal, was by Xu Yang, eighteenth-century painter from Suzhou, China. It depicts the flourishing commercial scene on the Grand Canal (大运河). The first construction of the canal dates to the fifth century BC, but the various sections were linked during the Sui dynasty (581–618 AD). Since then, the later dynasties restored and rebuilt the canal and altered its route to supply their capital. It spans 1,100 miles [1,770 km], making it the longest canal system in the world. The canal provided safe transportation for China by insulating from the threats of storms and pirates on the high seas.

In 1770, Franklin grasped the importance of canals in the colonies as well. He told Thomas Gilpin (1728–1778), a Quaker merchant and manufacturer, of "the Advantages of Canals for internal Navigation in our Country, to which I heartily wish Success."[16] Franklin then told Gilpin that he was extremely pleased at the idea "of the Practicability of navigating down Sasquehanah."[17]

Gouverneur Morris (1752–1816), a prominent founder of the republic, further studied China's Grand Canal. With his encouragement, the New Yorkers built the Erie Canal, connecting New York to the Midwest. The canal played a role in New York City's rise, triggered an explosion in canal building, facilitated economic growth, and linked the Northeast with the region of the new nation that would later be known as the Midwest.[18]

As an agrarian society during the Early Republic years, the founders turned to China, a nation with a remarkably successful agriculture, to learn from some techniques that Chinese farmers invented in their farming experience. James Madison revealed to American farmers that, according to Chinese farming experience, perpetual fertility was compatible "with an uninterrupted succession of crops."[19] He expressed to members of the Agricultural Society of Albemarle that the Chinese would laugh at

> at the idea that land needs rest, as if, like animals, it had a sense of fatigue. Their soil does not need rest, because an industrious use is made of every fertilizing particle that can contribute toward replacing what has been drawn from it.[20]

He continued that "the Chinese example, where the cultivated crop is restored to the earth, all pronounce that such would be the effect."[21]

Finally, some Chinese artisan technologies were used to advance certain political agendas even before American independence. For example, some colonial leaders viewed porcelain manufacturing as essential to national economic self-reliance. Chinese porcelain, like tea, had been a major colonial import. Benjamin Rush was among the first group of people who advocated building a porcelain factory in North America with the intent of overcoming the colonies' dependence on British imports. The excerpt that follows from one of Rush's letters illustrates porcelain to be but one component of a grand strategy:

> I have many schemes in view with regard to these things. I have made those mechanical arts, which are connected with chemistry the particular objects of my study and not without hopes of seeing a china manufactory established in Philadelphia in the course of a few years. Yes, we will be revenged by the mother country. For my part, I am resolved to devote my head, my heart, and my pen entirely to the service of America, and promise myself much assistance from you in everything of this kind that I shall attempt through life.[22]

The colonists' pursuit of domestic Chinese porcelain ware became a powerful call for patriotic support of American economic independence. Franklin, in London when Rush was promoting colonial porcelain production, echoed this sentiment in a letter to his wife: "I am pleased to find so good progress made in the China Manufactory. I wish it Success most heartily."[23] The American China Manufactory in Philadelphia became noted for its quality, and more importantly, succeeded in cultivating patriotism as it challenged Britain's monopoly of the product and indirectly contributed to the struggle for independence.

Explicit examples of Chinese architectural influences are present in one of America's most historic buildings. Jefferson developed a new type of architecture by incorporating certain Chinese designs into his famous neoclassical-style home, Monticello. Jefferson used Chinese lattices in many buildings, including Barboursville, the home he designed in Orange County,

Virginia. Jefferson also planned to build a Chinese pavilion when he remodeled Monticello in the last decade of the eighteenth century.

BENJAMIN FRANKLIN, GEORGE WASHINGTON, AND THE GREAT WALL OF CHINA, 1756–1776

The Great Wall of China—an iconic symbol of Chinese civilization—has enjoyed an unexpected and yet substantial impact. In recent years, the idea of the Great Wall has frequently been employed in the context of former president Donald Trump's controversial Mexico-U.S. border wall. However, the notion of the "Chinese Wall" extends beyond this context and into fields as disparate as business, education, and the military. The Great Wall has cultural roots originating in America's colonial era, when Founding Fathers Benjamin Franklin and George Washington recommended that a similar barrier be constructed to protect and maintain independence. Alexander Hamilton fully realized the example of the Great Wall to China's border safety. In 1777, he told his fellow Americans the Chinese "immense wall of 600 leagues long" served as "a barrier against the tartars."[24]

I will examine the Great Wall's influence on American culture, with the intent of exploring how broader Chinese cultural elements have imprinted the nation's history. I will begin this chapter with a brief history of the Chinese wall, and then discuss its impact on the young United States prior to and immediately following the American Revolution.

A Brief History of the Great Wall of China

The Great Wall of China, as the world's largest defensive structure, stretches over approximately 6,400 kilometers (4,000 miles). The earliest foundations of the Great Wall can be traced to China's Warring States period (481–221 BC), a tumultuous era in which seven rival kingdoms battled for territorial advantage. Many of the smaller walls built by these states to protect their borders would lay the groundwork for the eventual Great Wall. Construction of a unified wall began under the reign of Emperor Qinshihuang (259–210 BC), who conquered the rival states and began the Qin dynasty (221–206 BC). As the first emperor to unify China, he had sections of earlier fortifications extended to form the Great Wall, a coordinated defense system against raids by Hunic, Mongol, Turkic, and other nomadic tribes from the north. Construction continued for more than a thousand years until the Ming dynasty (1368–1644 AD). Subsequent Chinese rulers would continue to build, modify, and extend the wall that had started to form under Emperor Qinshihuang.

The immediate impact of the wall was to safeguard farmlands from northern invaders, thereby improving the stability of ancient Chinese culture and society. In later centuries, the Great Wall promoted the transmission of goods and information between China and her trade partners by defending key routes, including the Silk Road. The Great Wall would become a symbol representing the "nation's spirit, [its] working people's wisdom, their perseverance to become stronger, and the ability to fend off enemies' intrusion."[25] In addition to its military influence, the Great Wall has played an important role in the evolution of Chinese civilization.

Like a giant belt, the wall has held China together, unifying the country from past to present. The importance of unification has been a continuing theme since the construction of the Great Wall. Yet somewhat paradoxically, the wall also served as a physical and metaphorical divide between civilizations. It served to insulate imperial China from what were regarded as inferior nomadic and European cultures.

The Great Wall of China in the West before the End of the Eighteenth Century

The earliest Western records of the Great Wall can be found in brief descriptions from Roman and Arabic manuscripts extending as far back as the fourth century. Ammianus Marcellinus, a historian who wrote one of the earliest accounts of the Roman Empire, recounted "summits of lofty walls" enclosing the land of Seres, the country that the Romans believed to lie at the end of the Silk Road.[26] Later Arab writers and travelers, such as Rashid-al-Din Hamadani (1248–1318) and Ibn Battuta (1304–1377), would also mention the Great Wall of China.[27]

Interestingly, Italian explorer Marco Polo (1254–1324), the first European to have left a detailed chronicle of China, neglects to mention the Great Wall in his *Book of the Marvels of the World*.[28] Polo's accounts were not unique in this regard; many European visitors to China during the Middle Ages, including John of Plano Carpini, William of Rubruck, Giovanni Marignolli, and Odoric of Pordenone, seem to have left no records of the wall. A possible explanation for this apparent discrepancy is that Polo and others stayed in China under the Yuan dynasty (1279–1368), which had been established by the Mongolians. The ruling class may have been reticent to show Europeans the structure that had been constructed to keep them out.

European records of the Great Wall became more widespread during China's Ming dynasty, during which the kingdom increased commercial activities with foreign states. Gaspar da Cruz's (c. 1520–1570) *A Treatise of China and the Adjoining Regions* notes "a Wall of a hundred leagues in length."[29] Another early account by Bishop Juan González de Mendoza (1550–1620) reported a wall spanning five hundred leagues, but advised that only one hundred leagues were man-made, with the rest being natural rock formations.[30] The Jesuit priest Matteo Ricci (1552–1610) described "a tremendous wall four hundred and five miles long" that formed part of the Ming Empire's northern defenses.[31] The book *1563 Asia* postulated that the wall had been constructed to defend against Mongolian invaders. In 1754, English antiquarian William Stukeley (1687–1765) described the Chinese wall as "a considerable figure upon the terrestrial globe [which] may be discerned at the moon."[32]

Perhaps the first recorded instance of a European entering China via the Great Wall occurred in 1605, when the Portuguese Jesuit brother Bento de Góis (1562–1607) reached the northwestern Jiayu Pass from India.[33] In a separate account sixty years later, Jesuit Martino Martini (1614–1661) described atypical stretches of the Great Wall and generalized such fortifications to exist along China's entire northern frontier in his *Atlas Sinensis*. Martini believed that the entire wall had been built under the Qin dynasty, which historical records suggest was a common misperception at the time.[34]

The Great Wall would later draw the attention of several philosophers during the European Enlightenment of the eighteenth century. For example, French revolutionary Voltaire proclaimed the Great Wall to be "a monument to fear" in the same manner that the Great Egyptian Pyramids were "monuments to vanity and superstition."[35] Jean-Baptiste Du Halde (1674–1743) offered a more tempered perspective: "Two hundred and fifteen years before the Coming of Christ this prodigious Work was built, by order of the First Emperor of the Family of Tsin, to defend three great Provinces against the Irruption of the Tartars."[36]

Westerners would again explore the Great Wall during the 1793 McCartney Embassy, the first British diplomatic mission to China. The envoy, led by George McCartney (1737–1806), surveyed the wall to gather intelligence.[37] McCartney would later envision China during the time of construction as not only a "powerful empire, but also a very wise and virtuous nation."[38]

However, several negative perceptions of the Great Wall also existed in the West. For some, the wall was the emblem of an inward-looking people, a closeted "Middle Kingdom." German philosopher Johann Gottfried Herder (1744–1803) disparaged it as the symbol of the feudal autocracy. Others would dismiss it as a display of "Chinese exceptionalism."

The Great Wall in North America, 1700–1800

The British Parliament endorsed the idea of a "Great Wall" along the Appalachians with the intent of maintaining order among its colonies, specifically by limiting potential territorial conflicts with Native American tribes. The colonial Americans were, at times, similarly drawn to the prospect of barricading their cultivated soil from the boundaries of nature. Such a wall might prevent the "incalculable loss of life and property" and, in their view, the "lust of territory [and] wealth . . . which has poured out streams of innocent blood."[39]

The Founding Fathers recommended the construction of such a wall on the eve of the American Revolution and again after the fledgling nation won independence from England. During the French and Indian War (1754–1763), Franklin introduced the notion of the Great Wall of China into the public debate, maintaining that building an American Great Wall was the most efficient way to protect the thirteen colonies. Franklin again raised the notion of the Great Wall during the Revolutionary War.[40] George Washington also found the value of the Great Wall in keeping the newborn United States a consolidated nation. Although no wall was ever constructed, one can better appreciate the founders' mindset by surveying the background from which such ideas were formed.

Proclamation of 1763: Great Britain's Plan to Contain the Colonists

The rapid growth and unification of the thirteen colonies during the 1700s set the stage for a momentous shift in the balance of power between England and her North American provinces.[41] In 1700, England had twenty subjects for each colonist; only seventy-five years later, the colonial population had ballooned to 2.5 million, approximately a third the size of the English. The thirteen colonies had also established close trade relations with each other, cultivating a sense of shared American identity. Early displays of unity were evident in instances such as the 1754 Albany Congress, during which Benjamin Franklin proposed the creation of a union for the colonies' joint defense.[42]

Throughout the 1700s, the colonists also began venturing further from the Atlantic seaboard. Pennsylvania, Virginia, Connecticut, and Maryland had all laid claim to territory in the Ohio River Valley, with elite families investing in the Ohio Company to promote settlement of the region.[43] The colonists' steady encroachment drew the ire of Native Americans. In 1763, a coalition of American Indians known as the Ottawa Nation campaigned to drive the colonists from the region, leading to the death of thousands of settlers and British soldiers. Parliament passed a series of stringent edicts to curtail further attacks and recoup financial losses suffered from the Ottawa, in conjunction with the recently ended French and Indian War. Among these edicts was the Royal Proclamation of 1763, which prohibited westward expansion beyond the Appalachians; the Stamp Act, an internal tax levied on all printed paper used by the colonists; and an order to retain a large standing army in North America.

These edicts caused tensions to flare between England and its colonies. Many colonists decried the new taxes that had been imposed, in part, to pay for Britain's unsolicited standing army. Many colonists also ignored the Royal Proclamation. In 1773, the *Virginia Gazette* proclaimed that not even "a second Chinese wall" could "prevent the settlement of the lands on [the] Ohio [River] and its dependencies."[44] Throughout the mid-eighteenth century, various settlements continued to form beyond the Appalachians in disregard of England's new laws.

Parliament eventually responded by passing the Quebec Act of 1774, which reinforced its 1763 Royal Proclamation and punished the colonists for various transgressions that had transpired over the past decade, including the Boston Tea Party. The Quebec Act expanded the boundaries of the Quebec province to include land in the Ohio River Valley and west of the Mississippi River, effectively voiding the colonists' land claims in the region. The Quebec Act sent a clear message to the colonists by establishing a "border beyond which, for the advantage of the whole empire, [the colonists] would not extend [themselves]."[45]

Many colonists opposed the Quebec Act, both because the edict had been intended as a punishment and because it degraded the "proper superiority of Protestant Britons by favoring [the Quebec] Catholics."[46] In October 1774, Founding Father Richard Henry Lee (1732–1794) declared the Quebec Act to be the "the worst grievance" suffered by the colonists.[47] Some British politicians supported Lee's stance. Charles Pratt, Earl of Camden (1714–1794), proposed a bill in the House of Lords to repeal the Quebec Act.[48] Camden believed that if Britain were to draw "the limits of that province close along the interior settlements of all the old English colonies, so as to prevent their further progress," then it would effectively oppose "the further extension of civil liberty and Protestant religion."[49]

The colonists rejected parliamentary authority soon after the passage of the Quebec Act, leading to the outbreak of the American Revolution in 1775. To the colonists, the proposed Appalachian wall—like the Great Wall of China—did more than just separate territories and civilizations. Both walls could be seen as manifestations of the political ideologies of the ruling class. Just as the Great Wall helped metaphorically insulate China from external influences, the "American Wall" was perceived as an extension of "the shackles of arbitrary power and of Property over all the future settlements and colonies of America."[50]

Benjamin Franklin and the Great Wall of China, 1756–1776

The newly declared United States faced tremendous military pressure, for Great Britain had mobilized its considerable military to suppress the rebellion. The Founding Fathers were faced with the seemingly impossible task of protecting the nascent nation. Franklin turned to Chinese military strategy immediately following the beginning of the American Revolution.

Benjamin Franklin had recommended that a fortification like China's Great Wall be constructed in North America before the founding of the United States. During the French and Indian War, Pennsylvania came under threat from the French Indians shortly after the war broke in 1754, and the leaders of the colony were debating between active retaliation and defense fortification. In this time, Franklin suggested before the British Parliament that the best means to protect the colonists' interests was to construct a great wall like that of China.[51] In 1760, Franklin stated (figure 2.2),

> The second kind of security—A security of our planters from the inroads of savages, and the murders committed by them—will not be obtained by such forts, unless they were connected by a *wall* like that of *China*, from one end of our settlements to the other.[52]

Franklin often applied practical and valuable elements from Chinese civilization in his effort to build a flourishing new society in North America.[53]

Figure 2.2 Allen Well, the Only Relics of Franklin's Great Wall. Following the order of the governor of Pennsylvania, Franklin went to the front and built Fort Allen, which included two blockhouses and a well. It was used as a base of supplies and as a rendezvous for troops during the period of the French and Indian War in the winter of 1756. The well is the only trace left of the fort. (Photo by the author.)

Given Franklin's propensity to often draw insight from Chinese civilization, it is unsurprising that he turned to Chinese military strategy in a time of need. However, Franklin's recommendation of a great wall raises several important questions, the most important being why Franklin thought such a proposal was necessary. To understand this, it is necessary to review the historical context behind Franklin's plan.

The eighteenth century saw the rapid expansion of the British colonies in North America. In 1700, the Caucasian population in the English colonies was 250,000; just twenty years later, the population had almost doubled. While this period was one of rapid growth, it was also filled with various hardships and conflicts. The French and Indian War began in the Ohio River Valley in 1754, and Pennsylvania was under threat by the French Indians a year later. Franklin's letters from separate occasions indicate that he was familiar with China's Great Wall. For instance, Franklin had once sent rhubarb seeds to his friend, botanist John Bartram, with the message that the seeds had come from near the Chinese wall.[54] From his personal experiences constructing fortifications in the Blue Mountain region, combined with accounts of China's Great Wall, Franklin believed that connecting individual turrets into a line of forts would provide the greatest security.

The leaders of Pennsylvania were split between two approaches on how to most effectively protect the colony. Some leaders advocated a policy of aggressive retaliation, believing that they should invade French Indian territory. Others advocated for a defensive "chain of forts" to safeguard the British colonists from attack. Franklin left us the vivid description of the debate:

> The Commissioners were of Oppinion, that the best means of Securing our Inhabitants, was to Carry the warr into the Enemys Country, and hunt them in all their Fishing, Hunting, Planting and dwelling places: But having sent for Croghan and others, in order to obtain their Oppinion; and they Advising that by *a Chain of forts* the Frontier should first be in some degree secured before we Acted Offencively, the same was agreed to, and the Building of Forts immediately set about, which took up much more time than was expected.[55]

Franklin did not agree with bringing the war into Indian Territory. While Franklin sided with the second idea, he was not satisfied with the chain of forts; instead, he imagined a "line of forts." Governor Harris of Pennsylvania endorsed Franklin's approach and entrusted him with the authority to make decisions on defensive affairs.[56]

Realizing the speed with which he had to implement his strategy, Franklin immediately rushed to the front, "which was infested by the Enemy."[57] He was to build a line of forts between the Delaware and Susquehanna Rivers. Along the Blue Mountains, some forts had already been built to defend the colonies. As the commander for defense, Franklin envisioned connecting these forts to form a barrier between the French Indians and the British. However, it was impossible for him to establish a new line of forts with the French Indians rapidly approaching.

Pressed for time, Franklin decided to "execute more speedily the first Design of erecting a Fort near Gnadenhutten." So on January 14, 1756, Franklin arrived with more than two hundred men in force to the devastated New Gnaden Huetten settlement to build Fort Allen, the first of his defensive structures. With this force, Franklin hoped to complete construction within three weeks. Upon his arrival at New Gnaden Huetten, he expressed his optimism to his wife, Deborah: "I hope in a Fortnight or three Weeks, God willing, to see the intended Line of Forts finished."[58]

By January 26, Franklin had almost finished the construction of Fort Allen. He relayed this progress in his letter to Samuel Rhoads (1711–1784).[59] He told Rhoads that they had constructed a "pretty strong Fort," and they were going to complete two more forts in a week. Franklin hoped that they would "compleat the projected Line from Delaware to Susquehanah."[60]

In order to "complete the Projected Line," Franklin would have to build two more forts. After he finalized construction of Fort Allen, Franklin sent his troops to build Fort Norris and Fort Franklin. Therefore, as soon as Captain Hays returned with the Convoy of Stores and Provisions, Franklin decided to "send Orndt and Hays to Haeds to join Capt. Trump in erecting the middle Fort there."[61] He reasoned that

> with those two Forts may be finished and the Line of Forts compleated and garrisoned, the Rangers in Motion, and the internal Guards and Watches disbanded, as well as some other Companies; unless they are permitted and encouraged to go after the Enemy to Sasquehannah.[62]

After Franklin erected the three forts between the Susquehanna and Delaware Rivers, he effectively created a line of forts and strengthened the defensive fortifications. Franklin believed that the defense line for Philadelphia was consolidated and was better "than that of any other Colony on the Continent." The reason was that it was "being guarded by a Line of Forts at no great Distance from each other, all strongly garrisoned."[63]

After Franklin finished construction on Forts Allen, Norris, and Franklin, both he and the governor realized that it was no longer necessary for Franklin to remain there.[64] And so, Franklin left Fort Allen after entrusting its defense to Colonel Clapham, a man skilled in military affairs. Franklin believed that as soon his line of forts was completed, the people in the area "may be secur'd." He assured the governor, it was "absolutely necessary to get the Ranging Line of Forts completed." He reasoned that otherwise, "the Expence and Loss to the Province will be intolerable."[65]

After leaving the frontline, Franklin was still concerned about Fort Allen. In 1758, two years after the forts were completed, Franklin asked for information regarding the fort from Charles Thomson (1729–1824),[66] a supporter of Franklin's policies in the French and Indian War.[67] On January 4, 1760, shortly before he made his recommendation for constructing fortification similar to the Great Wall of China public, Franklin exchanged information on Fort Allen with Isaac Norris (1671–1735).[68] Norris told him, "At our last sitting in December our House reduced our Forces to 150 Men intended to Garrison Fort Augusta Littleton and Fort Allen with a Design to protect our Indian Trade."[69]

Within nineteen days, Franklin had effectively established a line of forts in Lehigh Valley by constructing Forts Allen, Norris, and Franklin. This line was comparable to a great wall; indeed, many would regard this as Franklin's version of the Great Wall of China. Franklin would later use his personal experience with his line to strengthen his argument for a great wall in the colonies.

Certain people, both in the North American colonies and in the English Parliament, believed that the colonies would be "sufficiently secure" if they would simply "raise English forts." However, Franklin argued that more needed to be done. From his personal experiences constructing a line of fortifications in the Blue Mountain region, Franklin believed that the security of the colonies "will not be obtained by such forts" unless they should be connected into "a *wall* like that of *China,* from one end of our settlements to the other." Franklin supported his assertion by drawing from the French and Indian War:

> They [the Indians] go to war, as they call it, in small parties, from fifty men down to five. Their hunting life has made them acquainted with the whole country, and scarce any part of it is impracticable to such a party. They can travel thro' the woods even by night, and know how to conceal their tracks. They pass easily between your forts undiscover'd; and privately approach the settlements of your frontier inhabitants. They need no convoys of provisions to follow them; for whether they are shifting from place to place in the woods, or lying in wait for an opportunity to strike a blow, every thicket and every stream furnishes so small a number with sufficient subsistence. When they have surpriz'd separately, and murder'd and scalp'd a dozen families, they are gone with inconceivable expedition thro' unknown ways, and 'tis very rare that pursuers have any chance of coming up with them. *In short,*

long experience has taught our planters, that they cannot rely upon forts as a security against Indians.[70]

Franklin described the dangers faced by the colonists in order to alert the public to their need of a great wall. The French Indian strategies described by Franklin were exactly the same as those used by the nomadic intruders who plundered Chinese settlers. The patterns of warfare that the colonists confronted in North America were similar to those the Chinese faced before the completion of the Great Wall. Franklin's recommendation demonstrated his knowledge of Chinese history. He not only understood the wall's function but was also knowledgeable about its historical context, according to his correspondence with John Bartram, dated August 22, 1772.[71]

Although Franklin never completed his vision during the French and Indian War, he would continue to draw inspiration from China's Great Wall. More than a decade later, in the midst of the American Revolution, Franklin again proposed the idea in a letter to Chevalier de Kermorvan (1740–1817), an engineer in the Continental Army. Kermorvan was involved with fortifications at Billingsport, located below Philadelphia along the Delaware River, and at Perth Amboy, located opposite Staten Island.[72] However, Kermorvan "made himself 'disagreeable' to General Washington and his army staff with his criticism of all military operations" during the 1777 Philadelphia Campaign, and was invited to leave Washington's army before any further action could have been taken.[73]

In his reply to Franklin, Chevalier de Kermorvan ridiculed the recommended great wall. Kermorvan believed Franklin lacked full knowledge on the history of the Great Wall of China. In his letter, Kermorvan told Franklin that the great wall was useless, for the Great Wall of China "did not preserve this empire from being conquered by the Tartar ones."[74]

It is unclear whether Franklin ever responded to the Chevalier. The chevalier's knowledge was flawed. The Tartars, or the Manchu people, successfully entered the China proper because the Han Chinese who defended the wall willingly opened the doors for the invaders. Their invasion was not due to the ineffectiveness of the Great Wall itself. In any case, Franklin continued to regard the Great Wall of China as a valuable example for safeguarding American interests during the Revolution.

Several circumstantial differences existed between Franklin's two recommendations, owing to dramatic political changes between the French and Indian War and the American Revolution. Yet looking beyond such differences, Franklin's proposal of a "Chinese wall" reflected his understanding of the wall's function in defending China. Franklin's proposal remained a constant throughout his transformation from a subject of the British Empire to an American Founding Father, suggesting the enduring applications of such a wall.

George Washington and the Great Wall

Following America's successful War of Independence, the Founding Fathers were confronted with the challenge of maintaining unity within their fledgling nation. George Washington, the primary architect of American foreign policy during the founding era, feared that continued conflicts with Native American neighbors would threaten the independent nation. His concern was not unfounded. Shortly after the Treaty of Paris ended the war in 1783, some American settlers made inroads into Native American territories in disregard of prior negotiated treaties. Washington was concerned about the ramifications of this unchecked westward expansion beyond the Appalachian Mountains.

Washington appreciated the importance of maintaining viable relationships with powerful Native American confederacies and spent much of his first term in diplomacy with various tribes. He understood that if the federal government failed to "restrain the turbulence and disorderly conduct" of its citizens, then the new nation could not expect peace with the Native Americans.[75] Managing westward expansion might also provide an opportunity to "force the state-based members of the confederation to behave collectively, thereby giving the political foundation for the nation-in-the-making."[76] As such, in the summer of 1790, Washington signed the Treaty of New York with twenty-six other chieftains to establish a Creek Nation and set aside new lands for American expansion. Shortly thereafter, Washington issued the Proclamation of 1790, an executive order that forbade private citizens, corporations, and states from encroaching upon Indian lands.

However, the frontier states generally disregarded the federal government's management of Indian affairs. Many Indian tribes were suspicious of Washington, the so-called Great Father. During the Revolutionary War, Washington attacked perhaps as many as forty Native American villages allied with the British.[77] In addition, Britain retained several outposts in limited U.S. territories following the war and "continued to incite Indian tribes into the Ohio Valley to attack American frontiersmen."[78] Confronted with these circumstances, Washington sent statesman John Jay (1745–1829) to broker a treaty with Britain and avoid another war. For many Americans, this treaty, signed in November 1794, was a humiliation. However, Washington believed that such a treaty was necessary; another serious conflict would jeopardize the new nation.

Washington lacked the manpower to adequately defend the western front. According to Secretary of War Henry Knox (1750–1806), the new nation needed five thousand soldiers to patrol the border, but had less than half at the time.[79] By 1796, a much-discouraged Washington had begun to doubt that the federal government was capable of establishing a lasting peace with the Native American peoples. It was in this grave time that Washington suggested that the federal government might control the situation by building a wall like China's. Washington said to Secretary of State Thomas Pickering (1745–1829), "I believe scarcely anything short of a Chinese wall or a line of troops will restrain land jobbers and the encroachment of settlers on Indian Territory."[80] In 1796, Washington instructed Pickering to consider the proposal and revert with a recommendation on when such work should commence.[81]

For Washington, such a wall would be mutually beneficial by demarcating the border. It occurred to him that this wall could help keep Americans on their side of the border and maintain peace with the natives. As he expressed, "The Indians urge this; the Law requires it; and it ought to be done."[82]

Washington's recommendation of a wall should not be taken out of context. Washington sought to manage, but not curb, the western expansion. He worried that a "widely dispersed westward migration" would weaken the country's defenses against British power.[83] Like the Great Wall, Washington's proposed American wall might separate the two civilizations and preserve the cultural integrity of his fledgling nation. It was also because Washington had read about China. For example, he owned a copy of Louis le: Compte's Travels thro. China—1 vol. [Louis Daniel Le Comte. Memoirs and remarks . . . made in above ten years travel through the empire of China. London, 1738.].[84]

Summary

The impact of China's Great Wall on the young United States was more metaphorical than architectural. For the British, this psychological wall was employed as a means of maintaining control of its colonies and shielding against the Native Americans. Benjamin Franklin and George Washington had similar visions for a wall that could secure the young nation against external threats—in Franklin's case, both the natives and the English—while simultaneously serving as a unifying force.[85]

From its beginning, the United States embraced an "us-against-them" mindset reflected in its approach. The intention behind building the wall changed with the situation. The founders tore down the wall that restricted the country's expansion while simultaneously building another for protection. Despite distance in time and space, the founders' wall directly echoes the framework of the Great Wall of China. Even today, the wall mindset continues to penetrate American beliefs. On the one hand, the United States believes that it should build a wall to keep "us as a quiet home-dwelling under our vine and fig tree"; on the other, it also firmly believes that "there is for us no Chinese wall against trade or intercourse or political influences."[86]

THOMAS JEFFERSON AND CHINESE ARCHITECTURAL AND GARDEN DESIGNS

Chinese influence on American architecture arrived through Europe in the early eighteenth century. Some residents built their houses with "Chinese trim." Others adopted the style known as Chinese Chippendale. Some followed the designs of British builders called Chinoiserie—a style of ornamentation that "represented an Occidental interpretation of China."[87]

Initiated in 1755, Chinese Chippendale patterns started appearing in many homes in Southern colonies like South Carolina and Virginia, which "displayed Chinese fretwork or trellis railings on roof, porches and stairways."[88] In the 1760s, the influence of Chippendale's "Chinese" manner was apparent in roof balustrades. An advertisement in the *South Carolina Gazette*, dated April 1, 1757, shows that at that time some Americans had used Chinese-style design as a great attraction to potential buyers. The advertisement describes the James Reid house offered for sale, as the "new-built, strong and modish" house built "after the Chinese taste." The house was "remarkably commodious in many respects; it is both warm in winter and deemed the most airy in summer of any house in the province."[89]

At Woodside House, Berkshire in 1752, Hugh Hamersley brought Gothic style by laying out a Rococo-style wildness with an elegant Chinese kiosk. This seems to have been inspired by the House of Confucius at Kew, which was designed by Chambers and decorated by the fan-painter Joseph Goupy. The decoration of the Miles Brewton House, completed in 1769, is full of Chippendale motifs, in which Rococo, "Gothic," and "Chinese" are mingled. Some researchers prove that Jefferson preferred such forms of construction in 1782.[90]

Chinoiserie took inspiration from the irregularity of Chinese gardening, particularly temples. Numerous pattern books on how to build Chinese gardens were produced at this time. Among them were William Halfpenny's *New Designs for Chinese Temples &c* (1750) and *Chinese and Gothic Architecture Properly Ornamented* (1752).[91] Burlington's purchase of Ripa's engravings in 1724 confirmed the style, and some "remarkable fruit" began to appear in the 1740s and 1750s. At Grove House, Old Winds, Dickie Bateman (c. 1705–1773) had lived like a "pseudo-Mandarin" during the 1730s and by the end of the decade had laid out a whimsically designed irregular garden adorned with a Chinoiserie bridge and a China House that combined Chinese and English styles.

The Chinese influence on architecture remained conspicuous after the formation of the United States. At Croyden, close to Philadelphia, Andreas Everardus van Braam Houckgeest (1739–1801), a member of the American Philosophical Society, built a home known as China's Retreat during the 1790s. The building adopted a Chinese-style cupola on the roof. The windows, similar to screens in Chinese homes, were double leaves that slid into pockets in the walls. The buildings that used Chinese "touches" added "decorative embellishments to an otherwise Occidental plan and structure."[92] Julian Ursyn Niemcewicz, a Polish visitor, described the house as "immense, surmounted with a cupola and decorated with golden serpents in the Chinese manner. Six tabourets of porcelain were arranged in a circle in the peristyle."[93]

Jefferson had a great affection for architecture, regarding it as "a passion of country gentleman in all countries and ages." Jefferson was also interested in gardening as a natural extension of architecture and studied various Chinese garden styles as he began to construct a garden in his own estate. Jefferson especially loved a particular style of Chinese railing design popularized by Chippendale and Chambers. He decided on a garden in which "objects are intended only to adorn . . . the Chinese style."[94] He used the railings below the dome of his main building and surrounding the walkways.[95] Jefferson treasured the Chinese railing so much that he applied the technique throughout his estates from 1756, such as the Woodford, Schuyler, Orne, and Morris houses, and onward after the Revolutionary War concluded.

Monticello is widely considered one of the greatest architectural treasures in the United States.[96] Jefferson considered Monticello his "architectural ideas and experiments."[97] He made Chinese railings a recurring motif at Monticello. In his main building, Jefferson adopted the Chinese style, making drawings of Chinese lattices in the early 1770s.[98] In the late 1790s and early 1800s, he designed Chinese lattices for houses in Edgehill, Farmington, and Barboursville. In the Swan House in Dorchester, the open panels contained Chinese lattices, which Jefferson continued to use in balcony railings until his death in 1826.[99]

In addition to the lattice, Jefferson considered building one of his rooms with a Chinese roof.[100] In 1771, Jefferson recorded a plan to build "a square 'Chinese Temple,' . . . two stories high with four columns on a side in the lower story." He then decided to "set back behind a balustrade also of Chinese form." Later, Jefferson wrote, "I think I shall prefer to these Chinese temples two regular Tuscan ones."[101] Jefferson also intended to build a few Chinese pagodas on his property.[102]

The vast numbers of memos dealing with temples indicate Jefferson's deep interest in and aesthetic appreciation of this Chinese style. In his 1804 memo, Jefferson planned to build a number of different temples. "At the Rocks" was to be "a turning Tuscan temple 10 f., diam. 6. Columns. Proportions of Pantheon," and over the offices, he planned to erect "the Chinese pavilion of Kew garden." Then along the lower edge of the garden he proposed to place four small temples: models of the Gothic style; the Pantheon, which he regarded the masterpiece of spherical building; a "model of cubic architecture," such as the Maison Carree; and "a specimen of Chinese" architecture.[103] Jefferson also planned to build a Chinese pavilion when he worked to remodel Monticello in the last decade of the eighteenth century and built the university in the second decade of the nineteenth century.[104]

Jefferson fell in love with designing gardens immediately after his inheritance of Monticello in 1757.[105] Jefferson wanted to construct the gardens of Monticello from his own naturalistic point of view. Under the influence of *Designs of Chinese Building* by William Chambers, Jefferson decided to have "a specimen of Chinese" architecture in his garden. He thought of constructing a Chinese Ting and Chinese temples when he made plans for this garden.[106] In fact, Jefferson indeed built a Chinese pavilion "at the center of the long walk."[107] The pavilion made of bricks fell in 1828. It "was twelve feet, six inches square, with arches on all four sides covered by a pyramidal roof with a Chinese railing"[108] (figures 2.3 and 2.4).

As the first great architectural style in North America, Jeffersonian architecture is well known. It was particularly popular during the early American period. These designs typically feature octagonal forms, red bricks, and Chinese railings. It is still very popular today, as evidenced by publications

Figure 2.3 Chinese Pavilion in William Chambers's *Designs of Chinese Buildings, Furniture, Dresses, Machines and Utensils*, Published in London in 1757. The pictures of the Chinese Pavilion that Jefferson used as references when he built his pavilion.

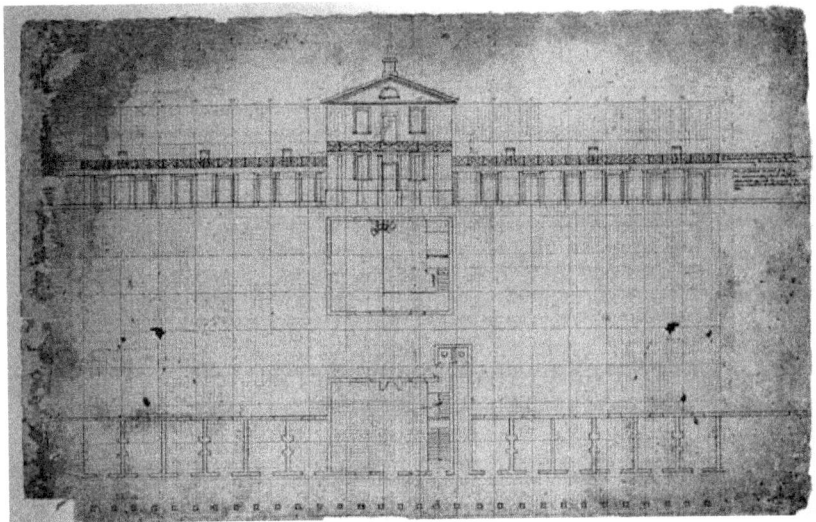

Figure 2.4 Thomas Jefferson's Drawing of a Typical Pavilion the Albemarle Academy in 1814. Jefferson's August 1814 drawing of a typical pavilion for the Albemarle Academy. N-309, Albert and Shirley Small Special Collections Library, University of Virginia.

such as *Taunton's Fine Homebuilding Journal* that continue to introduce the style to the American people.[109]

However, the implication of Jefferson using the Chinese railing goes beyond the architecture itself. He deemed that architecture was "the heart of the American cause." For him, "a building was not merely a walled structure, but a metaphor for American ideology."[110] In other words, to construct a building was akin to creating a nation. Therefore, "the architecture of any American building should convey the American desire to break cultural—as well as political—ties to Europe."[111] The implicit consensus among the founding generation of American statesmen was to "pursue a political destiny separate from Europe."[112] Jefferson was determined to make a new nation in North America rather than a replica of a European country. He understood that the elements from Chinese culture could play a particularly important and positive role in his efforts to develop the new nation. He viewed the integration of Chinese elements in his own building as an attempt to develop a new identity for the nation. He purposely incorporated Chinese designs into his buildings and refused to copy English styles.

Jefferson had "a national audience in mind" when he built his home at Monticello.[113] He told James Madison,

> You see, I am an enthusiast on the subject of the arts. But it is an enthusiasm of which I am not ashamed, as its object to improve the taste of my countrymen, to

increase their reputation, to reconcile them to the rest of the world, and procure them its praise.[114]

As the principal writer of the Declaration of Independence, Jefferson's formation of the new style with Chinese architectural features has captivated many Americans. As a founder of the United States with national prominence, he was visited daily by numerous guests from all over the country. It was at this point that one author stated that the Chinese railing included on the exterior of Monticello "became a public expression of Jefferson's regard for Chinese culture through its inclusion in the private space of his home."[115]

BENJAMIN FRANKLIN'S EFFORTS TO PROMOTE SERICULTURE IN NORTH AMERICA

Americans have always loved silk. By the twentieth century, the United States had become the leading customer for raw silk, and New York had become the leading international silk center.[116] According to the Silk Association of America's report, the United States had imported about 60 percent of the total silk trade internationally.[117] Benjamin Franklin would have been happy to hear such fashion headlines as Alice Roosevelt getting married in a wedding gown of American silk,[118] or the selection of a new range of silk colors for the inaugural gowns of Mrs. Woodrow Wilson and her three daughters.[119]

Silkworms were first imported to Virginia as early as 1613.[120] During the colonial era, Chinese silk was widely admired by wealthy colonists. George Washington wrote numerous times that he bought some Chinese silk in 1764.[121] By the middle of the eighteenth century, silk consumption in the colonies had reached "considerable proportions."[122]

Franklin worked tirelessly and consistently to promote the sericulture, or silk production, in North America as early as 1729. At the age of twenty-three, Franklin bound the value of silk making to the economic and social progress of the colonies. He told his fellow colonists that if they thought that "raising Wheat proves dull, more may (if there is money to support and carry on new Manufactures) proceed to the raising and manufacturing of silk.[123] He told the colonists,

> If it is asked, what can such farmers raise, wherewith to pay for the manufactures they may want from us? I answer, that the inland parts of America in question are well-known to be fitted for the production of hemp, flax, potash, and above all silk.[124]

In order to make his proposal more valid and attractive, Franklin used the success of sericulture in China as an example to encourage the colonists to engage in the business. He told them sericulture was so developed in China that the country "clothes its Inhabitants with Silk, while it feeds them plentifully and has besides a vast Quantity both of raw and manufactured to spare for Exportation."[125]

Franklin recognized that encouragement with the example of China was not powerful enough to have sericulture developed in North America. People would say that sericulture had developed in China for 2,500 years already. It was crucial to borrow the experience from other countries that had introduced Chinese sericulture successfully. In 1749, Franklin took the opportunity in England and visited the Derby silk factory.[126] He published his portrayal of the achievements the British businessmen had achieved in the *Pennsylvania Gazette*: "there are 26,586 wheels, 97,746 movements; 73,728 yards of silk wound every time the water-wheel goes round, which is three times every minute; 318,504,960 yards of silk in one day and night; and consequently 99,373,547,550 yards of silk in a year."[127]

For the purpose of inspiring the colonists to be interested in sericulture, Franklin relayed the history that silk culture transmitted from China to other parts of the world. He wrote an essay titled "Memoirs *of the Culture of SILK*" based on his research and published it in the *Pennsylvania Gazette*. Franklin told his readers:

> About 2,500 years before Christ, the Empress Siling began the Culture of Silk in China, where it was confined near 2,000 years, before it reached India and Persia.
>
> A.D. 555 This Silk Culture first brought into Greece, particularly Athens, Thebes, and Corinth.
>
> 1130 Roger, King of Sicily, established it at Palermo and Calabria, by Work men brought from Athens and Corinth, at the Time of the Crusades.
>
> 1300 The Italians received it from Sicily.
>
> 1600 It was established in France.
>
> 1740 Begun in America.[128]

Franklin further pointed out the significance of sericulture. American colonists learned from Franklin that sericulture had been an important economic factor in China for centuries, and that the potential for it to be so in the American colonies was substantial. He revealed that the Chinese imperial court received over 955,000 lbs. as revenue annually.[129] He recommended the planting of mulberry trees in Pennsylvania. Franklin predicted, if "One Million of Trees disposed into Mulberry Walks, in Pennsylvania," in a few years, the colony would "enable a yearly Remittance to Great-Britain of a Million Sterling, and no Ways interfere with the other necessary Branches of Labour in the Community."[130]

Knowing the history and understanding the economic significance of sericulture were vital in Franklin's advocacy. However, the more crucial factor was to provide the American colonies with the technology for sericulture to be successful. Without it, cultivating silk in North America would have been an empty pursuit. Franklin paid particular attention to silk cultivation technology in China and emphasized Chinese expertise in sericulture. Mulberry tree leaves are important elements in keeping silkworms strong. Over the centuries, Chinese silk keepers had developed successful standard industry practices. Franklin shared the results of his research with some colonists who were interested in the field. He informed them that the Chinese

> prune their Mulberry Trees once a year as we do our Vines in Europe, and suffer them not to grow up to high Trees, because thro' long Experience they have learn'd that the leaves of the smallest and youngest Trees make the best Silk.[131]

He also advised interested colonists on how to find "a good deal on the Chinese Management of the Silk Business."[132]

Franklin tried everything he could to support the colonists in their endeavors to master Chinese technology in silk cultivation. He provided with them all the related information he could obtain. On December 7, 1763, Franklin sent Ezra Stiles (1727–1795), president of Yale College, "the Prints copied from Chinese Pictures concerning the Produce of Silk."[133] In 1764, Franklin followed up on the pictures he sent and made sure that Mr. Stiles had received "a Set of Chinese Prints, or rather Prints taken from Chinese Pictures, relating to the Culture of Silk in that Country."[134] Stiles conducted experiments with silkworms and production, going so far as to give some of his worms monikers such as General Wolfe and Oliver Cromwell.[135] In February 1772, Franklin told Cadwalader Evans that he had some knowledge of the technology of Chinese silk in the form of pictures. He told Mr. Evans that "Dr. Fothergill has a number of Chinese drawings, of which some represent the process of raising silk, from the beginning to the end."[136] Franklin told him that he had tried to get the pictures and Dr. Fothergill promised to "send them as a present to the Silk Company."[137] In 1773, Franklin strove to make an arrangement for Joseph Clark, a silk technician, to go to Philadelphia to help with the advancement of its sericulture. He wrote a letter to the Committee of the Managers of the Philadelphia Silk Filature:

> I beg leave to recommend him to the Notice and Encouragement of the Silk Committee, as far as they may find him deserving. For tho' it may be most advantageous for our Country, while the Bounty continues so high, to send all our raw Silk hither; yet as the Bounty will gradually diminish and at length

cease, I should think it not amiss to begin early the laying a Foundation for the future Manufacture of it; and perhaps this Person, if he finds Employment, may be a means of raising Hands for that purpose. His Name is Joseph Clark.[138]

With Franklin's encouragement, sericulture started to flourish in Pennsylvania. In November 1771, the managers of the Philadelphia Silk Filature reported the progress of their silk industry to Franklin. According to the report, "Managers of the Contributions for promoting the Culture of silk in Pennsylvania" had achieved such a great success that "in the course of the last Season," they had secured "at the Filature erected here such a quantity of Cocoons as have produced about 155 lbs. of raw Silk proper for Exportation."[139]

Despite early successes, there was no easy way for American colonists to develop the silk industry. Franklin had grasped that they needed constant assistance and inspiration. He appealed to them not to be deterred by difficulties (figure 2.5):

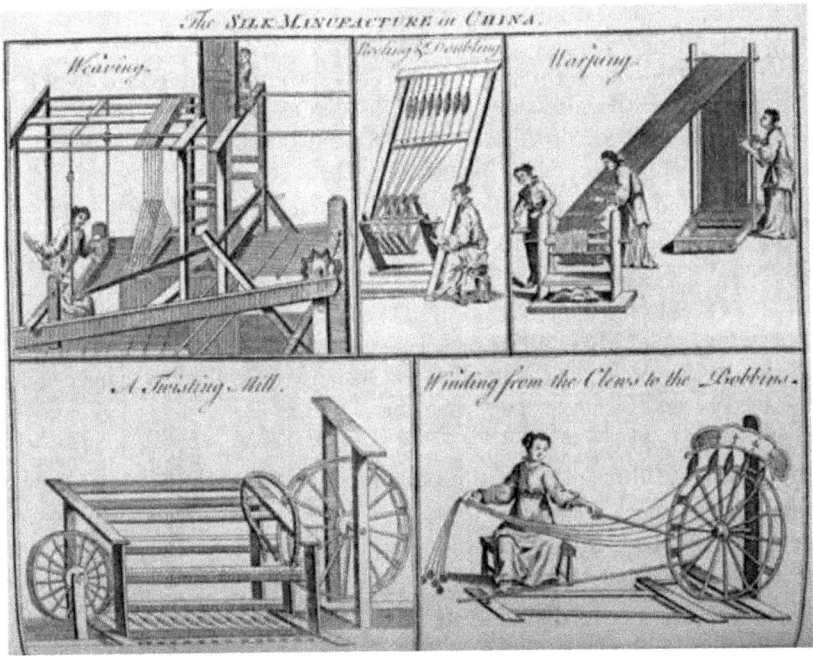

Figure 2.5 Silk Production in China in the Eighteenth Century. John Greene and Thomas Astley, "The Silk Manufacturing in China," c. eighteenth-century engraving, New York Public Library Collection.

> I hope our People will not be disheartened by a few Accidents, and such Disappointments as are incident to all new Undertakings, but persevere bravely in the silk Business till they have conquer'd all Difficulties. *By Diligence and Patience the Mouse ate in twain the Cable.* It is not two Centuries since it was as much a Novelty in France as it is now with us in North America, and the People as much unacquainted with it.[140]

The objective of an industry is to find a market for its product. It was no different for silk production. In order to facilitate sericulture, Franklin personally searched for silk markets. The following quote illustrates Franklin's efforts at acquiring a market for silk products in North America:

> Two Months' Time was given to the Buyers, and I have now received the Money. You may therefore draw for the Ballance of the Account £210 10s. 5½d. on me, or in Case of my Absence on Browns & Collinson, Bankers, with whom I shall leave an Order to honour your Bill. I hear by several Hands that our Silk is in high Credit; we may therefore hope for rising Prices, the Manufacturers being at first doubtful of a new Commodity, not knowing till Trial has been made how it will work.[141]

With a remarkably busy schedule in Europe, Franklin did not have time to locate potential buyers. He worked with brokers in promoting the sale of silk. One time he told the silk company that the American silk he received should be sold soon. Following recommendations from a broker, Franklin "has sorted it into 4 Parcels, according to his opinions of its Difference in Perfection."[142]

In 1782, at the age of seventy-six, Franklin remained concerned about marketing silk produced in North America. He commented to Edmund Clegg, a silk manufacturer, information on the silk prices in Europe. He told him that

> when I was in London I had several Trunks of it consign'd to me for sale, and I remember it fetched at a publick Sale as high a Price within 6d. in the pound weight, as the Italian sold at the same time.[143]

Franklin's efforts in promoting silk production in North America won him appreciation and respect from silk businessmen. Rebecca Haydock Garrigues, a silk businesswoman in Philadelphia, summarized their sentiments by saying that "I shall always esteem myself much obliged by Doctor Franklin's kindness, in taking so much Trouble as he has done in getting the Silk made."[144] The Committee of the Managers of the Philadelphia Silk Filature were moved by Franklin's efforts and showed their appreciation in a letter addressed to him:

We are sensible how much the promoters of the Culture of Silk are Obliged to Doctor Franklin for the trouble he has taken in the business; in their behalf, we thankfully Acknowledge it, and remain with perfect Esteem, his Assured ready Friends.[145]

Franklin had the whole of North America in his concern when he advocated for sericulture. For Franklin, having silk in Philadelphia and New England was not enough. He tried to push production throughout the colonies in North America. He pointed out that in Carolina and further south, "there is good hope for silk, as mulberry trees can grow even in New England. The bounty for silk culture continues."[146] In order to stimulate sericulture in New Jersey, he wrote to his son from London in May 1772: "I am glad to find such a Progress in [the making?] of Silk in Pennsylvania. I hope your Pro[vince will] take a Part in it. I think you sh[ould encou]rage the raising Cocoons in all your Towns."[147]

In 1831, forty years after Benjamin Franklin passed away, J. H. Cobb published a manual on sericulture. The Congress of the United States bought copies of the manual and distributed it to its members. From that point on, "there was a determined effort to establish silk culture on a firm basis in the United States. This interest in silk culture soon led to what was known as the 'Mormus multicaulis craze.'"[148]

Above, we briefly introduced Franklin's great contribution to developing sericulture in North America. A question that might come to a reader's mind would be why Franklin made such a great effort to push sericulture in North America. The readers who are familiar with Franklin know that silk had contributed to Benjamin Franklin's scientific research in the field of electricity. In 1752, Franklin made an important experiment with electricity. The important instrument—the kite—was made of silk. Franklin well understood that "silk is fitter to bear the Wet and Wind of a Thunder Gust without tearing."[149] However, this episode of Franklin's personal use of silk cannot alone answer this question. The best answer is from his correspondence with the Committee of the Managers of the Philadelphia Silk Filature. In Franklin's mind, sericulture was a "great service to our country."[150]

FRANKLIN USED CHINESE HEATING TECHNOLOGY AND MEDICAL THEORY TO IMPROVE HIS STOVE

During colonial times most Americans warmed their homes by building a fire in a fireplace. It was dangerous, and much wood was needed. Franklin surmised that there had to be a more efficient means for heating homes.[151]

By the 1740s, the growing population of the Colonies resulted in noticeable inroads on the great forests, which supplied fuel. The heating of houses was growing more expensive, while the wood used was very inefficient. This led to much of the heat—five-sixths, Franklin estimated in many cases—being lost up the chimney.[152]

Franklin carefully studied the Chinese technology of heating houses in the cold winters. He found that the northern Chinese had an ingenious method of warming their ground floors. Franklin told Jan Ingenhousz (1730–1799), a Dutch physiologist, biologist, and chemist, that

> Europeans may still learn something about the use of stoves . . . from the Chinese, whose country being greatly populous and fully cultivated, has little room left for the growth of wood, and having not much fuel that is good, have been forced upon many inventions during a course of ages, for making a little fire go as far as possible.[153]

In the process of working on a new and efficient heating system, Franklin explored Chinese heating technology. In August 1785, he learned:

> It is said the northern Chinese have a method of warming their ground floors, which is ingenious. Those floors are made of tiles, a foot square and two inches thick, their corners being supported by bricks set on end, that are a foot long and four inches square; the tiles, too, join into each other, by ridges and hollows along their sides. This forms a hollow under the whole floor, which on one side of the house has an opening into the air, where a fire is made, and it has a funnel rising from the other side to carry off the smoke. The fuel is a sulphurous pit coal, the smell of which in the room is thus avoided, while the floor, and of course the room is well warmed.[154]

Franklin did not just copy the Chinese technology. He examined it first, and then adopted the most suitable part of the technology. He noticed that the Chinese heating technology had some problems. For instance, "the underside of the floor must grow foul with soot, and a thick coat of soot prevents much of the direct application of the hot air to the tiles."[155] Franklin found the cause of this problem. Franklin found that the colonists' way of warming their houses by "burning the smoke by obliging it to descend through red coals" was the reason.[156]

Franklin was not satisfied with finding the reason. He continued to investigate to find the solution to make Chinese heating systems more effective. He thought, if "the funnel close to the grate" was erected and "only an iron plate between the fire and the funnel, through which plate, the air in the funnel being heated, it will be sure to draw well, and force the smoke to descend."[157]

Based on his analysis of Chinese heating technology, Franklin invented the Pennsylvania Fireplace. He dealt with the problem by integrating a number of passages and vents so that the apparatus drew in cold fresh air from outside the building and, after warming the air in a passage kept hot by the escaping gases of the fire, finally discharged it into the room.[158]

The main advantage of his new stove, Franklin maintained, was that the whole room was equally warmed; therefore, "people need not crowd so close round the fire, but many sit near the window, and have the benefit of the light for reading, writing, needle-work, &c." People would be able to "sit with comfort in any part of the room."[159]

It is interesting to imagine that Franklin used traditional Chinese medical theory as a guide when he renovated his stove. He told the colonists of the theory from the Tchang seng (The Art of Procuring Health and Long Life), a Chinese medical book:

> As of all the Passions which ruffle us, Anger does the most Mischief; so of all the malignant Affections of the Air, a Wind that comes thro' any narrow Passage, which is cold and piercing, is most dangerous; and coming upon us unawares, insinuates itself into the Body, often causing grievous Diseases. It should therefore be avoided, according to the Advice of the ancient Proverb, as carefully as the Point of an Arrow.[160]

Franklin then informed his readers that his newly invented Pennsylvania Fireplace aimed to avoid "these harms"[161] This is fascinating. It would be a hasty conclusion to say that Franklin mastered traditional Chinese medical theory based on this single case. However, it is astonishing that Franklin was so familiar with the theory that he could apply it adroitly to justify the benefits of improving his fireplace. His improvement aimed to keep people not only warm in the cold winters, but physically healthier as well.

BENJAMIN FRANKLIN AND CHINESE NAVIGATION AND PAPERMAKING TECHNOLOGY

Franklin recognized the potential of Chinese technologies to improve their Western counterparts. Even near the end of his life, Franklin was impressed by Chinese navigation technology, and in particular, the traditional Chinese practice of "[dividing] the hold of a great ship into a number of separate chambers by partitions tightly caulked."[162] He recognized immediately that this Chinese technique of making vessels safer could be used to boost interaction between people in the world. "This being known would be a great encouragement to passengers."[163]

He likened the method of "the division of ships into watertight sections to a proposal to institute passenger service between France and the United States."[164]

Franklin stated that since the bottoms of vessels were used to "be laden with goods," therefore, "their holds may without inconvenience be divided into separate apartments after the Chinese manner, and each of those apartments caulked tight so as to keep out water."[165] In a time when "a leak should happen in one apartment, that only would be affected by it, and the others would be free." As a result, "the ship would not be so subject as others to founder and sink at sea."

Franklin then wrote down Chinese innovations in shipbuilding and sent to a friend of his that using the Chinese method in ship making "had come to him in the seven times he had crossed the Atlantic."[166]

Besides shipbuilding technology, Franklin also researched Chinese knowledge on rowing a boat. For Franklin, rowing a boat was not something new. He had showed his capability "to manage a boat" when he was a child.[167] In old age, he was astonished by the Chinese way of rowing a boat. He recognized that the Chinese approach "differed from that customary in the West." In the Chinese way, "the oars being worked two a-stern as we scull, or on the sides with the same kind of motion, being hung parallel to the keel on a rail and always acting in the water." In Europe, rowing was perpendicular to the sides and lifted out at every stroke. As a result, the traditional European way "is a loss of time, and the boat in the interval loses motion."[168] In the end, Franklin concluded, the Chinese "see our manner, and we theirs." However, neither the Chinese nor the Americans "are disposed to learn of or copy the other."[169]

Franklin was not content with European paper manufacturing. He studied in detail the procedures, techniques, and equipment that Chinese workers used to make paper. Franklin wrote down the complete process of papermaking in China. First, the Chinese workers prepared "two large vats, each five ells long and two ells wide, made of brick, lined with a plaster that holds water." Then they made pulps ready by the side. Next, between the vats was a kiln or stove with two sloping sides larger than the sheet of paper. The sloping covers were "with a fine stucco that takes a polish, and are so contrived as to be well heated by a small fire circulating in the walls."[170] He carefully examined the mold. He observed that

> the mould is made with thin but deep sides, that it may be both light and stiff: It is suspended at each end with cords that pass over pullies fastened to the ceiling, their ends connected with a counterpoise nearly equal the weight of the mould.[171]

The most important part was the operating procedure. He discovered that in China's paper mills, two workers at each end of the mold would lift "it out of the water by the help of the counterpoise, turn it and apply it with the stuff for the sheet, to the smooth surface of the stove, against which they press it." After the paper was dried by the hot wall, a worker would take off "the dried sheet by rolling it up." Because of that "the side next the stove receives the even polish of the stucco, and is thereby better fitted to receive the impression of fine prints."[172] Because the kiln had two polished sides and the two vats by the side, therefore, "the same operation is at the same time performed by two other men at the other vat; and one fire serves."[173] The operation would allow workers to get a great sheet of smooth and well-sized paper, with as a result "a number of the European operations saved."[174]

To conclude, Chinese knowledge had produced deep and far-reaching influence on American society during the colonial and early republic periods. China became an essential center of resources for the founders' search for suggestions on technical innovation. When Franklin intended to upgrade certain technologies that the Americans carried over from Europe, he would seek illumination from the East. They would find whether there was any related information from China that could benefit them with their efforts. In order to establish the silk industry in North America, Benjamin Franklin put great energy into familiarizing himself with Chinese silk technology. The scope of his borrowing from Chinese inventions was extremely broad, from daily necessities, such as candles, bean curd, and vinegar, to essential industry, including silk production, heating, and navigation technologies. The time span over which Franklin used Chinese technology stretched from his youth to his senior years. The fact that Franklin studied Chinese navigation and papermaking technologies in his senior years, merely a couple of years before his death, tells that Franklin had trained in himself a habit of looking for insight from Chinese sources throughout his life.

When assimilating Chinese architectural design into his work, Jefferson understood that the elements from Chinese culture could play a particularly important and positive role in his efforts to develop the new style of architecture. He viewed the integration of Chinese elements in his own building as an attempt to develop a new identity for the nation. Therefore, he refused to copy the English style in his buildings. All these activities illuminate the Founding Fathers' initiative in using Chinese civilization to facilitate social development in North America.

NOTES

1. Leonard W. Labaree and William B. Willcox, eds., *The Papers of Benjamin Franklin* (New Haven: Yale University Press, 1959–), 9:82, 10:182–88, 389, 11:230, 12:11–12, 17:107, 18:188, 19:69, 136, 138, 268, 20:442–43; Albert

H. Smyth, ed., *The Writings of Benjamin Franklin* (New York: MacMillan, 1905–1907), 8:24; John Bigelow, ed., *The Works of Benjamin Franklin* (New York: G. P. Putnam's Sons, 1904), 11:177–78; Jonathan Goldstein, *Philadelphia and the China Trade, 1682–1846: Commercial, Cultural, and Attitudinal Effects* (University Park: Pennsylvania State University Press, 1978), 7, 15; George W. Coner, ed., *The Autobiography of Benjamin Rush* (Princeton, NJ: American Philosophical Society, 1948), 175–76. Others outside Philadelphia also looked to China as a model. James Madison took an interest in the intensive agricultural techniques of the Chinese. *The James Madison Letters* (New York, 1884), 3:80, 90, 209.

2. Kenneth Latourette, *The History of Early Relations between the United States and China* (New Haven: Yale University Press, 1917), 124.

3. The three eclipses noted here are also listed in *Poor Richard* for 1761 or 1762, with Philadelphia times very roughly corresponding to those given here after allowing for the difference in longitude from Canton. See "Notes on Reading an Account of Travel in China, [1762?]," Founders Online, National Archives, https://founders.archives.gov/documents/Franklin/01-10-02-0098. Original source: *The Papers of Benjamin Franklin*, ed. Leonard W. Labaree, vol. 10, *January 1, 1762, through December 31, 1763* (New Haven and London: Yale University Press, 1959), 182–83.

4. "From Benjamin Franklin to Peter Franklin, [1762?–1764]," Founders Online, National Archives, https://founders.archives.gov/documents/Franklin/01-10-02-0099. Original source: *The Papers of Benjamin Franklin*, ed. Leonard W. Labaree, vol. 10, *January 1, 1762, through December 31, 1763* (New Haven and London: Yale University Press, 1959), 183–84.

5. "From Benjamin Franklin to Thomas Gilpin, March 18, 1770," Founders Online, National Archives, https://founders.archives.gov/documents/Franklin/01-17-02-0053. Original source: *The Papers of Benjamin Franklin*, ed. William B. Willcox, vol. 17, *January 1 through December 31, 1770* (New Haven and London: Yale University Press, 1973), 103–9.

6. "From Benjamin Franklin to John Bartram, 11 January 1770," Founders Online, National Archives, https://founders.archives.gov/documents/Franklin/01-17-02-0010. Original source: *The Papers of Benjamin Franklin*, ed. William B. Willcox, vol. 17, *January 1 through December 31, 1770* (New Haven and London: Yale University Press, 1973), 22–23.

The account he mentioned was by Domingo Fernandez Navarrete (1618–1686), a Jesuit missionary to China, who published his work in Spanish in 1676. It was translated into English by Awnsham and John Churchill, published in 1704, and subsequently republished; Franklin probably encountered it in the third edition: *A Collection of Voyages and Travels* . . . (6 vols., London, 1744–1746), i, 1–311. Tau-fu or teufu was there described (p. 252) as a paste of kidney beans, as it was in the original Spanish; where bf got hold of garavances we have no idea. (The above notes from original source: *The Papers of Benjamin Franklin*, ed. William B. Willcox, vol. 17, *January 1 through December 31, 1770* (New Haven and London: Yale University Press, 1973), 22–23.

7. "Notes on Reading an Account of Travel in China, [1762?]," Founders Online, National Archives, https://founders.archives.gov/documents/Franklin/01-10-02-0098. Original source: *The Papers of Benjamin Franklin*, ed. Leonard W. Labaree, vol. 10, *January 1, 1762, through December 31, 1763* (New Haven and London: Yale University Press, 1959), 182–83.

8. "From Thomas Jefferson to Benjamin Franklin Bache, 29 September 1794," Founders Online, National Archives, https://founders.archives.gov/documents/Jefferson/01-28-02-0121. Original source: *The Papers of Thomas Jefferson*, ed. John Catanzariti, vol. 28, *1 January 1794–29 February 1796* (Princeton: Princeton University Press, 2000), 168–69.

9. "Margaret Bayard Smith's Account of a Visit to Monticello, (July 29–August 2, 1809)," Founders Online, National Archives, https://founders.archives.gov/documents/Jefferson/03-01-02-0315. Original source: *The Papers of Thomas Jefferson, Retirement Series*, ed. J. Jefferson Looney, vol. 1, *4 March 1809 to 15 November 1809* (Princeton: Princeton University Press, 2004), 386–401.

10. "Pay Book of the State Company of Artillery, [1777]," Founders Online, National Archives, https://founders.archives.gov/documents/Hamilton/01-01-02-0350. Original source: *The Papers of Alexander Hamilton*, ed. Harold C. Syrett, vol. 1, *1768–1778* (New York: Columbia University Press, 1961), 373–412.

11. "September 1784," Founders Online, National Archives, https://founders.archives.gov/documents/Washington/01-04-02-0001-0001. Original source: *The Diaries of George Washington*, ed. Donald Jackson and Dorothy Twohig, vol. 4, *September 1, 1784–June 30, 1786* (Charlottesville: University Press of Virginia, 1978), 1–54.

12. Ibid.

13. Ibid.

14. "[July 1774]," Founders Online, National Archives, https://founders.archives.gov/documents/Washington/01-03-02-0004-0013. Original source: *The Diaries of George Washington*, ed. Donald Jackson, vol. 3, *January 1, 1771–November 5, 1781* (Charlottesville: University Press of Virginia, 1978), 259–64.

15. Craig R. Hanyan, "China and the Erie Canal," *Business History Review* 35, no. 4 (1961): 558–66. https://www.jstor.org/stable/3111758?seq=1.

16. "From Benjamin Franklin to Thomas Gilpin, March 18, 1770," Founders Online, National Archives, https://founders.archives.gov/documents/Franklin/01-17-02-0053. Original source: *The Papers of Benjamin Franklin*, ed. William B. Willcox, vol. 17, *January 1 through December 31, 1770* (New Haven and London: Yale University Press, 1973), 103–9.

17. Ibid.

18. Hanyan, "China and the Erie Canal."

19. "Address to the Agricultural Society of Albemarle, May 12, 1818," Founders Online, National Archives, https://founders.archives.gov/documents/Madison/04-01-02-0244. Original source: *The Papers of James Madison, Retirement Series*, ed. David B. Mattern, J. C. A. Stagg, Mary Parke Johnson, and Anne Mandeville Colony, vol. 1, *March 4, 1817–January 31, 1820* (Charlottesville: University Press of Virginia, 2009), 260–85.

20. Ibid.

21. Ibid.

22. Benjamin Rush to Thomas Bradford, April 15, 1768, in *Letters of Benjamin Rush*, ed. L. H. Butterfield (Princeton: Princeton University Press, 1951), 1:54.

23. Philadelphia Museum of Art Exhibition, Colonial Philadelphia Porcelain: The Art of Bonnin and Morris, March 8–June 1, 2008.

24. "Pay Book of the State Company of Artillery, [1777]," 373–412.

25. See https://cn.nytimes.com/china/20161230/great-wall-china/en-us/.

26. Arthur Waldron, "The Problem of The Great Wall of China," Harvard Journal of Asiatic Studies 43, no. 2 (1983): 652.

27. Arthur Waldron, The Great Wall of China: From History to Myth (Cambridge and New York: Cambridge University Press, 1990), 203–4; J. A. Boyle, "The Alexander Legend in Central Asia," *Folklore* 85, no. 4 (1974).

28. Livre des merveilles du monde (Book of the Marvels of the World, also known as The Travels of Marco Polo).

29. Waldron, Great Wall of China, 204.

30. Ibid.

31. Ibid.

32. Private letter published in the *Family Memoirs of the Rev. William Stukeley* (1887), vol. 3, *1754*, 142.

33. Henry Yule, ed., "Cathay and the way thither: being a collection of medieval notices of China." Works issued by the Hakluyt Society, issues 36–37 (London: T. Richards, 1866), 579. This section is the report of Góis's travel, as reported by Matteo Ricci in De Christiana expeditione apud Sinas (published 1615, annotated by Henry Yule).

34. Waldron, *Great Wall of China*, 206.

35. Voltaire, *The Philosophical Dictionary*, selected and trans. H. I. Woolf (New York: Knopf, 1924), https://history.hanover.edu/texts/voltaire/volancie.html.

36. J. B. Du Halde, The General History of China (London: J. Watts, 1741), II:76.

37. Alain Peyrefitte, *The Immobile Empire* (New York: Knopf Doubleday, 2013), 183–85.

38. George L. Staunton, An Authentic Account of an Embassy from the King of Great Britain to the Embassy of China (London: G. Nicol, 1797), 184.

39. Mercy Otis Warren, History of the Rise, Progress, and Termination of the American Revolution (Indianapolis: Liberty Fund, 1805), 313–14.

40. Dave Wang, "Benjamin Franklin and the Great Wall of China," *Franklin Gazette* 18, no. 1 (Spring 2008).

41. David M. Kennedy and Lizabeth Cohen, The American Pageant, vol. 1 (Boston: Cengage Learning, 2012), 78.

42. Richard Middleton and Anne Lombard, Colonial America: A History to 1763, 4th ed. (Hoboken, NJ: Wiley-Blackwell, 2011), 390–91.

43. Daniel Richter, Before the Revolution: America's Ancient Pasts (Cambridge, MA: Belknap Press, 2011), 373–74.

44. A friend to the true interests of Britain in North America, Williamsburg Virginia Gazette, January 14, 1773. Jonah Bader, *The Failure of America's First "Chinese Wall,"* http://thepolitic.org/the-failure-of-americas-first-chinese-wall/;

Benjamin Lieberman, *Remaking Identities: God, Nation, and Race in World History* (Lanham, MD: Rowman & Littlefield, 2013), 173.

45. Alan Taylor, *American Revolutions: A Continental History, 1750–1804* (New York and London: Norton, 2016), 85.

46. Ibid.

47. Ibid, 86.

48. Great Britain, The Proceedings Before the Judicial Committee of Her Majesty Imperial Privy Council on the Special Case Respecting the Westerly Boundary of Ontario: Argued 15*th*, 16*th*, 17*th*, 19*th*, 21*st* and 22*nd* July 1884, with Notes of Explanation and Correction. Printed by Order of the Legislative Assembly of [Ontario].

49. Great Britain, *The Parliamentary History of England from the Earliest Period to the Year 1803*, vol. 18 (London: T. C. Hansard, 1813), 657.

50. Ibid.

51. "To Benjamin Franklin from the Chevalier de Kermorvan, [August 12, 1776?]," Founders Online, National Archives, http://founders.archives.gov/documents/Franklin/01-22-02-0328.

52. Benjamin Franklin, *The Interest of Great Britain Considered, with Regard to her Colonies, And the Acquisitions of Canada and Guadaloupe. To which are added, Observations concerning the Increase of Mankind, Peopling of Countries, &c*. London: Printed for T. Becket, at Tully's Head, near Surry-Street in the Strand. MDCCLX. (Yale University Library); draft (five scattered pages only): American Philosophical Society, http://franklinpapers.org/franklin/framedVolumes.jsp.

53. As for Franklin's efforts to draw positive elements from Chinese civilization in his efforts to build North American colonies, please see Dr. Dave Wang's published papers in the following: "Exploring Benjamin Franklin's Moral Life," Franklin Gazette, Spring 2007; "Benjamin Franklin and Chinese Civilization," U.S.–China Relation Series, No. 2 (New York: Outer Sky Press, August 2006); "Benjamin Franklin's Attitude toward Chinese Civilization," Social Science Journal of Harbin Institute of Technology, Issue 4, 2006; "Benjamin Franklin and China: A Survey of Benjamin Franklin's Efforts at Drawing Positive Elements from Chinese Civilization during the Formative Age of the United States," which is published since 2005 by the Official Website of the Tercentenary Commission, http://www.benfranklin300.org/etc_essays.htm.

54. Benjamin Franklin, to John Bartram, ALS: Central Library, Salford, England; draft: American Philosophical Society, London, August 22, 1772, in the Papers of Benjamin Franklin, http://franklinpapers.org/franklin/framedVolumes.jsp.

55. Benjamin Franklin, Provincial Commissioners to Robert Hunter Morris, June 13, 1756. Pennsylvania Historical and Museum Commission.

56. *Memoirs of the Life & Writings of Benjamin Franklin* (London: J. M. Dent & Sons Ltd.; New York: E. P. Dutton & Co., 1908), 174.

57. Ibid.

58. Benjamin Franklin, to Deborah Franklin, ALS: American Philosophical Society Bethlehem, January 15, 1756.

59. His brief biography is available at http://en.wikipedia.org/wiki/Samuel_Rhoads.

60. Benjamin Franklin, to Samuel Rhoads, reprinted from the Historical Magazine, 2nd series, I (May 1867), 284–85. Fort Allen, January 26, 1756.

61. Benjamin Franklin, to Robert Hunter Morris, Pennsylvania Historical and Museum Commission. Fort Allen at Gnadenhutten, January 26, 1756.

62. Ibid.

63. Benjamin Franklin, Pennsylvania Assembly: Reply to the Governor, Printed in Votes and Proceedings of the House of Representatives, *1755–1756* (Philadelphia, 1756), 92.

64. *The Autobiography of Benjamin Franklin, Poor Richard's Almanac and Other Papers* (Reading, PA: Spencer Press, 1936), 196–97.

65. Benjamin Franklin, to Robert Hunter Morris, LS: Historical Society of Pennsylvania Bethlehem, January 14, 1756.

66. His brief biography is available at http://en.wikipedia.org/wiki/Charles_Thomson.

67. Benjamin Franklin, to William Parsons ALS: American Philosophical Society Philadelphia, February 22, 1757.

68. His brief biography is available from http://en.wikipedia.org/wiki/Isaac_Norris.

69. From Isaac Norris, Fairhill, January 4, 1760, Letterbook copy: Historical Society of Pennsylvania, in the Papers of Benjamin Franklin.

70. Franklin, *Interest of Great Britain Considered.*

71. Benjamin Franklin, to John Bartram, ALS: Central Library, Salford, England; draft: American Philosophical Society London, August 22, 1772. In The Papers of Benjamin Franklin, http://franklinpapers.org/franklin/framedVolumes.jsp.

72. The correspondence from Chevalier de Kermorvan (1740–1817) tells that he received Franklin's recommendation that a wall like the Great Wall of China should be erected in defending the independent nation. Franklin's letter has disappeared. See "To Benjamin Franklin from the Chevalier de Kermorvan, [12 August 1776?]," Founders Online, National Archives (http://founders.archives.gov/documents/Franklin/01-22-02-0328).

73. See "The French Volunteers and Supporters of the American Revolution," http://xenophongroup.com/mcjoynt/volunt.htm.

74. Chevalier de Kermorvan, from the Chevalier de Kermorvan, ALS: American Philosophical Society [August 12? 1776.]. In *The Papers of Benjamin Franklin*, http://franklinpapers.org/franklin/framedVolumes.jsp.

75. Harrison Clark, *All Cloudless Glory: The Life of George Washington*, vol. 2: *Making a Nation* (Washington, DC: Regnery Publishing 1996), 197.

76. Joseph J. Ellis, *American Dialogue: The Founding Fathers and Us* (New York: Alfred A. Knopf, 2018), 181.

77. Roger Ginn, New England Must Not Be Trampled On: The Tragic Death of Jonathan Cilley (Lanham, MD: Rowman & Littlefield, 2016), 14.

78. Robert Remini, A Short History of the United States (New York: Harper Perennial, 2008), 61.
79. Ellis, American Dialogue, 191.
80. "From George Washington to Timothy Pickering, July 1, 1796," Founders Online, National Archives, http://founders.archives.gov/documents/Washington/99-01-02-00674. This is an Early Access document from *The Papers of George Washington*.
81. Ibid.
82. Ibid.
83. Ellis, American Dialogue, 180.
84. "Appendix D. Inventory of the Books in the Estate, c.1759," Founders Online, National Archives, https://founders.archives.gov/documents/Washington/02-06-02-0164-0026. Original source: *The Papers of George Washington, Colonial Series*, ed. W. W. Abbot, vol. 6, *September 4, 1758– December 26, 1760* (Charlottesville: University Press of Virginia, 1988), 283–300.
85. Great Britain, Parliamentary History of England.
86. Albert Bushnell Hart, "The Monroe Doctrine and the Doctrine of Permanent Interest," American Historical Review 7, no. 1 (October 1901): 77–91.
87. William J. Brinker, "Commerce, Culture, and Horticulture: The Beginnings of Sino-American Cultural Relations," in Aspects of Sino-American Relations since 1784, ed. Thomas H. Etzold (New York and London: New Viewpoints, A Division of Franklin Watt, 1978), 5.
88. Ellen Paul Denker, *After the Chinese Taste: China's Influence in America, 1730–1930* (Salem, MA: Peabody Museum, 1985), 7.
89. Alice R. Huger Smith and D. E. Huger Smith, The Dwelling Houses of Charleston, South Carolina (Philadelphia and London: J.B. Lippincott Company, 1917), 357–58.
90. Fiske Kimball, Domestic Architecture of the American Colonies and of the Early Republic (New York: Charles Scribner's Sons, 1927), 138. See Kimball, *Thomas Jefferson: Architect, Original Designs in the Coolidge Collection of the Massachusetts Historical Society with an Essay and Notes* (New York: Da Capo Press, 1968), 35.
91. David Watkin, The English Vision—The Picturesque in Architecture, Landscape and Garden Design (London: Breslich & Foss, 1982), 31–33.
92. Brinker, "Commerce, Culture, and Horticulture," 11–12.
93. Julian Ursyn Niemcewicz, *Vine and Fig Tree: Travels Through America 1797–1799, 1805 with some Further Account of Life in New Jersey*, trans. and ed. with an introduction and notes by Metchie J. E. Budka (Elizabeth, NJ: Grassmann Publishing Company, Inc, 1965), 62–63.
94. Marie Kimball, Jefferson: The Road to Glory, 1743 to 1776 (New York: Coward-McCann, Inc., 1943), 148; Thomas Whately, Observations on Modern Gardening (London: Boydell Press, 1770), 120 and 127–28.
95. Kiesten Larsen Davis, "Secondhand Chinoiserie and the Confucian Revolutionary: Colonial America's Decorative Arts 'after the Chinese Taste'" (master's thesis, Brigham Young University, 2008), 17.

96. "Architectural Side of Thomas Jefferson," *USA Today Magazine* 122, no. 2583 (December 1993), 8.

97. Ibid.

98. Kimball, *Thomas Jefferson: Architect*, 130.

99. Kimball, *Domestic Architecture*, 234.

100. Kimball, *Jefferson: The Road to Glory*, 162.

101. Kimball, *Thomas Jefferson: Architect*, 126.

102. Thomas Jefferson, *Thomas Jefferson Papers* (Boston: Massachusetts Historical Society), 2003.

103. Kimball, *Thomas Jefferson: Architect*, figs. 161–62.

104. Karl Lehmann, *Thomas Jefferson: American Humanist* (New York: Macmillan, 1947), 170.

105. "Attending to My Farm"—Thomas Jefferson's Monticello, https://www.monticello.org/thomas-jefferson/a-day-in-the-life-of-jefferson/attending-to-my-farm/.

106. Claus Daufenbach, "Jefferson's Monticello and the Poetics of Landscape Gardening," *Soundings: An Interdisciplinary Journal* 78, no. 3/4 (Fall/Winter 1995): 405–6.

107. Ibid., 406.

108. Ibid.

109. Scott McBride, "Building a Chinese Railing," *Taunton's Fine Homebuilding*, July 2006, 76–77.

110. *Thomas Jefferson: The Architect of a Nation*, http://xroads.virginia.edu/~cap/jeff/jeffarch.html.

111. Ibid.

112. Robert W. Tucker and David C. Hendrickson, "Thomas Jefferson and American Foreign Policy," *Foreign Affairs* 69, no. 2 (Spring 1990): 136.

113. Kenneth Hafertepe, "An Inquiry into Thomas Jefferson's Ideas of Beauty," *Journal of the Society of Architectural Historians* 59, no. 2 (June 2000), 221.

114. To James Madison, September 20, 1785, *The Papers of Thomas Jefferson*, ed. Julian Boyd, vol. 8, *February 1785 to October 1785* (Princeton: Princeton University Press, 1953), 535.

115. Davis, "Secondhand Chinoiserie," 61.

116. Silk Association of America, Annual Report, 1900, 32; Silk Association of America, *Annual Report, 1908*, 923–24.

117. Ibid., 1917, 19.

118. Ibid., 1906, 69.

119. Ibid., 1913, 36.

120. Bob Wyss, *Connecticut's Mulberry Craze*, https://connecticuthistory.org/connecticuts-mulberry-craze/.

121. "Enclosure: Invoice of Goods to Robert Cary & Company, September 27, 1763," Founders Online, National Archives, https://founders.archives.gov/documents/Washington/02-07-02-0153-0002. Original source: *The Papers of George Washington, Colonial Series*, ed. W. W. Abbot and Dorothy Twohig, vol. 7, *January 1, 1761–June 15, 1767* (Charlottesville: University Press of Virginia, 1990), 253–57.

"Invoice from Robert Cary & Company, February 13, 1764," Founders Online, National Archives, https://founders.archives.gov/documents/Washington/02-07-02-0175. Original source: *The Papers of George Washington, Colonial Series*, ed. W. W. Abbot and Dorothy Twohig, vol. 7, *January 1, 1761–June 15, 1767* (Charlottesville: University Press of Virginia, 1990), 287–95.

122. Charles M. Andrews, *The Colonial Period of American History, England's Commercial and Colonial Policy, With a New Introduction by Leonard W. Labaree* (New Haven and London: Yale University Press, 1969), 330.

123. Benjamin Franklin, *The Nature and Necessity of a Paper-Currency*, A Modest Enquiry into the Nature and Necessity of a Paper-Currency. Philadelphia: Printed and Sold at the New Printing-Office, near the Market. 1729. (Historical Society of Pennsylvania). In *The Papers of Benjamin Franklin*, http://franklinpapers.org/franklin/framedVolumes.jsp.

124. Franklin, *Interest of Great Britain Considered.*

125. Benjamin Franklin, to Cadwalader Evans, reprinted from Samuel Hazard, ed., Hazard's Register of Pennsylvania, XVI, no. 5 (August 1, 1835): 66–67, extract in American Philosophical Society Minutes. London, September 7, 1769. In *The Papers of Benjamin Franklin*, http://franklinpapers.org/franklin/framedVolumes.jsp.

126. In the eighteenth century, Thomas Lombe built the famous silk-throwing mill at Derby—built allegedly with Italian designs smuggled to England by his brother. This mill employed hundreds of workers and set the pattern for the spinning factories of future years. See M. Dorothy George, England in Transition, rev. ed. (Baltimore: Pelican, 1953), 103. See also Lilian M. Li, *China's Silk Trade: Traditional Industry in the Modern World, 1842 1937* (Cambridge, MA: Harvard University Press, 1981), 66.

127. Benjamin Franklin, Poor Richard improved: Being an Almanack and Ephemeris...for the Year of our Lord 1749 . . . By Richard Saunders, Philom. Philadelphia: Printed and Sold by B. Franklin, and D. Hall (Yale University Library). In *The Papers of Benjamin Franklin*, http://franklinpapers.org/franklin/framedVolumes.jsp.

128. Ibid.

129. Benjamin Franklin, "Memoirs of the Cultures of Silk," in The Papers of Benjamin Franklin, ed. Leonard Labaree, vol. 12 (New Haven and London: Yale University Press, 1968), 12.

130. Ibid.

131. Benjamin Franklin, to Cadwalader Evans, London, July 18, 1771, reprinted from Samuel Hazard, ed., Hazard's Register of Pennsylvania, XVI, no. 5 (August 1, 1835): 92–93. In *The Papers of Benjamin Franklin*, http://franklinpapers.org/franklin/framedVolumes.jsp.

132. Ibid.

133. Benjamin Franklin, to Ezra Stiles, ALS: Universitätsbibliothek Leipzig, Sammlung Kestner, Philadelphia, December 12, 1763. In *The Papers of Benjamin Franklin*, http://franklinpapers.org/franklin/framedVolumes.jsp.

134. Ibid.

135. Wyss, *Connecticut's Mulberry Craze.*

136. Benjamin Franklin, to Cadwalader Evans, Reprinted from Jared Sparks, ed., The Works of Benjamin Franklin . . . (10 vols., Boston, 1836–1840), VIII, 3–4. London, February 6, 1772. In *The Papers of Benjamin Franklin*, http://franklinpapers.org/franklin/framedVolumes.jsp.

137. Ibid.

138. Benjamin Franklin, to a Committee of the Managers of the Philadelphia Silk Filature ALS (letter book draft): Library of Congress, London, March 15, 1773. In *The Papers of Benjamin Franklin*, http://franklinpapers.org/franklin/framedVolumes.jsp.

139. From the Managers of the Philadelphia Silk Filature to Franklin and John Fothergill LS: American Philosophical Society, Philadelphia, November 8, 1771, http://franklinpapers.org/franklin/framedVolumes.jsp.

140. Benjamin Franklin, to Cadwalader Evans, London, July 4, 1771, reprinted from Samuel Hazard, ed., Hazard's Register of Pennsylvania XVI, no. 5 (August 1, 1835): 92–93. In *The Papers of Benjamin Franklin*, http://franklinpapers.org/franklin/framedVolumes.jsp.

141. Benjamin Franklin, to a Committee of the Managers of the Philadelphia Silk Filature ALS: Historical Society of Pennsylvania; letter book draft: Library of Congress, London, July 14, 1773. In *The Papers of Benjamin Franklin*, http://franklinpapers.org/franklin/framedVolumes.jsp.

142. Benjamin Franklin, to Cadwalader Evans, ALS (letterbook draft): Library of Congress, London, April 6, 1773. In *The Papers of Benjamin Franklin*, http://franklinpapers.org/franklin/framedVolumes.jsp.

143. Benjamin Franklin, to Edmund Clegg, ALS: Elisha K. Kane, Pennsylvania (1956), Passy, April 26, 1782, http://franklinpapers.org/franklin/framedVolumes.jsp.

144. From Rebecca Haydock Garrigues, "ALS: American Philosophical Society, Philadelphia 5th Mo 20th 1773." In *The Papers of Benjamin Franklin*, http://franklinpapers.org/franklin/framedVolumes.jsp.

145. From a Committee of the Managers of the Philadelphia Silk Filature, LS: American Philosophical Society Philadelphia, November 17, 1772, http://franklinpapers.org/franklin/framedVolumes.jsp.

146. Gottfried Achenwall, "Some Observations on North America from Oral Information by Dr. Franklin," translated from "Einige Anmerkungen über Nordamerika, und über dasige Grosbritannische Colonien. (Aus mündlichen Nachrichten des Hrn. Dr. Franklins.)," Hannoverisches Magazin, 17tes, 18tes, 19tes, 31tes, 32tes Stücke (Feb. 27, Mar. 2, 6, Apr. 17, 20, 1767), cols. 257–96, 482–508 (Princeton University Library), http://franklinpapers.org/franklin/framedVolumes.jsp.

147. Benjamin Franklin, to William Franklin, ALS (letterbook draft): American Philosophical Society, London, May 5, 1772, http://franklinpapers.org/franklin/framedVolumes.jsp.

148. For more information regarding the history of the sericulture, see Sericulture by Dr. Ron Cherry, http://www.insects.org/ced1/seric.html.

149. Benjamin Franklin, "The Kite Experiment, I." Printed in The Pennsylvania Gazette, October 19, 1752; also copy: The Royal Society. II. Printed in Joseph

Priestley, The History and Present State of Electricity, with Original Experiments (London, 1767), 179–81, Franklin's Statement, Philadelphia, October 19. In *The Papers of Benjamin Franklin*, http://franklinpapers.org/franklin/framedVolumes.jsp.

150. Benjamin Franklin, to a Committee of the Managers of the Philadelphia Silk Filature. ALS: Historical Society of Pennsylvania; letterbook draft: Library of Congress, London, July 14, 1773. In *The Papers of Benjamin Franklin*, http://franklinpapers.org/franklin/framedVolumes.jsp.

151. Benjamin Franklin: *Glimpses of the Man*, https://www.fi.edu/benjamin-franklin/resources.

152. Ronald W. Clark, *Benjamin Franklin: A Biography* (New York: Random House, 1983), 55.

153. Albert Henry Smyth, ed., *The Writings of Benjamin Franklin*, vol. IX, *1783–1788* (New York: McMillan, 1906), 434.

154. John Bigelow, ed., *The Complete Works of Benjamin Franklin* (New York: G. P. Putnam's Sons, 1888), 243–45.

155. Ibid., 244.

156. Ibid., 243–45.

157. Ibid., 244.

158. Clark, *Benjamin Franklin: A Biography*, 55.

159. Ibid.

160. "An Account of the New Invented Pennsylvanian Fire-Places, [November 15, 1744]," Founders Online, National Archives, https://founders.archives.gov/documents/Franklin/01-02-02-0114. Original source: *The Papers of Benjamin Franklin*, ed. Leonard W. Labaree, vol. 2, *January 1, 1735, through December 31, 1744* (New Haven: Yale University Press, 1961), 419–46. See also Du Halde, *General History of China*, IV:75.

161. Ibid.

162. Benjamin Franklin, to Julien-David LeRoy (unpublished), 1784. In *The Papers of Benjamin Franklin*, https://franklinpapers.org/framedVolumes.jsp.

163. Ibid.

164. Ibid.

165. Ibid.

166. Edmund S. Morgan, *Benjamin Franklin* (New Haven and London: Yale University Press, 2002), 7–8.

167. Louis P. Masur, ed., *The Autobiography of Benjamin Franklin with Related Documents*, 2nd ed. (Boston and New York: Bedford/St. Martin's, 2003), 34.

168. Benjamin Franklin, to Julien-David LeRoy.

169. Ibid., 89.

170. Benjamin Franklin "Description of Making Paper in the Chinese Manner" (unpublished) Friday, June 20, 1788. In *The Papers of Benjamin Franklin*, https://franklinpapers.org/framedVolumes.jsp?tocvol=45.

171. Ibid.

172. Ibid.

173. Ibid.

174. Ibid.

Chapter 3

Plants from the East

The Founders' Efforts to Transplant Chinese Plants to North America

Americans have a long history of introducing plants from other parts of the world. As early as 1699, on the banks of the Ashley River in South Carolina, an experimental farm was established by colonists interested in transferring plants to the North American colonies. In spring 1733, James Edward Oglethorpe (1696–1785), the founder of the colony of Georgia, set up an experimental garden for botanical purposes and for testing agricultural plants. The Royal Botanical Gardens at Kew in West London also made many contributions in transplanting plants to North America.[1]

During the colonial period, China was considered a rich source of new plants and was viewed as "a botanical and zoological wonderland."[2] Some American colonists realized that "many valuable trees, unknown in Europe, grow in the northern provinces of China" and could thrive well "in the colonies."[3] They took measures to introduce and naturalize Chinese plants into North America (table 3.1).[4] For example, paper mulberry was brought into North America in 1754.[5]

As a country with a long history of flourishing agriculture, China became an indispensable source for the founders. Below I will explore the actions the founders took to bring in agricultural, economic, and ornamental plants from China to North America. First, I will briefly probe the founders' attempt to have Chinese plants growing in the new nation. Then I will review how Benjamin Franklin made his attempts to introduce various Chinese economically viable plants in the colonial era. Third, I will focus on my survey of Washington's efforts to propagate Chinese flowers. Finally, I will examine how Jefferson proliferated Chinese flowers at Monticello.

Table 3.1 List of Chinese Plants That John Ellis Recommended Should Be Brought into North America

Chinese Names	Latin Names	English Names	Observations
Yeqi Shu	Croton Sebiferum	Tallow tree of China	This plant grows in moist places in China and is of great use in the country.
Zhuteng	Arundo Bambo	The true Bamboo cane	Of great use in China and might be also in our American islands.
Chashu	Thea	Tea	From China and Japan.
Ezihua	Gardenia Florida	Umky of the Chinese	Used in dyeing in China. The pulp that surrounds the seeds gives in warm water a most excellent yellow color, inclining to orange.
Sangshu	Morus papyrifera	Paper Mulberry tree	Used for making paper in China and Japan. This has been some time in English gardens.
Boqigen	Similax China	China Root	In China and in New Spain.
	Leechee	Leechee of China	This fruit is highly commended by all persons who have been to China.

THE FOUNDERS AND CHINESE PLANTS

Agriculture was the major component of the American colonial economy. It employed 90 percent of the workforce population. As the founders searched for foreign plants to improve agriculture, China was considered a rich source of possible valued additions. There was a continuous endeavor to acquire Chinese plants to North America starting from the colonial era to the early republic period. George Washington, Benjamin Franklin, John Jay, James Madison, even Abigail Smith Adams—John Adams's wife—made substantial efforts to introduce and propagate Chinese plants.

During the colonial era, some realized that many valuable trees, unknown in Europe, grew in the northern provinces of China and could be transplanted. Numerous plants were brought into North America. In 1765, Franklin encountered Chinese soybeans in England and sent some to John Bartram, the famous colonial botanist. In 1772, Franklin also sent Chinese rhubarb seeds and Chinese tallow trees to North America. Tallow trees, which were incredibly useful in the manufacturing of candles, soap, cooking oil, and herbal remedies, spread widely throughout the Southern colonies.

George Washington had a lifetime preoccupation with agriculture. He conducted personal experiments to sow Chinese flowers at his plantation, Mount Vernon. He recorded his experiments in his diary in detail, suggesting how much he valued his effort. Thanks to Washington's seriousness with his experiments, we can trace his efforts.

After American independence was secured, John Jay reported to Washington in 1794 that South Carolina introduced certain Chinese cotton. He described further the original region of the cotton, which "came from the Nanjing region of China."[6] James Madison acquired some "Seeds of chinese hemp" from John Coakley Lettsom (1741–1815), an English physician and philanthropist.[7] James Madison also ordered Chinese flower seeds.[8] Abigail Smith Adams proudly told her daughter, Abigail Amelia Adams Smith, that in her garden, "Chinese Chatterer grows daily more interesting."[9]

In 1805, Jefferson told William Hamilton (1745–1813) that the latter's nephew provided Jefferson "the plant of the Chinese silk tree in perfect good order."[10] Jefferson told him, "I shall nurse it with care until it shall be in a condition to be planted at Monticello."[11] In 1809, Madame de Tessé (1741–1813), a French salon holder and letter writer, sent Thomas Jefferson some tree seeds. She told Jefferson that the seeds "come from northern China. It was first called Paulinia aurea."[12] According to her letter, the tree "grows very quickly, does not grow tall, its foliage is beautiful, its blossom pleasant."[13]

In April 1811, Jefferson sowed the seeds of the silk plant—also known as China grass, Chinese silk plant, or ramie (Boehmeria nivea). The silk plant was cultivated for its long fibers or ramie, which could be woven.[14]

What was important to the founders was to obtain Chinese plants for propagation in North America. Their intention was well reflected in Jefferson's statement, "The greatest service which can be rendered to any country is, to add a useful plant to its [agri]culture, especially a bread grain."[15]

BENJAMIN FRANKLIN AND CHINESE PLANTS

Franklin showed an extensive interest in agriculture, helping to introduce several Chinese plants to the United States. In his *A Proposal for Promoting Useful Knowledge Among the British Plantations in America*, Franklin aggregated knowledge about general farming innovations and various newly discovered plants, including methods for effective propagation and cultivation.

In order to promote the development of North America's agricultural economy, colonists made efforts to obtain plants from other lands. China was considered a rich source of new plants and was viewed as "a botanical and zoological wonderland."[16] Some colonists had realized that "many valuable trees, unknown in Europe, grow in the northern provinces of China . . . that climate, though in 40 degrees of North latitude, . . . is liable to more severe cold than" North American colonies in winter. Trees from northern China "would thrive well in the colonies."[17] The colonists made their efforts to introduce China's agricultural plants into North America. Numerous Chinese plants were brought into North American colonies.[18]

Franklin sought to bring into the colonies "all new-discovered plants, herbs, trees, roots, their virtues, uses, etc; methods of propagating them, and making such as are useful." Additionally, he wanted to learn from other nations "new mechanical inventions for saving labor, as mills and carriages, all new arts trades, and manufactures, introducing other sorts from foreign countries."[19] Franklin was inspired by many Chinese inventions. Franklin considered his *Proposal for Promoting Useful Knowledge among the British Plantations in America* his own leading line.

In 1761, Franklin sent Joshua Babcock (1707–1783), a physician and general in the American Revolutionary War, some Chinese seeds of the true Tartarian Rhubarb.[20] Franklin, who at the time served as the North American representative to France, sent Chinese soybean seeds back to the colonies.[21]

Franklin sent from London to North America Chinese rhubarb seeds in 1772. He was assured that the seeds would flourish well in North America, "where the Climate is the same with that of the Chinese Wall, just without which it grows in plenty and of the best Quality."[22] He was anxious about their cultivation.

In October of the same year, Franklin sent from London some "Seeds of the Chinese Tallow Tree" to John Bartram, the famous botanist in North America.[23] Franklin told Bartram to have good taken care of the plant and expressed his confidence that the tallow tree "may grow under your skillful Care."[24] He told Bartram, "Remember that for Use the Root does not come to its Perfection of Power and Virtue in less than Seven Years."[25] Later, he gave Bartram the example he found in London, "The Physicians here who have try'd the Scotch, approve it much, and say it is fully equal to the best imported."[26] At the same time, Franklin also sent "a few Seeds of the Chinese Tallow Tree" to Noble Wimberly Jones (1723–1805), an American physician and statesman in Savannah, Georgia. He told Jones that "I believe grow and thrive with you. 'Tis a most useful plant."[27] The tallow tree spread widely throughout the south.[28]

In 1765, Franklin acquired some Chinese soybeans in England and sent the soybeans—"Chinese Garavance"—to John Bartram in the same year.[29] When he served as ambassador to France, Franklin, who had been a member of the French Academy of Science since 1772, sent soybean seeds back to the United States and urged that "they be given a trial."[30]

GEORGE WASHINGTON AND CHINESE FLOWERS

From the onset of the introduction of Chinese plants to Americans, ornamental plants such as the gardenia, the camellia, and the Cherokee rose were brought from China and grew well in the Southern states. A few handsome trees were also introduced, such as the ginkgo and the camphor.[31]

George Washington showed great enthusiasm in the agricultural development of the United States. Born and raised in the country, Washington had a special bond with the soil. In his annual message to Congress in 1796, he advocated "a federal appropriation to stimulate enterprise and experiment in agriculture."[32] Simultaneously, he tried to "draw to the national center the results of individual skill and observation, and to spread the collected information far and wide throughout the nation."[33]

Led by his interest in farming, Washington turned his attention to agricultural developments in the wake of the victory of the American Revolution. In 1783, Washington returned to Mount Vernon "with every hope and intention of spending the rest of his days there."[34] He told his fellow Americans that the advancement of agriculture in the United States "by all proper means, will not I trust need recommendation."[35] Believing that "with reference either to individual, or National Welfare, Agriculture is of primary importance,"[36] Washington had made agriculture his "favorite subject" by the late 1790s.[37] At Mount Vernon, Washington indulged himself in agricultural experiments and "entirely devoted [himself] to the care of his farm."[38]

One of Washington's great preoccupations was finding the right crops for the soil, climate, and practical needs of his Mount Vernon estate.[39] In December 1788, he informed Arthur Young, the most scientific farmer of his day and the editor of *the Annuals of Agriculture*, that "the more I am acquainted with agricultural affairs, the better I am pleased with them; inasmuch that I can nowhere find so great satisfaction as in those innocent and useful pursuits."[40]

Experimentation was one of Washington's chief delights as a farmer. He worked hard to transplant Chinese flowers to North America. Washington's journal records suggest that he experimented with best practices such as the distance between rows, different rates of seeding, and drilling instead of broadcasting the seed. He was meticulous in detailing these processes, revealing the extent to which he valued this type of agricultural research.

Washington varied the distance between rows. He attempted different rates of seeding.[41] He recorded his experiments in his diary, suggesting how much he valued this kind of transplanting research. He wrote of the procedure in detail by which he sowed the flowers as well as information on the kinds of flowers he sowed.

According to his diary, on Friday, July 8, 1785, Washington chose a good place next to the garden wall in his "well cultivated and neatly kept" botanical garden[42] and sowed "one half the Chinese Seed given by Mr. Porter and Doctr. Craik. [James Craik, a physician at Mount Vernon]." Washington documented an incredibly detailed record of the procedures he used to plant the seeds. The following record from his diary shows that Washington sowed the flowers in three rows.

First Row

> Between the 1st. & 2d. pegs 1 *1 Muc qua fa*;
> betwn. the 2d. & 3d. Do. 1 *Pungton leea fa*; 6 & 7 2 *In che fa*
> 3 & 4th *1 Ting litt fa* 7 & 8 *Cum hung fa*. 4 Seeds
> 4 & 5 *1 Iso pung fa* 8 & 9 2 *Hung co fa*
> 5 & 6 *1 Ci chou la fa* 9 & 10 5 *Be yack fa*
> 10 & 11 7 *Hou sun fa* 18 & 19 *Pain ba fa*
> 11 & 12 *Sung sang fa yung* 19 & 20 *Cu si fa*
> 12 & 13 *Pu yung fa* 20 & 21 *Tu me fa*
> 13 & 14 *Mon Tan fa* 21 & 22 *All san fa*
> 14 & 15 *Cum Coak fa* 22 & 23 *Yong san con fa*
> 15 & 16 *Pung ke Cuun* 23 & 24 *Hou Con fa*
> 16 & 17 *Cin yet cou* 24 & 25 *Hoak sing fa*
> 17 & 18 *Se me fa* 25 & 26 *1 sit Ye muy fa*

Second Row

> 1st & 2nd *Tits swe fa* 10 & 11 *Ling si qui*
> 2 & 3 *An lee pung fa* 11 & 12 *Yuck soy hung seen fa*
> 3 & 4 *Se lou fa* 12 & 13 *Yuck sou cou fa*
> 4 & 5 *Lung Ci fa* 13 & 14 *Sing si qui fa*
> 5 & 6 *Tiahung seen fa* 14 & 15 *Bea an Cou*
> 6 & 7 *Lam Coax fa* 15 & 16 *Brey hung fa*
> 7 & 8 *Iny hung fa* 16 & 17 *Si fu he Tons*
> 8 & 9 *Jien pien cou fa* 17 & 18 *No name*
> 9 & 10 *Pung qui fa*

Third Row

> 1st & 2 *Cum Seen fa*
> 2 & 3 *Top pu young*
> 3 & 4 No name—like a 2d. bla. Bead.
> 4 & 5 *Ditto*—like but large. than Cabbage seed
> 5 & 6 larger and redder than Clover Seed.[43]

Washington sowed the seeds of the Chinese flowers corresponding to the above pattern at his River Plantation on July 13. Ten days later, he observed that "a few Plants of the Pride of China (the Seed of which were Sowed on the 13th. of June) to be coming up." He also discovered that the *Jien pien cou fa* and the other kinds of Chinese flower he sowed according to "Chinese sowing" had "been up several days."[44]

After that, Washington departed home. Twenty days later, on August 13, when he returned to Mount Vernon, Washington noticed that two kinds of Chinese flowers, which had sprouted earlier, had vanished. He assumed that they might have been "destroyed either by the drought or insects."[45] Seeing some flowers were "eradicated" while others were broken near the ground, Washington was incredibly sad and disappointed. He was anxious about whether they could "recover." Washington tried to figure out what had happened to the seeds. One explanation he entertained was that bugs might have eaten them, upon remembering that, at the time he left home, "some kind of fly, or bug, had begun to prey upon the leaves."[46]

By April 6, 1786, Washington acknowledged that his experiment had failed. He did not see any flowers sowed with the seeds from China coming up, even though some of them had germinated the previous year. He could not understand why these seeds failed to grow in his garden. From his diary, we understand that he sought to fathom reasons responsible for their disappearance. He did not know "whether these plants are unfit for this climate, or whether covering and thereby hiding them entirely from the Sun the whole winter occasioned them to rot."[47]

The year 1785 was not a good year for Washington to conduct experiments due to poor weather conditions. The rains were few and far between, resulting in drought conditions. The crops suffered, the wheat yield was poor, and chinch bugs attacked the corn to the degree that "hundreds of them & their young [were found] under the blades and at the lower joints of the Stock."[48]

Due to the severe drought conditions that year, Washington's experiment was not very positive. However, his efforts provide strong evidence of Washington's attempts at transplanting Chinese flowers in North America. As Paul Leland Haworth (1876–1936), an American author, educator, explorer, and politician, pointed out, the record of Washington's failures was "much greater than of successes." It is the experience of "every scientific farmer of horticulture who ventures out of the beaten path."[49] Evidently, this experiment exposed George Washington's endeavors to bring in Chinese flowers to the newly independent United States that he fought for (figure 3.1).

THOMAS JEFFERSON AND CHINESE FLOWERS

Jefferson considered the garden his "main business," and naturalized with all his "might when the interruptions permit" various kinds of foreign plants in his gardens at Monticello. His gardens reflected his efforts to realize his horticultural dreams.[50]

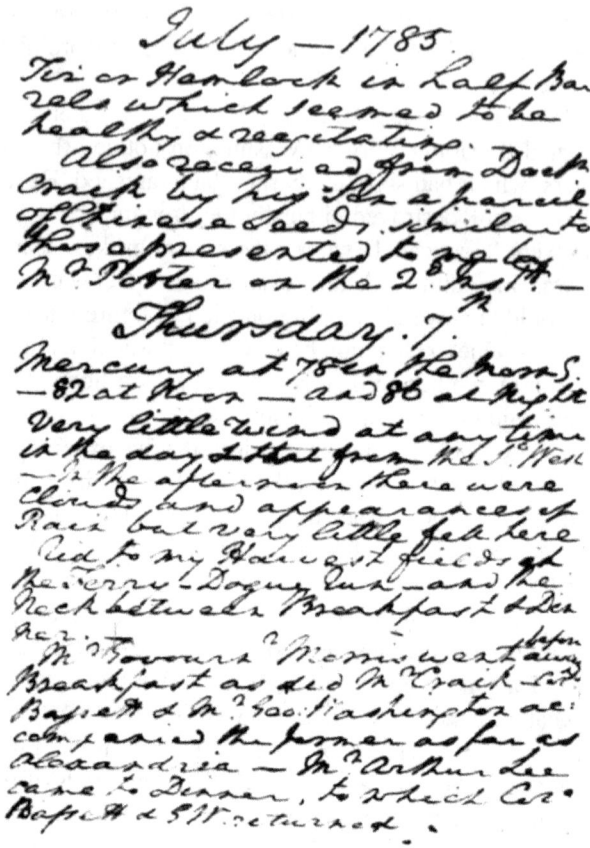

Figure 3.1 George Washington's Handwriting in His Diaries. George Washington Papers, Manuscript Division, Library of Congress, Washington, DC. A letterpress edition of all the diaries and diary fragments that could be located was edited by Donald Jackson and Dorothy Twohig and published in six volumes as The Diaries of George Washington (Charlottesville: University Press of Virginia, 1976–1979).

Thomas Jefferson's project of transplanting flowers from China into his garden at Monticello was so crucial to American botanical history that it was called the "China Revolution."[51] Jefferson fell in love with designing gardens immediately after he inherited Monticello in 1757.[52] Jefferson wanted to design and construct the gardens of Monticello from his own naturalistic point of view. He gathered a variety of seeds from around the world. His passion for gardening was widely known among his friends, who often sent him seeds and plants. As early as 1766, Jefferson started to document records on his naturalistic observations in his Garden Book.[53]

Unsurprisingly, Jefferson turned his eyes to China—the nation with a long history of botanical cultivation. He discerned Chinese flowers when he cultivated and designed his Monticello gardens.[54] In the late 1700s, European old roses, such as the Albas, Damasks, and Gallicas, were still immensely popular in North America. One of the shortcomings of those flowers was that they had a short blooming season. The main beauty of the rose garden was confined only to spring and was called "the metaphor for evanescent beauty."[55]

Jefferson first planted "China pinks" at Shadwell, his birthplace, in 1767. The flower was introduced from China and had been cultivated in Europe and America since the early eighteenth century. John Bartram planted Dianthus chinensis, China pink, in his garden.[56] When Jefferson received seeds of Blackberry Lily from nurseryman Bernard McMahon (1775–1816), an Irish American horticulturist settled in Philadelphia, he sowed them in a Monticello flower garden and mentioned them as "Chinese Ixia" in 1807. Later, Jefferson planted them in an east front oval flowerbed at Monticello.[57] In the twenty-first century, one can see it all over the grounds at Monticello. Traditional Chinese medical doctors used it as an ingredient in some Chinese medicine.[58] Jefferson planted Althaea (rose of Sharon) seeds at Shadwell in April 1767 and set out plants at Monticello in March 1794 and also at Poplar Forest in December 1812.[59]

The introduction of China roses brought new fashion to North America. The practice of growing only European roses that were carried across the Atlantic Ocean and that bloomed in spring only changed forever. The roses from China resulted in an extended blooming season in North America. From the early nineteenth century on, all American nurserymen began a "hybridizing odyssey attempting to fuse the genes of the China's with hardier species. The journey would take them from the first Hybrid Chinas, through Noisettes and Bourbons, to the Hybrid Perpetuals, and then the Hybrid Teas."[60]

Jefferson made long-term plans to transplant and naturalize the Pride of China, the goldenrain tree. The goldenrain tree (Koelreuteria paniculata), originally from China, was introduced in Europe in 1747. Common names include goldenrain tree,[61] and China tree.[62] French Jesuit Pierre d'Incarville (1706–1751), a missionary to China, sent seeds back to France in the mid-eighteenth century. In 1786, Jefferson asked Antonio Giannini (a gardener and vigneron at Monticello from 1778 to 1782) to send him seeds of the China tree (Pride of China).[63]

In June 1809, Madame de Tessé (1741–1813), a French salon holder and letter writer, sent Jefferson some seeds of goldenrain trees.

> I am enclosing a few seeds of a tree that seems to come from northern China. It was first called Paulinia aurea. I have kept this name though it has been given a new one lately. It grows very quickly, does not grow tall, its foliage is beautiful,

its blossom pleasant. I persuaded myself that you were lacking it because I wanted you to be kind enough to single it out with interest as a token of the cult in which I venerate you.[64]

On October 5, 1809, Jefferson planted the enclosed seeds of the Paulinia aurea (Koelreuteria paniculata), or goldenrain tree. Two years later, in his letter to de Tessé, Jefferson happily told her that the seeds had successfully germinated.[65] The tree is now "naturalized" on the grounds of Monticello. This is probably the first time it was grown in North America.[66]

Jefferson's efforts to transplant the Pride of China were fully reflected in several of his correspondences from 1798 to 1817, including his letter to Thomas Mann Randolph (1768–1828), an American planter, soldier, and politician from Virginia, dated March 22, 1798,[67] a letter from Raphaelle Peale (1774–1825), considered the first professional American painter of still life, dated January 19, 1806,[68] and his letter to Joel Yancey (1773–1838) a U.S. representative from Kentucky, dated March 6, 1817.[69]

With other plants that he transplanted from other parts of the world, Jefferson made his Monticello garden a Revolutionary American garden. His efforts still inspire Americans today to make the United States a great beautiful garden with flowers blooming all year round.

The founders' determination in transplanting Chinese plants persisted for many years during the colonial and early republic eras. In the colonial era, the founders, such as Franklin, mainly emphasized transplanting various plants valued for their economic benefits. After independence was secured, the founders primarily focused on ornamental plants. By then most Chinese economic and agricultural plants had been naturalized and were booming in North America.

NOTES

1. Nelson Klose, *America's Crop Heritage: The History of Foreign Plant Introduction by the Federal Government* (Ames: Iowa State College Press, 1950), 11.

2. Thomas H. Etzold, ed., *Aspects of Sino-American Relations Since 1784* (New York and London: New Viewpoints, A Division of Franklin Watt, 1978), 5.

3. John Ellis, "Directions for Bringing over Seeds and Plants, From the East Indies and Other Distant Countries, in A State of Vegetation: Together with a Catalogue of Such Foreign Plants as Are Worthy of Being Encouraged in Our American Colonies, For the Purposes of Medicine, Agriculture, and Commerce (1784)," in *Aphrodite's Mousetrap: A Biography of Venus's Flytrap with Facsimiles of an Original Pamphlet and the Manuscripts of John Ellis*, ed. E. Charles Nelson (Aberystwyth, Wales: published by Boethius Press, in association with Bentham-Moxon Trust and the Linnean Society, 1990), 2.

4. Table 3.1 shows a list of Chinese plants that John Ellis recommended should be brought into North America.
See Ellis, "Directions for Bringing over Seeds and Plants," 22–33.

5. Ibid., 13.

6. "To George Washington from John Jay, March 1, 1794," Founders Online, National Archives, https://founders.archives.gov/documents/Washington/05-15-02-0232. Original source: *The Papers of George Washington, Presidential Series*, ed. Christine Sternberg Patrick, vol. 15, *1 January–30 April 1794* (Charlottesville: University Press of Virginia, 2009), 302–3.

7. "To George Washington from John Coakley Lettsom, July 15, 1795," Founders Online, National Archives, https://founders.archives.gov/documents/Washington/05-18-02-0258. Original source: *The Papers of George Washington, Presidential Series*, ed. Carol S. Ebel, vol. 18, *April1–September 30, 1795* (Charlottesville: University Press of Virginia, 2015), 347–48.

8. "Seed Order for James Madison, Sr., March 26, 1791," Founders Online, National Archives, https://founders.archives.gov/documents/Madison/01-13-02-030

9. Original source: *The Papers of James Madison*, ed. Charles F. Hobson and Robert A. Rutland, vol. 13, *January 20, 1790– March 31, 1791* (Charlottesville: University Press of Virginia, 1981), 407–8.

9. "From Abigail Smith Adams to Abigail Amelia Adams Smith, April 17, 1808," Founders Online, National Archives, https://founders.archives.gov/documents/Adams/99-03-02-1668.

10. "From Thomas Jefferson to William Hamilton, November 6, 1805," Founders Online, National Archives, https://founders.archives.gov/documents/Jefferson/99 01-02-2587.

11. Ibid.

12. "Madame de Tessé to Thomas Jefferson, June 12, 1809," Founders Online, National Archives, https://founders.archives.gov/documents/Jefferson/03-01-02-0221. Original source: *The Papers of Thomas Jefferson, Retirement Series*, ed. J. Jefferson Looney, vol. 1, *March 4, 1809 to November 15, 1809* (Princeton: Princeton University Press, 2004), 271–74.

13. Ibid.

14. "George W. Erving to Thomas Jefferson, January 29, 1811," Founders Online, National Archives, https://founders.archives.gov/documents/Jefferson/03-03-02-0264. Original source: *The Papers of Thomas Jefferson, Retirement Series*, ed. J. Jefferson Looney, vol. 3, *12 August 12, 1810 to June 17, 1811* (Princeton: Princeton University Press, 2006), 342–43.

15. "Summary of Public Service, [after 2 September 1800]," Founders Online, National Archives, https://founders.archives.gov/documents/Jefferson/01-32-02-0080. Original source: *The Papers of Thomas Jefferson*, ed. Barbara B. Oberg, vol. 32, *June 1, 1800–February 16, 1801* (Princeton: Princeton University Press, 2005), 122–25.

16. Etzold, *Aspects of Sino-American Relations since 1784*, 5.

17. Ellis, "Directions for Bringing over Seeds and Plants," 2.

18. Ibid., 13.

19. Benjamin Franklin, "A Proposal for Promoting Useful Knowledge among the British Plantations in America," in *The Autobiography and Other Writings of Benjamin Franklin*, ed. Frank Donovan (New York: Dodd, Mead & Company, 1963), 303.

20. The Tartarian rhubarb (Rheum officinale) was introduced to Europe from China through Russia and promoted in Great Britain by Franklin's friend Sir Alexander Dick. It was highly prized for its medicinal uses. In 1774, the Society of Arts awarded its gold medal to Dick for his contribution. Robert Dossie, *Memoirs of Agriculture and other Economical Arts* (London, 1768–1782), ii, 258–91; iii, 208–25. See "From Benjamin Franklin to Joshua Babcock, December 10, 1761," Founders Online, National Archives, https://founders.archives.gov/documents/Franklin/01-09-02-0174. Original source: *The Papers of Benjamin Franklin*, ed. Leonard W. Labaree, vol. 9, *January 1, 1760, through December 31, 1761* (New Haven: Yale University Press, 1966), 396–98.

21. Walter T. Swingle, "Our Agricultural Debt to Asia," in *The Asian Legacy and American Life*, ed. Arthur E. Christy (New York: John Day Company, 1945), 87–88.

22. Benjamin Franklin, "To John Bartram, London, August 22, 1772," in *The Papers of Benjamin Franklin*, vol. 19, ed. William Willcox (New Haven and London: Yale University Press, 1975), 268.

23. Ibid.

24. Ibid.

25. Ibid.

26. Ibid.

27. Benjamin Franklin, "To Noble Wimberly Jones, London, October 7, 1772," in *The Papers of Benjamin Franklin*, vol. 19, ed. William Willcox (New Haven and London: Yale University Press, 1975), 324.

28. Ibid.

29. "From Benjamin Franklin to John Bartram, January 11, 1770," Founders Online, National Archives, https://founders.archives.gov/documents/Franklin/01-17-02-0010. Original source: *The Papers of Benjamin Franklin*, ed. William B. Willcox, vol. 17, *January 1 through December 31, 1770* (New Haven and London: Yale University Press, 1973), 22–23.

30. Swingle, "Our Agricultural Debt to Asia," 88.

31. Ibid., 85.

32. Charles A. Beard and Mary R. Beard, *The Rise of American Civilization*, vol. II (New York: Macmillan, 1927), 282.

33. Ibid.

34. Ralph K. Andrist, *The Founding Fathers: George Washington: A Biography in His Own Words* (New York: Newsweek Book Division, 1972), 289.

35. George Washington, "First Annual Address to Congress, January 8, 1790," in *Writings of George Washington from the Original Manuscript Sources 1745–1799*, ed. John C. Fitzpatrick, vol. 30 (Washington, DC: U.S. Government Printing Office, 1939), 493.

36. George Washington, "Eighth Annual Address to Congress, December 7, 1796," in *Writings of George Washington from the Original Manuscript Sources*

1745–1799, ed. John C. Fitzpatrick, vol. 35 (Washington, DC: U.S. Government Printing Office, 1939), 315.

37. Julian Ursyn Niemcewicz, *Vine and Fig Tree: Travels Through America 1797–1799, 1805 with some Further Account of Life in New Jersey*, trans. and ed. with an introduction and notes by Metchie J. E. Budka (Elizabeth, NJ: Grassmann Publishing Company, Inc, 1965), 102.

38. Jacques-Pierre Brissot de Warville, *New Travels in the United States of America*, trans. Mara Sconceanu Vamos and Durand Echeverria; ed. Durand Echeverria (Cambridge, MA: Belknap Press, 1964). Reprint, 1972, 342–43.

39. Introduction to the *Diary of George Washington*, http://memory.loc.gov/amm em/gwhtml/4gwintro.html.

40. Paul Leland Haworth, *George Washington: Being an Account of His Life and Agricultural Activities* (Indianapolis: Bobbs-Merrill, 1925), 2–3.

41. Introduction, *Diary of George Washington*.

42. Niemcewicz, *Vine and Fig Tree*, 97. His Botanical Garden is a plot of ground lying between the flower garden and the spinners' house, where he made many experiments. According to Paul Leland Haworth, most of Washington's experiments did not succeed. However, Washington's experiment was "the experience of every scientific farmer of horicultures who ventures out of the beaten path." See Haworth, *George Washington*, 106–7.

43. The above are the Chinese names that were accompanied by characters or hieroglyphics; a concise description of the seeds are annexed to their names on the paper that enrolls them. See John C. Fitzpatrick, *The Diaries of George Washington, 1748–1799*, vol. IV, *1789–1799* (Boston and New York: Houghton Mifflin, 1925), 388–89.

44. Fitzpatrick, *Diaries of George Washington*, 392–93.

45. Ibid., 404–5.

46. Ibid.

47. Ibid., 37–38.

48. Haworth, *George Washington*, 104.

49. Ibid., 107.

50. Peter J. Hatch, "Jefferson's Retirement Garden," *Twinleaf Journal Archives*, 2009.

51. Douglas T. Seidel, *The China (Rose) Revolution*, https://www.monticello.org /house-gardens/center-for-historic-plants/twinleaf-journal-online/the-china-rose-rev olution/.

52. "Attending to My Farm"—Thomas Jefferson's Monticello, https://www.mon ticello.org/thomas-jefferson/a-day-in-the-life-of-jefferson/attending-to-my-farm/.

53. Edwin Morris Betts and Hazlehurst Bolton Perkins, *Thomas Jefferson's Flower Garden at Monticello* (Charlottesville: University of Virginia, 1971), 1.

54. "Monticello—Virginia Museum of History & Culture," www.vahistorical.org.

55. Seidel, *The China (Rose) Revolution*.

56. *Bartram's Garden—Core Collection Plant List*, ed. American Society of Botanical Artists, http://www.asba-art.org/.

57. See https://www.monticello.org/house-gardens/in-bloom-at-monticello/blackberry-lily/.

58. *A Leafy Indulgence*, http://leafychronicles.blogspot.com/2014/08/thomas-jeffersons-chinese-ixia.html.

59. See https://www.plantanswers.com/articles/Althaea-Althea-Rose_of_Sharon.asp.

60. Peter J. Hatch, "Thomas Jefferson's Legacy in Gardening and Food," *Twinleaf Journal Archives*, 2010, https://www.monticello.org/house-gardens/center-for-historic-plants/twinleaf-journal-online/thomas-jefferson-s-legacy-in-gardening-and-food/.

61. Natural Resources Conservation Service, U.S. Department of Agriculture.

62. Encyclopædia Britannica Online, https://www.britannica.com/plant/China-tree.

63. "From Thomas Jefferson to Antonio Giannini, with a List of Seeds Wanted, February 5, 1786," Founders Online, National Archives, https://founders.archives.gov/documents/Jefferson/01-09-02-0218. Original source: *The Papers of Thomas Jefferson*, ed. Julian P. Boyd, vol. 9, *November 1, 1785– June 22, 1786* (Princeton: Princeton University Press, 1954), 252–55.

64. "Madame de Tessé to Thomas Jefferson, 12 June 1809."

65. "Thomas Jefferson to Madame de Tessé, 27 March 1811," Founders Online, National Archives, https://founders.archives.gov/documents/Jefferson/03-03-02-0375. Original source: *The Papers of Thomas Jefferson, Retirement Series*, ed. J. Jefferson Looney, vol. 3, *12 August 1810 to 17 June 1811* (Princeton: Princeton University Press, 2006), 503–4.

66. "Madame de Tessé to Thomas Jefferson, 12 June 1809."

67. "From Thomas Jefferson to Thomas Mann Randolph, 22 March 1798," Founders Online, National Archives, https://founders.archives.gov/documents/Jefferson/01-30-02-0131. Original source: *The Papers of Thomas Jefferson*, ed. Barbara B. Oberg, vol. 30, *January 1, 1798–January 31, 1799* (Princeton: Princeton University Press, 2003), 192–94.

68. "To Thomas Jefferson from Raphaelle Peale, 19 January 1806," Founders Online, National Archives, https://founders.archives.gov/documents/Jefferson/99-01-02-3046.

69. "Thomas Jefferson to Joel Yancey, 6 March 1817," *Founders Online*, National Archives, https://founders.archives.gov/documents/Jefferson/03-11-02-0132. Original source: *The Papers of Thomas Jefferson, Retirement Series*, ed. J. Jefferson Looney, vol. 11, *January 19, to August 31, 1817* (Princeton: Princeton University Press, 2014), 178–79.

Chapter 4

The Influence of Chinese Material Culture on Early U.S. History

The connection between China and North America can be traced to the initial settlement by British colonists on the East Coast of North America in May 1609. These colonists, sent by the Virginia Company of London, landed on the north bank of a river they named the James and built Fort James—later to be renamed Jamestown. They believed the river's headwaters to be "the shortcut to China."[1] The choosing of Jamestown as the landing spot was not a chance decision, but was made in accordance with instructions given by the Virginia Company.[2] Even the "decisive and stern leadership" of John Smith (1580–1631) was not given "the authority to override" the instruction from the company, which believed that the James River could lead the colonists to "a shortcut to China."[3]

It seems a historical irony that China—an ancient, distant empire—also influenced the founding of the United States. Military support from France was one of the key factors in the colonists' victory in the American Revolutionary War. One reason the French royal court fought the British in North America was to prevent a monopoly of trade with China. The French court understood that it needed a victory to "destroy British hegemony, not only in North America but in the sugar-rich West Indies and the even richer market of India and China."[4]

Below I will provide a summary of the founders of the American colonies and Chinese material culture. Then I will examine two items: tea and porcelain ware, which had a remarkable social and political impact on American society in the colonial and early republic period.

THE AMERICAN FOUNDERS AND CHINESE MATERIAL CULTURE

Chinese material products, in particular tea and porcelain ware, were greatly influential on American society. Before American independence, Chinese goods enriched colonial "American life in many, many ways"[5] with the Chinese developing products that increased in popularity and "spread among less affluent sectors of American society."[6]

Throughout the mid-eighteenth century, affluent American colonists bought substantial amounts of "Chinese Chippendale" furniture, Chinese wallpaper, silk, and porcelain ware. Chinese tea had become the most popular drink for most colonists.[7] For some, China was a source of silk.[8] Countless Chinese trade products impressed the Americans. From letters and correspondence penned by some of the American founders, we can glean that abundant amounts of goods originating from China could be found in the colonies. These included "the Flour matting from China,"[9] "Chinese silk Netting,"[10] "Chinese Wall Papers,"[11] "Chinese porcelain table,"[12] "Chinese straw floor cloth,"[13] "Chinese pipe,"[14] "Linnen China, Glass kitchen furniture Plate,"[15] Cloth (Nankins),[16] "bundles of Nankeens imported from China,"[17] the "cotton fabrics of China,"[18] "Gong (bell),"[19] "fine Cambk Pockt Handfs of the Chinese sort,"[20] and more. Benjamin Franklin was "particularly fascinated by the huge sheet of Chinese paper, presumably rice paper."[21] George Washington bought "A Neat tortoise shell Comb & Case for the Pocket—small at one end & large at the other."[22] He also maintained "2 dozn pr large Chinese green Ivory Table knives & Forks."[23]

The founders discovered the importance of Chinese domestic animals. As a result, Chinese pigs also reached North America. In 1796, George Washington "purchased the Guinea, or Chinese Hogs"[24] and raised the "Chinese Hogs" at his mill."[25] Three years later, Washington told William Thornton (1759–1828) that he had "The true Chinese Hogs."[26] Washington went too far with trying to develop a certain breed of pig and needed more of the original species to start the process again. He told William Thornton that he thought his Chinese Hogs "have got so mixed, that a boar pig is desirable; & I would thank you for securing one for me, of the genuine kind, if to be had."[27] In 1811, Peter Carr (1770–1815), gave Jefferson "a very fine boar-pig of the Chinese or Parkinson breed."[28]

Tea and other Chinese products had become profoundly popular in colonial society, becoming an indispensable element of colonists' daily lives. The British monopoly of tea importation and the colonists' struggle against this changed the historical development of the colonies. The tax on tea and the resentment toward the tea monopoly by the East India Company were factors that led the colonists to rebel. Chinese porcelain ware not only greatly enriched American life but became the catalyst of the formation of American identity.

TEA: THE LEAVES THAT TRIGGERED THE AMERICAN WAR FOR INDEPENDENCE

On the night of December 16, 1773, a week away from Christmas Eve, colonial patriots disguised as Indians secretly entered Boston Harbor under the cover of night. They boarded three British ships in the harbor and dumped some 350 chests of Chinese tea. John Adams commended the destruction of the tea, calling it the "grandest Event" in the history of the colonial protest movement.[29] The Boston Tea Party was merely the first of a series of tea parties given by Americans at the expense of the East India Company and colonial tea importers.[30] Their action was a protest of taxation without representation and the monopoly granted to the East India Company—among other complaints against the British Empire. Chinese tea, which was transported from China to Britain and then re-exported to North American Colonies, formed part of Britain's contentious taxation agenda during the 1760s and 1770s.[31] George Washington stated, "Is it against paying the duty of three pence per pound on tea became burthensome? No, it is the right only, we have all along disputed."[32] Thomas Jefferson also echoed, "We must boldly take an unequivocal stand in the line with Massachusetts."[33] This protest brought Anglo-American relations to a boiling point.

The incident was an indicator that the importance of tea had developed to such a degree that it impacted the historical course of the North American colonies. Tea had become a basic element in North American colonial society. In the eighteenth century, drinking tea in the morning at home and socially in the afternoon or early evening became an "established custom." According to Benjamin Franklin, "at least a Million of Americans drink Tea twice a Day."[34] Another contemporary estimated that one third of the population drank tea twice a day.[35] Foreign travelers who visited there left vivid records about tea drinking in Pennsylvania and New York, "The favorite drink, especially after dinner, is tea."[36] The tea ceremony, with tea drinking, became the core of family life. A Swedish traveler found that there was "hardly a farmer's wife or a poor woman, who does not drink tea in the morning."[37] In Philadelphia women would rather go without their dinners than without "a dish of tea."[38] By the early 1780s, most American "had acquired the tea-drinking habit."[39]

As Samuel Shaw, the first American merchant to sail to China on new nation's first commercial ship—*Empress of China*—in 1784, observed, "The inhabitants of America must have Tea, the consumption of which will necessarily increase with the increasing population of our Country."[40]

Since the early 1700s, tea had been used as a social beverage in the colonies. Judge Samuel Sewall maintained good records of Boston life in the turn of the eighteenth century. The guests enjoyed tea in a meeting at the residence of Madam Winthrope, he wrote on April 15, 1709.[41] According to Peter Kalm (1716–1779), who toured North America in the mid-eighteenth century, tea had not only replaced milk as a breakfast beverage but also was drunk in the afternoon.[42] From the letter that Ms. Alice Addertongue wrote to Benjamin Franklin in 1732, we can tell that tea was widely used in social gatherings. Addertongue told Franklin, "The first Day of this Separation [with her mother] we both drank Tea at the same Time, but she with her Visitors in the Parlor."[43]

Tea had become the excuse for many a social gathering. Benjamin Franklin wrote a note showing his appreciation for Mr. Fisher's "Company to drink Tea at 5 o'clock this afternoon, June 4, 1745."[44] During the tea hour, social and economic affairs were discussed and interestingly, since teatime provided an ideal opportunity to get acquainted, young men and women enjoyed it very much. Being invited to drink tea became a special event for the colonists. The habit of tea drinking also had an impact on women's status in colonial society. The tea drinking,

> its ceremony and its equipage from pots to slop bowls to cups, that more than any other single ritual symbolized the new domestic world in which women were in charge of a home that was the center of social and family life.[45]

Benjamin Franklin also published advertisements for tea traders. In August 1745, the colonists read in the *Pennsylvania Gazette*, "Choice Bohea Tea to be sold by the Dozen or half Dozen Pound, at the Post-Office, Philadelphia."[46]

Realizing that it would be a great source for its national revenue, the British government began to impose a tax on tea, first through the Stamp Act of 1765 and later with the Townshend Act of 1767. Given their monopoly of the tea business, the British East India Company profited greatly. Benjamin Franklin reported that in the five years since the act passed, Americans "would have paid 2,500,000 Guineas, *for Tea alone*, into the Coffers of the Company."[47] The acts created serious dissatisfaction among the American colonists. Many colonists grew to dislike tea "due to what it supposedly represented-taxation without presentation and corruption of monopoly, both of which were reviewed as threats to political and economic freedom."[48] They tried to boycott the acts by avoiding tea and drinking herbal infusions. Benjamin Franklin tried to find some alternatives to Chinese tea. Peter Kalm had an interesting conversation with Franklin. He commented,

> Benjamin Franklin, a man now famous in the political world, told me that at different times he had drunk tea cooked from the leaves of the hickory with the bitter nuts. The leaves are collected early in the spring when they have just come out but have not yet had time to become large. They are then dried and used as tea. Mr. Franklin said that of all the species used for tea in North America, next to the real tea from China, he had in his estimation not found any as palatable and agreeable as this.[49]

Two weeks before the events in Boston Harbor, Franklin, then the representative from the North American colonies, found that the colonists' "steady refusal to take tea from hence for several years past has made its impressions"[50] in the British Parliament. In 1773, Parliament enacted a law in May 1773. This Tea Act authorized the drawback of duties paid on all tea above ten million pounds held by the East India Company in its warehouses before being exported to the colonies. Furthermore, it allowed the company to directly export this excess amount of tea to the colonies. There were about seventeen million pounds of tea on hand and some of it had been there more than seven years.[51] Franklin worked hard to convince Parliament to issue "a temporary license from the treasury to export tea to America free of duty."[52] Franklin took every step in his power to prevent the passage of the Stamp Act, but the tide was too strong.[53] They could gain nothing through peaceful negotiation. Smuggling tea could not meet the demand of the consumers.

Outraged colonists, including merchants, shippers, and the general masses, started demonstrations. This culminated in the famous Boston Tea Party of December 1773. General Thomas Gage (1718/9–1787), commander in chief of the army in America, was made governor of Massachusetts and was authorized to bring in troops to maintain order in the colony.[54] This imprudent step ignited more objections from the colonists. Just a year and a half after the patriots dumped the tea in Boston Harbor, Paul Revere's (1734/5–1818) ride and the first shots were fired at Lexington. The conflict caused by the justified right to drink tea without extra economic burden led to political hostilities, which in due course led to the American war for independence.

After independence, Americans enjoyed their gatherings again around the tea table. Moreau de Saint-Méry, a foreign visitor to Philadelphia in the 1790s, noted the warmth and hospitality of these events. Philadelphia families would usually unite at tea, "to which friends, acquaintances and even strangers are invited."[55] Nancy Shippen, a Philadelphian, mentioned in her journal between 1783 and 1786 that one afternoon in December 1783 she and other people "were honored with the Company of Gen Washington to Tea."[56]

As soon as the Americans were free of British control, they sent the ship of the *Empress of China* to Guangzhou (Canton) to bring tea back to North America. In 1785, the ship, carrying three hundred piculs of Hyson and Bohea Tea, returned to New York City. The era when Britain monopolized the tea trade in North America had gone forever. The Chinese-American tea trade increased steadily after 1785 (table 4.1). With the increase of population and increased national wealth, the American people demanded larger and larger quantities of tea. Exports of tea from Guangzhou to the United States increased from 6.6 million-ton pounds in 1822 to 19 million pounds in 1840.[57]

Table 4.1 American Ships and Exports of Tea at Guangzhou (Canton) 1785–1800 (in Pounds)

Year (based on season rather than calendar year)	Ships	Tea Exports to the United States
1785	2	880,100
1786	1	695,000
1787	5	1,181,860
1788	2	750,000
1789	4	1,188,800
1790	14	3,093,200
1791	3	743,100
1792	3	1,863,200
1793	6	1,538,400
1794	7	1,973,130
1795	7	1,438,270
1796	10	2,819,600
1797	13	3,450,400
1798	10	3,100,400
1799	13	5,674,000
1800	18	5,665,067
1801	23	4,762,866
1802	31	5,740,734
1803	20	2,612,436
1804	12	2,371,600
1805	31	8,546,800
1806	37	11,702,800
1807	27	8,464,133
1808	31	6,408,266
1809	6	1,082,400
1810	29	9,737,066
1811	12	2,884,400

Sources: Foster R. Dulles, *The Old China Trade* (Boston and New York: Houghton Mifflin, 1930), 210; Tyler Dennett, *Americans in Eastern Asia: Critical Study of the Policy of the United States with Reference to China, Japan, and Korea in the 19th Century* (New York: Macmillan, 1922), 45.

THE U.S. FOUNDERS AND CHINESE PORCELAIN WARE

Chinese porcelain ware—also called Chinaware—was very important to colonial life in the North American colonies. From Benjamin Franklin's "beautiful simile of the 'fine and noble China Vase the British Empire'" we can tell its importance in colonial Americans' minds.[58] By comparing the North American colonies as a "noble china vase," Franklin warned the British parliament it should deal with colonial issues with a fair attitude and reasonable policy—otherwise, sooner or later, the colonies would no longer belong to the British Empire:

Long did I endeavour with unfeigned and unwearied Zeal, to preserve from breaking, that fine and noble China Vase the British Empire: for I knew that being once broken, the separate Parts could not retain even their Share of the Strength or Value that existed in the Whole, and that a perfect Re-Union of those Parts could scarce even be hoped for.[59]

After the signing of the Treaty of Paris in 1783, the colonists won their desired independence and became the owners of the "noble china vase." Franklin told the American people, "There is sense enough in America to take care of their own china vase."[60]

Benjamin Franklin's simile indeed revealed the historical reality of the cherished nature of Chinese porcelain ware in colonial America and the fledgling United States. In the following I will introduce you to the Founding Fathers' fondness for and their effort to obtain Chinese porcelain. It is believed that their love of chinaware "attested to individual and national taste in a pivotal period of American cultural history."[61]

Chinese porcelain ware made its way into the North American colonies through Europe during the eighteenth century. New Englanders also learned about Chinese porcelain ware. The direct trade between China and the United States opened the channel that allowed the flow of large quantities of chinaware into North America. Chinese porcelain, "standing preeminent in its picturesqueness and grace," almost "wholly displaced all other wares, whether metal, leather, or glass."[62] For instance, in Elias Hasket Derby's house in Salem, Massachusetts, almost every corner "was adorned with Chinese pottery, while one closet contained china estimated as worth $371."[63]

A personal story that Benjamin Franklin told in his well-read autobiography reveals chinaware's popularity in the colonial society (figure 4.1):

Being call'd one Morning to Breakfast, I [Benjamin Franklin] found it in a *China* Bowl with a Spoon of Silver. They had been bought for me without my Knowledge by my Wife, and had cost her the enormous Sum of three and twenty Shillings, for which she had no other Excuse or Apology to make, but that she thought her Husband deserv'd a Silver Spoon and *China* Bowl as well as any of his Neighbours. This was the first Appearance of Plate and *China* in our House, which afterwards in a Course of Years as our Wealth encreas'd augmented gradually to several Hundred Pounds in Value.[64]

Washington and Jefferson also displayed their fondness for Chinese porcelain ware. Throughout his life, Washington treasured his porcelain. The history of his affection for Chinese porcelain can be traced back as early as his youth. From 1757 through 1772, he sent numerous orders for Chinese

Figure 4.1 Franklin's Chinaware in the Franklin Museum. The bowl is in the collections of the Franklin Institute, Philadelphia, in proximity to the photo representation. (Photo by the author.)

porcelain to Bristol and London.[65] During this period, Washington obtained Chinese porcelain from a famous Chinese dealer.[66] A survey of the invoices sent to Washington by Robert Cary (1730–1777), Virginia merchant of London and Hampstead, from 1759 to 1772, reveals that Richard Farrer (1692/93–1775) supplied an extraordinary range of Chinese porcelain to Washington.[67] Washington's use of Chinese porcelain ware for the wedding ceremony at his marriage in the White House on the Pamunkey River[68] set "the vogue for men of means to celebrate their wedlock with beautiful collections of chinaware."[69]

Among Chinese porcelain ware, Washington had a special attachment for blue-and-white porcelain. There are at least nine recorded references to his purchase of blue-and-white Chinese porcelain in Washington's papers.[70] Samuel Fraunces (ca. 1722–1795), realizing that Washington loved this, found an assortment of blue-and-white china for Washington.[71] As the War of Independence ended and American officers and troops turned toward their civilian futures, Washington began to search for a large set of chinaware for Mount Vernon. He wrote to Daniel Parker (a partner with William Duer and John Holker in a company formed to provision the Continental Army) in occupied New York and requested "a neat and complete sett of blue and white table China."[72] With the help of Samuel Fraunces, Parker collected

205 pieces of blue-and-white porcelain before September.[73] Edward Nicole Jr. also provided some blue and white pieces for Washington.[74] Washington learned through an advertisement in the *Maryland Gazette and Baltimore Advertiser* on August 12, 1785, that the *Pallas*, which was coming directly back from China, would be selling its cargo, including blue and white Chinese porcelain. He wrote to Tench Tilghman, his former military aide, and asked him to inquire about the conditions of sale and price.[75] Five days later Washington, at Mount Vernon, learned that "the Cargo is to be sold at public Venue, on the first of October," and wrote a letter to Tilghman in which Washington asked him to buy "a set of *large* blue and White China Dishes with the badge of the Society of the Cincinnati" and the best Hyson Tea, one dozen small blue and white porcelain bowls and best nankeens.[76] In July 1790, when two ships had just arrived in New York from Canton, Tobias Lear asked Clement Biddle to purchase and send to Mount Vernon blue and white china tea and coffee services for twenty-four persons with three or four matching slop bowls for tea dregs. A week later Biddle sent to Mount Vernon a box marked GW containing three dozen china cups and saucers, two dozen coffee cups and saucers, and four slop bowls by the sloop *Dolphin*, Captain Carhart, on August 6, 1790.[77]

Washington used Chinese porcelain as precious gifts to his friends and guests. In 1797, he gave Mrs. Samuel Power a Chinese porcelain cooler, liner, and cover, with an underglaze-blue river scene with gilt handles and rims.[78] On June 9, 1798, Mrs. Washington made Julian Ursyn Niemcewicz, a Polish journalist then visiting Mount Vernon, a gift of Chinese porcelain cup with her name and the name of the United States.[79]

Washington's appreciation for Chinese porcelain ware created unlimited influence on other Americans since a stream of visitors to the headquarters were served with the ware at the commander in chief's table. Washington once called his home "a well-resorted tavern."[80] Some existing records confirm his statement. According to household documents, Washington dined with his wife alone only twice in the last twenty years of his marriage. Ordinary American citizens and friends "flocked to see the President, and with customary grace, he welcomed them to home, not only for meals but to spend the night."[81]

Before direct trade between China and the United States, Europe was the main source of Chinese porcelain for Americans. Thomas Jefferson made good use of his stay in France to acquire Chinese porcelain ware. On May 7, 1784, Jefferson was appointed the European commissioner, replacing John Jay. In August 1784, Jefferson went to take his position in Paris. As soon as he arrived, he bought some Chinese porcelain ware including one dozen coffee cups, saucers, and teacups when he still lived "in temporary quarters."[82] In the following year, he ordered more Chinese porcelain ware. On March 6,

1786, Jefferson left France and before departing he acquired "larger quantities of Chinese export porcelain" in Paris. Among the things he wanted to take back with him to the United States were "a set of table furniture consisting in China, silver & and plated ware."[83]

Like most who ordered stock Chinese porcelain in the eighteenth century, Jefferson relied on the tenacity of middlemen, and the nature of the current inventory in China. After he came back from Paris, Jefferson gave a "second large order of Chinese export porcelain."[84]

The process through which Thomas Jefferson transported Chinese porcelain from Europe to North America served as an indicator of the value of the Chinese porcelain ware. In order to protect Chinese porcelain ware from being broken in the process of transportation, Jefferson bought creamware made by English potters. He clearly stated out that the purchase was to protect the Chinese porcelain ware from harm. Then he put them outside of the Chinese porcelain ware as a protective layer. Jefferson's action led an author to conclude that the role of English creamware was changing and its "aesthetic and qualitative value was waning."[85]

Later, in 1789, Jefferson ordered more Chinese porcelain from Edward Dowse, a Boston merchant engaging in Chinese trade. In April 1790, Dowse sent the porcelain ordered by Jefferson to New York where Jefferson was serving as the first secretary of state.[86] In the interim, the porcelain ware he ordered in France arrived, including 120 porcelain plates, 58 cups, 39 saucers, 4 tureens, saltcellars, and various platters. He used these in New York and Philadelphia, and what remained was eventually shipped to Monticello.[87] In 1793, Jefferson had all his Chinese porcelain transported to Monticello.[88]

The Americans wanted to reduce their reliance on taxed imports and ultimately their need for other goods controlled by England. Their pursuing self-supply of Chinese porcelain ware became a powerful call for the patriotic support of American economic independence. Some colonists attempted to establish a porcelain manufactory company in Philadelphia in 1769. They established the factory on Prime Street "near the present day navy yard, intended to make china at a savings of 15,000 £."[89] Benjamin Franklin, who was in London at the time, showed his happiness seeing the achievement made by his countrymen. He said, "I am pleased to find so good progress made in the China Manufactory. I wish it Success most heartily."[90]

The American China Manufactory became noted for the porcelain ware it produced. More importantly, it succeeded in cultivating patriotic support. It set in motion "an intense competition between the young American factory and its English contemporaries."[91] Although the porcelain factory only lasted until 1772, it challenged Britain's monopoly of the Chinese products and ultimately contributed to the winning of American independence. Benjamin

Rush (1745–1813) stated clearly, "There is but one expedient left whereby we can save our sinking country, and that is by encouraging American manufactures. Unless we do this, we shall be undone forever."[92]

As one author aptly observed, "the sense of national independence was not confined to politics; it overflowed political channels and spread over the whole area of life. Independence, and its corollary, self-sufficiency, sought expression in industry and commerce and in culture."[93] The demand for Chinese porcelain and the efforts to shake off Great Britain's control over it helped to create the national conscience of the patriots. Benjamin Rush was among the first group of colonists who wanted to build a porcelain factory in North America.[94] For Dr. Rush, colonial production of porcelain ware was one of the means to overcome dependence on Great Britain for goods and trade. The building of such a factory was far beyond the porcelain only. It proved the colonists' determination to be independent from their motherland.

> Go on in encouraging American manufactures. I have many schemes in view about these things. I have made those mechanical arts which are connected with chemistry the particular objects of my study and not without hopes of seeing a china manufactory established in Philadelphia in the course of a few years. Yes, we will be revenged by the mother country. For my part, I am resolved to devote my head, my heart, and my pen entirely to the service of America, and promise myself much assistance from you in everything of this kind that I shall attempt through life.[95]

The above analysis of the Founding Fathers' outlooks toward and exertions to acquire Chinese porcelain ware reveals the significant impact of Chinese porcelain or tea on social and political life in North American colonies. Their meaning was far beyond common instruments for daily life in the colonists. They became political tools for the founders to bring up the national awareness of the colonists. It is fair to conclude that Chinese goods left a deep mark in the social and political history in the foundational age of the United States.

NOTES

1. Bob Deans, *The River Where American Began: A Journey Along the James* (Lanham, MD and New York: Rowman & Littlefield, 2007), 59.

2. "Should they happen upon more than one suitable river, the colonists were instructed to if the difference was not great, make a choice of that which bendeth most toward the North-West for that way you shall soonest find the other sea. You must observe if you can, whether the river on which you plant doth spring out of mountains or out of lakes. If it be out of any lake, the passage to the other sea will be more easy, and [it] is like enough, that out of the same lake you shall find some spring which

run[s] the contrary way towards the East India Sea." The Instructions for the Virginia Colony, 1606, http://www.let.rug.nl/usa/documents/1600-1650/instructions-for-the-virginia-colony-1606.php.

3. Deans, *The River Where American Began*, 94.

4. With the accession of King Louis XVI, Charles Gravier Comte de Vergennes (1717–1787) became foreign minister. He believed that the power of the states on the periphery of Europe, namely Great Britain and Russia, was increasing and should be checked. His rivalry with the British and his desire to avenge the failure of the Seven Years' War led to his support of the Americans in their war for independence. In 1777, he told the thirteen colonies' commissioners that France acknowledged the United States and was willing to form an offensive and defensive alliance with the new nation. It was also due to his encouragement that King Louis sent expeditions to Indochina. Thomas Fleming, *The Perishes of Peace: America's Struggle for Survival After Yorktown* (New York: Smithsonian Books, 2007), 57.

5. C. Martin Wilbur, "Modern America's Cultural Debts to China," *Issues & Studies: A Journal of China Studies and International Affairs* 22, no. 1 (January 1986): 127.

6. Warren I. Cohen, *America's Response to China: A History of Sino-American Relations* (New York: Columbia University Press, 1990), 2.

7. Dave Wang, "Chinese Civilization and the United States: Tea, Ginseng, Porcelain Ware and Silk in Colonial America," *Virginia Review of Asian Studies* (Summer 2011): 114–18.

8. Dave Wang, "Benjamin Franklin's Efforts to Promote Sericulture in North America," *Franklin Gazette* 18, no. 2 (Summer 2008): 3–7.

9. "From George Washington to Robert Morris, 15 January 1789," Founders Online, National Archives, https://founders.archives.gov/documents/Washington/05-01-02-0180. Original source: *The Papers of George Washington, Presidential Series*, ed. Dorothy Twohig, vol. 1, *September 24, 1788–March 31, 1789* (Charlottesville: University Press of Virginia, 1987), 245–46.

10. "Invoice from Robert Cary & Company, 13 February 1765," Founders Online, National Archives, https://founders.archives.gov/documents/Washington/02-07-02-0222. Original source: *The Papers of George Washington, Colonial Series*, ed. W. W. Abbot and Dorothy Twohig, vol. 7, *January 1, 1761–June 15, 1767* (Charlottesville: University Press of Virginia, 1990), 353–57.

11. "Invoice from Richard Washington, 10 November 1757," Founders Online, National Archives, https://founders.archives.gov/documents/Washington/02-05-02-0031. Original source: *The Papers of George Washington, Colonial Series*, ed. W. W. Abbot, vol. 5, *October 5, 1757–September 3, 1758* (Charlottesville: University Press of Virginia, 1988), 49–51.

12. "To George Washington from Tobias Lear, 24 October 1790," Founders Online, National Archives, https://founders.archives.gov/documents/Washington/05-06-02-0271. Original source: *The Papers of George Washington, Presidential Series*, ed. Mark A. Mastromarino, vol. 6, *July 1, 1790–November 30, 1790* (Charlottesville: University Press of Virginia, 1996), 573–79.

13. "From Thomas Jefferson to Thomas Claxton, 18 June 1802," Founders Online, National Archives, https://founders.archives.gov/documents/Jefferson/01-37-02-0504. Original source: *The Papers of Thomas Jefferson*, ed. Barbara B. Oberg, vol. 37, *March 4–June 30, 1802* (Princeton: Princeton University Press, 2010), 615–16.

14. "Inventory of President's House, 19 February 1809," Founders Online, National Archives, https://founders.archives.gov/documents/Jefferson/99-01-02-9835.

15. "Abigail Adams to John Adams, 16 May 1789," Founders Online, National Archives, https://founders.archives.gov/documents/Adams/04-08-02-0189. Original source: *The Adams Papers, Adams Family Correspondence*, ed. C. James Taylor, Margaret A. Hogan, Jessie May Rodrique, Gregg L. Lint, Hobson Woodward, and Mary T. Claffey, vol. 8, *March 1787–December 1789* (Cambridge, MA: Harvard University Press, 2007), 354–56.

16. "To Alexander Hamilton from Gouverneur Morris, 17 August 1792," Founders Online, National Archives, https://founders.archives.gov/documents/Hamilton/01-12-02-0174. Original source: *The Papers of Alexander Hamilton*, ed. Harold C. Syrett, vol. 12, *July 1792–October 1792* (New York: Columbia University Press, 1967), 220–22.

17. "To James Madison from John Mitchell, 12 August 1803," Founders Online, National Archives, https://founders.archives.gov/documents/Madison/02-91-02-0802.

18. "From James Madison to James Monroe, 20 May 1807," Founders Online, National Archives, https://founders.archives.gov/documents/Madison/99-01-02-1706.

19. "To Thomas Jefferson from Henry Remsen, 19 November 1792," Founders Online, National Archives, https://founders.archives.gov/documents/Jefferson/01-24-02-0623. Original source: *The Papers of Thomas Jefferson*, ed. John Catanzariti, vol. 24, *June 1–December 31, 1792* (Princeton: Princeton University Press, 1990), 640–41.

20. "Enclosure: Invoice to Robert Cary & Company, 20 July 1767," Founders Online, National Archives, https://founders.archives.gov/documents/Washington/02-08-02-0007-0002. Original source: *The Papers of George Washington, Colonial Series*, ed. W. W. Abbot and Dorothy Twohig, vol. 8, *June 24, 1767–December 25, 1771* (Charlottesville: University Press of Virginia, 1993), 12–14.

21. "To Benjamin Franklin from John Baskerville, 24 August 1773," Founders Online, National Archives, https://founders.archives.gov/documents/Franklin/01-20-02-0202. Original source: *The Papers of Benjamin Franklin*, ed. William B. Willcox, vol. 20, *January 1 through December 31, 1773* (New Haven and London: Yale University Press, 1976), 375–76.

22. "Enclosure: Invoice to Robert Cary & Company, 23 June 1766," Founders Online, National Archives, https://founders.archives.gov/documents/Washington/02-07-02-0295-0002. Original source: *The Papers of George Washington, Colonial Series*, ed. W. W. Abbot and Dorothy Twohig, vol. 7, *January 1, 1761–June 15, 1767* (Charlottesville: University Press of Virginia, 1990), 447–50.

23. "Enclosure: Invoice to Robert Cary & Company, 15 July 1772," Founders Online, National Archives, https://founders.archives.gov/documents/Washington/02-09-02-0050-0002. Original source: *The Papers of George Washington, Colonial Series*, ed. W. W. Abbot and Dorothy Twohig, vol. 9, *January 8, 1772–March 18, 1774* (Charlottesville: University Press of Virginia, 1994), 64–67.

24. "From George Washington to Bushrod Washington, 14 February 1796," *Founders Online*, National Archives, https://founders.archives.gov/documents/Washington/05-19-02-0370. Original source: *The Papers of George Washington, Presidential Series*, ed. David R. Hoth, vol. 19, *October 1, 1795–March 31, 1796* (Charlottesville: University Press of Virginia, 2016), 463.

25. "From George Washington to Bushrod Washington, 10 February 1796," Founders Online, National Archives, https://founders.archives.gov/documents/Washington/05-19-02-0355. Original source: *The Papers of George Washington, Presidential Series*, ed. David R. Hoth, vol. 19, *October 1, 1795–March 31, 1796* (Charlottesville: University Press of Virginia, 2016), 447–48.

26. "From George Washington to William Thornton, 1 December 1799," *Founders Online*, National Archives, https://founders.archives.gov/documents/Washington/06-04-02-0379. Original source: *The Papers of George Washington, Retirement Series*, ed. W. W. Abbot, vol. 4, *April 20, 1799–December 13, 1799* (Charlottesville: University Press of Virginia, 1999), 434–35.

27. Ibid.

28. "Peter Carr to Thomas Jefferson, 31 August 1811," *Founders Online*, National Archives, https://founders.archives.gov/documents/Jefferson/03-04-02-0105. Original source: *The Papers of Thomas Jefferson, Retirement Series*, ed. J. Jefferson Looney, vol. 4, *June 18, 1811 to April 30, 1812* (Princeton: Princeton University Press, 2007), 109–10.

29. John E. Ferling, *John Adams: A Life* (Knoxville: University of Tennessee Press, 1992), 92.

30. John C. Miller, *Origins of the American Revolution: With a New Introduction and a Biography* (Stanford, CA: Stanford University Press, 1943), 350.

31. Simon Hill, "China and the American Revolution," *Journal of the American Revolution* (December 7, 2017). https://allthingsliberty.com/2017/12/china-american-revolution/.

32. "George Washington, To Bryan Fairfax, July 20, 1774," *Writings of George Washington*, ed. John C. Fitzpatrick, vol. 3 (Washington, DC: U.S. Government Printing Office, 1939), 232. Also John Frederick Schroeder, ed., *Maxims of Washington: Political, Social, Moral, and Religious* (Mount Vernon, VA: Mount Vernon Ladies Association, 1942), 18.

33. Jon Meacham, *Thomas Jefferson: The Art of Power* (New York: Random House, 2012), 71.

34. Benjamin Franklin, "Preface to Declaration of the Boston Town Meeting," in *The Votes and Proceedings of the Freeholders and Other Inhabitants of the Town of Boston* (London, 1773), i–vi, http://franklinpapers.org/franklin/framedVolumes.jsp.

35. Letter from Gilbert Barkly to directors of the East India Company, May 26, 1773. *Tea Leaves: Being a Collection of Letters and Documents*, ed. Francis S. Drake (Boston, 1884), 200.

36. Jacques-Pierre Brissot de Warville, *New Travels in the United States of America, 1788*, trans. Mara Sconceanu Vamos and Durand Echeverria; ed. Durand Echeverria (Cambridge, MA: Belknap Press, 1964).

37. Peter Kalm, *Peter Kalm's Travels in North America*, ed. and trans. Adolf B. Benson (New York: Wilson-Erickson, 1937), 1:361.

38. Miller, *Origins of the American Revolution*, 275.

39. Michael H. Hunt, *The Making of a Special Relationship: The United States and China to 1914* (New York: Columbia University Press, 1983), 7.

40. "To John Jay from Samuel Shaw, 31 December 1786," Founders Online, National Archives, https://founders.archives.gov/documents/Jay/01-04-02-0208. Original source: *The Selected Papers of John Jay*, ed. Elizabeth M. Nuxoll, vol. 4, *1785–1788* (Charlottesville: University Press of Virginia, 2015), 448–59.

41. Samuel Sewall, *Diary of Samuel Sewall, 1674–1729*, reprinted in *Collections of the Massachusetts Historical Society*, 1879, ser. 5, vol. 6, 253.

42. Peter Kalm, "The America of 1750," in *Peter Kalm's Travels in North America*, ed. and trans. Adolf B. Benson (New York: Wilson-Erickson, 1937), 1:346 and 2:605.

43. *Pennsylvania Gazette*, September 12, 1732, http://franklinpapers.org/franklin/framedVolumes.jsp.

44. Benjamin Franklin, to Denial Fisher, June 4, 1745, http://franklinpapers.org/franklin/framedVolumes.jsp.

45. Stephanie Grauman Wolf, *As Various as Their Land: The Everyday Lives of Eighteenth-Century Americans* (New York: HarperCollins, 1993), 80.

46. *Pennsylvania Gazette*, August 8, 1745.

47. Franklin, "Preface to Declaration."

48. Hill, "China and the American Revolution."

49. Peter Kalm, "Conversation with Benjamin Franklin," *Franklin Papers*, https://franklinpapers.org/framedVolumes.jsp?vol=4&page=053a.

50. Benjamin Franklin, to Joseph Galloway, London, November 3, 1773. Reprinted from William Temple Franklin, ed., *Memoirs of the Life and Writings of Benjamin Franklin, L.L.D., F.R.S., &c* . . . (3 vols., London, 1817–1718), II, https://franklinpapers.org/framedNames.jsp.

51. Lawrence Henry Gipson, *The Coming of the Revolution, 1763–1775*, in the New American Nation Series, ed. Henry Steele Commager and Richard B. Morris (New York: Harper & Row, 1954), 217.

52. Benjamin Franklin, to Joseph Galloway, London, November 3, 1773.

53. Carl Van Doren, *Benjamin Franklin* (New York: Viking, 1938; third printing 1968), 322.

54. John Richard Alden, *The American Revolution, 1775–1783*, New American Nation Series, ed. Henry Steele Commager and Richard B. Morris (New York: Harper & Row, 1954), 7.

55. Mederic Louis Elie Moreau de Saint-Méry, *Moreau de St. Méry's American Journey*, translated and edited by Kenneth Roberts and Anna M. Roberts (Garden City, NY: Doubleday, 1947), 266; Beth Carver Wees, *Coffee, Tea and Chocolate in Early Colonial America*, http://www.metmuseum.org/toah/hd/coff/hd_coff.htm.

56. Nancy Shippen, *Nancy Shippen, Her Journal Book*, edited by Ethel Armes (Philadelphia: Lippincott, 1935), 167–243.

57. Yen-P'ing Hao, "Chinese Teas to America—a Synopsis," in *America's China Trade in Historical Perspective: The Chinese and American Performance*, ed. Ernest R. May and John K. Fairbank (Cambridge, MA and London: Harvard University Press, 1986), 14.

58. From Amelia Barry, ALS: American Philosophical Society, Tunis 3d. July 1777. In *The Papers of Benjamin Franklin*, http://franklinpapers.org/franklin/framedVolumes.jsp.

59. Benjamin Franklin, to Lord Howe, Copy: Henry E. Huntington Library; other copies: British Museum; Library of Congress Philada. July 20, 1776. In *The Papers of Benjamin Franklin*, http://franklinpapers.org/franklin/framedVolumes.jsp.

60. Benjamin Franklin, to David Hartley (unpublished) Passy, October 22, 1783. In *The Papers of Benjamin Franklin*, http://franklinpapers.org/franklin/framedVolumes.jsp.

61. Susan Gray Detweiler, *George Washington's Chinaware* (New York: Harry N. Abrams, Inc., 1982), 8.

62. Ping Chia Kuo, "Canton and Salem: The Impact of Chinese Culture Upon New England Life During the Post-Revolutionary Era," *New England Quarterly* III (1930): 429.

63. Esther Singleton, *Furniture of Our Forefathers* (New York: Doubleday, Page & Company, 1901), 2:548–53.

64. Benjamin Franklin, *The Autobiography of Benjamin Franklin*, Part Eight, in *The Papers of Benjamin Franklin*, http://franklinpapers.org/franklin/framedVolumes.jsp.

65. Detweiler, *George Washington's Chinaware*, 9.

66. The term was used in the eighteenth century to describe merchants who specialized in imported Chinese porcelain. There were over a hundred such Chinamen in London between 1711 and 1774. See Detweiler, *George Washington's Chinaware*, 43.

67. Ibid.

68. Ibid., 37.

69. Kuo, "Canton and Salem," 430.

70. Detweiler, *George Washington's Chinaware*, 52.

71. Samuel Fraunces was a keeper of the Queen's Head Tavern in New York. He used to serve as a steward to President Washington in New York and Philadelphia. See Detweiler, *George Washington's Chinaware*, 77.

72. Ibid.

73. Ibid.

74. Ibid.

75. Ibid.

76. John C. Fitzpatrick, ed., *The Writings of George Washington from the Original Manuscript Sources 1745–1799*, volume 30, *June 20, 1788–January 21, 1790* (Washington, DC: U.S. Government Printing Office, 1939), 223.

77. Lear to Biddle, 18, July 25 and August 1790, all in PHi: Washington-Biddle Correspondence; Biddle to Lear, 21, and July 29, 1790, and Biddle to George A. Washington, 8 August 1790, all in PHi: Clement Biddle Letter Book.

78. Detweiler, *George Washington's Chinaware*, 145.

79. See Niemcewicz's letter of thanks for his stay at Mount Vernon, in Eugene Kuisielewicz, "Niemcewicz in America," *Polish Review* V (1960): 71–72. As for the cup, see Samuel W. Woddhouse Jr., "Martha Washington's China and Mr. Van Braam," *Antiquaries* XXVII (May 1935): 186; Julian Ursyn Niemcewicz, *Vine and Fig Tree: Travels Through America 1797–1799, 1805 with some Further Account of Life in New Jersey*, trans. and ed. with an introduction and notes by Metchie J. E. Budka (Elizabeth, NJ: Grassmann Publishing Company, Inc, 1965), 104.

80. Anne Petri, *George Washington and Food*, http://www.house.gov/petri/gw003.htm.

81. Ibid.

82. Susan R. Stein, *The Worlds of Thomas Jefferson at Monticello* (New York: Harry N. Abrams, Inc., 1993), 23. (Jefferson's Memorandum Books shows records of these purchases between August 21 and September 6, 1784.)

83. Thomas Jefferson to Rayneval, March 3, 1786, in *Jefferson Papers* (Boston: Massachusetts Historical Society, 2003), 9:312–13; Stein, *Worlds of Thomas Jefferson*, 27.

84. Stein, *Worlds of Thomas Jefferson*, 348.

85. George L. Miller, "A Revised Set of CC Index Value for Classification and Economic Scaling of English Ceramics from 1787 to 1880," *Historical Archaeology* 25 (1991): 1; Stein, *Worlds of Thomas Jefferson*, 346.

86. This china may be the double bordered Nanking pattern with an armorial shield with the initial "TJ" that was found in Boston in the late nineteenth century. It was acquired by Thomas Jefferson Coolidge Jr.

87. Martha Jefferson Randolph to Thomas Jefferson, January 16, 1791, *Family Letters*; see Stein, *Worlds of Thomas Jefferson*, 68.

88. Martha Jefferson Randolph to Thomas Jefferson, June 23, 1808 (Boston: Massachusetts Historical Society); see Stein, *Worlds of Thomas Jefferson*, 86–87.

89. John Fanning Watson, ed., *Annals of Philadelphia* (Philadelphia and New York: E. L. Carey & A. Hart, 1830). See also Michael K. Brown, "Piecing Together the Past: Recent Research on the American China Manufactory, 1769–1772," *Proceedings of the American Philosophical Society* 133, no. 4 (1989). 555.

90. Benjamin Franklin to Deborah Franklin, January 28, 1772. In *The Franklin Papers*, http://www.franklinpapers.org/franklin/framedVolumes.jsp.

91. Brown, "Piecing Together the Past," 573.

92. Benjamin Rush to probably Jacob Rush, January 26, 1769, in L. H. Butterfield, ed., *Letters of Benjamin Rush* (Princeton: Princeton University Press), 1:74. Also in *Pennsylvania Journal* 1374 (April 6, 1769).

93. John Spargo, *Early American Pottery and China* (Rutland, VT: Charles E. Tuttle, 1974), 97–98.

94. Brown, "Piecing Together the Past," 557.

95. Benjamin Rush to Thomas Bradford, April 15, 1768, in L. H. Butterfield, ed., *Letters of Benjamin Rush* (Princeton: Princeton University Press), 1:54.

Chapter 5

Trade with the East
The Founders' Efforts to Open China Trade

The opening of commercial trade between the newly independent United States with China was pivotal. Below I will first review the founders' ideas on their backing and inaugural trade with China. Then I will discuss ginseng, initially the most significant product. Finally, I will discuss how American society was influenced by American ginseng, the most welcomed of goods in the trading relationship with China.

THE FOUNDING FATHERS AND MARITIME TRADE WITH CHINA

Embodying the hopes and aspirations of Americans, the *Empress of China*—the first postindependence American international commercial ship—departed New York City for Canton, China on February 22, 1784.

Immediately before the departure of the *Empress of China*, the president of Yale College told George Washington:

> Navigation will carry the American flag around the globe itself, and display the *thirteen stripes and new constellation*, at Bengal and Canton, on the Indus and Ganges, on the Whang-ho and the Yang-ti-king; and with commerce will import the wisdom and literature of the East.[1]

Efforts to build direct commercial relations with China began during a critical period following the American Revolution. The new national government, operating under the Articles of Confederation (1781–1789), was grappling with the consolidation of thirteen independent states while the economy and nation's finances were on the brink of chaos. With traditional trading partners now closed to America, new ones had to be cultivated; otherwise, political independence might well have proven to be a barren victory. John Adams was among the founders who comprehended the significance of opening trade with China. In 1780, Adams told the president of Congress, "It will not be long after their Establishment as an Empire, before they will be found trading in the south Sea and in China."[2]

Immediately after the founding of the United States, traditional trade partners closed their doors to the new nation under British pressure. France, Holland, and other European countries were willing to export goods, but not purchase American products. This attracted some Americans to view China favorably. John Ledyard, with the ambition to "take the lead of the greatest commercial enterprise, that has never been embarked on in this country" came to talk to Robert Morris about his suggestions of opening trade with China.[3] To engage in trade with China had occupied Ledyard's "thoughts ever since his return from Cook's expedition."[4] Morris, who was appointed by Congress as superintendent of finance in February 1781, felt the suggestion a great idea and took the lead in arranging the *Empress of China* venture by personally financing much of the voyage. On November 27, 1783, Morris told John Jay that "I am sending some Ships to China in order to encourage others in the adventurous pursuits of Commerce."[5] Washington was directly involved in the venture. He recommended Samuel Shaw (1754–1794) to be the ship's supercargo—the officer in charge of the critical task of sales and purchases of cargo.

About a month after the *Empress of China* departed, Washington told Jefferson that "From trade our citizen will not be restrained."[6] Washington's words had significant meaning for the fledgling United States. The successful sailing of *the Empress of China* not only symbolized the hope of trade itself but made a statement to the world—the United States was now a sovereign nation. When the *Empress of China* returned from its successful maiden voyage, John Adams told John Jay that "there is no better Advice to be given to the Merchants of the United States, than to push their Commerce to the East Indies as fast and as far as it will go."[7]

The *Empress of China* arrived in New York City on May 11, 1785, after a round trip voyage of fourteen months and twenty-four days. As soon as the *Empress of China* arrived, Robert Morris met with the crew members, and happily reported to John Jay "Our Ship from China does tollerably well for the Concerned & she has opened new objects to all America A Mandarine."[8] Richard Henry Lee wrote to Thomas Jefferson, Samuel Adams, and James Madison, respectively, about the experience. In his letter to Jefferson, Lee stated, "The enterprise of America is well marked by a successful Voyage made by a ship from this City—A ship has gone to, and returned from Canton in fourteen months with a valuable Eastern cargo and met with the most friendly treatment from the Chinese—Other Vessels are gone and are expected back in the continuation."⁹ To James Madison, Lee expounded his pondering of the trade. He told Madison, "The Chinese were kind to our people and glad to see a new source of Commerce opened to them from a New People, as they called us."¹⁰ He continued that European nations were "astonished at the rapidity of our movements, especially the English."¹¹ The circumstance that the whole country was in a favor of trade with China, in this situation, led to Lee's worry, "I fear that our Countrymen will overdo this business." He recommended setting up some regulations to ensure "a regulated & useful commerce with that part of the World."¹² Hamilton also recognized that when "the trade to China being now well established, a moderate regulation of this nature, duly proportioned to the Tonnage of each vessel, might perhaps be conveniently enacted."¹³

Later, Lee informed Samuel Adams that the success of the voyage was "a proof of American enterprise, and will probably mortify, as much as it will injure our old oppressor, the British."¹⁴ Encouraged by the success of the *Empress of China*'s voyage, Lee even planned to open up the Potomac River and the James River to build ports for the China trade. Secretary of the Treasury Alexander Hamilton also closely followed the U.S.-China trade and requested that Thomas Randall, the American vice consul at Canton, provide him with specific information on the trade. Randall, who had served as the "joint supercargo" of the *Empress of China*, sent incredibly detailed reports to Hamilton. Assistant Secretary of the Treasury Tench Coxe (1755–1824) testified to Hamilton that "the trade to China being now well established."¹⁵ In 1791, Thomas Randall, the joint supercargo in the *Empress of China*, sent to Hamilton a detailed report on the sail. He told Hamilton that the *Empress*'s cargo "consisted of Spanish dollars, about four hundred peculs of genseng, a pecul being 133⅓ lb English Avoirdu poids, some cordage, wine, lead, iron a few furs, with other trifling articles not worth enumerating."¹⁶

From his post in London, Adams did his part to encourage and facilitate the China trade in which ships and sailors from Massachusetts came to play a prominent role.¹⁷ Adams analyzed the trade between China and Europe and found that the United States could gain an advantage in China. He told John Jay,

> East India Manufactures in Silk and Coton &c are prohibited in England, and as we have no Such Prohibitions in America, because We have no Such manufactures for them to interfere with, We may take them to a great advantage.¹⁸

In the same letter to Jay, Adams suggested that "the Tobacco and Peltries as well as the Ginseng of the United States, are proper Articles for the China Markett, and have been found to answer very well, and many other of our

Commodities may be found in demand there."[19] In 1786, assuring that the new nation would pursue its trade with China, Jay told Adams,

> Three Vessels will sail from this Port for Canton the first fair Wind. vizt. The Ship *Empress of China* Capt. Green, the Ship *Hope* Capt. Mc.Gee—and the Brigantine *Betsey* Capt. Neal Mc.Henry—one is also ready to sail from Philadelphia vizt. the Ship *Canton* Captain Truxton.[20]

Washington timely appointed Major Samuel Shaw as American consul for Canton in China.[21] Fully realizing the importance of his position, Shaw happily accepted the appointment. He told Washington,

> The commerce of a nation being one of the principal objects of the attention of its rulers, I hope it will not be deemed inconsistent with the duties of the office with which you have been pleased to honor me.[22]

After the achievements of the *Empress of China*, William Grayson (1732–1790), a statesman from Virginia, told James Madison that the American merchants "were treated with as much respect as the Subjects of any other nation."[23] Most businessmen in Virginia agreed that American trade with China "can be carried on, on betters from America than Europe." He told Madison confidently, "I could heartily wish to see the merchts. of our State engaged in this business."[24]

President Washington became even more interested in U.S.-China trade and attempted to collect as much related information as possible. As president, Washington continued to understand the significance of the flourishing China trade. Washington told the Marquis de Lafayette, "Our government is now happily carried into operation." What distracted him was financial difficulty. "A funding system is one of the subjects which occasions most anxiety and perplexity."[25] Washington then cheerfully articulated to Lafayette that the financial issues had been solved by the trade with China. He described some examples:

> A single vessel just arrived in this port pays $30,000 to government. Two vessels fitted out for the fur trade to the northwest coast of America have succeeded well. The whole outfits of vessels and cargoes cost but $7,000. One is returning home loaded with India produce, the other going back to the coast of America; and they have deposited $100,000 of their profits in China.[26] I mention this to shew the spirit of enterprize that prevails.[27]

Washington toured "west to inspect his vacant bounty lands on the Ohio and Kanawha rivers" in September 1784. This happened just one month after the *Empress of China* reached China's shore. Washington made a trip to find out "the possibilities for convenient water transportation between the Ohio Valley and the eastern seaboard, especially via the Potomac River."[28] Washington detailed clearly, "Gentlemen came here to see me & one object of my journey being to obtain information of the nearest and best communication between the Eastern & Western Waters; & to facilitate as much as in me lay the Inland Navigation of the Potomack."[29] In 1787, Washington sent David Stuart (1754–1813), a relation and correspondent of his, to survey the Potomac River to locate an ideal place to build a harbor to be used for trade with China.[30] Five years after the sail of *the Empress of China* to Canton, Washington followed the trade status carefully. He asked for "a list of the Ships that were in Canton in China the last year which you were so good as to send me on the 30th of June."[31]

Thomas Jefferson as well had a substantial interest in U.S.-China trade. For Jefferson, the United States was an agricultural-commercial nation. With its internal trade undeveloped and its industrial base extremely narrow, the United States "must cherish its navigation and expand international market."[32] While serving as an American representative in France in 1785, Jefferson obtained a complete report concerning the *Empress of China*. As Washington's secretary of state, Jefferson suggested exploration to find a shorter trade route to East Asia. Later, shortly after the Louisiana Purchase, President Jefferson sent the famed explorers Louis and Clark west in hopes of finding a quicker route to China. During Jefferson's administration (1801–1809), U.S.-China trade reached new heights, with the number of involved American ships having increased from two in 1785 to forty-two in 1806. U.S.-foreign trade was severely limited in the brief period after President Jefferson signed the 1807 Embargo Act, supposedly prohibiting all American exports, in his attempt to keep the United States out of the war between Great Britain and France. Even though only eight American ships sailed to China between 1808 and the first months of 1809, Jefferson understood China's importance to the new nation and viewed strengthening U.S.-China trade as a strategy to force European countries to recognize American interests and sovereignty.

In 1808, a specific event occurred during the second year of Jefferson's Embargo Act that afforded the president the opportunity to proffer his thoughts on U.S.-China relations. With Jefferson's permission, New York-based merchant John Jacob Astor succeeded in getting one of his vessels to China despite the current trade embargo. Jefferson firmly believed that Astor's deed provided the United States an opportunity. He expressed his opinion in a letter to secretary of the Treasury Albert Gallatin: "The opportunity hoped from that, of making known through one of its own characters of note, our nation, our circumstances and character, and of letting that [Chinese] government understand at length the difference between us and the

English, and separate us in its policy, rendered that measure a diplomatic one in my view, and likely to bring lasting advantage to our merchants and commerce with that country"[33] (figure 5.1).

Jefferson's pronouncement remained fundamental in American dealings with China long into the future. At least one authority on U.S.-East Asian

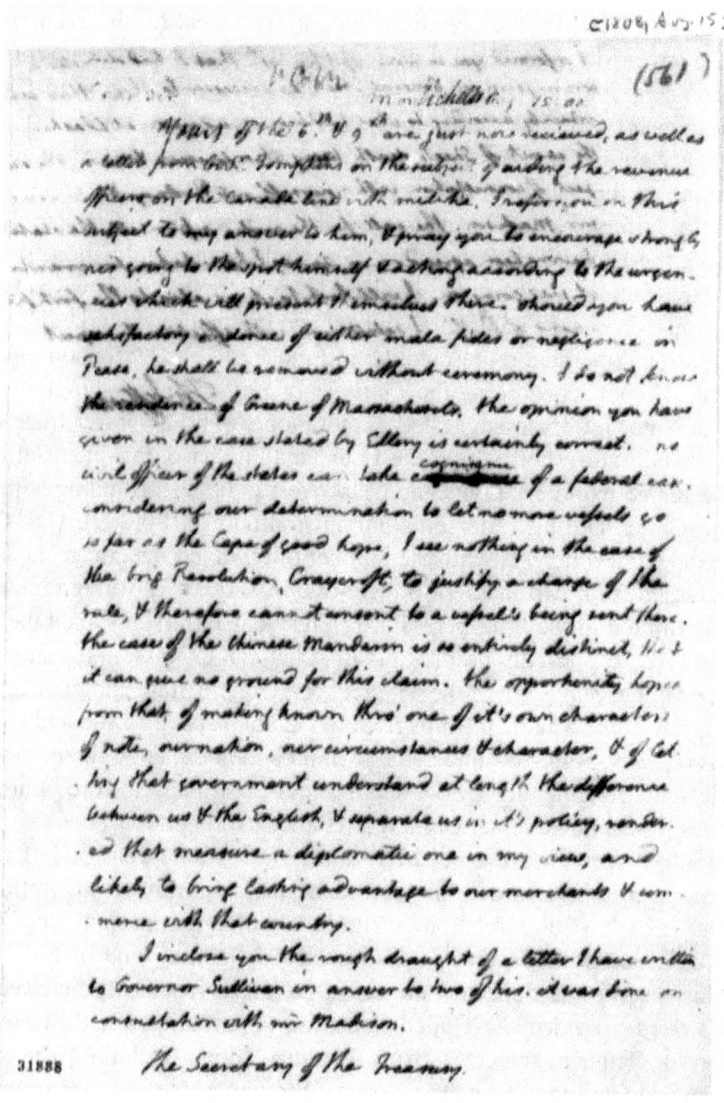

Figure 5.1 Thomas Jefferson's Handwriting, Jefferson to Albert Gallatin, August 15, 1808. Thomas Jefferson Papers at the Library of Congress, Manuscript Division.

relations acclaimed the statement as "the nearest to an official opinion on American policy."[34]

American success that began with the *Empress of China* not only was profitable but also contributed to the new nation's international economic and political ascendancy. Fueled by political support and entrepreneurs' responses to a huge domestic demand for Chinese products, U.S.-China trade grew rapidly. By 1795—only a little over a decade after the *Empress of China* voyage—the United States had already passed all European rivals except Great Britain in the volume of its China trade. Port cities such as Salem, New York, and Boston benefited significantly from the China trade, earning investment funds for new industry. Factory towns sprang up, and Americans began to experiment with the techniques of mass production. The United States began to lay the groundwork that contributed to post–Civil War industrialization.

China trade helped to change the U.S. political map, moving much of American power from Virginia to New York City and New England. In the early 1790s, in part because of China profits and newly affluent business concerns, Hamilton had the power to establish a stronger financial role for the federal government. This strengthened New York and New England commercial and financial elites and weakened the previously powerful great Virginia planters. The China trade was a joint determination by the Founding Fathers. Robert Morris financed the first American commercial ship to China. George Washington helped choose the business manager. Richard Henry Lee and Rufus King supported the first attempts to build an economic relationship with China. Thomas Jefferson used successful American trade with China as an opportunity to move toward establishing a distinct American national identity in China that was clearly separate from the United Kingdom.

The China trade added significant stimulus to the western expansion in U.S. history. Edmond Kelly told Madison,

> In short this trade to India & China that great & patriotic statesman Mr. Jefferson also attempted to render profitable by projecting settlements on the shores of the Pacific Ocean & on the banks of the Misouri & Columbia Rivers—forming settlements on their banks establishing Furr Companies & Exporting the furrs to China.[35]

In 1784, when the *Empress of China* reached Chinese shores, the United States was a feeble, underdeveloped country. "Its leaders sought security—from external threats and for internal developments."[36] John Adams soundly understood the significance of the trade and correctly stated that American trade with China was far beyond the commerce itself. To establish a friendly relationship with China would have significant influence on America's position in the world. He told John Jay,

> We Should attend to this Intercourse with the East, with the more Ardour, because the Stronger Footing We obtain in those Countries, of more importance will our Friendship be, to the Powers of Europe who have large Connections there.—The East Indies will probably be the Object and The Theatre of the next War, and the more familiar We are with everything relative to that Country, the more will the contending Parties desire to win Us of their Side, or at least, what We ought to wish for most, to keep Us neutral.[37]

GINSENG: THE CHINESE HERB THAT HELPED THE UNITED STATES ENTER INTERNATIONAL COMMERCE

In 1784, when the first American trading ship, the *Empress of China*, entered your waters, my country was unknown to you. We were a new republic, eager to win a place in international commerce.[38]

One day in the mid-seventeenth century some Chinese soldiers of the Qing dynasty (1644–1911) started to build the Willow Palisade along the entire south boundary of northeast China. The Willow Palisade was built under the order of Emperor Shunzhi (r. 1644–1661) to discourage ginseng diggers from other parts of China to search for ginseng in the region. This structure was intended to discourage diggers of ginseng, a valuable herb, from searching in northeastern China. Emperor Shunzhi never imagined that China's fashion for ginseng would have an impact on American efforts to win legitimacy in international trade. Ginseng was beneficial to the U.S. economy and trade, unexpectedly allowing American farmers in rural mountainsides to grow this herb for trade with China.

In 1783, the British signed the Paris Treaty with American representatives. The Americans rightfully celebrated and enjoyed their hard-won victory. However, the euphoric feeling of victory was quickly overshadowed by economic challenges. Depression and inflation quickly drained away the jubilation of victory from the Founding Fathers and the fighters of the Revolutionary War. Britain, which had just lost the war, was trying hard to suppress America through economic coercion. All old trade routes were forced to close to the Americans. Britain adopted the strategy of seeking to put enough economic pressure on individual states to force them, one by one, to "return to Mother England."[39]

It seemed that the British policy was really working, and the Americans were feeling bitter over the victory. They hardly had time to enjoy their freedom from Britain when the national fiscal system was on the brink of collapse. Inflation was unbearable, the cost of tea reaching a lofty $100. By comparison, an army private's salary was $4 per month. People were using the paper money as wallpaper. In the streets of Philadelphia, men were seen in a procession wearing the bills as cockades in their hats accompanied by a dog covered with a coat of tar in which the paper money was thickly set. When Congress demanded people pay tax, it was paid in its own money, a worthless paper from its own printing machine.[40]

There was no encouraging news from continental Europe. American representative Benjamin Franklin (1706–1790) was not able to secure any more loans from the French government. There was no good news from John Jay (1745–1829), the American representative in Madrid, or John Adams, the American representative in the Netherlands.[41]

Americans desperately needed to trade. Political independence without economic independence might well prove an unfruitful victory. As the first minister of Finance of the United States, Robert Morris (1734–1806) worked hard to find a new trade partner that was beyond Britain's control. China became his first choice. However, what could Americans trade with China? As an agricultural society, the United States lacked the capability to provide anything that would sell in China; therefore, ginseng became the main commercial product that the Americans could trade with the Chinese. Thomas Jefferson was told that as the Chinese market was opened to the United States, ginseng "might be brought to a very, great vallue, and the State of Virginia alone could supply the whole of the China market with this Article."[42] John Adams also recommended to John Jay that "the Ginseng of the United States, are proper Articles for the China Markett."[43]

Since the Chinese imperial government closed northeast China—the main source for ginseng—Chinese merchants had to search for ginseng from other sources. This created an opportunity for North America. In 1709, Emperor Kangxi (1661–1722) hired French Jesuit priest Father Petrus Jartoux (1668–1720) to investigate the Changbai Mountain in northeast China. During that time he learned about the value of ginseng and wrote a letter, in which he predicted that ginseng could be found in Canada due to the similar environment of French Canada to northeast China.[44] In 1714, Father Lafitau received the letter and started to look for ginseng in French Canada. He discovered ginseng growing near the Montreal area. Realizing the potential profit with the trade with China from ginseng, Jesuits sent missionaries to Canada to collect ginseng. For many years, the Jesuits shipped tons of Canadian ginseng to China.[45] Ginseng had become a profitable commodity for French Canada. Ginseng was available at twenty-five cents a pound in Canada and sold at five dollars a pound in China.[46]

Benjamin Franklin testified to the availability of ginseng in the British colonies. On July 22, 1738, Franklin told his fellow Americans, "We have the pleasure of acquainting the World, that the famous Chinese or Tartarian Plant, called *Ginseng*, is now discovered in this Province."[47] John Bartram also reported that ginseng was found on the Susquehanna River in the same year.[48] Quoting from a French book, Neil Jamieson told Jefferson that the Chinese loved ginseng so much "that they never think they can Pay too dear for it."[49] Gouverneur Morris (1752–1816) acclaimed that "we have Ginseng too, which going hence immediately it's freshness will give us a preference."[50] In the same year when the *Empress of China* was on her way to China, Thomas Jefferson also looked for ginseng on his Monticello estate. He gave ginseng found there to a Mr. St. John.[51] In November 1784, Jefferson reminded Nicolas Lewis not to forget the ginseng.[52] From Paris on November 27, 1785, Jefferson listed in a letter to John Adams, "Ginseng. we can furnish them with enough to supply their whole demand for the E. Indies."[53] Samuel Shaw (1754–1794), the supercargo of the *Empress of China*, reported to John Jay,

> The advantages peculiar to America in this instance are striking, and the manner in which her Commerce has commenced, and is now going on with this Country, has not a little alarmed the Europeans. Such are the advantages which America derives from her Genseng. With respect to the demand in this Country for the Genseng of America, which might perhaps be rendered as beneficial to her Citizens as her mines of Silver and Gold have been to the rest of Mankind, the world has been much mistaken. Until the American flag appeared in this quarter, it had been generally supposed that forty or fifty peculs* ^ [in margin] a pecul is 133 1/3 lb. English^ were equal to the annual consumption; But experience has proved the contrary. Upwards of four hundred and forty peculs were brought here by the first American Ship in 1784, which did not equal the quantity brought from Europe the same Season; the greatest part of which must have been previously sent there by Citizens of the United States. The present year more than eighteen hundred peculs have been sold, one half of which came in the American Vessels. Notwithstanding the increased quantity since 1784, the sales have not been materially affected by it, and it is probable there will always be a sufficient demand for the Article to make it equally valuable.[54]

He then suggested to John Jay that it "be for the interest of America to prevent the exportation of it in any but American bottoms directly to this Country, may be objects not unworthy of national attention."[55]

Ginseng helped greatly in the development of international trade between China and America. The entire country was connected by trade with China. Not only merchants in New York, Boston, and Philadelphia, but also isolated farmers in deep mountains had learned that they could earn money selling this valuable plant grown on the northern slope of the mountains. About the same time when the *Empress of China* unloaded the ginseng at China, Washington met some people who were doing ginseng business in Virginia. He recorded in his diary, "I met numbers of Persons & Pack horses going in with *Ginseng*: & for salt & other articles at the Market Below."[56] One month before the *Empress of China* reached Canton, China, in July 1874, Neil Jamieson reported to Thomas Jefferson that "the Article of Ginsang may become one of considerable value to the State of Virginia there has been exported previous to the late war to the value of 30,000 ℔.[57]

The *Empress of China* left New York on February 22, 1784, and returned triumphantly to New York on May 11, 1785. Her successful voyage brought a measure of prosperity and was seen as an American economic salvation. The voyage had been a remarkable financial success. It was a win-win two-way trade. The ship profited on her investment about 30 percent.[58] The success of the voyage stimulated American merchants. Other traders were quick to see the value of economic exchange with China. The great success enjoyed by the *Empress of China* aroused so much enthusiasm that the report about her sail was read in Congress. Three years after the sail, George Washington happily stated, "The Maritime Genius of this Country is now steering our Vessels in every ocean, to the East Indies."[59]

The U.S. government encouraged China trade by maintaining favorable tariff policies.[60] Under the support of the political leaders, American trade with China grew rapidly. By the first half of the nineteenth century, the Chinese port of Canton saw about forty American ships a year loading and unloading. America's purpose to win a place in international commerce was realized successfully.[61] Naturally, the voyage of the *Empress of China* has been claimed as "the brightest chapter in the maritime history of the United States."[62]

AMERICAN GINSENG AND ITS EFFECTS ON AMERICANIZATION

American ginseng, nicknamed "Flower Flag Ginseng," was the most important commercial trade good between China and the United States during the late 1700s and early 1800s. The search for ginseng, the most lucrative American export to China, was a significant driving force behind westward expansion. The search for ginseng inspired migration from the Eastern Seaboard to the Midwestern territories of the United States.

Historical records show that ginseng was first found in northeast China more than 5,000 years ago. About 3,000 years ago, traditional Chinese doctors began to use it as medicine. According to Chinese books of traditional medicine, ginseng boosts the spirit, brightens the eyes, strengthens the heart, and expels evil. If taken for a long period of time, ginseng invigorates the body and prolongs life.[63]

During the Qing dynasty, ginseng had become so popular that the royal family monopolized it in northeast China. For the purpose of preserving ginseng for the imperial court, Emperor Qianlong (1711–1799) established the Ginseng Monopoly Bureau to make policies and regulations on managing ginseng affairs. Emperor Qianlong even wrote many poems to applaud ginseng, demonstrating the level to which the Chinese treasured the herb.[64]

Ironically, Chinese royal restrictions on collecting ginseng and huge commercial demands created a valuable trade opportunity for the Americans. John Ledyard (1751–1788), an American explorer and adventurer who had sailed to the Pacific with British explorer Captain James Cook, brought the trade news to the newly independent United States. Robert Morris (1734–1806) grasped China's great craving for ginseng as a valuable prospect to break the economic embargo imposed by Britain. Upon learning that American ginseng was welcomed in China, he decided to dispatch it to China in an attempt to establish direct trade relationship with the Chinese.

When the American ginseng carried by the *Empress of China* reached Canton, it immediately sold out for substantial profits. Shortly after, the joint supercargo reported to secretary of the Treasury Alexander Hamilton (1755–1804):

> In the year of 1784, on the 22d of February, the ship *Empress of China*, being the first ship that ever sailed from United States for China, was sent to Canton by a company of American merchants; her cargo consists of Spanish dollars, about four hundred peculs of Genseng [(Ginseng], a piculs being 133/⅓ lb English Avoirdu poids, some cordage, wine, lead, iron a few furs, with other trifling articles not worthy enumerating.[65]

In the era when the United States was a small and developing country with few products to sell in the Chinese market, ginseng naturally became a major—and by far the most lucrative—American export to China.

After the influx of American ginseng, the Chinese gradually discovered the variances between American ginseng and its Chinese counterpart. They learned that Chinese ginseng is warm and good for people who have recovered from a serious illness and need to regain their strength. On the other hand, American ginseng has cooler properties and is normally used to cool down fevers or summer heat. The Chinese considered it good for people with deficient *yin* or excessive *yang*.[66] Therefore, American ginseng was welcomed all the time even when plenty of Chinese ginseng was available.

Unlike other commercial goods, there is a complementary rather than a competitive relationship between Chinese and American ginsengs.

Much has been written about ginseng's contributions to the American effort to open trade with China. Its impact on social development has been neglected. American ginseng helped transform American society in the early republic period. The westward expansion was promoted by the pioneers who looked for exploitable natural resources and new profitable opportunities. Driven by the need to gather enough ginseng worthy for the long-distance journey to China, ginseng diggers and traders were soon found in the Appalachian Mountains and other areas where ginseng was readily available. After gathering them, the merchants would transport the herbs from the interiors of Pennsylvania and Virginia to Philadelphia, New York, or Boston. "This proved to be an important educational influence, since it was almost the only way in which the pioneer learned what was going on in the East."[67] As a result, the huge numbers of ginseng diggers, traders, and transporters reformed society. "Mobility of population is death to localism, and the western frontier worked irresistibly in an unsettling population. The effect reached back from the frontier and affected profoundly the Atlantic coast and even the Old World."[68]

American ginseng's role in promoting western expansion is evident by how the amount of ginseng shipped to China increased proportionally to the American expansion to the west. During the Washington administration of 1789–1797, the United States exported 374,792 pounds of ginseng to China. However, during John Adams's short administration, 1797–1801, the United States exported 337,192 pounds, close to that of the much longer Washington administration. During the Thomas Jefferson administration of 1801–1809, American merchants sent 1,617,594 pounds to China. Compared with that of Washington's administration, the export of ginseng increased 4.3 times. In the James Madison administration, 1809–1817, the United States exported 1,000,660 pounds to China. During the last presidency of the Founding Father generation, the James Monroe administration (1817–1825), the amount of American ginseng exported to China reached 2,868,062 pounds.[69]

The search for ginseng became an imperative dynamic force of westward expansion. From the East Coast areas all the way to Minnesota, Missouri, and Iowa, searching for ginseng became a preoccupation. Daniel Boone (1734–1820), the well-known pioneer of America's westward expansion, accumulated a huge amount of ginseng on his way to the west. Many generations of American families in the Atlantic coast areas from New York to Georgia "relied on Ginseng as a source of cash income."[70] In Thomas Jefferson's record of North American plants in *Notes on the State of Virginia*, his only published book, he recorded species "he deemed valuable to early Americans"[71] Jefferson listed ginseng (*Panax quinquefolium L.*) in the book.[72]

In addition to its economic impact on society, American social life was also influenced by the ginseng drive. Some parents sent their children to excavate the roots in the Appalachian Mountains, the Midwest, and Northeast, and wherever ginseng grew. There are some folk tales and songs that reflect the life of the young ginseng diggers or collectors. Through scrutinizing these kinds of historical materials, we can find how ginseng changed their livelihoods. The following traditional song provides a vivid story of a Carolinian young man's personal experience with digging the roots:

Ain't a-gonna dig no ginseng,
Well I ain't a-gonna hunt no crow,
Ain't gonna do a doggone thing[73]

American ginseng's impact on life and culture went far beyond the field of international commodities. It also affected the social progress of the United States and helped to stimulate westward expansion. The initiative for ginseng facilitated a new American society. "Moving westward, the frontier became more and more American."[74]

The ginseng enterprise also helped popularize tea drinking from the upper class to the rest of society. Tea drinking in the colonies had been very popular before the huge amount of tea shipped directly by the citizens of the United States. The British exported the habit from England to North America, and the colonists quickly adopted their tastes for tea. Tea houses following London models to become powerful social catalysts, providing an excellent forum for the exchange of ideas and the distribution of news.[75] Indeed, the taxes that the British imposed on the colonists' tea spurred their demands for independence in the American Revolution.[76] However, before 1784, tea was mainly a luxury reserved for affluent colonists due to its high price. However, large amounts of tea carried over oceans from China to North America by the *Empress of China* and other American ships after 1784 popularized the drink by making it more affordable to ordinary Americans.

The United States sought to build direct commercial relations with China as it grappled with a domestic economy on the brink of chaos. The opening of American direct trade with China realized two purposes. It symbolized the fledgling nation's hopes of improving its beleaguered postwar economy, and separately established the United States as a legitimate, sovereign nation. Alexander Hamilton pointed out that U.S. trade with China was beneficial to American financial stability.[77] George Washington also understood that U.S. trade with China affected not only economic growth but also the status of the United States in the world. In 1787, he articulated happiness seeing the achievements of the trade. He expressed "his hearty wishes" for Joseph Barrell, a merchant who engaged in trade with China, to wish him to succeed in his enterprise with China trade. Washington expressed that he hoped "the day will arrive (at no very distant period) when the sources of commerce shall be enlarged and replenished; and when the new Constellation of this Hemisphere shall be hailed and respected in every quarter of the terraqueous globe."[78]

NOTES

1. John Frederick Schroeder, ed., *Maxims of Washington: Political, Social, Moral, and Religious* (Mount Vernon, VA: Mount Vernon Ladies Association, 1942), 174.
2. "I. To the President of Congress, No. 49, 19 April 1780," Founders Online, National Archives, https://founders.archives.gov/documents/Adams/06-09-02-0115-0002. Original source: *The Adams Papers, Papers of John Adams*, ed. Gregg L. Lint and Richard Alan Ryerson, vol. 9, *March 1780–July 1780* (Cambridge, MA: Harvard University Press, 1996), 164–96.
3. Kenneth Munford, *John Ledyard: An American Marco Polo* (Portland, OR: Binfords & Mort, 1939), 178.
4. Jared Sparks, *The Life of John Ledyard: The American Traveler, Comprising Selections from His Journals and Correspondence* (Cambridge, MA: Hilliard and Brown, 1828), 154.
5. "To John Jay from Robert Morris, 27 November 1783," Founders Online, National Archives, https://founders.archives.gov/documents/Jay/01-03-02-0211. Original source: *The Selected Papers of John Jay*, ed. Elizabeth M. Nuxoll, vol. 3, *1782–1784* (Charlottesville: University Press of Virginia, 2013), 523–24.
6. Letter from George Washington to Thomas Jefferson, March 29, 1784, Library of Virginia, http://www.lva.virginia.gov/lib-edu/education/psd/nation/gwtj.htm.
7. "From John Adams to John Jay, 11 November 1785," Founders Online, National Archives, https://founders.archives.gov/documents/Adams/06-17-02-0302. Original source: *The Adams Papers, Papers of John Adams*, ed. Gregg L. Lint, C. James Taylor, Sara Georgini, Hobson Woodward, Sara B. Sikes, Amanda A. Mathews, and Sara Martin, vol. 17, *April–November 1785* (Cambridge, MA: Harvard University Press, 2014), 584–85.
8. "To John Jay from Robert Morris, 19 May 1785," Founders Online, National Archives, https://founders.archives.gov/documents/Jay/01-04-02-0042. Original source: *The Selected Papers of John Jay*, ed. Elizabeth M. Nuxoll, vol. 4, *1785–1788* (Charlottesville: University Press of Virginia, 2015), 90–91.
9. Richard Henry Lee, "The Letters of Richard Henry Lee, 2," National Society of the Colonial Dames of America (New York: Macmillan, 1914), 358.
10. "To James Madison from Richard Henry Lee, 30 May 1785," Founders Online, National Archives, https://founders.archives.gov/documents/Madison/01-08-02-0158. Original source: *The Papers of James Madison*, ed. Robert A. Rutland and

William M. E. Rachal, vol. 8, *10 March 1784–28 March 1786* (Chicago: University of Chicago Press, 1973), 288–90.

11. Ibid.

12. Ibid.

13. "Alexander Hamilton's First Draft of the Report on the Subject of Manufactures, [27 January–4 February] 1790," Founders Online, National Archives, https://founders.archives.gov/documents/Hamilton/01-10-02-0001-0003. Original source: *The Papers of Alexander Hamilton*, ed. Harold C. Syrett, vol. 10, *December 1791–January 1792* (New York: Columbia University Press, 1966), 23–49.

14. "The Letters of Richard Henry Lee, 2," 360.

15. "Tench Coxe's Second Draft, [September 1790]," Founders Online, National Archives, https://founders.archives.gov/documents/Hamilton/01-26-02-0002-0311-0003. Original source: *The Papers of Alexander Hamilton*, ed. Harold C. Syrett, vol. 26, *May 1, 1802–October 23, 1804, Additional Documents 1774–1799, Addenda and Errata* (New York: Columbia University Press, 1979), 632–47.

16. "To Alexander Hamilton from Thomas Randall, 14 August 1791," Founders Online, National Archives, https://founders.archives.gov/documents/Hamilton/01-09-02-0040. Original source: *The Papers of Alexander Hamilton*, ed. Harold C. Syrett, vol. 9, *August 1791–December 1791* (New York: Columbia University Press, 1965), 38–55.

17. "Americans Engage in the China Trade: Editorial Note," Founders Online, National Archives, https://founders.archives.gov/documents/Jay/01-04-02-0043. Original source: *The Selected Papers of John Jay*, ed. Elizabeth M. Nuxoll, vol. 4, *1785–1788* (Charlottesville: University Press of Virginia, 2015), 91–95.

18. "From John Adams to John Jay, 11 November 1785," Founders Online, National Archives, https://founders.archives.gov/documents/Adams/06-17-02-0302. Original source: *The Adams Papers, Papers of John Adams*, ed. Gregg L. Lint, C. James Taylor, Sara Georgini, Hobson Woodward, Sara B. Sikes, Amanda A. Mathews, and Sara Martin, vol. 17, *April–November 1785* (Cambridge, MA: Harvard University Press, 2014), 584–85.

19. Ibid.

20. "To John Adams from John Jay, 3 February 1786," Founders Online, National Archives, https://founders.archives.gov/documents/Adams/06-18-02-0071. Original source: *The Adams Papers, Papers of John Adams*, ed. Gregg L. Lint, Sara Martin, C. James Taylor, Sara Georgini, Hobson Woodward, Sara B. Sikes, Amanda M. Norton, vol. 18, *December 1785–January 1787* (Cambridge, MA: Harvard University Press, 2016), 140–42.

21. "Diary entry: 8 February 1790," Founders Online, National Archives, https://founders.archives.gov/documents/Washington/01-06-02-0001-0002-0008. Original source: *The Diaries of George Washington*, ed. Donald Jackson and Dorothy Twohig, vol. 6, *1 January 1790–13 December 1799* (Charlottesville: University Press of Virginia, 1979), 29–30.

22. "To George Washington from Samuel Shaw, 7 December 1790," Founders Online, National Archives, https://founders.archives.gov/documents/Washington/05-07-02-0020. Original source: *The Papers of George Washington, Presidential Series*,

ed. Jack D. Warren Jr., vol. 7, *December 1, 1790–March 21, 1791* (Charlottesville: University Press of Virginia, 1998), 35–39.

23. "To James Madison from William Grayson, 28 May 1785," Founders Online, National Archives, https://founders.archives.gov/documents/Madison/01-08-02-015 5. Original source: *The Papers of James Madison*, ed. Robert A. Rutland and William M. E. Rachal, vol. 8, *10 March 1784–28 March 1786* (Chicago: University of Chicago Press, 1973), 284–85.

24. Ibid.

25. "From George Washington to Lafayette, 3 June 1790," Founders Online, National Archives, https://founders.archives.gov/documents/Washington/05-05-02-0292. Original source: *The Papers of George Washington, Presidential Series*, ed. Dorothy Twohig, Mark A. Mastromarino, and Jack D. Warren, vol. 5, *January 16, 1790–June 30, 1790* (Charlottesville: University Press of Virginia, 1996), 467–69.

26. John C. Fitzpatrick, ed., *George Washington Writings*, 39 vols. (Washington, DC, 1931–1944), XXXI:45; John C. Miller, *Origins of the American Revolution: With a New Introduction and a Biography* (Stanford, CA: Stanford University Press, 1943), 231n37; James Thomas Flexner, *George Washington and the New Nation (1783–1793)* (Boston and New York: Little, Brown, 1969), 249.

27. "From George Washington to Lafayette, 3 June 1790," Founders Online, National Archives, https://founders.archives.gov/documents/Washington/05-05-02-0292. Original source: *The Papers of George Washington, Presidential Series*, ed. Dorothy Twohig, Mark A. Mastromarino, and Jack D. Warren, vol. 5, *January 16, 1790–June 30, 1790* (Charlottesville: University Press of Virginia, 1996), 467–69.

28. "September 1784," Founders Online, National Archives, https://founders.archives.gov/documents/Washington/01-04-02-0001-0001. Original source: *The Diaries of George Washington*, ed. Donald Jackson and Dorothy Twohig, vol. 4, *September 1, 1784–June 30, 1786* (Charlottesville: University Press of Virginia, 1978), 1–54.

29. "September 1784," Founders Online, National Archives, https://founders.archives.gov/documents/Washington/01-04-02-0001-0001. Original source: *The Diaries of George Washington*, ed. Donald Jackson and Dorothy Twohig, vol. 4, *September 1, 1784–June 30, 1786* (Charlottesville: University Press of Virginia, 1978), 1–54.

30. Fitzpatrick, *Writings of George Washington*, 29:211–12; Dorothy Twohig et al., *The Letters of George Washington*, Confederate Series, 5:172.

31. "From George Washington to John Barry, 6 July 1789," Founders Online, National Archives, https://founders.archives.gov/documents/Washington/05-03-02-0058. Original source: *The Papers of George Washington, Presidential Series*, ed. Dorothy Twohig, vol. 3, *June 15, 1789–September 5, 1789* (Charlottesville: University Press of Virginia, 1989), 120.

32. Merrill D. Peterson, "Thomas Jefferson and Commercial Policy, 1783–1793," *William and Mary Quarterly* 22, no. 4 (October 1965): 585.

33. Thomas Jefferson to the secretary of the Treasury (Albert Gallatin), Monticello, August 15, 1808, *Jefferson's Works: Correspondence* XII:134.

34. Tyler Dennett, *Americans in Eastern Asia; a Critical Study of the Policy of the United States with Reference to China, Japan and Korea in the 19th Century* (New York: Macmillan, 1922), 77.

35. "To James Madison from Edmond Kelly, 24 December 1820," Founders Online, National Archives, https://founders.archives.gov/documents/Madison/04-02-02-0160. Original source: *The Papers of James Madison, Retirement Series*, ed. David B. Mattern, J. C. A. Stagg, Mary Parke Johnson, and Anne Mandeville Colony, vol. 2, *February 1, 1820–February 26, 1823* (Charlottesville: University Press of Virginia, 2013), 187–90.

36. Warren I. Cohen, "American Perception of China," in *Dragon and Eagle: United States-China Relations: Past and Future*, ed. Michael Oksenberg and Robert B. Oxnam (New York: Basic Books, 1973), 50.

37. "From John Adams to John Jay, 11 November 1785," Founders Online, National Archives, https://founders.archives.gov/documents/Adams/06-17-02-0302. Original source: *The Adams Papers, Papers of John Adams*, ed. Gregg L. Lint, C. James Taylor, Sara Georgini, Hobson Woodward, Sara B. Sikes, Amanda A. Mathews, and Sara Martin, vol. 17, *April–November 1785* (Cambridge, MA: Harvard University Press, 2014), 584–85.

38. Ronald Reagan, *Remarks to Chinese Community Leaders in Beijing, China, April 27, 1984*, http://www.reagan.uttexas.edu/resource/speeches/1984/42784a.htm.

39. Frank T. Reuter, *Trials and Triumphs: George Washington's Foreign Policy* (Fort Worth: Texas Christian University Press, 1983), 17–18.

40. Jim Powell, "The Man Who Financed the American Revolution," http://www.libertystory.net/LSACTIONROBERTMORRIS.htm.

41. Lisa Rogers, "Our Man in Paris," *Humanities* 23, no. 4 (July/August 2002): 12. See also Powell, "Man Who Financed the American Revolution."

42. "To Thomas Jefferson from Neil Jamieson, 12 July 1784," Founders Online, National Archives, https://founders.archives.gov/documents/Jefferson/01-07-02-0277. Original source: *The Papers of Thomas Jefferson*, ed. Julian P. Boyd, vol. 7, *March 2, 1784–February 25, 1785* (Princeton: Princeton University Press, 1953), 365–75.

43. "From John Adams to John Jay, 11 November 1785," Founders Online, National Archives, https://founders.archives.gov/documents/Adams/06-17-02-0302. Original source: *The Adams Papers, Papers of John Adams*, ed. Gregg L. Lint, C. James Taylor, Sara Georgini, Hobson Woodward, Sara B. Sikes, Amanda A. Mathews, and Sara Martin, vol. 17, *April–November 1785* (Cambridge, MA: Harvard University Press, 2014), 584–85.

44. See http://www.huarenworldnet.org/members-contribution/ginseng--us-commerce.

45. B. L. Evans, *Proceedings of the 1994 International Ginseng Conference*, July 17–22, Vancouver, British Columbia, Canada, 305–12. In 1750 American ginseng trade reached a peak. In 1770, the colonies exported 74,605 pounds of ginseng. See http://www.herbalgram.org/wholefoodsmarket/herbclip/review.asp?I=43463.

46. Kim Young-sik, "The Ginseng 'Trade War,'" Part III from *A Brief History of the US-Korea relations Prior to 1945*, http://www.asianresearch.org/articles/1438.html.

47. *Pennsylvania Gazette*, July 22, 1738.

48. See http://www.kouroo.info/kouroo/thumbnails/B/JohnBartram.

49. "To Thomas Jefferson from Neil Jamieson, 12 July 1784," Founders Online, National Archives, https://founders.archives.gov/documents/Jefferson/01-07-02-0277. Original source: *The Papers of Thomas Jefferson*, ed. Julian P. Boyd, vol. 7, *March 2, 1784–February 25, 1785* (Princeton: Princeton University Press, 1953), 365–75.

50. "IX. Abstracts of Gouverneur Morris' Letters on Commerce, [May 1784]," Founders Online, National Archives, https://founders.archives.gov/documents/Jefferson/01-07-02-0262-0011. Original source: *The Papers of Thomas Jefferson*, ed. Julian P. Boyd, vol. 7, *March 2, 1784–February 25, 1785* (Princeton: Princeton University Press, 1953), 350–55.

51. "From Thomas Jefferson to Nicholas Lewis, 1 July 1784," Founders Online, National Archives, https://founders.archives.gov/documents/Jefferson/01-07-02-0267. Original source: *The Papers of Thomas Jefferson*, ed. Julian P. Boyd, vol. 7, *March 2, 1784–February 25, 1785* (Princeton: Princeton University Press, 1953), 356.

52. "From Thomas Jefferson to Nicholas Lewis, 11 November 1784," Founders Online, National Archives, https://founders.archives.gov/documents/Jefferson/01-07-02-0366. Original source: *The Papers of Thomas Jefferson*, ed. Julian P. Boyd, vol. 7, *March 2, 1784–February 25, 1785* (Princeton: Princeton University Press, 1953), 502–3.

53. "To John Adams from Thomas Jefferson, 27 November 1785," Founders Online, National Archives, https://founders.archives.gov/documents/Adams/06-17-02-0314. Original source: The Adams Papers, *Papers of John Adams*, ed. Gregg L. Lint, C. James Taylor, Sara Georgini, Hobson Woodward, Sara B. Sikes, Amanda A. Mathews, and Sara Martin, vol. 17, *April–November 1785* (Cambridge, MA: Harvard University Press, 2014), 609–14.

54. "To John Jay from Samuel Shaw, 31 December 1786," Founders Online, National Archives, https://founders.archives.gov/documents/Jay/01-04-02-0208. Original source: *The Selected Papers of John Jay*, ed. Elizabeth M. Nuxoll, vol. 4, *1785–1788* (Charlottesville: University Press of Virginia, 2015), 448–59.

55. Ibid.

56. John C. Fitzpatrick ed., *The Diaries of George Washington, 1748–1799*, ed. Donald Jackson and Dorothy Twohig, vol. 4 (Boston and New York: Houghton Mifflin, 1978).

57. "To Thomas Jefferson from Neil Jamieson, 12 July 1784," Founders Online, National Archives, https://founders.archives.gov/documents/Jefferson/01-07-02-0277. Original source: *The Papers of Thomas Jefferson*, ed. Julian P. Boyd, vol. 7, *March 2, 1784–February 25, 1785* (Princeton: Princeton University Press, 1953), 365–75.

58. Oscar Theodore Barck, *New York City During the War for Independence: With Special Reference to the Period of British Occupation* (New York: Columbia University Press, 1931), 227.

59. George Washington, to Comte de Moustier, August 17, 1788, *Writings of George Washington*, 30:46; see also Schroeder, *Maxims of Washington*, 105.

60. "Thomas Jefferson to (Albert Gallatin) the Secretary of the Treasury, Monticello, August 1808," *Jefferson's Works: Correspondence*, XII:134.

61. William Milburn, *Oriental Commerce* (London: Black, Parry & Co., 1813); Kenneth Scott Latourette, *Voyages of American Ships to China, 1784–1844* (New Haven: Connecticut Academy of Arts and Sciences, 1927); and Foster Rhea Dulles, *The Old China Trade* (Boston and New York: Houghton Mifflin, 1930).

62. Dulles, *Old China Trade*, 4.

63. Zhou Chuncai and Han Yazhou, *The Illustrated Yellow Emperor's Canon of Medicine* (Beijing: Dolphin Books, 2002).

64. More information on the imperial regulations forbidding collecting Ginseng in northeast China is available from Dave Wang, "Ginseng; the Herb that Helped the United States to Enter International Commerce," http://www.huarenworldnet.org/members-contribution/ginseng--us-commerce.

65. From Thomas Randall, New York, August 14, 1791. In *The Papers of Alexander Hamilton* (New York: Columbia University Press, 1961), 38–39.

66. See http://www.itmonline.org/arts/ginsengnature.htm.

67. Frederick Jackson Turner, *The Significance of the Frontier in American History*, 11, http://xroads.virginia.edu/~hyper/turner.

68. Ibid., 19.

69. The sources are from Samuel Blodget, *Economica: Statistical Manual for the United States of America* (Washington, DC: Kelley, 1806); J. D. B. Debow, *Statistical View of the United States, Being a Compendium of the Seventh Census to which We Added the Results of Every Previous Census, Beginning with 1790* (Washington, DC: Beverly Tucker, 1854); Isaac Smith Homans Jr., *An Historical and Statistical Account of the Foreign Commerce of the United States* (New York: Putnam, 1857); Hosea Ballou Morse, *The Chronicles of the East India Company Trading to China 1635–1834* (5 vols.; Cambridge, MA: Harvard University Press, 1926–1929); Timothy Pitkin, *A Statistical View of the Improvements, Together with that of the Revenues of the General Government* (New Haven: Durrie & Peck, 1835); Adam Seybert, *Statistical Annals; Embracing View of the Population, Commerce, Navigation, Fisheries, Public Lands, Post-Office Establishment, Revenue, Mint, Military and Naval Establishments, Expenditures, Public Debt, and Sinking Fund of the United States of America* (New York: Burt Franklin, 1818); and Paul E. Fontenoy, "Ginseng, Otter Skins, and Sandalwood: The Conundrum of the China Trade," *Northern Mariner* 7, no. 1 (January 1997).

70. Kristin Johannsen, *Ginseng Dreams: The Secret World of America's Most Valuable Plant* (Lexington: University Press of Kentucky, 2006), 7.

71. "Jefferson's Botanical Catalog in *Notes on the State of Virginia*," *Twinleaf Journal Archives*, 2009.

72. Thomas Jefferson, *Notes on the State of Virginia* (Philadelphia: Printed and Sold by Richard and Hall, in Market Street, between front and second streets, M.DCC.LXXXVIII), 36.

73. Lyle Lofgren, *Remembering the Old Songs: Ginseng Blues*, http://www.lizlyle.lofgrens.org/RmOlSngs/RTOS-GinsengBlues.html.

74. Turner, *Significance of the Frontier in American History*, 3.

75. Beth Carver Wees, *Coffee, Tea and Chocolate in Early Colonial America*, http://www.metmuseum.org/toah/hd/coff/hd_coff.htm.

76. Dave Wang, "Tea: The Leaves that Triggered the American War for Independence," *Huaren E-Magazine* (Australia), September 2007.

77. "Final Version of the Report on the Establishment of a Mint [28 January 1791]," Founders Online, National Archives, https://founders.archives.gov/documents/Hamilton/01-07-02-0334-0004. Original source: *The Papers of Alexander Hamilton*, ed. Harold C. Syrett, vol. 7, *September 1790–January 1791* (New York: Columbia University Press, 1963), 570–607.

78. "From George Washington to Joseph Barrell, 8 June 1788," Founders Online, National Archives, https://founders.archives.gov/documents/Washington/04-06-02-0283. Original source: *The Papers of George Washington, Confederation Series*, ed. W. W. Abbot, vol. 6, *January 1, 1788–September 23, 1788* (Charlottesville: University Press of Virginia, 1997), 316–17.

Chapter 6

Confucianism in the Making of U.S. Democracy

In the preceding chapters, I have introduced the effects of Confucian moral philosophy in the American colonial era. In the founding and the early republic eras, when the founders were contemplating the direction of the newly independent United States, they found the value of Confucianism and adopted some aspects of Confucian social and political principles to assist in their efforts to build a democratic system of government.

After the victory of the American Revolution, the founders took Confucian ideas and used them to frame new political institutions. I will also investigate how Confucian merit-based avenues were actualized to transform the American civil service system. Finally, I will examine Confucian educational principles and Thomas Jefferson's revolution of the American educational system.

The founders' efforts to pursue some of the positive Confucian moral, social, and political approaches were part of a broader ideological shift. These sought to replace the historic Western emphasis on birthright with systems of merit-based succession. Their efforts contributed to the emergence of a "[distinct] American character with new sets of values,"[1] one that was further removed from its European roots and was prepared to craft its own national identity.

CONFUCIAN VIRTUE AND THE FOUNDERS' EFFORTS TO CREATE A NEW VIRTUE FOR THE NEW NATION

At first glance, Confucius and the founding of the United States do not seem to be related. Confucius, the Latinized name of Kongzi (孔子) (550–476 BC), was a great philosopher and educator who lived at the end of "the

Spring and Autumn Period" (771–476 BC) in China. The American decision to declare independence in 1776 initiated a period in which the founders waged their death-or-life struggle to expel the imperialist rule of Great Britain. However, despite their differences, a close relationship existed. The American founders applied many values from Confucian moral philosophy to the formation of the United States.[2] Their recognition of Confucian ideas can be seen in places such as Montpelier, the house of James Madison, the father of the Constitution and the Bill of Rights, which displayed a portrait of Confucius. In addition, Thomas Paine, author of *Common Sense*, considered the Chinese sage to be in the same category as Jesus and Socrates.[3] Benjamin Franklin, the creator of the American Spirit, made the solemn statement that Confucian moral philosophy was valuable to human beings in general.[4] Thomas Jefferson, the principal author of the Declaration of Independence, also promoted Confucian moral principles in his inaugural speech in 1801. In his personal scrapbook, Jefferson placed a poem about an ideal Chinese prince that was recommended by Confucius.

Other founders such as John Adams and Benjamin Rush (1746–1813) also regarded Confucius highly in their efforts to formulate a blueprint for the new nation. These founders urged the citizens of the United States to adopt positive elements from Confucian moral philosophy and follow these moral examples to cultivate and advance their own virtues.[5]

The shared reverence of Confucius by the American founders has stimulated my curiosity. Why did they find Confucius's moral teachings so important? The American Revolution was a political revolution that marked the birth of the United States as a new nation. Additionally, it was simultaneously a moral revolution. While the founders were concerned with preserving their civil liberties and economic freedom as expressed by "no taxation without representation," they were also concerned with public morality. They fully understood that the American Revolutionary War was as much a battle against "the corruption of 18th century British high society" as it was against financial oppression.[6] As a result, the Founding Fathers were determined to create new virtues better responsive to the interests of the new nation. Having seen the consequences of moral corruption in the old world, the founders worked diligently to use all valuable moral resources available for them to create distinctly American virtues for the newly independent nation.

A Good Moral Position Is Life or Death to the New Nation

Virtue is the basis and foundation of an empire and the source from whence flows whatever may render it flourishing.[7]

The end of the Revolutionary War in 1783 brought freedom to the former British colonists in the thirteen colonies, but with this freedom also came greater opportunities to misbehave. During the late eighteenth century, moral issues caused by a culture of pleasure and freedom blossomed in American cities. According to some existing historical records, one could find a public place to engage in illicit activities on nearly every block in every eighteenth-century American city. John Adams realized that "we may look up to Armies for our defense, but virtue is our best security. It is not possible that any state should long remain free, where virtue is not supremely honored."[8]

Alarmed by those problems and other social issues, the founders reached a consensus that moral construction was not only a necessity to make the fruit of the revolution sustainable but also it should be considered a priority. The founders believed that only virtuous people could live in a free society. Almost every Founding Father testified to the link between liberty and virtue. George Washington (1732–1799) told Americans, "It is essentially true that virtue or morality is a main and necessary spring of popular or republican governments."[9] Benjamin Rush stated, "Without virtue there can be no liberty."[10] Benjamin Franklin warned, "Only a virtuous people are capable of freedom. As nations become corrupt and vicious, they have more need of masters."[11] Thomas Jefferson told his fellow Americans, "A nation as a society forms a moral person, and every member of it is personally responsible for his society."[12]

John Adams told the Americans that while the success of the revolution made the former colonies free, "they will not obtain a lasting Liberty" without good virtues.[13] He continued, "If Virtue & Knowledge are diffused among the People, they will never be enslav'd. This will be their great Security."[14] Adams repeatedly warned, "Liberty can no more exist without virtue and independence than the body can live and move without a soul."[15] To prevent corruption became John Adams's main concerns. He told his compatriots,

> We have no government armed with power capable of contending with human passions unbridled by morality and religion. Avarice, ambition, revenge, or gallantry would break the strongest cords of our constitution as a whale goes through a net. Our Constitution was made only for a moral and religious people.[16]

James Madison echoed the sentiment with the statement that the aim of U.S. Constitution was to find "men who possess most wisdom to discern, and most virtue to pursue, the common good of society," and in the meantime "to take the most effectual precautions for keeping them virtuous whilst they continue to hold their public trust."[17]

As the main creators of the new nation, the founders knew that it took more than a perfect plan of government to maintain liberty. They needed some moral principles accepted by the people to encourage them to obey laws voluntarily. They recognized that a free government should be supported by people who could act morally without compulsion and would not willfully violate the rights of others. Benjamin Franklin passionately believed that "laws without morals are in vain."[18] Cultivating new virtues for the fledgling United States, therefore, became one of the most significant themes during this time of social and political transformation. The founders turned to Confucian moral philosophy.

Private Virtue and Confucian Moral Philosophy

Public virtue was regarded as a foundation of freedom. Private virtue was considered the most important element of public virtue. As early as 1776, John Adams emphasized the significance of private virtue. He explained to his fellow Americans that the new American government's principles were "great and excellent among Men. But its Principles are as easily destroyed, as human Nature is corrupted." Therefore, "public Virtue is the only Foundation of Republics." However, "Public Virtue cannot exist in a Nation without private, and there must be a positive Passion for the public good, the public Interest,"[19] James Madison also emphasized the significance of private virtue. For him, "To suppose liberty or happiness without any virtue in the people is a chimerical idea."[20] Thomas Jefferson also told the Americans,

> When virtue is banished, ambition invades the minds of those who are disposed to receive it, and avarice possesses the whole community. . . . The order of nature [is] that individual happiness shall be inseparable from the practice of virtue.[21]

Jefferson understood that leaders had to establish role models for the nation to continue its success.

Private virtue meant being a person of integrity. Such qualities essential to private virtue included being honest in one's dealings with others, being faithful in one's duties to one's family, and controlling one's appetites. The qualities that private virtue emphasized could be found in the values that Confucius promoted. For instance, one of the main tenets of Confucian moral philosophy is a positive passion for the public good and public interest.

Moral philosophy is one of the most important components of Confucianism, which is regarded as the crystallization of ancient Chinese traditional culture. Confucius taught,

You will find Men capable of Governing happily the Kingdom of the Earth. You will see some that will have Magnanimity enough to refuse the most considerable Dignities and Advantages: There will be some also that will have Courage enough to walk on Naked Swords: But you will find few, that are capable of keeping a just Mean. That to arrive hereat, Art, Labor, Courage and Virtue are requir'd.[22]

Confucius taught that a perfect leader could create a perfect world through moral strength and example. Confucius viewed a leader as a moral person. Anyone who foresaw serving in a role of leadership as result of either desire or social status should rigorously mold and polish personal character, or *Te* (德). *Te* in this sense was not just personal power but also positive human qualities such as honesty and loyalty. Confucius believed that personal self-cultivation should be practiced for the benefit of society. For Confucius, a leader "ought always to be master of his own Heart, and Actions; He must not suffer himself to be corrupted by the Conversation, or Examples of loose and effeminate Persons."[23]

The founders understood that respectable and benevolent men were more likely to support the universal pursuit of happiness. An affectionate man would not only be more likely to live in harmony with his neighbors but also be able to understand the mutual sacrifices required for the success of the new nation. The founders drew from Confucius's moral teachings for private virtue that the new nation required.

The main tenets of Confucian moral philosophy provided what the founders wanted to develop: the new private virtue for its citizens and future leaders. These founders dreamed of creating truly virtuous people brought up by the Confucian standards of a gentleman. As a result, Confucian moral philosophy became important to the founders and the cause they fought for.

CONFUCIAN MORAL PHILOSOPHY IN NORTH AMERICA AROUND THE REVOLUTION

In eighteenth-century colonial society, the impact of Confucius was widely discussed in the North American colonies. Some eminent colonists, including Benjamin Franklin, expressed their respect for the philosopher. Franklin followed Confucius's practices and measures for moral cultivation, developing his own virtues as early as 1727.[24] Franklin saw it as his responsibility to spread Confucius's moral teachings. He published some excerpts from *Morals of Confucius* in his widely circulated *Pennsylvania Gazette* in 1737.[25] Franklin also made it clear that he regarded Confucius as his role model in 1749.[26] In August 1775, on the eve of American independence, Thomas Paine revealed a critical and meaningful interest in China. He published a series of works about China in the *Pennsylvania Magazine*.[27]

Other prominent figures of the day also recognized the value of Confucian teachings. John Bartram (1699–1777), a well-known botanist in the colonies, was very interested in Chinese philosophy, particularly in the personality of Confucius.[28] Bartram's paper, *Life and Character of the Chinese Philosopher Confucius*, introduced Confucius's life to his readers.[29] James Logan (1674–1751), another very influential colonist in Philadelphia, acquired a copy of the first European printing of Confucius's philosophy for his personal library in 1733.[30] Logan was not satisfied with the translation by the Jesuits and showed his desire to obtain the "true sense" of Confucianism.[31] Joel Barlow (1754–1812), an American poet and diplomat, considered Confucius to be one of the wisest philosophers in the history of antiquity.[32] Jedidiah Morse (1761–1826), a notable geographer, praised *Daxue* (大学 *Great Learning*) and *Zhongyong* (中庸 the *Doctrine of the Mean*), two of the four classics of Confucius. Morse extolled the two classics as "the most excellent precepts of wisdom and virtue, expressed with the greatest eloquence, elegance and precision."[33] Morse also compared Confucius with Socrates. He pointed out that Confucius was "very striking, and which far exceeds, in clearness, the prophecy of Socrates."[34] A contemporary author found that Morse's high praise of the Chinese sage "is especially significant" because Morse wrote his *Geography* for the youth of America and "considered it a means of instructing students in patriotism and morality."[35]

In May 1788, an article published in *Columbian Magazine* discussed Confucian morals related to filial piety.[36] One author loved Confucius's philosophy so much that he published a paper under the pen name *Confucius Discipulus*, introducing Confucius and Confucian moral teachings. In his paper, carried in the September 1793 edition of *New Hampshire Magazine*, this author gave "a concise History of Confucius, a famous Chinese philosopher." He also declared to his readers that Confucius was "a character so truly virtuous."[37]

Among women in the fledging United States, Confucian moral philosophy was also read and appreciated. Mrs. Elizabeth Drinker in Philadelphia was deeply impressed by Confucian moral teachings. Mrs. Drinker believed that people in her era should follow Confucius to cultivate their virtues. After studying the *Morals of Confucius*, she wrote in her diary on May 28, 1795,

> I have been pleased by reading The Morals of Confucius, a Chinese Philosopher, who flourished about five hundred and fifty years before the coming of Christ—said to be one of the choicest pieces of Learning remaining of that nation. A

sweet little piece it is. If there were such men in that day, what ought to be expected in this more enlightened Age!³⁸

The Founders' Efforts to Use Confucius's Moral Philosophy in their Efforts to Build New Virtue

The founders of the United States promoted Confucian moral teachings and urged these principles to be applied in the development of the nation. Benjamin Franklin cherished Confucian virtue so much that planned to build a United Party for Virtue. He announced to his readers,

> There seems to me at present to be great occasion for raising a United Party for Virtue, by forming the virtuous and good men of all nations into a regular body, to be governed by suitable good and wise rules, which good and wise men may probably be more unanimous in their obedience to, than common people are to common laws.³⁹

Franklin used Confucian moral principles as a guideline to examine social phenomena after the conclusion of the Revolutionary War. By using Confucian moral principles, Franklin opposed an idea raised by some revolutionary veterans who wanted to hand down glory to their descendants. In the wake of America's victory, these veterans of the Revolutionary War wanted to establish a hereditary aristocracy to "distinguish themselves and their posterity from their fellow citizens." These veterans wanted to form an order of hereditary knights and organized the Society of Cincinnatus hoping to let their descendants inherit their honor.⁴⁰ Franklin drew from Chinese examples to fight against this idea. In China, social promotion was based on "the Education, Instruction, and good Example afforded him by his Parents that he was rendered capable of Serving the Publick."⁴¹ He divulged to new American citizens that the way of Chinese social promotion should be adopted. The European hereditary system "is not only groundless and absurd, but often hurtful to that Posterity."⁴²

Confucius asserted that the people should be led by leaders who governed through their virtue rather than using their laws. He believed that if a government rested its rule entirely on laws, its people would try to escape punishment and have no sense of shame. Therefore, he reasoned that if the people were led by virtue, they would possess a sense of shame and follow their leaders through their own will.⁴³

In 1778, two years after the colonists declared their independence, Franklin addressed the significance of morality. He pointed out the necessity of governing with morality, especially for the leaders of the United States. He enjoined his fellow Americans that laws were not enough for the new nation. He asked, "What can laws do without morals?" Without virtue, the new nation "will in a course of minutes become corrupt like those of other and older Bushes, and consequently as wretched."[44]

Thomas Paine, the famous polemicist of republicanism, regarded Confucius as one of the world's great moral teachers. In his "Age of Reason, 1791–1792," Paine listed Confucius in the ranks of Jesus and the famous Greek philosophers. Paine reiterated this point in an article he wrote a decade later for *The Prospect*, a New York magazine. He stated that "Confucius, the Chinese philosopher, who lived five hundred years before the time of Christ says, 'acknowledge thy benefits by the turn of benefits, but never revenge injuries.'"[45] In his political disagreements with the federalists, Paine used Confucian ideas to criticize their moral faults. He enjoined these federalists to follow Confucian teachings so they could be honest.[46]

> As to the hypocritical abuse thrown out by the federalists on other subjects, I recommend to them the observance of a commandment that existed before either Christian or Jew existed.
>
> "Thou shalt make a covenant with thy senses,
> "With thine eye, that it beholds no evil.
> "With thine ear, that it hear no evil.
> "With thy tongue, that it speak no evil.
> "With thy hands that they commit no evils."[47]

For John Adams, the purpose of government is to promote the pursuit of happiness. Such happiness lies not merely in "ease, comfort, [and] security" but also characteristics such as virtue, humility, industry, and goodwill. Adams confidently declared "Confucius . . . agreed in this" goal of happiness through virtue.[48] Adams also realized that virtue ennobled individual character and lifted the entire society. Adams's statement conveys the significance of virtue for a good government and the significance of Confucius's moral philosophy in Adams's own efforts to bring up "the minds of the people." John Adams showed his high regard for Confucian virtues and believed that any good Americans should possess these traits.

In a letter to Jefferson, Adams criticized the English theologian and natural philosopher Joseph Priestley for ignoring Confucius in his writing. He said that "Priestley ought to have given us a sketch of the religion and morals of Zoroaster, of Sanchuniathon, of Confucius."[49]

Dr. Benjamin Rush, an ardent patriot, asserted in a 1798 essay on education in the new republic that "the only foundation for a useful education in a republic is to be laid in Religion. Without this there can be no virtue, and without virtue there can be no liberty, and liberty is the object and life of all republican governments." Having expressed his veneration for Confucianism, which "reveals the attributes of the Deity," Rush declared that he had rather see the opinions of Confucius "inculcated upon our youth, than see them grow up wholly devoid of a system of religious principles."[50]

As one of the main founders of the new nation, Jefferson eventually became the third president after his victory in the election of 1800. For Jefferson, who tired of metaphysics, a practical religion that advanced private virtue, such as Confucianism, had definite appeal. As president, Jefferson realized the importance of Confucian values to keep his ideals alive and move the country forward. His inaugural speech manifested his thoughts on how to make the United States a great nation. Remarkably, Jefferson showed his confidence in using Confucian moral values in his efforts to lead the new nation in 1801. In front of the representatives celebrating his victory, Jefferson told his fellow citizens that the new nation had been "enlightened by a benign religion, professed indeed and practised in various forms, yet all of them inculcating honesty, truth, temperance, gratitude and the love of man."[51]

Jefferson admired Voltaire, the French leader of the Age of Enlightenment. Voltaire regarded Confucianism as a superior system of morals, and Confucius as the greatest of all sages. From Jefferson's speech, it is evident that Jefferson accepted the Confucian concept of the true gentleman, and the belief that a good moral foundation was the foundation of a good government. Jefferson's vision for a better United States was largely based on a benign religion and a wise government. The morals Jefferson listed in his inauguration speech were the same moral principles that Confucius maintained. Jefferson also enshrined the Confucian moral principle that a ruler loses his mandate if the people don't approve in the Declaration of Independence: "We hold these truths to be self-evident. . . . That whenever any form of government becomes destructive of these ends, it is the right of the people to alter or to abolish it."[52] Furthermore, through careful examination of the Declaration of Independence and the First Great Pronouncement of King Wu,[53] one author has identified that Jefferson had imitated the First Great Pronouncement of King Wu.[54]

During his presidency, Jefferson included an ancient Chinese poem from *Shijing* (诗经 *The Book of Odes*) in his scrapbook.[55] This poem is about an ancient Chinese prince who was set up as an example for other leaders of the nation to follow.[56] Jefferson's inclusion of this specific Chinese poem is significant and reveals his close ties to Confucian ideals. Confucius pointed out, "He who governs by means of morality is like the North Star, which keeps its place with all the other stars gathering around it."[57]

Jefferson aimed to make himself this "North Polar Star." Therefore, it was not a surprise that Thomas Jefferson regarded the Chinese prince, whom Confucius considered to be one of the ideal rulers, his role model.[58]

The poem pays tribute to Prince Wu from the State of Wei, who was loved and respected by the people of his state.[59] Confucius praised Prince Wu when he quoted this poem in his famous book, *The Great Learning*, to provide a standard to aspire to other princes and leaders of various states.[60] Jefferson's choosing to position this poem in his personal scrapbook indicates his determination to be as great a leader as Prince Wu. Therefore, "His mem'ry of eternal prime, Like truth defies the power of time!" Jefferson wanted himself to be "in manners goodly great, Refine the people of the state." Jefferson used Prince Wu to encourage himself to be a leader loved by the future American people, just as Prince Wu was praised and remembered by all posterity.

In the section, "Poems of Nation," Jefferson included certain commentary on his presidency. The "Poems of Nation" shows that Jefferson viewed his legacy as intertwined with the success of the republican experiment. Believing that he should help the United States to maintain his political, moral, and personal values in the history of the American Revolution, Jefferson collected documents, books, newspapers, and other materials so that later historians could construct a right and comprehensive history of the American Revolution.[61] Jefferson was very serious about preserving his personal legacy. His inclusion of the ancient Chinese poem in his scrapbook shows that Jefferson valued Confucianism highly and used some of the principles to build the new nation in the new land with rich natural resources. With the help of Confucianism, Jefferson was confident that he could achieve his goal. Jefferson had long regarded Confucius in the same rank as Jesus. During his years of retirement at Monticello, he recalled that he had classed Jesus "with the great men of antiquity—Zoroaster, Socrates, Confucius, &c." in his correspondence with Dr. Rush.[62]

Summary

During the founding era, the American Founding Fathers "managed to establish a set of ideas and institutions that, over the stretch of time, became the blueprint for political and economic success for the nation-state in the modern world."[63] My intent is to bring to light the founders' efforts to adopt some principles of Confucian moral philosophy and include them in the fiber of the newly independent United States as a free and democratic society. The founders tried to develop dependable morals, ensuring that a democratic system would function in the correct direction. They attempted to use Confucian moral philosophy to safeguard the democratic system, build private virtue, and bring up citizens with good morals to serve the new nation. Through the founders' efforts, Confucian moral philosophy contributed greatly to the formation of American virtue.

CONFUCIANISM IN THE MAKING OF THE AMERICAN DEMOCRATIC SYSTEM

Immediately following the conclusion of the American War of Independence in 1783, the Founding Fathers faced the challenge of creating stable political institutions to preserve the hard-earned fruits of their revolution. As John Adams (1735–1826) described this daunting task, "It is much easier to pull down a government, in such a conjuncture of affairs as we have seen, than to build up at such season as present."[64] Some founders were worrying that "their enemies might have been right—America was ungovernable."[65] The American Revolution entered an uncharted course. In a sense, it went into a second phase and the constitutional settlement of 1787–1788 became "a second founding moment, along with the original occasion of 1776."[66]

The Founding Fathers of the United States appreciated the gravity and unprecedented nature of their actions as they established the country's charter during the Constitutional Convention of 1787. Unsurprisingly, the Constitution was a controversial document. Following its completion, critics "condemned it as a betrayal of the core principles of the American Revolution" while defenders of the Constitution saluted it as a "sensible accommodation of liberty to power and a realistic compromise with the requirements of a national domain."[67]

The Founding Fathers, raised under Western schools of thought, were influenced by ideas regarding the role of government as expounded during the European Enlightenment. The founders were receptive to the concept of popular rule promoted by Enlightenment philosophers. One such philosopher was John Locke (1632–1704), who expressed his influential social contract theory in his *Two Treatises on Government* (1689 and 1690). This theory opposed the divine right of kings in favor of government grounded on the consent of the governed, so long as the latter agreed to forfeit certain liberties in exchange for basic rights to life, liberty, and property. Among the founders, Benjamin Franklin, Thomas Jefferson, George Washington, and James Madison "were acquainted with Montesquieu."[68] However, as Professor Russel Blaine Nye has recognized, "it is misleading to assume that eighteenth-century America was merely a reflection of eighteenth-century Britain, or Europe."[69]

Perhaps somewhat unexpectedly, several figureheads of the Enlightenment, such as Locke and Voltaire (1694–1778), held Confucian governing principles in high regard. For instance, Locke agreed that the governed have the right of rebellion, consistent with Confucian political theory. Locke reasoned that if a government failed to protect its subjects' natural rights, then those subjects had a right to revolt and establish a new ruling class.[70] The founders expressed similar convictions on how the fundamental purpose of government was to serve its people. Simultaneously, the ruling class had to check the commoners. Founders such as James Madison (1751–1836) expressed concern that ceding too much political power to the uneducated and impoverished might destabilize society from a social and political perspective.[71] Alexander Hamilton also considered that popular passion "spread like wild fire and become irresistible."[72]

The United States, guided by the founding principles set forth in its Constitution, has often been hailed as an example of modern democracy. However, the American system is not a pure democracy. The nation's president is appointed through an "indirect popular election" based on the Electoral College, rather than via a direct majority vote. The Electoral College was an innovation created by the founders to reduce the power of the general public, thereby addressing the concerns expressed by Madison and his compatriots. Under the Electoral College system, a presidential candidate who wins the popular vote is not guaranteed the keys to the White House. Instead, the president is elected through a majority of electoral votes.[73]

The role of Confucianism in the crafting of American democracy is perhaps one of the most conspicuous absences in the lists of founding influences. Evidence suggests that the Founding Fathers frequently drew on Confucian political philosophy when crafting a new and unique American political system. Noah Webster (1758–1843), known as the father of American scholarship and education, went so far as to proclaim Confucianism as one of the most influential forces in the development of the U.S. Constitution.[74]

In this section, I will examine how the founders introduced Confucian ideas of government in their creation of a new political institution in the United States. I will provide a brief overview of Confucian philosophies regarding government, and then discuss Benjamin Franklin's political theory and the founders' efforts to apply Confucian principles in their creation of a new government system.

An Introduction to Confucian Governing Ideas

Confucius (551–479 BC) was a Chinese philosopher, teacher, and political figure whose works were posthumously installed as the nation's official philosophy during the Han dynasty (206–220 AD). One of the guiding principles of Confucianism was that moral cultivation should originate from the leader of a nation. Remarkably, given the violent nature of his time, Confucius believed that rulers should govern subjects through education and personal example rather than through force. Confucius also maintained that government should exist for the people; between the ruler and his people, the latter was viewed as the more precious and important.[75]

Confucius believed that a ruler's good virtue was the primary prerequisite for leadership. Virtue, pronounced in Chinese as "*dé*," was seen as a moral force that enabled rulers to gain the loyalty of others without physical coercion.[76] As Confucius noted, "Lead them by means of regulations and keep order among them through punishments, and the people will evade them and will lack any sense of shame. Lead them through moral force [*dé*] and keep order among them through rites ['*li*'], and they will have a sense of shame and will also correct themselves."[77] Confucius stated, "If the rulers lived by the highest principles, the people would then follow, and there would be reform from the greatest to the least."[78] The virtuous ruler was analogous to a "polestar" around which the lesser stars would orbit.[79]

Notably, Confucius taught the democratic principle that sovereign rule originated from the people.[80] He compared the ruler to a boat and the people to water: "Water can carry the boat, and it can upset the boat."[81] In other words, the ruler's right to govern was made possible through the consent of the people. Yet Confucius also believed that the moral character of the ruler had a sure and inevitable effect on his subjects. The moral power of the ruler could be represented as the wind, and the people as the grass: wherever the wind blew, the grass would be sure to bend.[82]

In addition, Confucius opposed the misuse of official positions to enrich oneself. He said, "To act with an eye to personal profit will incur ... resentment."[83] One of his foundational tenets was that leaders should set moral examples. He said, "Exemplary persons [junzi] understand what is appropriate; petty persons understand what is of personal advantage."[84] As Confucius further explained:

> Wealth and honor are what people want, but if they are the consequence of deviating from the way [dao], I would have no part of them. Poverty and disgrace are what people deplore, but if they are the consequence of staying on the way, I would not avoid them. Wherein do the exemplary persons [junzi] who would abandon their authoritative conduct [ren] warrant that name? Exemplary persons do not take leave of their authoritative conduct even for the space of a meal. When they are troubled, they certainly turn to it, as they do in facing difficulties.[85]

Finally, Confucius also helped pioneer the concept of meritocracy, the notion that the selection of a ruler should be based on talent, effort, and achievement rather than heredity or wealth. The modern concept of political meritocracy is based on this framework, demanding first that political leaders are capable and virtuous, and second that such individuals are elected as governmental officials.

Having East Combining with the West—Benjamin Franklin's Political Theory

The Founding Fathers were heavily influenced by the European Enlightenment, which demarcated a dramatic shift in Western thought.[86] Confucian principles had a meaningful impact on the Enlightenment and, by extension, the formation of the American political system.

Since the introduction of Confucianism into the West by the Jesuits in the seventeenth century, European intellectuals have advocated many of Confucius's ideals regarding ethics, social conduct, and the role of government.[87] With an increased volume of translations of Confucian classics during the Age of Enlightenment, the philosopher's principles of political meritocracy increasingly won the admiration of the European intellectuals, who encouraged the adoption of the Confucian system.[88] Voltaire and François Quesnay (1694–1774) were two such intellectuals: Voltaire claimed that Confucius created "perfected moral science" while Quesnay advocated an economic and political system modeled after Confucianism.[89] The Enlightenment intellectuals' emphasis on "reason and virtue," influenced by Confucianism, spread across the Atlantic Ocean and reached the American colonies during the first half of the eighteenth century.[90]

It was around this period that Benjamin Franklin, unsatisfied with the corruption of the British government, formulated his theory for transforming the Western political system. For Franklin, the ideal political system was one that combined Confucian government principles with Western social traditions. Franklin described his theory in a letter to George Whitefield (1714–1770), a well-known Christian minister during the Great Awakening, in which he summarized the government-led Confucian social progress model with the masses-initiated Western one:

> I am glad to hear that you have frequent opportunities of preaching among the great. If you can gain them to a good and exemplary life, wonderful changes will follow in the manners of the lower ranks; for, ad Exemplum Regis, &c. On this principle Confucius, the famous eastern reformer, proceeded. When he saw his country sunk in vice, and wickedness of all kinds triumphant, he applied himself first to the grandees; and having by his doctrine won them to the cause of virtue, the commons followed in multitudes. The mode has a wonderful influence on mankind; and there are numbers that perhaps fear less the being in Hell, than

out of the fashion! Our more western reformations began with the ignorant mob; and when numbers of them were gained, interest and party-views drew in the wise and great. Where both methods can be used, reformations are like to be more speedy. O that some method could be found to make them lasting! He that shall discover that, will, in my opinion, deserve more, ten thousand times, than the inventor of the longtitude.[91]

In his letter, Franklin expressed three points that would have a meaningful impact on the nascent American political system. First, Franklin believed leaders should be the "cause of virtue." Second, Franklin recognized that the modes of social progress were different between the East and West; the former was characterized by good government and the latter by "the ignorant mob." Finally, combining the Western mode of social progress with Eastern governing traditions was essential to political progress. The interplay of these three points, which served as the foundation of Franklin's theory, is illustrated (figure 6.1):

In the East, social progress was achieved through the elite leading the masses—in Franklin's words, the wise and great (cause of virtue) would lead the commons (ignorant mobs) to social progress. This dynamic was reversed in the West, where the commons pushed the wise and great to social progress. John Adams shared Franklin's opinion on Western social progress: "The most Atheistical Philosophers of France and of Europe encouraged in secret this engine to work upon popular Credulity and excite popular passions."[92]

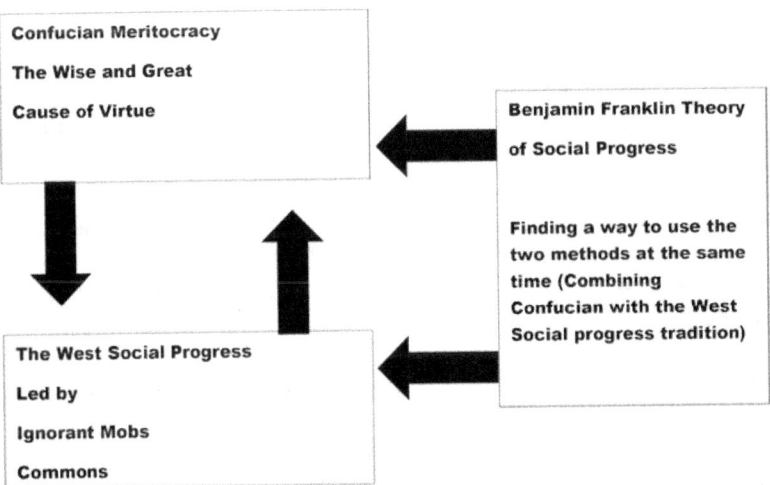

Figure 6.1 Benjamin Franklin's Theory Chart. Source: Created by author.

Franklin viewed neither mode as complete in itself. A combination of the two would create a superior framework. Practically speaking, Franklin's theory emphasized the importance of three elements. The first was a strong central government. In addition, leaders in the central government should be virtuous examples for the public to follow. Finally, the power dynamic between the government and public should be controlled by a system of checks and balances.

Franklin's references to Confucian principles of government were unsurprising. This Founding Father had long been familiar with the Chinese philosopher's teachings. For example, a decade earlier in his widely circulated *Pennsylvania Gazette*, Franklin had proclaimed his favoritism of Confucius's teachings as requirements for colonial leaders:

> His will inclining only to good, his soul will be entirely rectified, there will not be any passion that can make him destroy his rectitude: The soul being thus rectified, he will be employed in his exterior, nothing will be observed in his person that can offend complaisance. His person being thus perfected, his family, forming it fell according to this model, will be reformed and amended. His family being arrived at this perfection, twill serve as an example to all the subjects of the particular kingdoms and the members of the of the particular Kingdoms to all those that compose the body of the empire. Thus the whole empire. Thus the whole empire will be well governed and justice will reign: we shall there enjoy a profound peace, twill be a happy and flourishing empire.[93]

Confucius taught that the leaders should shoulder responsibility for the actions and welfare of their people. As he described, "the famine of my people is my own famine. My people's sin is my own sin."[94] Franklin similarly espoused the importance of good virtue. At the Constitutional Convention of 1787, he emphasized the significance of virtue in government to fellow delegates:

> Much of the Strength and Efficiency of any Government in procuring and securing Happiness to the People depends on Opinion, on the general Opinion of the Goodness of that Government as well as of the Wisdom and Integrity of its Governors.[95]

Franklin ardently believed that moral citizenry was necessary for a healthy society and held himself responsible for instilling virtue in the nation's youth. He believed that a populace's wisdom and virtue were more important than its military and financial success. As in times of weak government, situations of excessive military and wealth could lead to sociopolitical instability. In this sense, a few virtuous leaders could hold sway over huge masses. Franklin wrote:

> Nothing is of more importance for the public weal, than to form and train up youth in wisdom and virtue. Wise and good men are, in my opinion, the *strength* of a state: much more so than riches or arms, which, under the management of Ignorance and Wickedness, often draw on destruction, instead of providing for the safety of a people. And though the culture bestowed on *many* should be successful only with a *few*, yet the influence of those few and the service in their power, may be very great.[96]

Franklin also appreciated the importance of checks and balances to discourage misbehavior in both leaders and the general public. Such measures were meant to counteract human nature, as Franklin believed government was derived "not from a voluntary human contract, but from human weakness and necessities."[97]

Franklin resided in England from 1757 to 1762 and 1764 to 1775 as colonial representative for Pennsylvania, Georgia, New Jersey, and Massachusetts, during which he began to formulate his theory of ideal government. Franklin underwent a "political metamorphosis" in London.[98] In particular, he began to lose confidence in the British Parliament during this time. This was partly due to his realization that the British courts represented a departure from the Confucian virtues that he held in high regard. Franklin's previously conservative attitudes began to align more closely with the radicalism of the American revolutionaries, and he would eventually become a stalwart patriot and one of the key founders of the United States.

Franklin would express his concerns about the colonial government on the eve of the American Revolution. He had witnessed many poor colonial governors. As he had also lost faith in Great Britain's political system, he found little guidance from across the Atlantic.[99] In a letter dated September 1769, two decades after he had first elaborated on his theory of government, Franklin pointed out that without proper governance, "sending soldiers to Boston always appeared . . . a dangerous step [for Great Britain]; [the soldiers] could do no good, they might occasion mischief." However, Franklin recognized that the colonies also bore their share of responsibility for conflicts with Mother England; its affairs were often poorly managed by local rulers.[100]

The colonists' struggle for independence encouraged Franklin's hope that the American Revolution would provide a catalyst for a superior system of government. In 1777, Franklin stated regarding the Revolution, "it is a common observation here that our cause is the cause of all mankind, and that we are fighting for their liberty in defending our own."[101]

The following year, Franklin admonished his fellow Americans that "only a virtuous people are capable of freedom. As nations became corrupt and vicious, they need masters."[102] He emphasized the importance of a virtuous government for the new nation:

> What the political struggle I have been engag'd in for the good of my compatriots, inhabitants of this bush; or my philosophical studies for the benefits of our race in general! For in politics, what can laws do without morals? Our present race of ephemeras will in a course of minutes become corrupt like those of other and older Bushes, and consequently as wretched.[103]

In summary, Franklin recognized the importance of introducing Confucian principles during the formative years of the United States. His political theory was an amalgamation of the East and West with the former based on Confucian political theories regarding effective government.

Using Confucian Meritocracy to Check European Aristocratic Inheritance

Franklin found an opportunity to guide the new sociopolitical environment in the United States toward certain Confucian ideals of good government. He appreciated the unprecedented nature of his situation, claiming "It is a singular Thing in the History of Mankind, that a great People have had the Opportunity of forming a Government for themselves."[104]

Several conflicts within the fledgling United States began to resurface following the cessation of hostilities, occupying the attention of the Founding Fathers. About 6,000 loyalists moved to Canada, with some starting insurgencies such as Shay's Rebellion in 1786. By the mid-1780s, the new nation threatened to collapse only several years after it had gained independence. Many states were roiled by social conflicts between the wealthy and the commoners, often over financial issues of credit. The country was divided religiously, with significant populations of Anglicans, Roman Catholics, Calvinists, Huguenots, Lutherans, Quakers, Jews, agnostics, and atheists. The country faced socioeconomic stratification as well from the landed aristocracy to indentured servants.[105] George Washington remarked that the thirteen states were united only "by a rope of sand."[106]

During this time, delegates at the Second Continental Congress (1775–1781) and Confederation Congress (1781–1788) were unable to achieve consensus on how the nation should be governed and what powers the individual states ought to retain. The founders were anxious to create a system of government that could sustain the nation through the ages.

Regarding the nation's new government, some revolutionaries were convinced that it was within the nation's best interest to establish a system resembling European monarchy.[107] In a similar vein, some Revolutionary War veterans sought to establish a hereditary aristocracy in order to "distinguish themselves and their posterity from their fellow citizens." In 1784, these veterans formed an order of hereditary knights and organized the Society of Cincinnatus.[108]

Franklin used this opportunity to introduce Confucian meritocracy. Based on these principles, Franklin decried the members of the Society of Cincinnatus as directly opposing the "solemnly declared Sense of their Country." Instead, Franklin posited the Confucian system of meritocracy to the new nation:

> Thus among the Chinese, the most antient, and, from long Experience, the wisest of Nations, Honour does not *descend* but *ascends*. If a Man from his Learning, his Wisdom or his Valour, is promoted by the Emperor to the Rank of Mandarin, his Parents are immediately intitled to all the same Ceremonies of Respect from the People, that are establish'd as due to the Mandarin himself; on this Supposition, that it must have been owing to the Education, Instruction, and good Example afforded him by his Parents that he was rendered capable of Serving the Publick. This *ascending Honour* is therefore useful to the State as it encourages Parents to give their Children a good and virtuous Education. But the *descending Honour*, to Posterity who could have had no Share in obtaining it, is not only groundless and absurd, but often hurtful to that Posterity, since it is apt to make them proud, disdaining to be employed in useful Arts, and thence falling into Poverty and all the Meannesses, Servility and Wretchedness attending it; which is the present case with much of what is called the *Noblesse* in Europe.[109]

John Adams, John Jay (1745–1829), Thomas Jefferson (1743–1826), and other founders supported these meritocratic ideas. They condemned the Cincinnati Society "as an attempt to establish hereditary nobility in the American Republic."[110] Jefferson revealed to Washington that his stay in Europe had convinced him that the Society of Cincinnati was a real threat to American government. He said, "because it would produce an hereditary aristocracy—not in his lifetime, perhaps, but eventually; it would change the form of American governments from the best to the worst in the world."[111] In 1784, Washington echoed that "unless the grounds of popular complaint were eliminated," the Society of Cincinnatus should be terminated.[112]

Confucian meritocracy was influential among other founders. Alexander Hamilton (1757–1804), known to be foreign born and illegitimate, had risen to a position of prominence in the United States when he would have otherwise "[languished] in obscurity" across the Atlantic.[113] Hamilton's political viewpoints were well respected and debated among the founders. He was regarded as a symbol of how meritocracy could triumph over European aristocratic tradition.[114] Jefferson had realized that the aristocracy "could not long maintain its high sense of public obligation on its existing foundation. The trouble was that it was based, not on merit, but on inherited privilege."[115]

Using Virtue to Check Public Officials

The American Founding Fathers were faced with justifying the doctrine of popular sovereignty as the basis of their new government. During the colonial era, the founders had leveraged this doctrine to rally the colonists against the British. In the aftermath of the war, the founders sought to balance the principles of popular rule while simultaneously maintaining a stable government that would preserve the rights and liberties of its citizens.[116] The Constitutional Convention, held in Philadelphia from May to September 1787, was intended to craft such a government for a nation that had been built by its people. Franklin seized the opportunity at this convention to advance the political theory that he had developed.

Since returning to America in 1785, Franklin had devoted himself to laying the foundation of the new nation's government. Just before he reached Philadelphia for the Constitutional Convention, Franklin received a letter from Charles de Butré, then the secretary of the Society of Agriculture of Strasbourg and one of the most important collaborators of the physiocrat workshops. In this letter, de Butré referenced China as an example for Franklin during this critical juncture: the United States should "read its laws drawn by its plows; like yao, chum, and yu, had taken them there in China over 40 centuries ago or they still exist, and will last as long as the centuries since they conform to eternal decrees which are unalterable."[117]

Franklin was one of the most influential members of the convention. If his health permitted, Franklin might have been the only delegate other than George Washington in consideration to serve as chair of the convention.[118] Despite being eighty-one years old and facing fragile health, Franklin worked tirelessly for over four months to secure the fruits of the revolution, bringing crucial strengths and perspectives as the oldest member of the party. He described the significance of failure during the convention as such: "Mankind may hereafter, from this unfortunate instance, despair of establishing government by human wisdom, and leave it to Chance, War and Conquest."[119]

To illustrate effective government, Franklin contrasted the state government of Massachusetts with that of Pennsylvania. Franklin was alarmed by the dangerous Shay's Rebellion in the former state. His reaction was consistent with the Confucian principle that effective governments would guarantee their citizens against revolution.[120] In contrast to that of Massachusetts, the Pennsylvania government was well organized with a prudent system of checks and balances. The Pennsylvania government was characterized by two parties, one for "preserving the Constitution as it was, and the other for adding an upper house as a check to the Assembly."[121]

Franklin acknowledged that although the Convention did not seek to establish a kingdom for the new nation, there was a "natural Inclination in Mankind to Kingly Government." [122] For example, Alexander Hamilton and others had recommended a single executive appointed for life. Franklin opposed, contending that because the government of the United States "derives all its powers directly or indirectly from the great body of the people," its president should hold office for a limited rather than permanent period. James Madison echoed Franklin's sentiment, claiming that "an elective despotism was not the government we fought for."[123]

Franklin cautioned fellow citizens that the way to delay the "catastrophe" of monarchy was to establish government positions as "Posts of Honor."[124] He also emphasized the importance of virtue. If men lacking good virtue were put in "a [Post] of *Honor*," they would make their positions "a Place of *Profit*."[125] Franklin believed that immoral persons had ruined the British government by making it "so tempestuous."[126] The struggles for various British government positions were "the true Source of all those Factions which are perpetually dividing the Nation, distracting its Councils, hurrying it sometimes into fruitless, and mischievous Wars, and often compelling a Submission to dishonorable Terms of Peace."[127] With his overseas experiences in mind, Franklin was determined in his crafting of early American government that "The first man at the helm will be a good one."[128]

Throughout the convention, Franklin consistently emphasized the importance of good virtue for the leaders of the new nation. He would note to other delegates that ambition and avarice were the "two passions which have a powerful influence on the affairs of men"; the combination of these two traits might produce "the most violent effects."[129] Franklin cautioned that if individuals with such traits were in positions of power, they might "perpetually [divide] the nation, [distract] its councils, [hurry] sometimes into fruitless & mischievous wars, and often [compel] a submission to dishonorable terms of peace."[130] As Franklin noted:

> It will not be the wise and moderate, the lovers of peace and good order, the men fittest for the trust. It will be the bold and the violent, the men of strong passions and indefatigable activity in their selfish pursuits. These will thrust themselves into your Government and be your rulers. And these too will be mistaken in the expected happiness of their situation: For their vanquished competitors of the same spirit, and from the same motives will perpetually be endeavouring to

distress their administration, thwart their measures, and render them odious to the people.[131]

The Constitutional Convention of 1788, held with these principles in mind, sought to design a centralized national government with the authority to oversee a federation of states.

Using the Electoral College to Check the Populace

The founders distrusted strong central government from their own experiences with the British. However, they appreciated that the new government needed the authority to enforce its edicts over a diverse federation of states. Confronted with meaningful social, political, and economic disorder in the wake of the revolution, the founders reached a consensus in early 1787 to amend the Articles of Confederation in favor of a more centralized system.

At the convention, representatives considered several methods to elect the president. Such proposals included direct popular election, selection by one of Congress, the governors of the states, state legislatures, or a special group of members of Congress chosen by lot. One such proposal was James Madison's Virginia Plan, which proposed that a "National Executive be chosen by the National Legislature for the terms of years." Franklin opposed the Virginia Plan, believing it to be a violation of the separation of power: a system in which the National Legislature participated in the election of another branch would ensure that the elected executive be heavily swayed by the interests of that electoral branch.

In lieu of Madison's Virginia Plan, the founders devised a system in which each state received presidential "electors" equal to the number of its senators and congressional representatives. These electors, chosen by whatever means each state decided, would each vote for two men. The candidate with the majority of electoral votes became president, while the second-place finisher became vice president. This structure was noted in Article II, Section 1, of the U.S. Constitution as such:

> Each State shall appoint, in such Manner as the Legislature thereof may direct, a Number of Electors, equal to the whole Number of Senators and Representatives to which the State may be entitled in the Congress: but no Senator or Representative, or Person holding an Office of Trust or Profit under the United States, shall be appointed an Elector.[132]

This system, to be known as the Electoral College, was originally proposed by James Wilson (1742–1798). Wilson was selected to be one of six delegates who reported the final document for acceptance, an honor in recognition of his role as one of the proposal's chief architects. Although Wilson had promoted the idea that the committee meet in secret, there was enough reason to believe that Franklin was involved in the plan given the close relationship that the two had shared.[133] At the convention, Wilson acted as Franklin's speaker; it is possible that Franklin had his ideas transmitted by James Wilson among the delegates. On the last day of the convention, September 17, 1787, Franklin had Wilson read his final speech to the audience. Immediately after ratification, the College of Philadelphia, founded by Franklin, hired James Wilson to give a series of lectures explaining and analyzing the Constitution. In 1790, Wilson received an honorary LLD degree from the College of Philadelphia and became its first professor of law. In 1906, President Theodore Roosevelt had Wilson's casket carried to Philadelphia and buried next to Franklin's (figure 6.2).[134]

The president was selected by the Electoral College, which was "originally composed of electors selected by methods left up to the various state legislature."[135] The Electoral College reflected a compromise between the Enlightenment ideal that the "nation should govern itself" and the necessity of having a system of checks and balances. The establishment of the Electoral College reflected how Franklin and other delegates did not fully trust the population to elect the most capable candidate. Franklin hoped that

Figure 6.2 Franklin and His Friends at the Constitutional Convention. Allyn Cox: The Constitutional Convention, oil on canvas mural by Allyn Cox, 1973–1974; in the House of Representatives wing of the U.S. Capitol building, depicting (from left) Alexander Hamilton, James Wilson, James Madison, and Benjamin Franklin.

the chosen electors would be able to ensure that the most qualified person became president. James Madison advocated for Franklin's position, stating, "A dependence on the people is, no doubt, the primary control on the government; but experience has taught mankind the necessity of auxiliary precautions."[136] Madison hoped to minimize the abuses of majority rule.[137] For Madison, the entire point of political representation is "to refine and enlarge the public views, by passing them through the medium of a chosen body of citizens, whose wisdom may best discern the true interest of their country, and whose patriotism and love of justice, will be least likely to sacrifice it to temporary or partial considerations."[138] He also reasoned that "it may well happen that the public voice pronounced by the representatives of the people, will be more consonant to the public good, than if pronounced by the people themselves convened for the purpose."[139] Alexander Hamilton also reiterated that the genuine selection of the president should be made

> by men most capable of analyzing the qualities adapted to the station, and acting under circumstances favourable to deliberation and to a judicious combination of all the reasons and inducements, which were proper to govern their choice. A small number of persons, selected by their fellow citizens from the general mass, will be most likely to possess the information and discernment requisite to so complicated an investigation.[140]

By 1787, many of the founders were similarly realistic about the importance of relying on institutional checks rather than on individual virtue as the most effective means of maintaining liberty.[141]

The Electoral College reflected Franklin's theory of combining Eastern with Western influences. As Franklin expressed to la Rochefoucauld, the new nation presented an opportunity to experiment in politics.[142] Franklin warned that for those who still clung to Western traditions, the introduction of new cultural elements was "natural and unavoidable."[143] Franklin worked to communicate the merits of various non-Western influences to various representatives, and advised that the proposed Constitution would lead the nation to be "well administered for a Course of Years."[144]

Carl Van Doren declared that Franklin "was the author of the compromise which held the delegates together" in July 1787.[145] Throughout the convention, Franklin had helped lay the foundation for the democratic republic that the Constitution would enshrine.[146] As one of the most influential members of the Constitutional Convention, Franklin helped draft the Constitution and create the Electoral College. As such, he was called Sage of the Constitutional Convention, and the ratification of the Constitution was described as his "great victory in the Convention."[147]

John Adams Agreed with Confucian Principles: The Purpose of the Government Was to Serve the People

John Adams served in London as an ambassador during the Constitutional Convention of 1787, so he did not have as direct an impact on the drafting of the Constitution. However, Adams influenced the formation of U.S. government through his political writings. Two examples of such writings were "Thoughts on Government" (1776) and *A Defense of the Constitutions of the United States of America* (1778), which helped develop the principles of American government that Franklin, Madison, and other delegates applied at the 1787 Constitutional Convention. Adams was an ardent supporter of the new Constitution.[148]

Adams, one of the premier American political minds, often referred to Confucian philosophies regarding government during the formative period of the new nation's political system. Adams was known to discuss the nature and application of Confucian governmental principles. He was unsatisfied with the English translations of Confucius and would instead read the original Latin translations.[149] In 1808, he confessed to his fellow founders that "Having named Voltaire I may now explain my long silence. For three or four months I have been in company with such great Personages as Moses, Zoroaster, Sanchuniathon, Confucius, Numa, Mahomet and others of that Rank."[150]

Adams believed that in determining the means of government, the United States ought to first consider the ends. He noted that throughout history, "all Divines and moral Philosophers will agree that the happiness of the individual is the end of man." From his perspective, the best system of government would be that which brought "happiness to the greatest number of persons, and in the greatest degree." He continued that humans "ancient and modern, Pagan and Christian, have declared that the happiness of man, as well as his dignity consists in virtue. Confucius, Zoroaster, Socrates, Mahomet, not to mention authorities really sacred, have agreed in this."[151]

Like Franklin, Adams agreed with the Confucian principle that "the wise and brave" should be the leaders of the nation. For Adams, a simple, perfect democracy "had never yet existed."[152] Adams reasoned,

> In a large society, inhabiting an extensive country, it is impossible that the whole should assemble, to make laws: The first necessary step then, is, to depute power from the many, to a few of the most wise and good.[153]

Adams also emphasized the importance of virtue in a republic: "the dignity and stability of government in all its branches, the morals of the people and every blessing of society, depends so much upon an upright and skillful administration of justice."[154]

In early January 1787, Adams had rushed the first installment of his efforts, titled *A Defence of the Constitutions of Government of the United States of America*, to a London printer. In addition to supporting Franklin's call for virtuous leaders to oversee the new nation, Adams attempted to devise systems to check the balance of power between rulers and commoners. Adams was wary of pure democracy, warning that such systems might lead to disaster:

> There never was a Democracy Yet, that did not commit suicide. It is in vain to Say that Democracy is less vain, less proud, less selfish, less ambitious or less avaricious than Aristocracy or Monarchy. It is not true in Fact and no where appears in history. Those Passions are the same in all Men under all forms of Simple Government, and when unchecked, produce the same Effects of Fraud Violence and Cruelty.[155]

Notably, other founders such as James Madison agreed with Adams. Madison claimed,

> Pure democracies have ever been spectacles of turbulence and contention; have ever been found incompatible with personal security, or the rights of property; and have, in general, been as short in their lives as they have been violent in their deaths.[156]

These founders viewed unchecked democracy as akin to mob rule and questioned the ability of such masses to collectively make informed decisions.

In conclusion, John Adams and James Madison shared Benjamin Franklin's respect for Confucian governing principles, specifically with respect to the purpose of government and the importance of virtuous leaders.

Jefferson Used Confucian Political Virtue to Help Him Establish Cultural Independence

Jefferson declared cultural independence from Great Britain on more than one occasion. The poems he gathered from American newspapers reveal his distaste for the English monarchy.[157] Although Jefferson was in France serving as minister for the United States when the Constitution was drafted in 1787, he was able to influence the development of the federal government through his correspondence with his fellow founders. Franklin "advanced many of the positions that the younger Virginian likely would have championed."[158] Like John Adams, Jefferson was delighted to learn the achievement of the convention. He recalled in his autobiography that he "received a copy [of the Constitution] early in November, and read and contemplated its provisions with great satisfaction."[159]

Jefferson preferred republican government.[160] In his *Notes on the State of Virginia*, published in Europe in 1785, Jefferson spent a great deal of time pondering constitutional issues. While in Paris prior to the Constitutional Convention, Jefferson closely followed developments in the United States and corresponded with facilitators such as James Madison, a fellow driving force behind the 1787 Constitutional Convention and an author of the Federalist Papers.[161]

One of Jefferson's most important contributions to the formation of American democratic institutions was his promotion of Confucian moral values for the leaders. Jefferson aspired to be the type of virtuous leader that Confucius held on a pedestal—despite having already established himself as one of the principal Founding Fathers who would eventually be elected the nation's third president.[162] Jefferson was so influenced by the Confucian emphasis on virtue that during his presidency he included an ancient Chinese poem, edited by Confucius, in his personal scrapbook.[163]

The poem praised an ancient Chinese prince whom Confucius used as an example for other leaders. Jefferson's inclusion of this specific Chinese poem provides evidence for his positive attitudes toward Confucian ideals.[164] The poem was taken from the *Great Learning*, which has been called a *Handbook on Good Government* or *Instructions to Rulers*.[165]

In the same period as when he preserved this poem in his scrapbook, Jefferson created a personal Bible that was partially inspired by Confucian morals. He titled this personal Bible *The Life and Morals of Jesus of Nazareth*. This name likely referenced *The Morals of Confucius*, a popular book among the European intellectuals that was published in 1689.[166] Jefferson created this Bible to save passages that he believed would best represent Jesus as a moral person.[167] In a letter to Charles Thomson, Jefferson described how he would cut certain texts out of the Bible and rearrange them in a blank book, ordered by time or subject. Jefferson would proudly describe this arrangement as "a more beautiful or precious morsel of ethics I have never seen."[168]

A separate poem from Jefferson's scrapbook reveals his attitude toward Confucian meritocracy and the church. The poem disparaged the church as the place where human wisdom and virtue were destroyed. Interestingly, this assertion was juxtaposed with meritocracy: "Merit [never] yet found favor with the Church."[169]

For Jefferson—who tired of metaphysics—Confucianism was an appealing, practical doctrine that advanced private virtue. His acceptance of Confucianism was consistent with his general religious beliefs. On the one hand, Jefferson rejected some forms of organized religion and certain of its doctrines. On the other, he embraced several of Christianity's moral precepts. As Jefferson expressed to his fellow Americans, "A nation as a society forms a moral person, and every member of it is personally responsible for his society."[170]

Jefferson realized the importance of Confucian moral philosophy in creating a sound and progressive government infrastructure for the United States. He made his efforts to affirm government as "an affirmative obligation to promote the conditions under which the truly meritorious, from all ranks of society, could rise."[171] Jefferson was confident that the new political institutions created by the founders would appropriately serve the new nation. In front of the representatives celebrating his [presidential] victory, Jefferson made the following statement regarding the American government system and good virtues: "inculcating honesty, truth, temperance, gratitude and the love of man, acknowledging and adoring an overruling providence" the new nation would have great future and the Americans would be "a happy and a prosperous people."[172]

Summary

During the American Revolution, Benjamin Franklin formulated his theory of combining Confucian political ideas with the traditions of Western social progress. His main role in the making of the Constitution was evidenced by the fact that when General Washington arrived in Philadelphia on May 13, 1787, "his first act was to pay a call on Franklin."[173] Franklin had an unprecedented opportunity to apply this theory during the formation of the U.S. government. Franklin was able to translate and combine Confucian political ideas with the Western tradition of social progress into political reality. His theory of social progress was possibly the vital guide in composing the Constitution. Several other founders were similarly inspired by the revival of Confucian principles during the European Enlightenment. They drew upon the Chinese philosopher's ideas to craft a novel and sound political system for the fledgling nation. Franklin would become regarded as "the most influential in investing the type of society America would become" because of his role in formulating the American Constitution.[174]

Indisputable evidence shows that the founders took Confucian political ideas to shape the American political system. Benjamin Franklin, John Adams, and Thomas Jefferson were the staunchest advocates of Confucian principles of political meritocracy. Together, these founders labored to introduce Confucian governing principles to the new nation. As part of a collective effort, Franklin formulated the theory of combining Confucian governing principles with the Western mode of social progress. Adams focused on Confucian ideals regarding the purpose of government. Jefferson espoused the importance of virtuous leaders. Through the founders' efforts, Confucian political ideas joined the intellectual force of European Enlightenment to reform public institutions, thereby laying a foundational basis for American democracy.

These founders' understanding of Confucian ideas was ahead of its time. Franklin's theory would help guide the founders in creating a stable government. Based on Franklin's theory and drawing from Enlightenment principles, the founders crafted new political mechanisms such as the Electoral College and the separation of power among three branches of government. The founders also set forth a tradition of meritocracy that would become a cornerstone of the American political system. In this way, the founders' regard for and application of Franklin's theory helped spread Confucian principles into American democracy.

Taking a step back, one might wonder why the founders turned to Confucius at all. A significant reason was that the founders sought to establish cultural independence from England following the American War of Independence. They were worried that Europeans would continue to "seek to exploit America" for their own advantage, an anxiety that spurred efforts to devise a sound form of government.[175] In Thomas Jefferson's words, in order to better establish itself as a distinct entity, the United States would need to "fall off the parent stem."[176] John Adams also expressed his dislike of British character. He wrote, "I Said I was not a British Subject: that I had renounced that Character many years ago, forever, and that I Should rather be a Fugitive in China or Malabar, than ever reassume that Character."[177]

At the Constitutional Convention, Franklin explained to the delegates why the new nation could benefit from Confucian governing wisdom. He told his fellow representatives,

> We indeed seem to feel our own Want of political Wisdom, since we have been running all about in search of it. We have gone back to ancient History for Models of Government, and examin'd the different forms of those Republicks, which, having been originally form'd with the Seeds of their own Dissolution, now no longer exist. And we have view'd modern States all round Europe, but find none of their constitutions suitable to our circumstances.[178]

Among the key founders, Franklin was not alone in his desire to look beyond Western traditions of government. Both Adams and Jefferson had concluded that Britain was "too far gone in corruption to be seen with anything but suspicious and hostility."[179] As Jefferson stated:

> I confess then I can neither see what Cicero, Cato &. Brutus, united and uncontrouled, could have devised to lead their people into good government, nor how this aenigma can be solved, nor how further shewn. why it has been the fate of that delightful country never to have known to this day & through a course of

five & twenty hundred years, the history of which we possess one single day of free & rational government.[180]

Furthermore, one might wonder why descriptions of Confucian influences on the foundation of the American democratic system tend to be absent from history books and classrooms. As Adams noted, Confucian political ideas were still too foreign for the general populace. If a person quoted Confucius in an argument, he would be "ridiculed and abused."[181] In the colonial era, John Bartram was disavowed by the Quakers after he wrote the biography of Confucius in 1758.[182]

Franklin and Jefferson may have privately shared his sentiment that "pure and simple deism" was the best religion for the fledgling republic. But they were reluctant to publish incendiary materials in a devoutly Christian America.[183]

As a result, the founders used alternative terms for Confucian ideas. They made great efforts to find similar ideas from Western works that conveyed Confucian political ideas. It was with originality that Jefferson cut his Bible to reframe passages on morality. Adams would separately use the book of Revelation to promote Christian ideas, stating,

> It has been usual with zealous men, to ridicule and abuse all those who dare on this point, to quote the Chinese Philosopher; but instead of supporting their cause; they would Shake it if it could be shaken by their uncandid Asperity; for they ought to remember, that one great end of Revelation, as it is most expressly declared, was not to instruct the wise and few, but the many and unenlightened.[184]

John Adams, Thomas Jefferson, and James Madison cited Montesquieu and Blackstone as authorities to justify certain arrangements and procedures that they favored in the making of the American political system.

The formulation of the American Constitution "was a matter of doctrine, ideas, and comprehension."[185] With the help of Confucian governing ideas, the great concert of the founders created the foundation of the great and unique American political system. George Washington acclaimed that the constitution "is the best Constitution that can be obtained in this Epocha."[186] Upon seeing that great and unique political institution born in the meeting between the East and West, Benjamin Franklin had tears streaming down his face at the conclusion of the Constitutional Convention.[187]

CONFUCIAN MERIT SYSTEM AND AMERICAN CIVIL SERVICE REFORM

Most Western countries have adopted some form of the Confucian merit system, one of China's greatest contributions to modern democracy. Despite now being one of the cultural icons of the West, the United States adopted the Confucian system later than many of its European peers.[188] It was only in 1884 that Congress passed the Pendleton Act, alternatively known as the Civil Service Reform Act, which initiated a long-overdue reform of the U.S. civil service system. The passage of the Pendleton Act marked the U.S. federal government's embracement of the Confucian merit system.

Although the passage of the Pendleton Act represented the first time the Confucian system gained legal credence within the United States, it was not the first time such a change had been suggested. About a century earlier, Benjamin Franklin had proposed that the fledging nation look to the ancient Chinese merit system for selecting public servants. Unfortunately for Franklin, the nineteenth century marked the rise of cronyism and nepotism within the U.S. government in a period that became notoriously known as the Century of Corruption. Until reform efforts began in 1884, it was the norm for government representatives to exchange public office positions for fees and bribes.[189]

This section explores some of the reasons the United States went full circle on its stance regarding the Confucian merit-based system of electing civil servants. It will address Benjamin Franklin's original proposal and why it was neglected, the state of government and bureaucracy in the United States prior to 1884, and why the United States ultimately revisited Franklin's plan after nearly a century of neglect.

Benjamin Franklin and the Chinese Merit System, 1784

During the 1780s, the founders of the young American republic faced the tremendous challenge of creating a stable political system to preserve their hard-earned national independence. Soon after the conclusion of the War for Independence, the Founding Fathers realized that the election of capable public servants would be one of the major factors that determined the destiny of their new nation. Many of the founders believed that the ideal government official would not only have a strong educational background but also display exemplary moral virtue.[190]

However, this sentiment was not shared by all citizens. In particular, some veterans of the War for Independence sought to establish certain systems that would enable them to pass their honors to their descendants. In 1783, these veterans organized the Society of Cincinnati to counter the prevailing beliefs of the founders.[191] Franklin had been aware of the Society of the Cincinnati since at least mid-December, when Pierre-Charles L'Enfant (1754–1825), a French American military engineer, arrived in Paris to deliver George Washington's letters and began to create a French branch. In March, Lafayette would inform George Washington that "most of the Americans Here are indecently Violent Against our Association. . . . Doctor Franklin Said little. But Jay, Adams, and all the others warmly Blame the Army."[192]

Benjamin Franklin expressed uneasiness with the society's desire to mimic the European hereditary tradition by forming "an order of hereditary knights."[193] Franklin warned that the people who made the recommendation realized that it was not right to "distinguish themselves and their Posterity from their Fellow Citizens, and form an Order of hereditary Knights." He pointed out that their idea and action were directly in "opposition to the solemnly declared Sense of their Country."[194]

Franklin drew examples from Chinese civilization to counter the European heritage-based system. Franklin believed that in China, "honour does not descend but ascends."[195] Franklin proposed that the fledging nation should look to the Chinese merit system as a model of appointing public employees. He was especially attracted to the notion that a Chinese public servant earned his position based on "his Learning, his Wisdom, or his Valour."[196] The only channel through which public servants were able to secure their jobs "must have been owing to the Education, Instruction, and good Example afforded him by his Parents that he was rendered capable of Serving the Publick."[197] He was confident that the Chinese method of selecting public employees would encourage education and moral virtue.[198]

The Chinese merit system—the first civil servant program of its kind—was designed according to Confucian political philosophy as a method of ensuring competent and sustainable governance. This system recruited government officials based on merit rather than on familial or political ties and has thus been heralded as one of the world's first democratic systems.[199] The Chinese Confucian merit system developed during a time of chaos and disunion known in Chinese history as the Six Dynasties Period (220–589 AD). This period began with the collapse of the Han dynasty (206 BC–220 AD), which left China controlled by aristocratic families on the local and state level,[200] and ended after the Sui dynasty (581–681 AD) assumed power. The Sui rulers established the merit system to reduce the prevalence of hereditary aristocratic power. The following Tang dynasty (681–907 AD) built upon the foundation of the Sui rulers by using the merit system to further curb the generational passage of power. The Tang emperors appointed individuals who passed the civil servant examinations to important positions. Officials who gained their positions through familial ties were scorned by society. Later dynasties continued to use the same civil service system to ensure that the best and brightest were selected to work for the central government.[201]

There were unsurprising parallels between the context of the development of the Chinese civil service system and the unstable period of American history when Franklin gave his proposal. Franklin's proposal was not unprecedented, for he had sought guidance from Chinese civilization in prior occasions. Franklin had circulated Confucian moral philosophy in the British colonies long before the war, most notably publishing several chapters of Confucian works in his weekly newspaper, the *Pennsylvanian Gazette*, in 1737. Franklin also regarded Confucius as his moral example.[202] As such, it was natural that Franklin sought guidance from Confucian ideals in response to the surge of European aristocratic traditions in the years following American independence (figure 6.3).

Figure 6.3 Chinese Civil Service Examination in 1590. A detail of a sixteenth-century CE painted scroll showing students taking the civil service examinations that were used to select government officials throughout the history of imperial China. Beijing Palace Museum. 棘院秉衡，余壬、吳鉞描繪，徐顯卿題詠，時年三十八至四十七，北京故宮博物院藏 《徐顯卿宦跡圖》, 1590 by Yu Ren, Wu Yue, The Official Career of Xu Xianqing, Peking Palace Museum.

Public Service Positions Should Be Reserved for Federalists: John Adams's Midnight Appointments

The role of the U.S. federal government was initially limited. The Washington administration was composed only of Secretary of State Thomas Jefferson, Secretary of the Treasury Alexander Hamilton, Secretary of War Henry Knox (1750–1806), and Attorney General Edmund Randolph (1753–1813).[203] Washington believed that only "the best qualified" should work as government officials and chose to pick most of his federal employees from within the budding Federalist Party.[204] Given the early stages of party politics within the states, Washington's pro-Federalist policy was uncontroversial. However, even with his limited government, Washington found that choosing the best civil servants was "the most difficult and delicate part" of his work.[205]

By the time John Adams succeeded George Washington as the second president of the United States, party dynamics had begun to exert greater influence on the American political sphere. As a federalist himself, Adams continued Washington's practice of appointing only Federalists to government positions. However, by 1800, the Federalist Party had suffered from irreparable internal divisions under the leadership of Alexander Hamilton.[206] Radicals in the Federalist Party accused Adams of failing to enforce the Alien & Sedition Acts, which led to the rise of Thomas Jefferson and his Democratic-Republican Party.[207] Jefferson would succeed Adams as the third president, and the Democratic-Republican Party would control both Houses of Congress as well.[208]

To the sitting lame duck Adams, president-elect Jefferson threatened the power of the Federalists. In his final days before Jefferson's inauguration on March 4, 1801, Adams took action to preserve as much of the Federalist Party as he could. He passed the Judiciary Act of 1801, which established ten new court districts, three new circuit courts, and forty-two new justices, and took immediate action to appoint Federalists to these new positions. This event would later be known as the Midnight Appointments because Adams employed his judges the night before Jefferson's inauguration.[209]

Adams's Midnight Appointments served as the precedent for selecting public employees based on political affiliations. In this way, Adams might be credited with creating the foundation of what would later be a political patronage system. However, the institutionalization of this American patronage system, later known as the spoils system, can be traced to the presidency of Thomas Jefferson.[210]

Thomas Jefferson's Response to John Adams's Midnight Appointments

President Thomas Jefferson was inaugurated on March 4, 1801; unsurprisingly, Adams did not attend his ceremony.[211] Once in power, Jefferson set out to rescind Adams's Judiciary Act of 1801 and replace the Federalist judges with supporters from his own Democratic-Republican Party. However, although Jefferson reaped many benefits from his political patronage system, he also could not help but damage his reputation permanently when he rejected a request from a job seeker who had been one of his supporters in the election.

The presidential election of 1800 had been an uphill battle for Jefferson. Adams had defeated him four years prior, so the election of 1800 was hard-fought and bitter. The Federalist and Democratic-Republican parties used newspapers and brochures to deliver both personal and political attacks toward the other. Jefferson was on the weaker side of this battlefield of propaganda—during the late 1790s, there were about thirty papers that belonged to the Democratic-Republicans, compared to about 120 that belonged to the Federalists.[212]

As a result, Jefferson had to work diligently to find other means of support.[213] It was around this time that Jefferson met James Callender (1758–1803), a writer and publisher. Callender soon became a "tireless Jeffersonian propagandist."[214] In 1792, Callender wrote a piece regarding Hamilton's adulterous affair with a colleague's wife, to which Hamilton later confessed. It was later revealed that Jefferson and his Democratic-Republican allies had secretly funded this paper.[215] Callender would prove to be a devout and skilled propagandist for Jefferson. In his paper, "The Prospect Before Us," Callender told his readers that voting for Adams was endorsing "war and beggary," whereas supporting Jefferson would enable "peace and competency." However, Callender would also pay a price for discrediting the federalists, who convicted him of sedition and sentenced him to nine months' imprisonment.[216]

Callender believed that given his contributions to the Jefferson campaign, he would be rewarded with a high-ranking government position upon Jefferson's ascendency to the White House. Callender specifically desired that Jefferson appoint him as the U.S. Postmaster for Richmond, Virginia. The position was already filled, so Callender urged Jefferson to remove the current postmaster and give him the job instead. However, when Jefferson refused Callender's request, Callender flew into rage and responded, "I now begin to know what ingratitude is."[217] He launched a series of virulent attacks against Jefferson from 1801 to 1803. He described Jefferson as a person of "dishonesty, cowardice, and gross personal immorality."[218] In the *Richmond Recorder*, Callender published "The President, Again," charging that Jefferson "keeps, and for many years past has kept, as his concubine, one of his own slaves."[219] Callender alleged that this slave was named Sally, and that her son had features that were suspiciously similar to Jefferson's own. He detailed how Sally had gone to France with Jefferson and his two daughters, claiming that "the delicacy of this arrangement must strike every person of common sensibility . . . what a sublime pattern for an American ambassador to place before the eyes of two young ladies!"[220]

Callender's accusation of Jefferson's affair with Sally would be a tremendous blow to Jefferson's political reputation.[221] There had been some local rumors circulating about such a relationship, but Callender's article turned Jefferson's adultery into a widely circulated national story.

Jefferson's refusal to offer Callender the postmaster position would have significant ramifications on his political career. Callender had caused Jefferson to suffer in a fashion "which hardly encourages men in public life to be scrupulously upright."[222] Indeed, one scholar claims that almost every scandalous story about Jefferson today can be traced to Callender's writings; this scholar observed, "Had it not been for Callender, recently revived charges to the same effect probably would never have come to national attention."[223] Callender's charges have lasted through the centuries to represent a dark stain on Jefferson's career.

"To the Victor Belong the Spoils": Andrew Jackson and Institutionalization of the Spoils System

The next several presidents after Jefferson all followed in his footsteps by removing public employees based on their political leanings. Presidents James Madison (in office 1809–1817) and James Monroe (in office 1817–1825) were also part of the Democratic-Republican Party. President Monroe passed the Tenure of Office Act of 1820, which legalized the removal of all incumbent officials for the incoming president, regardless of their work performance. The federal government under Madison and Monroe remained small—most of the jobs were clerical and administrative positions in the major northeastern cities of Boston, New York, Philadelphia, and Washington, DC.

President Andrew Jackson (1767–1845) played another major role in institutionalizing the political patronage system. Jackson, a wealthy cotton planter from Tennessee, was an ardent Jeffersonian. His presidency from 1829 to 1837 was characterized by political corruption. Many governmental job seekers turned his inauguration into chaos; these job seekers were primarily Jackson's supporters who had been promised federal jobs as rewards for their loyalty during Jackson's campaign. In order to make good on these promises, Jackson fired about nine hundred government workers, or about 20 percent of all civic servants, at the beginning of his presidency.

The political patronage system received its nickname "the spoils system" during the Jackson administration. Jackson established the "Kitchen

Cabinet" by recruiting presidential advisors from among his friends and political allies. Democrat Senator William L. Marcy (1786–1857) of New York defended Jackson's political appointments, claiming that "to the victor belong the spoils of the enemy."[224] Marcy provided ideological justification for the patronage system and legitimized the practice of changing a significant portion of the American civil servant force based on mere political opinion.

Jackson used the spoils system to create opportunities through which he could bring his political cronies into office. At the time, the post office was the largest department in the federal government. In one year, Jackson fired 423 postmasters, most of whom had extensive records of good service.[225] He also removed 252 of 610 public employees in high positions, representing about 41 percent of the total. When including the lesser positions, Jackson had removed close to 20 percent of all public servants.[226]

The Jackson administration attempted to convince the public that the spoils system was for the benefit of all American citizens by making the government more efficient. The reality was that this cronyism led to corruption and graft. Because Jackson gave lucrative jobs to donors, friends, business associates, and other supporters with little qualifications for these jobs, his administration notably saw about $1.2 million embezzled from the New York City Customs House.

By the 1830s, the federal government had become complex due in large part to American's rapid growth and territorial expansion. With higher and more diverse populations, public demand for an efficient government system increased. However, the spoils system resulted in multitudes of incapable persons in government positions, resulting in corruption and outright theft.

Many believed that Jackson's use of the spoils system went too far. Thomas Jefferson felt uncomfortable seeing his abuse of the presidential appointing power. He complained that Jackson was a "man of violent passions and unfit for the presidency."[227]

The Spoils System Led to the Century of Corruption

The nineteenth century was widely recognized as the Century of Corruption in American history. The spoils system led directly to government corruption, which fed into regulatory and business corruption. The presidents during this era used the spoils system to reward their supporters and punish their adversaries. Public officials "worked largely behind the scenes to trade support and even subsidies for the tycoons of the day, for large sums of money, patronage, and other rewards."[228]

Although Jackson's political opponents initially condemned him for introducing political "proscription," they soon learned to follow his example.

Once later presidents were in power, they would take immediate action to imitate Jackson's precedent in appointing public employees.

In the early 1800s, no position within government was spared from the rapid transition between presidents. Every employee, from the Washington bureau chiefs to village postmasters, was at risk of losing his job after a new president took office. The spoils system became such that assigning jobs for party members who had made campaign contributions was a primary responsibility of the president-elect. Both Democrat and Whig presidents turned over thousands of jobs each presidential cycle, and each new administration saw thousands of job seekers besiege the White House.

The deficiencies of the spoils system had become obvious by the mid-1800s. One of the most prominent examples was that of Samuel Swartwout (1783–1856). As the Collector of the Port of New York, Swartwout had embezzled $210,000 during his first term of office under Jackson. Rather than being punished, Swartwout retained his position during the following van Buren administration. Later, Swartwout escaped to Europe with more than $1,250,000 in misappropriated public funds. Another similar perfidy was the case of Caleb J. McNulty, the Clerk of the U.S. House of Representatives (1843–1845), who also embezzled U.S. House funds.[229]

When William Henry Harrison (1773–1841) became president, about 40,000 office seekers gathered before the Capitol to scramble for about twenty thousand federal jobs. Those who ultimately received positions often did so through party connections; most were untrained for their responsibilities, and many were indifferent altogether.[230]

The historical record shows that the two parties had universally used the spoils system to explore their interests. The Harrison and Tyler administrations (1841–1845) fired 50 percent of the presidential class officials. When Democrat James K. Polk (1795–1849) won the office in 1845, he fired 37 percent of the presidential class employees. By this point, there remained only sixteen thousand postmasters in the country. President Polk reappointed almost fourteen thousand, which accounted for 84 percent of all positions. During the administration of Whig president Zachary Taylor (1849–1850), 58 percent of the presidential class officeholders were ousted and replaced.[231] When the Democrats returned to power in the subsequent election cycle, the Franklin Pierce administration (1853–1857) removed approximately 89 percent of the Whig presidential class appointees made by Taylor.[232]

The spoils system had tremendous negative impacts on American politics. Party member status became the primary determinant for whether an individual would receive or retain a public job. American political engagement was rising; many citizens were involved in a political party and its respective ideology. These citizens were fiercely loyal to their own parties and opposed to the other. In addition, given the level of bureaucratic expansion that had taken place over the last several decades, it had become the tedious norm for each new president to allocate positions to his party's office seekers.

Based on President Abraham Lincoln's correspondence and daily activities, it is fair to say that Lincoln also spent significant energy in applying the spoils system to provide his supporters with federal jobs. Lincoln's secretary, John G. Nicolay, complained of the size of the crowd looking for government jobs and was haunted "continually by someone who wants to see the President." These applicants came at all hours during the day to pursue "one of the many crumbs of official patronage."[233] President Lincoln and his predecessors realized the role of patronage in building and maintaining their political parties.[234] Lincoln took advantage of the special situation created by the Civil War (1861–1865) to expand the application of the spoils system to military forces. With more military offices at his disposal during the war, Lincoln used "the appointing power at his command as deliberately as he could have been used for practical, and usually partisan, political purpose."[235]

As such, the Lincoln administration discharged many experienced Democrats for primarily political reasons.[236] Lincoln appointed Grenville M. Dodge (1831–1916), an Iowan political leader and railroad entrepreneur, to the position of general in gratitude for his support in the Republican Convention in 1860. The newly hired General Dodge used Lincoln's Union Army to drive Native Americans out of the prospective path of the Union Pacific Railroad, of which Dodge was a founder. In 1862, the federal government gave the Union Pacific the first federal transcontinental railroad charter, which included massive land grants and monetary subsidies.[237]

In fact, the greatest employee turnover within the spoils system occurred within the Lincoln administration from 1861 to 1865. Lincoln ousted 1,457 of 1,520 presidential class appointees, representing 96 percent of the population. Prior to his presidency, Lincoln had been an attorney and lobbyist for the prominent Illinois Central Railroad. After entering the White House, Lincoln appointed George B. McClellan (1826–1885) to be commander of the Union Army. It was no coincidence that McClellan had been a chief engineer and vice president of Illinois Central prior to the war. Lincoln also appointed Ambrose Burnside (1824–1881), former treasurer of Illinois Central, to be McClellan's successor.[238]

Corruption was normal in both the Northern and Southern states during the Reconstruction Era (1865–1877) following the Civil War. In the South, dishonest scalawags and carpetbaggers grabbed every opportunity to funnel money into their own pockets.[239] In the North, the infamous Tweed Ring of New York City symbolized the extent of urban corruption.[240] In 1867, New Yorkers were shocked by their scandalous customer house and their corrupt state legislature, where "votes were bought and sold like meat in the market."[241]

A reporter who visited New York's City Hall in 1866 provided a vivid description of the job seekers as "idle men with their feet upon tables smoking cigars." He reported that no buildings in the world could compare with those in New York, "wherein the consumption of tobacco in all its forms goes on more vigorously during business hours than the City Hall of New York. . . . the 'Expectoration' is everywhere seen."[242]

The Grant administration (1869–1877), which followed the Lincoln presidency, was full of its share of scandals and fraudulent activities as well. Exemplified by the 1869 Black Friday gold speculation ring, it was clear that all federal departments within the Grant administration were corrupt during his eight-year presidency. Nepotism during this period was so widespread that the Grant administration was eventually referred to as Grantism. A significant number of government appointments and employees were essentially divided among forty family members.[243]

The Grant administration was a notable example of the spoils system run rampant. All of Grant's federal departments were faced with financial corruption charges or scandals at one point during his presidency. Grant was fiercely loyal and protective to those whom he had befriended; this fact, coupled with his inability to establish personal accountability within his cabinet and subordinates, expedited many scandals involving political appointees directly associated with the Grant administration.[244]

Returning to Franklin's Idea: The Confucian Merit System Was Adopted Eventually

As political corruption created by the spoils system became even more widespread in the 1850s, calls for reform—many of which had arisen from an earlier time—gathered more impetus. Critics of cronyism demanded that the appointment of public servants be removed from the influence of party politics. During the post–Civil War Reconstruction Era, civil service reform gained tremendous momentum. The high-profile scandals in the federal government during this time gave impetus to reformers including George W. Curtis (1824–1892),[245] Thomas Jenckes (1818–1875),[246] and Dorman B. Eaton (1823–1899).[247]

George W. Curtis believed that the spoils system "imperils not only the purity, economy, and efficiency of the administration of the Government, but . . . [also] destroys confidence in the method of popular government by party."[248] He told Americans that the spoils system "creates a mercenary political class, an oligarchy of stipendiaries, and bureaucracy of the worst kind."[249] Curtis would add that such a system "destroys the individual political independence which is the last defence of liberty."[250] His conclusion was based on the fact that the spoils system "excludes able men from public life, and makes a great many of the conspicuous names in politics little illustrative of the real leadership of American ability, enterprise, and progress."[251] He believed it was imperative to revoke such a system.

Reformers in the United States were inspired not only by domestic pressure but also by countries that had already adopted the Chinese merit system. By the 1800s, several western European countries had turned to a merit-based system of selecting their officials. American diplomats would bring home news regarding the success of these new European systems. Christopher Columbus Andrews (1829–1922), the American Minister to Sweden from 1869 to 1877, reported that European countries had started a "complete revolution" by introducing the Chinese merit system to civil service. Andrews attested, "Rigorous and impartial tests of qualification have been applied."[252] The system had a transformative role to civil service in Europe; after embracing merit-based selection, what was formerly described as an "incompetent, routine" system would become known for its "efficiency and fidelity."[253] The strengthening of the character of the civil service system was instrumental in the development of their public governance system and economy.

The American reformers used the European countries' experiences, particularly Great Britain's, to persuade the public of the benefits of accepting the merit system. Congressman Thomas A. Jenckes demonstrated to Congress that countries from England to Prussia were relying on merit-based systems. He admonished that the success in European countries that adopt the merit system "is so great and beneficial as to encourage the attempt to obtain the same end in our own."[254]

In his report on civil service in Great Britain, Dorman Eaton described how the enlightened European states had reformed their system since 1815. In many parts of Europe, a public employee was recruited according to "his fitness, and irrespective of his birth or party affiliation, to tender his claim upon that service and have its merits impartially considered."[255]

John Stuart Mill (1806–1873), the prominent English philosopher, political economist, and thinker, was also very critical of the American spoils system; indeed, Mill believed that "the appointments to office, without regard to qualifications, are the worst side of American institutions."[256] He reasoned that the Chinese merit system would reduce political corruption in the United States. He believed that if public positions were given by open competition rather than political affiliation, then the American culture of corruption would necessarily cease.[257]

Under increasing pressure to reform the crony system, Congress passed a resolution in 1851 to consider some plan to make the promotion of clerks "upon due regard to their qualifications and services."[258] This legislation was the first major indicator that the federal government was willing to address some of the negative externalities created by the spoils system.

By the late 1860s, civil service reform had become more mainstream. Inspired by the reformers, citizens from all social classes lent their support to the rallies for change. The public had become disgusted with the rising number of scandals and the increasing cost of government under existing party practices. Merchants, attorneys, teachers, and scholars alike called for a major restructuring of the government hiring system. The *New York Times* criticized the spoils system as "costly, inefficient, wasteful and corrupt," and echoed public demand to bring efficiency into government.[259] The *Nation*[260] concluded that there was no reform so much needed as that of the social service sector,[261] and indicated that competitive examinations would fill government posts with the most qualified people.[262]

Congressman Thomas Jenckes was regarded as "the nation's most prominent leader of the civil service reform movement"[263] and "the father of the civil Service Reform."[264] Jenckes began to work on legislation that would reform the state of civil service in 1864.[265] In December 1865, Jenckes introduced his civil service bill,[266] which unfolded the efforts to introduce China's "open competitive examinations for selecting civil service appointees" to the United States.[267]

Jenckes defended his bill in Congress on May 14, 1868, where he warned that the spoils system had penetrated every nook and cranny of the American political system. Unless this corruption was thoroughly eradicated, Jenckes predicted that the system would end in "political death."[268] The U.S. government could not sustain the regular turnover of more than fifty thousand federal employees for "mere opinion's sake."[269] Jenckes restated his belief that democracy could not coexist with the spoils system:

> The spoils system takes from the government employee those motives to fidelity which in private life are found universally necessary to secure it. As no degree of merit whatever can secure him in his place, he must be a man of heroic virtue who does not act upon the principle of getting the most out of it while he holds it. Whatever fidelity may be found in officeholders must be set down to the credit of unassisted human virtue. In a word, the spoils system renders pure, decent, orderly, and democratic government impossible.[270]

Jenckes alleged that the Chinese merit system would eliminate "inefficiencies of an overgrown and non-professional bureaucracy."[271] He told his fellow congressmen that the Chinese examination system "does away with all personal influence; bribery of all kinds, either by personal recommendation or political reward, becomes impossible."[272] He applauded his proposed merit system as "a wise and practical system regulating the appointments in the different departments of the civil service."[273] To institutionalize the merit system, Jenckes required that only those who had passed a competitive open examination were qualified for a civil service position. Such an examination would become thoroughly implemented if it represented "the sole channel to the acquirement of office and of political advancement."[274]

Before he completed his legislation in 1865, Jenckes had meticulously studied the Chinese civil service system. He had become familiar with not only the process of civil service examination in ancient China but also the content of the tests themselves. Chinese students who passed the test demonstrated their mastery of Confucian classics, as well as the nation's "Five Classics" and "Four Books."[275] These students also understood the authorized commentaries on all these texts.[276] Such knowledge represented the culmination of a grueling process that took years of dedication and hard work.

Jenckes acknowledged that as anywhere else in the world, corruption, venality, and the influence of rank and wealth also existed in China. However, in China public officers only being selected from the successful competitors was implemented. Therefore, "corruption and other sinister influences are, virtually, transgressions of the law."[277]

Very impressively, Jenckes was also familiarized with how the Chinese avoided the negative effects of the merit system:

> In addition to the division of power, and the checks upon Chinese officers already mentioned, there are other means adopted to prevent combination and resistance against the head of the state. One of them is the law forbidding a man to hold office in his native province, which, beside stopping all intrigue where it would best succeed, has the further effect of congregating all aspirants for office at Pekin, where they come in hope of obtaining some post or succeeding in the examination of literary degrees.[278]

He continued, in China, "no officer is allowed to marry in the jurisdiction under his control, nor own land in it, nor have a son, or brother, or near relative holding office under him." In the meantime, an official "is seldom continued in the same station or province for more than three or four years."[279]

Jenckes also realized that despite this examination system, not all Chinese students were on equal footing. Some of them had privileges, such as the students from the national institute and members of imperial and certain aristocratic families.[280] However, he believed that the system reduced the generational transfer of power because even those with privileges needed to pass the examination. Jenckes wrote that, in cases where favoritism existed in the appointment, equal examination "among the candidates is indispensable"; as a result, "the principle of intellectual qualification preponderates, on the whole, over all other considerations."[281] After they passed examinations, "the mandarins are watched with Argus eyes[282] and the ears of Dionysius;[283] an account of their merits and demerits is rigorously kept." Most importantly, to make sure that those officials implement their duties, "the examination of these merits and demerits is instituted every three years by the chamber of investigation."[284]

To Jenckes, the Chinese merit system gave individuals the opportunity to achieve the nation's highest honor. He called on Congress to provide civil service access to all citizens from all spheres of life. He frequently told congressmen that "qualification and merit, equal and exact justice to all, are what we are to seek and to do. Palmam qui meruit ferat . . . shall be the motto of the United States public service."[285]

To impress upon Congress the significance of the system he was proposing, Jenckes recounted how the Confucian merit system saved the Chinese from invasion by foreigners:

> Indeed, it may be safely asserted that if this prospect of government employment were not held out to accomplished men, and to them exclusively, letters would not be cultivated to the same extent. With equal truth it may be stated that, if the effect of excessive absolutism in the form of government, of excessive superstition in the form of religion, and of excessive dislike of innovation, had not thus been neutralized by culture and talent and the highest capacity in the civil and military service of the empire, Chinese civilization would have long ago perished beneath the walls that shut it off from the outer world, and the land of Confucius would have fallen a prey to barbarism.[286]

Jenckes's attempt at civil service reform faced opposition from those who benefited most under the status quo. One radical adversary to Jenckes was Frederic E. Woodbridge (1818–1888), a U.S. representative from Vermont. Woodbridge tried to highlight what he perceived to be flaws within Jenckes's bill. According to Woodbridge, the bill sounded great in theory but would crumble in practice; the merit system was suitable for a more aristocratic nation, such as Britain, Belgium, or France, where "the masses are mere machines; but in free America it will never work."[287]

Jenckes responded to Woodbridge by asserting that a meritocratic system was truly democratic, for under it, every citizen was entitled and given opportunity to "compete for office; it was the spoils system, built on favoritism, that deserves the term 'aristocratic.'"[288] Jenckes also retaliated that it was ridiculous to oppose the adoption of the merit system since China was a monarchy. Jenckes said:

> It has been most strangely objected to this salutary reform that it is in its tendency bureaucratic, exclusive, aristocratic, and that the system was formed under monarchic institutions. Nothing could be said more calumnious. It is our present system that is borrowed from that of monarchies, and gives us the will

and choice of the person having the appointing power, and not merit, as the passport to office, as under monarchies the king is the fountain of honor and the giver of employment. No measure could be more republican than that which we now present. The gates of the avenues to the public service are thrown open to all."[289]

Under the spoils system, it was almost impossible for one to ascend government ranks except through the influence or patronage of the privileged families. At the same time, those public employees did not have job security and continued to "cultivate the favor of the reigning favorites and governing families."[290] The practice of political patronage was contrary to the foundational principles of the United States as a democratic nation, "where the Government is of the people and for the people."[291] Therefore, as the U.S. government should serve the American people's will in the best and most effectual manner, the spoils system "is not a mere solecism, but a positive evil."[292] The spoils system was contrary to popular government.[293] The U.S. government should be administered for the benefit of the whole, with the best instruments, at the least expense, "without regard to the interests of any classes or class, or of persons or partisans."[294] He elaborated that to install the merit system in the U.S. government system was not temporary expediency, or to promote any partisan interest; its intention was to place "this Government in the hands of skillful and honest men, and thus to renew the health and life of the Republic."[295]

Jenckes opposed "centralization" under power-hungry presidents, but he also opposed the spoils of localism. In contrast to both, he praised nationalism and argued that civil service created a more integrated and balanced nation.[296] The Chinese merit system would stimulate education and bring the most talent into public service. In addition, the system would place service above all considerations of locality, favoritism, patronage, or party.[297]

Jenckes lost a close vote on his bill in Congress, but he was not discouraged by the setback. Instead, he revamped his approach by broadening his support within the business world.[298] Jenckes promoted the idea that civil service reform would reduce corruption and create a friendlier and more reliable business environment.[299] After his efforts, a businessman reported that after the election, some who had lost hope several months before "are quite sanguine now for an early favorable result."[300]

Jenckes's bill won a new round of endorsements from newspapers nationwide. Despite its earlier defeat in Congress, Jenckes's civil service reform continued to garner widespread support. Outgoing Secretary of the Treasury Hugh McCulloch (1808–1895) backed the passage of the legislation, as did the powerful Union League Club of New York and the American Social Science Association (ASSA).[301]

Preeminent scholar Ralph Waldo Emerson (1803–1882) also publicized his support of Jenckes's efforts at civil service reform. Emerson expressed an understanding of the Confucian merit system that was reminiscent of Benjamin Franklin. Emerson opined:

> China interests us at this moment in a point of politics. I am sure that gentlemen around me bear in mind the bill which the Hon. Mr. Jenckes of Rhode Island has twice attempted to carry through Congress, requiring that candidates for public offices shall first pass examinations on their literary qualifications for the same. Well, China has preceded us, as well as England and France, in this essential correction of a reckless usage; and the like high esteem of education appears in China in social life, to whose distinctions it is made an indispensable passport.[302]

Jenckes returned to Congress in 1869 optimistic that given his wide base of support, he would be able to influence change in the status quo. After the Johnson administration was replaced by the Grant presidency in 1869, Jenckes reintroduced his original proposal, giving the president power over the commission once again.

George William Curtis, another prominent leader of the reform movement, supported the Jenckes bill in his address at the annual meetings of ASSA in New York in October 1869.[303] That same month, Henry Adams (1838–1918) published his article on "Civil Service Reform" in the *North American Review*. He accused former presidents of carrying the spoils system to a new extreme. Adams pinpointed the politically powerful Civil War veterans' group, the Grand Army of the Republic, as aiding Grant in organizing a purge of administrative departments.[304]

In the third session of the forty-first Congress, the lame-duck session beginning in December 1870, Jenckes offered his most ambitious bill yet. Under his proposal, all government officers—except for cabinet members, ministers abroad, judges, and court clerks—would have to pass competitive examinations to qualify for their positions. Incumbent officers would also have to pass these tests; if they scored below a certain threshold, they would be automatically removed.[305] Jenckes's competitive exam model would apply to 80 percent of public servants, with the remaining 20 percent open to discretionary hires. However, President Grant still enjoyed the power of patronage politics, and Jenckes lost his congressional seat in November 1870.

As cries for reform gained even more momentum, President Grant was forced to offer some concessions. In 1871, Congress authorized President Grant to set regulations for admission to public service positions and appoint the Civil Service Commission. That same year, Grant chose Curtis to head the Civil Service Commission. By that time, civil service reform had become a forefront issue for the United States. Broad public masses had been mobilized to battle against the spoils system. In April 1872, the first competitive examination under the commission's rules was held for appointments in civil service positions in the cities of New York and Washington, DC.[306]

In 1872, President Grant managed to convince Congress to establish the U.S. Civil Service Commission, which was designed to set standards and qualifications for various federal jobs. In his annual message to Congress, Grant called for service reform. He claimed that the spoils system failed in selecting fit persons for public service in the United States. The reform of the civil service of the government "will be hailed with approval by the whole people of the United States."[307]

After the 1872 election, Congress cut off its funding to the Civil Service Commission while Grant simultaneously suspended it. Although Jenckes was ultimately unable to achieve anything lasting, his bill laid the foundation for the later Pendleton Act. Dorman B. Eaton succeeded Curtis as chair of the first Civil Service Commission and served from 1873 to 1875. During this time, the commission had become ineffectual after Congress had eliminated its funding.[308] In 1877, President Hayes entrusted Eaton with the responsibility of spearheading the continued efforts of reforming the spoils system. Eaton began to research the experiences of the British civil service system and realized soon thereafter that the system had its roots in China.

After several months of study in Great Britain, Eaton published his discoveries in his report, *Civil Service in Great Britain*. In this report, Eaton described the remarkable change that had occurred in Great Britain over the past century due to its adoption of the Chinese merit system.[309] For a lengthy period, there had been little corruption among Britain's public servants. Eaton noted that the merit system would sustain common justice and general education by eliminated patronage and the "old official monopoly."[310] George William Curtis praised Eaton's study" and continued that the unreformed civil service in the United States "was founded upon the theory of the feudal times, that the public services are the property of the ruler."[311]

The elections of 1882 demonstrated the American people's will to abandon the spoils system and install the merit system. Civil service reform became an important factor influencing the election in several congressional districts. In New York, Grover Cleveland (1837–1908) was elected governor, and Theodore Roosevelt (1858–1918) was elected to the State Assembly. Both of them supported civil service reform. However, the assassination of President James Garfield (1831–1881) was the last straw to bring the spoils system to collapse. Garfield's assassinator, Charles J. Guiteau (1841–1882), believed that he had been a primary contributor to Garfield's presidential victory and believed that he should be rewarded an ambassadorship. Guiteau was furious after several unsuccessful attempts to obtain this position and felt humiliated after he was told never to return to the White House again.

The assassination of President Garfield acted as the long-needed catalyst for change. It woke the nation and drove "into the heads of the most hardened political henchmen the idea that there was something disgraceful in reducing the Chief Executive of the United States to the level of a petty job broker."[312] The reformers held the spoils system responsible for the assassination of President Garfield. In September 1881, Curtis drafted a letter, pointing out the need of the civil service reform demonstrated by the murder of President Garfield. Former president Hayes and other eminent persons, such as Peter Cooper, signed the letter.

Chester A. Arthur (1829–1886) became president after Garfield's death. As a supporter of the movement, he continued the cause of civil service reform and lobbied Congress to pass the Pendleton Civil Service Reform Act in 1883.[313] Eaton drafted the Pendleton Civil Service Act of 1883, which essentially discarded the spoils system, which had been implemented by U.S. governments for a century. From then on, public office appointments were to be awarded on merit demonstrated through competitive examination.[314]

The passage of the Civil Service Act of 1883 marked the end of the spoils system and the acceptance of the Confucian merit system in public service.[315] For the first time in U.S. history, public service positions were opened to all citizens and the selection of public employees was done through competitive examinations. The Confucian merit system was accepted officially in the United States under the law.

Summary

The acceptance of the Confucian merit system changed the history of the United States. To accept the merit system "is not merely a mode of procedure and an economy, but has become a vital question of principle and public morality, involving the counterpoise and in no small degree the stability of the government itself."[316] The merit system elevated the United States to "a new and higher standard in official life."[317] It has been recognized that the adoption of the Pendleton Act "amounted to nothing less than [a] recasting of the foundations of national institutional power."[318]

Through the brief analysis above, the reader will have gained a basic comprehension of the course of events that led to the improvement of the U.S. civil service system from the early 1800s to the Pendleton Act of 1884. It was impossible to build a democratic society on the foundations of the spoils system. When applied to American politics, the spoils system caused tremendous turnover of federal employees with every new presidency. Public employees were chosen based on party affiliation rather than on their knowledge and dedication to their positions. As President Theodore Roosevelt aptly said, the spoils system was more fruitful of degradation in our political life than any other that could have possibly been invented. The spoils monger, the man who peddled patronage, inevitably bred the vote-buyer, the vote-seller, and the man guilty of misfeasance in office.[319]

It took a great, combined effort to eliminate the spoils system and return the United States to the democratic roots that Franklin had originally envisioned. During America's Century of Corruption, many presidents struggled with the inefficiencies of the system as well as disgruntled supporters who were denied government positions. Thomas Jefferson suffered a permanent blow to his reputation when he denied James Callender; James Garfield lost his life when he rejected Charles Guiteau. The civil service reform movement elevated the status of president beyond that of a "petty job broker" and restored faith in the nation's founding principles by allowing any qualified person to serve his or her country.

The reformers' interest in adopting a Chinese merit system led them to explore various European nations' experiences designing civil service systems suitable to the demands of their societies. The English influenced these reformers, but they were not completely satisfied by how Great Britain opened its examination to only select groups within its population. Instead, they turned to the creators of the original system, who had insisted that "all offices in China, from the highest to the lowest, [be] thrown open to all those classes of the people who have the requisite mental qualifications."[320] Therefore, in the United States, the entrance to public service was made available to all willing and able citizens.

CONFUCIAN EDUCATIONAL PRINCIPLES AND THOMAS JEFFERSON'S TRANSFORMATION OF THE AMERICAN EDUCATIONAL SYSTEM

Jefferson espoused the concept of universal education as early as 1779 in his *Bill for More General Diffusion of Knowledge*. Jefferson was ahead of his time, but his vision would eventually be realized by the 1900s as the nation approached a universal education system. In recognition of his pioneering efforts, Jefferson would become regarded as a "Founding Father" of both public and democratic education.

Confucius is regarded as one of the greatest teachers in Chinese history, one whose educational principles have influenced schools and pupils over many centuries across the world. In this section, I will examine how these Confucian principles were introduced to the United States and subsequently aided the development of the country's modern school system. Thomas

Jefferson, one of the nation's Founding Fathers and earliest presidents, was at the forefront of this Confucius-led transformation. Jefferson sought to apply two of Confucius's core educational principles, meritocracy and universal education, to what was, in his time, an unstandardized and European-centric school system emphasizing the classics.

In recognition of his pioneering efforts, Jefferson would become regarded as both "a founding father of public education"[321] and the "founding father of democratic education."[322]

This section discusses the process through which Jefferson introduced Confucian ideals to the United States following the American Revolution. It begins with a survey of Confucian educational principles, then examines how Jefferson was influenced by such principles.

Confucian Education Principles

Confucius was a teacher and philosopher during a tumultuous period of Chinese history known as the Spring and Autumn Period (770–476/403 BC).[323] This period was marked by a series of political, economic, and educational transformations as the country developed from a slave-ownership to feudal society. Three aristocratic families fought for control of Confucius's native state, a territory named Lu on the Shandong Peninsula in eastern China. In the context of this instability, Confucius began to appreciate the role of education in building a stable society; as such, he labored to use education as a tool to restore peace and prosperity.

Education is a Priority for the Nation

Confucius believed that education should be one of a nation's foremost priorities. Effective political governance should rely on not only strong laws and moral leaders but also a cultivated constituency. He cautioned that the former techniques might allow a ruler to garner a favorable reputation, but would be ineffective. The leaders who wished to improve society and build a lasting culture must instead "start from the lessons of the school."[324]

Confucius viewed moral education as the means through which one could improve one's life and contribute to society. He gave the younger generation three admonitions. The first is that when a youngster sees any virtuous action, he should practice it right away. The second is that when there is an "opportunity of doing a reasonable thing," he should "make use of it without hesitating." The third is that he should always endeavor to "extirpate and suppress vice."[325] He believed that one of the primary functions of education was instilling culture and virtue in future statesmen and government officials. Through preparing righteous leaders and citizens, a strong education system would lead to peace and prosperity. As Confucius indicates, "Education breeds confidence. Confidence breeds hope. Hope breeds peace."[326] Confucius's view of education was likely inspired by the tumultuous era in which he lived, one marked by conflict and disorder. He wanted to educate the people, particularly the leaders. For him, "if he could inspire them with the Sentiments of Virtue, their Subjects would become Virtuous after their Example."[327]

Confucius considered educational quality to be important not only at the individual level but also at the familial and national level. He states in *Great Learning* 《大学》, one of his four Classics, that good education fortifies self-cultivation, harmony within a family, prosperity of the nation, and development of the world.[328] His educational principles, edited into the *Analects* by his disciples, emphasized the importance of obtaining a moral education; in his canonical 《诗经》 *Book of Songs*, the first and perhaps most revered of his texts, Confucius discusses the process of cultivating strong moral character.[329]

Universal Education: The First Principle of Confucian Education

For most of Chinese history prior to Confucius, education had been restricted to the aristocratic elite. For example, under the Zhou dynasty (1046–250 BC),[330] only politically distinguished families could afford schools located in government offices and taught by officials. General education was a privilege for the nobility rather than a right for the commoner. Few teachers existed outside of bureaucratic circles.

Confucius rejected the ruling class's monopoly on education by proposing that it be transformed into a public good. He emphasized the importance of educational equity in individual and societal development. Such a system represented a radical shift from the political ideology, which held education as an aristocratic privilege. Confucius took a democratic approach to education, believing that effective teaching should address the differences in individual talents and abilities.[331]

Although there would be significant barriers to implementing such a system on a broader scale, Confucius set an important precedent when he declared his teaching "open to everyone, without distinction."[332] It is of great significance in the world of education; it opened the path for common people to receive education.

Meritocracy: The Second Principle of Confucian Education

One of the earliest examples of administrative meritocracy can be traced to the ancient Chinese civil service examination system.[333] The Chinese civil service examination system was used in imperial China to select candidates for the state bureaucracy. Confucius had advocated for the use of these examinations because they enabled the selection of statesmen based on merit rather than inheritance,[334] thereby cementing education as the key for social mobility.[335] The civil service examination system became institutionalized during the Qin dynasty (221–207 BC) as a way for the government to maintain power over a large, sprawling empire overseen by a complex network of officials.[336]

The Han dynasty (206 BC–220 AD) adopted Confucianism as the basis of its political philosophy. The Han dynasty expanded upon their Qin predecessors by further dividing the civil service exams into three levels: local, provincial, and national. To prepare for these exams, young men rigorously studied music, archery, horsemanship, arithmetic, and rituals. These disciplines would later also encompass military strategy, law, taxation, geography, and the Confucian classics.

The ideals embodied by the civil service exam spread from China to British India during the seventeenth century, before eventually venturing into continental Europe and the United States.[337] The British East India Company was the first European institution that used civil service–style exams to promote its employees. The concept of meritocracy, which reached intellectuals in the West during the Enlightenment, offered an attractive alternative to the traditional European aristocratic regime. Voltaire, one of the great leaders of the Enlightenment, and Francois Quesnay wrote favorably of the idea; Quesnay advocated for an economic and political system modeled after that of the Chinese, and Voltaire even went so far as to claim that the Chinese had "perfected moral science."[338]

Confucian Curriculum

The Confucian curriculum was well structured and progressive to facilitate the synthesis of a variety of subjects. The curriculum was broad and holistic, integrating six skills consisting of *Li* (礼, rites), *Yue* (乐, music), *She* (射, archery), *Yu* (御, chariot driving), *Shu* (书, calligraphy), and *Shu* (数, mathematics). Confucius considered these arts to be interconnected, mutually reinforcing, and practice oriented, and imparted them through a nine-year program that "systematically introduced students to a values-centered, rounded, and comprehensive curriculum." According to the program, students would first train their "learning aspirations" and ability to analyze texts, before developing the ability to work effectively with others. In later years, students would engage in ongoing dialogues with teachers and peers.[339]

Education in Colonial North America

In the American colonies during the eighteenth century, the education patterns followed the examples set by British tradition. Children were primarily educated in their homes, although some towns might have also offered "dame schools" provided by a woman of the town. Formal schools, while uncommon, were not unheard of—the Boston Latin School was founded in 1635, while the Mather School opened in Massachusetts in 1639.[340] These academies, typically supported by wealthy parents, would often teach the classics in Greek and Latin. The goal of most education was to provide basic literacy, especially for the purpose of reading the Bible. The great distances that disconnected homesteads scattered along the bays and rivers of Virginia and Maryland "made most of them inaccessible to such schools as were established."[341]

In the New England colonies, it was commonplace for wealthy colonists to hire tutors for their sons. Alternatively, such boys might have been sent to regional schools for the social elite.[342] The Southern colonies followed similar patterns, whereby families assumed the responsibilities of educating their own children and sometimes collaborated to set up communal "field schools." There were only about ten grammar schools in Georgia by 1770, most of which were taught by ministers. Local newspapers also showed advertisements for private teachers.[343]

The colonial education system often drew from British influences. Most schoolbooks from the period were either imported from England or based on English texts. The *New England Primer*, one of the most widespread educational texts, was reprinted from the *English Protestant Tutor*. Furthermore, pupils who continued formal education would typically attend Latin Grammar Schools, which were described as "direct copies" of their European counterparts.[344]

Thomas Jefferson's Educational Revolution

Thomas Jefferson had long been dissatisfied with the state of the colonial education system. He would often lament to John Adams that the postrevolutionary youths "acquired all learning in their mothers' wombs."[345] The current system was inadequate at imparting upon youths the foundation necessary for serious academic and intellectual pursuits. Jefferson saw a preponderance of petty academics sprouting upon across the nation, "where one or two men, possessing Latin, and sometimes Greek, a knowledge of the globes, and the first six books of Euclid, imagine and communicate this as the sum of science."[346]

Jefferson believed that the independence won through the American Revolution would be short-lived unless the citizens of the new nation could be "enlightened to a certain degree" such that they could be "safe depositories of their own [liberties]."[347] As such, Jefferson believed that educational reform was necessary. He committed to transforming the schooling system within his home state of Virginia, and eventually the entire nation. However, any proposals for improving education were daunting, especially for a fledgling nation in the wake of a prolonged domestic war for independence. The diversity of the new nation from both a cultural and geographical perspective compounded the difficulties of establishing an effective and unified school system.[348]

Jefferson began to develop his thoughts on the American education system when he served in the Virginia legislature in 1779. By 1820, he had formulated his views through four bills proposed to the General Assembly of Virginia (1779); a Bill for Establishing a System of Public Education (1817); his Rockfish Gap Report (1818); and in a series of letters to correspondents that included Peter Carr, John Banister, and John Adams. The consistent theme of all of Jefferson's works and musings was to promote educational equality and improve quality across the nation.

In 1779, Jefferson submitted the *Bill for More General Diffusion of Knowledge* to the Virginia State Legislature. This bill proposed a novel education system that would provide three years of general education for all "free children," regardless of gender. In 1781, Jefferson further documented his educational plan in the *Notes on the State of Virginia*, in which he expressed his belief that all children should receive an education. Some scholars have noted that these notes were "the most important scientific and political book written by an American before 1785."[349]

Jefferson's proposals typically followed several key themes. In particular, he believed that basic education should be available for all; that the talented should be able to pursue higher education through public support; and that education was critical for the individual and public good. Below, we consider Jefferson's principles in greater depth.

Education: The Vehicle for Instilling or Strengthening Virtue

Like Confucius, Jefferson viewed education as a vehicle for instilling and strengthening moral character.[350] Jefferson sought to reduce the role of the national government in its citizens' lives, but an effective system of limited governance would require an educational system that cultivated positive virtues and character. The education system would effectively replace the government's role in establishing order by imparting the knowledge and moral aptitude necessary for self-governance. Jefferson believed that democracy rested in education. He alleged that through education, "a majority would find its way to the right place."[351] Jefferson stressed the importance of education in cultivating moral virtues and protecting against the "germ of corruption."³⁵²

As Jefferson noted in his *Report of the Commissioners for the University of Virginia*, education enabled citizens "to form . . . habits of reflection and correct action, rendering them examples of virtue to others and of happiness within themselves": ³⁵³

> [In a republic, according to Montesquieu in Spirit of the Laws, IV, ch.5,] virtue may be defined as the love of the laws and of our country. As such love requires a constant preference of public to private interest, it is the source of all private virtue; for they are nothing more than this very preference itself. . . . Now a government is like everything else: to preserve it we must love it. . . . Everything, therefore, depends on establishing this love in a republic; and to inspire it ought to be the principal business of education; but the surest way of instilling it into children is for parents to set them an example.³⁵⁴

Jefferson Promoted Universal Education and Merit System

From 1779 until his death in 1826, Jefferson would repeatedly emphasize the importance of universal education and meritocracy. He maintained that all citizens, regardless of wealth, should have the same right to basic general education. To provide education to the poor and uneducated, Jefferson proposed a system of public schools subsidized through tax revenues. He believed that such a system would provide each citizen with "an education proportioned to the conditions and pursuits of his life."³⁵⁵ Basic learning would be important in allowing each man to judge and vote intelligently on matters of regional and national importance.³⁵⁶

During Jefferson's stay in Paris between 1781 and 1785, he corresponded with George Washington about his first education bill, which had made limited progress in the Virginia legislature since its introduction in 1779. Jefferson would repeatedly express the importance of a universal education system, once telling Washington, "It is an axiom in my mind that our liberty can never be safe but in the hands of the people themselves, and that too of the people with a certain degree of instruction."³⁵⁷

The general objective of Jefferson's educational scheme was to provide instruction adapted to each student's skills and ability to learn. Most students would receive a practical education that provides basic literacy and understanding of society. This basic system of education would ensure that citizens were educated enough to fulfill their needs and be sufficient for political participation. After graduating from general education, students would be expected to pursue vocations. Girls would learn homemaking from their mothers, while boys would learn trade skills from their fathers or through apprenticeships.[358]

For pupils who demonstrated evidence of belonging to the "learned class," elementary education would serve as the foundation for further study. These boys, whom "nature endowed with genius and virtue," would require more advanced preparation to qualify them for their varied pursuits and duties in a republican society.[359] Jefferson expressed his desire for a merit system in which the "highest degrees of education" would be "given to the [highest] degrees of genius."[360] A secondary education system would be implemented to ensure that the talented and virtuous, and not simply the wealthy and wellborn, would have opportunities to become statesmen. Jefferson summarized this part of his plan in his *Notes on the State of Virginia*, written in 1781. He reminded of the importance of "selecting the youths of genius from among the classes of the poor," because he believed that "the State of those talents which nature has sown as liberally among the poor as the rich, but which perish without use if not sought for and cultivated."[361]

In the early 1800s, Jefferson discussed a more elaborate educational proposal with John Adams. Jefferson described three tiers of students within his proposed scheme: the first consisted of students who developed basic literacy and arithmetic skills, the second of pupils who would receive higher education at the public expense, and the third of the brightest pupils who would learn "all the useful sciences" in universities.[362] Jefferson expanded his idea further in *A Bill for the More General Diffusion of Knowledge*:

> And whereas it is generally true that that people will be happiest whose laws are best, and are best administered, and that laws will be wisely formed, and honestly administered, in proportion as those who form and administer them are wise and honest; whence it becomes expedient for promoting the publick happiness that those persons, whom nature hath endowed with genius and virtue, should be rendered by liberal education worthy to receive, and able to guard the sacred deposit of the rights and liberties of their fellow citizens, and that they should be called to that charge without regard to wealth, birth or other accidental condition or circumstance; but the indigence of the greater number disabling them from so educating, at their own expence, those of their children whom nature hath fitly formed and disposed to become useful instruments for the public, it is better that such should be sought for and educated at the common expence of all, than that the happiness of all should be confided to the weak or wicked:[363]

Jefferson ultimately hoped to replace the aristocracy of wealth with a "natural aristocracy" based on virtue and talent. In his autobiography, Jefferson charged that the former brought "more harm and danger than benefit to society," and reasoned that the latter was "essential to a well-ordered republic."[364] He believed that replacing the monopoly of education opportunities was crucial for the "development of . . . a free society for people to have open minds," and sought to establish an accompanying merit system that rewarded intellectual ability rather than birthright.[365]

Jefferson wanted to replace the heritage aristocracies that had existed in the European tradition with the natural aristocracies that would form out of ability. On the one hand, he introduced a universal education system, and on the other hand, he planned to choose students according to their talents. Jefferson advocated universal K–12 education but sought to identify the best students at several levels and provide additional education to just the "most promising subjects."[366] Jefferson believed that merit would surface unless it was stifled by a system of class and privilege upheld by law.[367]

Jefferson's Curriculum: European Classics, History, Modern Language, and Science

Jefferson recommended a curriculum with specific focus on Roman and Greek literature, which likely reflected his affinity for the subjects stemming from his own childhood education. Many of Jefferson's contemporaries would have begun learning the classical languages by age eight; Jefferson himself started school when he was five, and was studying Latin, Greek, and French around age nine. He would later continue his studies of history, science, and philosophy at the College of William and Mary in Williamsburg.

Drawing from his own experience, Jefferson further prescribed a curriculum emphasizing science, history, and other practical skillsets. He also proposed that public school students learn the secular sciences rather than the Bible. While seemingly controversial, this suggestion was not unique. During this time, Benjamin Franklin had also expressed a desire to transform the "narrow, humanistic-religious-philosophical" American educational system into a modern structure focused on languages and sciences.[368]

Jefferson found value in providing the strongest students with a generalist education before having them specialize in any particular field. He noted that the subjects of American education should further include "classical knowledge, modern languages, chiefly French, Spanish, and Italian; Mathematics, Natural philosophy, Natural history, Civil history, and Ethics."[369] He explained his rationale for developing such a broad knowledge base to his friend, W. C. Rives: "Nothing can be sounder than your view of the importance of laying a broad foundation in other branches of knowledge whereon to raise the superstructure of any particular science. . . . Science is more important in a republic than in any other government."[370]

Jefferson's ideal curriculum incorporated European classical influences while simultaneously emphasizing the development of modern skills necessary to foster the development of the fledgling nation.

Jefferson's Educational Reforms Were Based on Confucian Educational Principles

In developing his educational principles, Jefferson was significantly influenced by the "experience of other ages and countries"; in his mind, ideas were "like fire . . . not to be confined in one country or on one continent."[371] The few surviving letters of Jefferson's youth (written between 1760 and 1764) tell us "nearly all we know about him firsthand before the age of twenty one, read much Society Page: the names in the social pageant are without exception those of the best Virginia families."[372] Although he was influenced by his own European upbringing, Jefferson recognized the flaws of the old system and opposed sending promising American youth to study overseas. Jefferson perceived a European education as detrimental to one's knowledge, morals, health, habits, and happiness.[373] He stated:

> Let us view the disadvantages of sending a youth to Europe. To enumerate them all would require a volume. I will select a few. If he goes to England he learns drinking, horse-racing and boxing. These are the peculiarities of English education. The following circumstances are common to education in that and the other countries of Europe. He acquires a fondness for European luxury and dissipation and a contempt for the simplicity of his own country; he is fascinated with the privileges of the European aristocrats, and sees with abhorrence the lovely equality which the poor enjoys with the rich in his own country: he contracts a partiality for aristocracy or monarchy; he forms foreign friendships which will never be useful to him, and loses the season of life for forming in his own country those friendships which of all others are the most faithful and permanent: he is led by the strongest of all the human passions into a spirit for female intrigue destructive of his own and others happiness, or a passion for whores destructive of his health, and in both cases learns to consider fidelity to the marriage bed as an ungentlemanly practice and inconsistent with happiness: he recollects the voluptuary dress and arts of the European women and pities and despises the chaste affections and simplicity of those of his own country; he retains thro' life a fond recollection and a hankering after those places which were the scenes of his first pleasures and of his first connections; he returns to his own country, a foreigner, unacquainted with the practices of domestic œconomy necessary to preserve him from ruin; speaking and writing his native tongue as a foreigner, and therefore unqualified to obtain those distinctions which eloquence of the pen and tongue ensures in a free country.[374]

Several other Founding Fathers corroborated Jefferson's distaste of the European system. For instance, Franklin also scorned European luxury[375] and claimed that a European upbringing would make an American "suspect to [his] own people."[376]

William Jarvis articulated to Jefferson the important role that Confucius played in Chinese education, "the comparative happy state of China, with the rest of Asia, does as much honor to his [Confucius's] Philosophical Wisdom as to the goodness of his intentions."[377]

It is likely that Jefferson sought some guidance from the principles of Confucian education when he considered reforms to the American system. Like Confucius, Jefferson sought to distinguish between laborers and the learned aristocracy by merit rather than birth or inherited wealth.[378] Also similar to Confucius, Jefferson believed that an ignorant citizenry would eventually succumb to tyranny. Jefferson proposed a democratic, merit-based system in which education was provided equitably based on an individual talent. By creating an educational system with high standards, Jefferson hoped to strengthen the foundations of democracy within his new nation. Scholars have identified similarities between Jefferson's proposed system and the Chinese civil service examinations, describing the former as the "keystone of the arch of our government."[379]

Jefferson was also inspired by Enlightenment philosophies, which were influenced by Confucianism. For example, during the Enlightenment period, European scholars discovered that the Chinese had already virtually abolished hereditary aristocracy. French and British anti-monarchists would draw from this precedent in their own quest to abolish hereditary privilege, thereby leveraging Confucianism to promote the rebirth of European democracy.[380]

From 1785 to 1789, Jefferson served as an American diplomat in Paris, which represented one of the centers of the Enlightenment during a period in which it was in full force. Jefferson agreed with the prevailing admiration of Confucius by several leading European intellectuals, including Voltaire. Jefferson was especially drawn to Voltaire and Confucianism; in 1814, Jefferson's personal library contained a set of Voltaire's complete works, as well as eight books related to China.[381] In his later years, Thomas Jefferson also managed through American diplomats in China to obtain books on China. He even bought a Chinese language book.[382] On July 19, 1818, Jefferson received two books, including Robert Morrison's *A View of China, for Philological Purposes; containing A Sketch of Chinese Chronology, Geography, Government, Religion & Customs. designed for the use of persons who study the Chinese Language*, Macao, 1817 and Morrison's *Dialogues and Detached Sentences in the Chinese Language; with a free and verbal Translation in English. collected from various sources. Designed as an Initiatory Work for the Use of Students of Chinese*, Macao, 1816.[383] He later expressed his appreciation for Charles J. Ingersoll (1782–1862), an American lawyer, writer, and politician. Jefferson told him, "I found here your favor of July 4. with the two Chinese works from mr Wilcox."[384] James Madison reported that Congress collected the book by Jean Baptiste Du Halde (1674–1743), *The General History of China*.[385]

In a letter to Adams, Jefferson conveyed his admiration for a meritocratic government system:

> I agree with you that there is a natural aristocracy among men. the grounds of this are virtue & talents. formerly bodily powers gave place among the aristoi. but since the invention of gunpowder has armed the weak as well as the strong with missile death, bodily strength, like beauty, good humor, politeness and other accomplishments, has become but an auxiliary ground of distinction. there is also an artificial aristocracy founded on wealth and birth, without either virtue or talents; for with these it would belong to the first class. the natural aristocracy I consider as the most precious gift of nature, for the instruction, the trusts, and government of society. and indeed it would have been inconsistent in creation to have formed man for the social state, and not to have provided virtue and wisdom enough to manage the concerns of the society.[386]

The impact of Confucian educational principles was also evident through Jefferson's praise of Chinese government for its ability to provide "the most effectually for a pure selection of these natural aristoi into the offices of government."[387] Jefferson's sentiment echoed those of Enlightenment intellectuals, who admired how the Chinese government was managed by a "group of highly educated scholars" rather than by an inefficient feudal aristocracy.[388] These intellectuals were further impressed by what they perceived as checks and balances within the Chinese government, wherein the Chinese emperor was "limited by [the Confucian] political philosophy that the people are the most important element in the state, the sovereign [the least]."[389]

The late Professor Herrlee G. Creel (1905–1994), a distinguished scholar on Confucius, compared the thoughts of Thomas Jefferson with those of Confucius. According to Dr. Creel, both men

> were alike in their impatience with metaphysics, in their concern for the poor as against the rich, in their insistence on basic human equality, in their belief in the essential decency of all men (including savages), and in their appeal not to authority by to "the head and heart of every honest man."[390]

Dr. Creel also pointed out, "Jefferson's statement that 'the whole art of government consists in the art of being honest' is amazingly like Analects 12.17, and other such examples could be cited."[391]

Jefferson's approval of Confucian educational principles was also based on his knowledge about China, as demonstrated through the various Chinese influences within his life. In addition to owning several books on Chinese culture at a time when China remained a distant entity, Jefferson had also drawn from Chinese architecture when designing the grounds of his Virginia home, Monticello. Jefferson had also once included a poem from the Confucian classics in his journal, demonstrating his familiarity with the scholarly works. Therefore, although limited direct records exist of the extent to which Jefferson studied Confucianism, there is enough piecemeal evidence to indicate that he was influenced by Chinese cultural works.

As Jefferson worked to refine his educational plan, he also searched for manuscripts on China in numerous Paris bookstores. He also sent James Madison a copy of *Conquista de la China por el Tartaro por Palafox*,[392] a book describing topics such as Chinese culture, religion, and mannerisms. Jefferson's gift to Madison provides further evidence that the former had significant familiarity with China.

Jefferson must have found that the Manchu, who occupied China, expressed their respect for the Chinese merit system and the officials selected by the system recorded by the book, the Manchu (Tartars)

> "kept up the Dignity of *Calao* and *Mandorin*; but none attain thereto, but by Merit and Election; and these ought all to be persons of high Reputation and Merit, of which the *Tartars* would be first well satisfied and informed."[393]

In the meantime, Chinese intellectual power must have left very deep impression on Jefferson when he pushed his educational revolution. In the book, he read that in 1647,

> there were above three hundred Scholars who took the degree of Doctor, in the City of *Nanking,* as heretofore they did at *Peking*; and above 600. Others were admitted as Licentiates, besides a great number of those who took the degree of Bachelor. It is not in Europe only, that there is such store of Doctors and Bachelors.[394]

Summary

Jefferson's educational revolution was ultimately idealistic for its time; Confucian educational principles were not widely acknowledged or accepted within the fledgling nation, and several of Jefferson's contemporaries considered him part of "the dissenting tradition in American education."[395] Jefferson was regarded as a "visionary and a dreamer,"[396] and his 1779 *Bill for the More*

General Diffusion of Knowledge was deemed too foreign for the Virginia House of Delegates.

Jefferson dreamed of creating an "aristocracy of worth and genius" [397] through a merit system that would replace the European monarchial tradition. He believed that only a well-educated populace would be able to maintain the hard-won independence that he had helped achieve from England. In thinking about the curricula of his education system, Jefferson designed holistic syllabi that drew from Roman and Greek classics, history, and science; he believed that by combining the Confucian educational principles with traditional European literature and modern scientific knowledge, he could cultivate productive future generations of U.S. citizens.

While Jefferson himself experienced little success to show for his efforts, his vision for American education eventually became a reality in the 1850s. Jefferson was influential as the starting point of this gradual movement, and later generations would build upon the foundation he set. For example, scholars such as Dustin Hornbeck have acknowledged the role of Horace Mann, the first superintendent of public schools in Massachusetts, in carrying on Jefferson's efforts to transform American education.[398]

However, although Jefferson's specific vision of education was ahead of its time, his general sentiments were consistent with the political and ideological climate within America. Many of the new nation's intellectual elite rejected the "luxury and corruption" of the Old World and sought to drive "rapid improvement in all of the arts that embellish human nature."[399]

Jefferson's educational principles were part of a broader ideological shift that replaced the historic Western emphasis on birthright with systems of merit-based succession. His efforts contributed to the emergence of a "[distinct] American character with new sets of values,"[400] one that was further removed from its European roots and was prepared to craft its own national identity.

NOTES

1. John E. Wise, *The History of Education: An Analysis Survey from the Age of Homer to the Present* (New York: Sheed and Ward, 1964), 350.

2. Dave Wang, "The U.S. Founders and China: The Origins of Chinese Cultural Influence on the United States," *Education About Asia* 16, no. 2 (Fall 2011): 5–11.

3. Gary Kowalski, "Confucius, Baseball and Apple Pie," *American Creation* (blog), March 26, 2010, http://americancreation.blogspot.com/2010/03/confucius-baseball-and-apple-pie.html.

4. Benjamin Franklin, Letter to George Whitefield, July 6, 1749, http://www.historycarper.com/1749/07/06/the-example-of-confucius.

5. Patrick Mendis, *Peaceful War: How the Chinese Dream and the American Destiny Create a Pacific New World Order* (New York: United Press of America, 2013), 50.

6. Marvin Olasky, *Fighting for Liberty and Virtue* (Washington, DC: Regnery, 1996), 142.

7. *The Morals of Confucius: A Chinese Philosopher, Who Flourished above Five Hundred Years before the Coming of our LORD and Saviour JESUS CHRIST. Being One of the Choicest Pieces of that Nation*, 2nd. ed. (London: Printed for T. Horne, at the South Entrance into the Royal Exchange, Cornhill, 1691), 61.

8. *The Founders' Constitution*, Volume 1, Chapter 18, Document 6, http://press-pubs.uchicago.edu/founders/documents/v1ch18s6.html, University of Chicago Press, *The Writings of Samuel Adams*, ed. Harry Alonzo Cushing, 4 vols. (New York: G. P. Putnam's Sons, 1904–1908).

9. Alexander Hamilton, "Washington's Farewell Address," *The Works of Alexander Hamilton* (Federal Edition), ed. Henry Cabot Lodge, vol. 8, *1774* (New York: G. P. Putnam's Sons, 1904).

10. Benjamin Rush, *The Selected Writings of Benjamin Rush*, ed. Dagobert D. Runes (New York: Philosophical Library, 1947).

11. Benjamin Franklin, *The Writings of Benjamin Franklin*, ed. Jared Sparks (Boston: Tappan, Whittemore and Mason, 1840), X:297, April 17, 1787.

12. Thomas Jefferson to George Hammond, 1792.

13. John Adams, Letter to Zabdiel Adams, June 21, 1776.

14. John Adams, Letter to Mercy Warren, April 16, 1776, http://www.revolutionary-war-and-beyond.com/john-adams-quotes-3.html#ixzz1xyBN7z8K.

15. John Adams, Novanglus Letters No. III, 1774.

16. John Adams, October 11, 1798, letter to the officers of the First Brigade of the Third Division of the Militia of Massachusetts. Charles Francis Adams, ed., *The Works of John Adams, Second President of the United States* (Boston: Little, Brown, and Co., 1854), 9:229.

17. James Madison, "The Alleged Tendency of the New Plan to Elevate the Few at the Expense of the Many Considered in Connection with Representation," *The Federalist* 57, New York Packet, Tuesday, February 19, 1788.

18. Benjamin Franklin, Motto of the University of Pennsylvania.

19. "John Adams to Mercy Warren, 16 Apr. 1776, Warren-Adams Letters 1:222–23," *The Founders' Constitution*, vol. 1, chap. 18, doc. 9, University of Chicago Press, http://press-pubs.uchicago.edu/founders/documents/v1ch18s9.html, *Warren-Adams Letters, Being Chiefly a Correspondence among John Adams, Samuel Adams, and James Warren*, vol. 2, 1778–1814. Collections of the Massachusetts Historical Society, vol. 73. (Boston: Massachusetts Historical Society, 1925).

20. James Madison, "Virginia Ratifying Convention," *The Founders' Constitution*, vol. 1, chap. 13, doc. 36, http://press-pubs.uchicago.edu/founders/documents/v1ch13s36.html.

21. Thomas Jefferson, "Jefferson's Literary Commonplace Book," in *The Papers of Thomas Jefferson*, Second Series (Princeton: Princeton University Press, 1989).

22. *Morals of Confucius*, 70.

23. Ibid., 72.

24. Dave Wang, "From Confucius to the Great Wall: Chinese Cultural Influence on Colonial North America," *Asia-Japan Journal*, 10th Anniversary Special Issue (March 2011): 117–25, Asia Japan Research Center, Kokushikan University; Wang, "Benjamin Franklin, George Washington, Thomas Jefferson and Chinese Civilization," *Virginia Review of Asian Studies* (2009), https://virginiareviewofasianstudies.com/archived-issues/2009-2/; Dave Wang, "Exploring Benjamin Franklin's Moral Life," *Franklin Gazette* 17, no. 1 (Spring 2007).

25. Benjamin Franklin, "From the *Morals of Confucius*," *Pennsylvania Gazette*, February 28 to March 7, 1738.

26. Franklin told Whitefield,

> I am glad to hear that you have frequent opportunities of preaching among the great. If you can gain them to a good and exemplary life, wonderful changes will follow in the manners of the lower ranks; for, Ad Exemplum Regis, &c. On this principle Confucius, the famous eastern reformer, proceeded. When he saw his country sunk in vice, and wickedness of all kinds triumphant, he applied himself first to the grandees; and having by his doctrine won them to the cause of virtue, the commons followed in multitudes. The mode has a wonderful influence on mankind; and there are numbers that perhaps fear less the being in Hell, than out of the fashion. Our more western reformations began with the ignorant mob; and when numbers of them were gained, interest and party-views drew in the wise and great. Where both methods can be used, reformations are like to be more speedy. O that some method could be found to make them lasting! He that shall discover that, will, in my opinion, deserve more, ten thousand times, than the inventor of the longitude.

Franklin to George Whitefield, Philadelphia July 6, 1649, reprinted from *The Evangelical Magazine* XI (1803), 27–28; also AL (fragment): American Philosophical Society, http://www.franklinpapers.org/franklin/framedVolumes.jsp.

27. Paine was the editor of the magazine. The works were composed based on the three works written by some seamen who had been to China, including *A Voyage to China and the East Indies*, *A Voyage to Suratte*, and *Account of the Chinese Husbandry*, were "published as a unit in Swedish in 1757." They were translated into German in 1765 and into English in 1771. A. Owen Aldridge, *The Dragon and the Eagle: The Presence of China in the American Enlightenment* (Detroit: Wayne State University Press, 1993), 34.

28. The Morgan Library in New York City possesses a manuscript in Bartram's hand titled *Life and Character of the Chinese Philosopher Confucius*.

29. According to John Bartram,

> Confucius had been the greatest moral as well as practical philosopher that ever lived, and he excelled Pythagoras (570–495 BC—writer) in pursuit of religion and morals. Confucius was of the most exemplary sobriety and chastity of life, was endured with every virtue and free from every vice, and showed the greatest equableness and magnanimity of temper even under the most unworthy treatment. His whole doctrine tended to restore human nature to its original dignity and that first purity and luster which it had received from heaven and which had been sullied and corrupted. He taught as means to obtain this

end to honor and fear the Lord of Heaven, to love our neighbor as ourselves, to subdue irregular passions and inclinations, to listen to reason in all things, and to do or say nothing contrary to it. He taught kings and princes to be fathers to their subjects, to love them as their children, and he taught subjects to reverence and obey their kings and governors with the honor and affection due to their parents. . . . In short, Confucius was the original ultimate end of all things and the one supreme holy, intelligent, and invisible being.

Cited in Aldridge, *Dragon and the Eagle*, 32.

30. Edwin Wolf, *James Logan, 1674–1751: Bookman Extraordinary, An exhibition of books and manuscripts from the library of James Logan, supplemented by his writings and documents relating to the history of the Bibliotheca Loganiana. In honor of the visit to Philadelphia of the seventh International Congress of Bibliophiles* (Philadelphia: The Library Company of Philadelphia, 1971), 41.

31. Ibid., 4.

32. A. Owen Aldridge, *American Literature: A Comparatist Approach* (Princeton: Princeton University Press, 1982), 289–90.

33. Jedidiah Morse, *The American Universal Geography; or a View of the Present Situation of the United States and of all the Empire, Kingdoms, States, and Republics in the Known World*, 2nd., vol. 2 (Boston: Isaiah Thomas and Ebenezer Andrews, 1796), 499.

34. Ibid.

35. Aldridge, *Dragon and the Eagle*, 37.

36. *The Columbian Magazine*, May 1788, 257–63.

37. According to the author, Confucius "recommended the contempt of riches and outward pomp; he endeavored to inspire magnanimity and greatness of soul" and to reclaim his countrymen from voluptuousness to reason and sobriety. "Kings were governed by his counsels, and people reverenced his as saint." *New Hampshire Magazine* 2 (1793): 199–203.

38. Elizabeth Drinker, *Extracts from the Journal of Elizabeth Drinker, Period from 1759–1807*, ed. Henry D. Biddle (Philadelphia: J. B. Lippincott, 1889), 267, https://archive.org/details/extractsfromjou00dringoog.

39. Benjamin Franklin, *The Autobiography of Benjamin Franklin*, http://www.ushistory.org/franklin/autobiography/.

40. In the years soon after the revolution, membership continued to expand. Members have served in all the major offices of the United States and many state governments. Some, including Thomas Jefferson, were alarmed at the apparent creation of a hereditary elite; membership eligibility is inherited through primogeniture and excludes enlisted men and in most cases militia officers, unless they were placed under "State Line" or "Continental Line" forces for a substantial period. Benjamin Franklin was among the society's earliest critics, although he would later accept its role in the republic and join the society under honorary membership after the country stabilized. He voiced concerns about not only the apparent creation of a noble order but also the society's use of the eagle in its emblem as evoking the traditions of heraldry.

41. Benjamin Franklin, to Sarah Bache (unpublished) Passy, Jan. 26th, 1784. In *The Papers of Benjamin Franklin*, ed. Yale University. See also http://www

.franklinpapers.org/franklin/framedVolumes.jsp; see also Mark Skousen, ed., *The Compleated Autobiography by Benjamin Franklin* (Washington, DC: Regnery, 2006), 311–12.

42. Ibid.

43. 朱熹，7; 吴国珍，16 and 杨伯峻, 17.

44. Benjamin Franklin, to Madame Brillon, "The Ephemera," Founders Online, National Archives, https://founders.archives.gov/documents/Franklin/01-27-02-0408.

45. Thomas Paine, "Of the Old and New Testament," *The Prospect* (March 31, 1804). See also *Complete Writings*, vol. 2, ed. Philip S. Foner (New York: Garden City Press, 1945), 805.

46. Ibid.

47. Thomas Paine, *The Political Works of Thomas Paine*, 2 vols. (Oxford: Oxford University Press, 1864), 15. Paine quoted from Confucius's following teaching maxims to Yan Yuan, one of his well-known students: "Look not at what is contrary to propriety; listen not to what is contrary to propriety; speak not what is contrary to propriety; make no movement which is contrary to propriety." (Section 12 of the Analects), http://wengu.tartarie.com/wg/wengu.php?no=294&l=Lunyu; see also 朱熹，93; and 杨伯峻, 174.

48. Thomas Paine, *Federal City, Lovett's Hotel*, 1802.

49. From John Adams, December 25, 1813, in *The Papers of Thomas Jefferson, Retirement Series*, vol. 7:28, *November 1813 to September 1814*, https://jeffersonpapers.princeton.edu/.

50. Benjamin Rush, "Of the Mode of Education Proper in a Republic, 1798," *The Selected Writings of Benjamin Rush*, ed. Dagobert D. Runes (New York: Philosophical Library, 1947), 87–89, 92, 94–96, http://press-pubs.uchicago.edu/founders/documents/v1ch18s30.html.

51. Thomas Jefferson, "First Inaugural Address," *The Papers of Thomas Jefferson*, vol. 33, *17 February to 30 April 1801* (Princeton: Princeton University Press, 2006), 148–52, http://www.princeton.edu/~tjpapers/inaugural/infinal.html.

52. America's Founding Documents, http://www.archives.gov/exhibits/charters/declaration_transcript.html.

53. King Wu of Zhou (周武王) was the first king of the Zhou dynasty of ancient China. The chronology of his reign is generally thought to have begun around 1046 BC and ended three years later in 1043 BC.

54. Sarah Schneewind, "Thomas Jefferson's Declaration of Independence and King Wu's First Great Pronouncement," *Journal of American-East Asian Relations* 19 (2012): 75–91.

55. Colin Wells, "Thomas Jefferson's Scrapbooks: Poems of Nation, Family, and Romantic Love Collected by America's Third President," *Early American Literature* 42, no. 3 (November 2007): 626.

56. For the Chinese poem that Jefferson collected, see ibid., 27.

57. 朱熹，7. 吴国珍, 16.

58. Dave Wang, "All Posterity Will Remember My Legacy: Thomas Jefferson and a Legendary Chinese Prince," *Huaren E-Magazine* (Australia), September 2008.

59. The Chinese character Feng, 风 "wind," has been interpreted as "mores" or "customs." The character may also be read as "influence." This is particularly the case of Confucian commentators who stress the poems' political significance. The section of the Wind of State contains 160 songs and is subdivided geographically into fifteen sections, one for each of fifteen states in ancient China. Most of them deal, however, with the lives of the common people—their work, play, festivities, joys, and hardships. The Wind of Wei (魏风) is number 10 from the "Wind of State （国风）." This poem as metaphor expresses the grateful sentiments of the people of Wei to Duke Hwan, who rescued them from invasion.

60. *Great Learning* is one of the four books edited by Confucius, including *The Doctrine of the Mean*, *The Analects*, and *The Mencius*.

61. Gene Allen Smith, "Thomas Jefferson: Reputation and Legacy," *Journal of American History* 94, no. 1 (June 2007): 260–61.

62. "Salma Hale's Notes on his Visit to Monticello, [after 1818]," Founders Online, National Archives, https://founders.archives.gov/documents/Jefferson/03-13-02-0015-0005. Original source: *The Papers of Thomas Jefferson, Retirement Series*, ed. J. Jefferson Looney, vol. 13, *22 April 1818 to 31 January 1819* (Princeton: Princeton University Press, 2016), 26–29.

63. Joseph J. Ellis, *American Creation: Triumph and Tragedies at the Founding of the Republic* (New York: Alfred A. Knopf, 2007), 3.

64. "From John Adams to James Warren, 9 January 1787," Founders Online, National Archives, https://founders.archives.gov/documents/Adams/06-18-02-0286. Original source: *The Adams Papers, Papers of John Adams*, ed. Gregg L. Lint, Sara Martin, C. James Taylor, Sara Georgini, Hobson Woodward, Sara B. Sikes, Amanda M. Norton, vol. 18, *December 1785–January 1787* (Cambridge, MA: Harvard University Press, 2016), 538–40.

65. Cokie Roberts, *Founding Mothers: The Women Who Raised Our Nation* (New York: HarperCollins, 2004), 190.

66. Joseph J. Ellis, *Founding Brothers: The Revolutionary Generation* (New York: Vintage, 2002), 9.

67. Ibid.

68. Paul Merrill Spurlin, *Montesquieu in America, 1760–1801* (Baton Rouge: Louisiana State University Press, 1940), 144.

69. Russel Blaine Nye, *The Cultural Life of the New Nation, 1776–1830* (New York: Harper & Brothers, 1960), 5.

70. Shane J. Ralston, *American Enlightenment Thoughts*, https://www.iep.utm.edu/amer-enl/.

71. Ibid.

72. Catherine Drinker Bowen, *Miracle at Philadelphia: The Story of the Constitutional Convention, May to September 1787* (Boston and Toronto: Little, Brown, 1966), 112.

73. There are several cases throughout U.S. history when candidates who won the popular vote did not become president. Back in 1824, Andrew Jackson won the popular vote; however, he could not win the electoral vote. In the end, John Quincy Adams won the election. Again in 1888, Benjamin Harrison, who lost the popular

vote, won the election by the Electoral College. In recent years, there were two presidential elections where the candidates who won the popular vote lost in the Electoral College. In the 2000 election, Al Gore received more than half a million more total votes nationally than George W. Bush. In 2016, Hillary Clinton won 2.9 million more votes than Donald Trump; both lost the election because they lost in the Electoral College.

74. Noah Webster, *An examination into the leading principles of the Federal Constitution proposed by the late convention held at Philadelphia. With answers to the principal objections that have been raised against the system* (Philadelphia: Printed and sold by Prichard & Hall, in Market Street the second door above Laetitia Court, M.DCC.LXXXVII [1787]).

75. Gilbert Reid, "Revolution as Taught by Confucianism," *International Journal of Ethics* 33, no. 2 (1923): 193.

76. Confucius, *Analects*, 2.1, http://www.confucius.org/lunyu/.

77. *Analects*, 3:19.

78. Patrick Zukeran, *A Brief Overview and Biblical Critique of Confucius*, https://evidenceandanswers.org/article/a-brief-overview-and-biblical-critique-of-confucius/.

79. *Analects*, 2.1.

80. Reid, "Revolution as Taught by Confucianism," 200.

81. 《荀子·王制》："传曰：'君者舟也，庶人者水也，水则载舟，水则覆舟。'此之谓也。"

"Xunzi·Wangzhi": It has been said, "rulers are like boats, people are like water, water can support boats, it can also overturn them."

82. Reid, "Revolution as Taught by Confucianism," 190.

83. *Analects*, 4.12.

84. *Analects*, 4.16.

85. *Analects*, 4.5.

86. Jennifer Ratner-Rosenhagen, ed., *The Ideas that Made America: A Brief History* (Oxford: Oxford University Press, 2019), 31.

87. Zukeran, *Brief Overview*.

88. Bill Schwarz, *The Expansion of England: Race, Ethnicity and Cultural History* (New York: Routledge, 1996).

89. Ibid.

90. Dave Wang, "Confucius in the American Making: The Founders' Efforts to Use Confucian Moral Philosophy in Their Endeavor to Create New Virtue for the New Nation," *Virginia Review of Asian Studies* 16 (2014): 11–26.

91. Benjamin Franklin, to George Whitefield, reprinted from *The Evangelical Magazine*, XI (1803): 27–28; also AL (fragment): American Philosophical Society. Philadelphia, July 6, 1749, https://founders.archives.gov/documents/Franklin/01-03-02-0156.

92. "From John Adams to Benjamin Rush, 22 December 1808," Founders Online, National Archives, https://founders.archives.gov/documents/Adams/99-02-02-5282.

93. Benjamin Franklin, "From the *Morals of Confucius*," *Pennsylvania Gazette*, 1728–1789, vol. 4, *1737–1740*, 74. Thanks to Mr. Roy Goodman, the former chief

librarian of American Philosophic Society, for his help in providing with me the *Pennsylvania Gazette*.

94. Ibid., 82.

95. From Benjamin Franklin: "Speech in the Convention on the Constitution" (unpublished) [September 17, 1787].

96. "From Benjamin Franklin to Samuel Johnson, 23 August 1750," *Founders Online*, National Archives, https://founders.archives.gov/documents/Franklin/01-04-02-0009. Original source: *The Papers of Benjamin Franklin*, ed. Leonard W. Labaree, vol. 4, *July 1, 1750, through June 30, 1753* (New Haven: Yale University Press, 1961), 40–42.

97. Benjamin Franklin, Marginalia in a Pamphlet by Allan Ramsay, MS notations in the margins of a copy in the Library of Congress of [Allan Ramsay,] *Thoughts on the Origin and Nature of Government, Occasioned by the Late Disputes between Great Britain and Her American Colonies: Written in the Year 1766* (London, 1769). Benjamin Franklin Papers, https://franklinpapers.org/framedVolumes.jsp.

98. See https://teachingamericanhistory.org/static/convention/delegates/franklin.html.

99. Louis J. Sirico Jr., *How the Separation of Powers Doctrine Shaped the Executive*, Working Paper Series, Villanova University Charles Widger School of Law, 2008, 10.

100. Benjamin Franklin, to George Whitefield, [Before Sept. 2, 1769], reprinted from Joseph Belcher, *George Whitefield: A Biography, with Special Reference to His Labors in America* (New York: [1857] 2016), 414–15.

101. "From Benjamin Franklin to Samuel Cooper, 1 May 1777," *Founders Online*, National Archives, https://founders.archives.gov/documents/Franklin/01-24-02-0004. Original source: *The Papers of Benjamin Franklin*, ed. William B. Willcox, vol. 24, *May 1 through September 30, 1777* (New Haven and London: Yale University Press, 1984), 6–7.

102. Skousen, *Compleated Autobiography by Benjamin Franklin*, 359.

103. Benjamin Franklin to Madame Brillon, "The Ephemera," Founders Online, National Archives, https://founders.archives.gov/documents/Franklin/01-27-02-0408.

104. To Count Castiglione (unpublished), Philadelphia, October 14, 1787.

105. The Basis of the American Republic, http://www.let.rug.nl/usa/outlines/government-1991/the-constitution-an-enduring-document/the-basis-of-the-american-republic.php.

106. American History: From Revolution to Reconstruction and Beyond, http://www.let.rug.nl/usa/outlines/history-2005/the-formation-of-a-national-government/constitutional-convention.php.

107. Willi Paul Adams, The First American Constitutions: Republican Ideology and the Making of the State Constitutions in the Revolutionary Era (Lanham, MD: Rowman & Littlefield, 2001), 128–29.

108. See note 40.

109. Benjamin Franklin, to Sarah Bache (unpublished), Passy, Jany. 26th. 1784, *Benjamin Franklin Papers*, https://franklinpapers.org/framedVolumes.jsp.

110. Broadus Mitchell, *Alexander Hamilton: The Revolutionary Years*, Leaders of the American Revolution Series, ed. North Callahan (New York: Thomas Y. Crowell, 1970), 305.

111. Dumas Malone, *Jefferson and the Rights of Man*, Jefferson and His Time Series, Volume II (Boston: Little, Brown, 1951), 156.

112. Ibid.

113. Ellis, *Founding Brothers*, 9.

114. Roberts, *Founding Mothers*, 190.

115. Dumas Malone, *Jefferson: The Virginian*, Jefferson and His Time Series, Volume I (Boston: Little, Brown, 1948), 251–52.

116. Richard R. Beeman, *Perspectives on the Constitution: A Republic, If You Can Keep It*, https://constitutioncenter.org/learn/educational-resources/historical-documents/perspectives-on-the-constitution-a-republic-if-you-can-keep-it.

117. From Charles de Butré with Franklin's Draft of a Reply (unpublished) Tue, March 8, 1785, The Papers of Benjamin Franklin, https://franklinpapers.org/framedVolumes.jsp.

118. Walter Isaacson, *Benjamin Franklin: An American Life* (New York: Simon & Schuster, 2003), 446.

119. Benjamin Franklin, Convention Speech Proposing Prayers (unpublished), June 28, 1787, *Benjamin Franklin Papers*, https://franklinpapers.org/framedVolumes.jsp.

120. Reid, "Revolution as Taught by Confucianism," 191.

121. Skousen, *Compleated Autobiography by Benjamin Franklin*, 356–57.

122. Benjamin Franklin, "Speech of June 4, 1787."

123. James Madison, *Federalist* 84, 1788.

124. Benjamin Franklin, "Speech of June 4, 1787."

125. Ibid.

126. Ibid.

127. Ibid.

128. Bowen, *Miracle at Philadelphia*, 60.

129. Records of the Federal Convention, Article 2, Section 1, Clause 7, http://press-pubs.uchicago.edu/founders/documents/a2_1_7s2.html.

130. Ibid.

131. *The Founders' Constitution*, vol. 3, article 2, section 1, clause 7, doc. 2, http://press-pubs.uchicago.edu/founders/documents/a2_1_7s2.html, University of Chicago Press, ed. Farrand, Max, *The Records of the Federal Convention of 1787*, rev. ed., 4 vols. (New Haven and London: Yale University Press, 1937).

132. *The Founders' Constitution*, vol. 3, article 2, section 1, clause 7, doc. 2, http://press-pubs.uchicago.edu/founders/documents/a2_1_7s2.html, University of Chicago Press.

133. See http://www.benjamin-franklin-history.org/constitutional-convention/.

134. George Taylor, *James Wilson*, Society of the Descendants of Signers of the Declaration of Independence, https://www.dsdi1776.com/signers-by-state/james-wilson/.

135. Stephen Macedo, "Meritocratic Democracy: Learning from the American Constitution," in *The East Asian Challenge for Democracy: Political Meritocracy*

in Comparative Perspective, ed. Daniel A. Bell and Changyang Li (New York: Cambridge University Press, 2013), 244.

136. James Madison, *Federalist* 51, 1788.

137. Noah Feldman, *The Three Lives of James Madison: Genius, Partisan, President* (New York: Random House, 2017), 98–99, 121–122.

138. James Madison, "*Federalist* 10, [22 November] 1787," Founders Online, National Archives, https://founders.archives.gov/documents/Madison/01-10-02-0178. Original source: *The Papers of James Madison*, ed. Robert A. Rutland, Charles F. Hobson, William M. E. Rachal, and Frederika J. Teute, vol. 10, *27 May 1787–3 March 1788* (Chicago: University of Chicago Press, 1977), 263–70.

139. Ibid.

140. "*Federalist* 68, [12 March 1788]," Founders Online, National Archives, https://founders.archives.gov/documents/Hamilton/01-04-02-0218. Original source: *The Papers of Alexander Hamilton*, ed. Harold C. Syrett, vol. 4, *January 1787–May 1788* (New York: Columbia University Press, 1962), 586–90.

141. Michael Kammen, ed., *The Origins of the American Constitution: A Documentary History* (New York: Penguin, 1986), xv.

142. Isaacson, *Benjamin Franklin: An American Life*, 457.

143. Benjamin Franklin to the editor of the *Federal Gazette* (unpublished), 1788, *Benjamin Franklin Papers*, https://franklinpapers.org/framedVolumes.jsp.

144. Isaacson, *Benjamin Franklin: An American Life*, 450.

145. Ibid.

146. Ibid.

147. See https://www.constitutionfacts.com/us-constitution-amendments/fascinating-facts.

148. See https://www.mtsu.edu/first-amendment/article/1156/john-adams.

149. "From John Adams to François Adriaan Van der Kemp, October 1, 1817," Founders Online, National Archives, https://founders.archives.gov/documents/Adams/99-02-02-6807.

150. From John Adams to Benjamin Rush, December 22, 1808," Founders Online, National Archives, https://founders.archives.gov/documents/Adams/99-02-02-5282.

151. Adams, "Thoughts on Government."

152. David McCullough, *John Adams* (New York and London: Simon & Schuster, 2001), 376.

153. Adams, "Thoughts on Government."

154. Ibid.

155. "From John Adams to John Taylor, December 17, 1814," Founders Online, National Archives, https://founders.archives.gov/documents/Adams/99-02-02-6371.

156. James Madison, *Federalist* 10, 1787.

157. Jonathan Gross, ed., *Thomas Jefferson's Scrapbooks: Poems of Nation, Family & Romantic Love, Collected by America's Third President* (Hanover, NH: Steerforth Press, 2006), 12.

158. Edward J. Larson, *Franklin & Washington: The Founding Partnership* (New York: William Morrow, 2020), 81.

159. Thomas Jefferson, *Autobiography, 1743–1790*, https://avalon.law.yale.edu/19th_century/jeffauto.asp.

160. Benjamin Rush, "Commonplace Book March 17, 1790," in *The Founders on the Founders: Word Portraits from the American Revolutionary Era*, ed. John P. Kaminski (Charlottesville and London: University of Virginia Press, 2019), 297.

161. For a quick look at Thomas Jefferson's constitutional legacy, https://constitutioncenter.org/blog/a-quick-look-at-thomas-jeffersons-constitutional-legacy.

162. Wells, "Thomas Jefferson's Scrapbooks," 626.

163. For the poem, please see ibid., 27.

164. Jefferson began the scrapbooks in 1801 and compiled them through his two terms as president.

165. Reid, "Revolution as Taught by Confucianism," 194.

166. J. David Gowdy, *Thomas Jefferson and the Pursuit of Virtue*, http://www.liberty1.org/TJVirtue.pdf.

167. Thomas Jefferson, *The Life and Morals of Jesus of Nazareth, Extracted Textually from the Gospels, Together with a Comparison of His Doctrines with Those of Others—The Jefferson Bible* (St. Louis, MO: N. D. Thompson Publishing Co., 1902).

168. "Thomas Jefferson to Charles Thomson, January 9, 1816," *Founders Online*, National Archives, https://founders.archives.gov/documents/Jefferson/03-09-02-0216. Original source: *The Papers of Thomas Jefferson, Retirement Series*, ed. J. Jefferson Looney, vol. 9, *September 1815 to April 1816* (Princeton: Princeton University Press, 2012), 340–42.

169. Gross, *Thomas Jefferson's Scrapbooks*, 12.

170. Thomas Jefferson to George Hammond, 1792.

171. Macedo, "Meritocratic Democracy," 249.

172. Thomas Jefferson, "First Inaugural Address," *The Papers of Thomas Jefferson*, vol. 33, *February 17 to April 30, 1801* (Princeton: Princeton University Press, 2006), 148–52, http://www.princeton.edu/~tjpapers/inaugural/infinal.html.

173. Isaacson, *Benjamin Franklin: An American Life*, 445.

174. Ibid., 492.

175. R. B. Bernstein, *The Founding Fathers Reconsidered* (Oxford: Oxford University Press, 2009), 26.

176. Thomas Jefferson, *Autobiography, 1743–1790*.

177. "From John Adams to Mercy Otis Warren, 8 August 1807," Founders Online, National Archives, https://founders.archives.gov/documents/Adams/99-02-02-5203.

178. Franklin, Convention Speech Proposing Prayers.

179. Bernstein, *Founding Fathers Reconsidered*, 32.

180. "From Thomas Jefferson to John Adams, 10 December 1819," *Founders Online*, National Archives, https://founders.archives.gov/documents/Jefferson/98-01-02-0953.

181. "From John Adams to François Adriaan Van der Kemp, 1 October 1817," *Founders Online*, National Archives, https://founders.archives.gov/documents/Adams/99-02-02-6807.

182. Ann Fishman, "The Greatest Naturist in the World," *Humanities: The Magazine of National Endowment of the Humanity*, January/February 1995, 33;

James E. Seely Jr., ed., *Shaping North America: From Exploration to the American Revolution*, 3 vols. (Santa Barbara, CA: ABC-CLIO, 2018), 92; Nina Reid, "Enlightenment and Piety in the Science of John Bartram," *Pennsylvania History: A Journal of Mid-Atlantic Studies* 58, no. 2 (April 1991): 128.

183. Thomas Paine, "Age of Reason, 1794–1795," in *The Ideas that Made America: A Brief History*, ed. Jennifer Ratner-Rosenhagen (Oxford: Oxford University Press, 2019), 58.

184. "From John Adams to François Adriaan Van der Kemp, 1 October 1817," *Founders Online*, National Archives, https://founders.archives.gov/documents/Adams/99-02-02-6807.

185. Bernard Bailyn, "Political Experience and Enlightenment Ideas in Eighteenth-Century America," in *The Causes of the American Revolution*, 3rd ed., ed. John. C. Wahlke (Lexington, MA: D. C. Heath, 1973), 95.

186. "From George Washington to Edmund Randolph, 8 January 1788," Founders Online, National Archives, https://founders.archives.gov/documents/Washington/04-06-02-0013. Original source: *The Papers of George Washington, Confederation Series*, ed. W. W. Abbot, vol. 6, *January 1, 1788–September 23, 1788* (Charlottesville: University Press of Virginia, 1997), 17–18.

187. See https://www.constitutionfacts.com/us-constitution-amendments/fascinating-facts/.

188. *History of Civil Service Merit System of the United States and Selected Foreign Countries, together with Executive Reorganization Studies and Personnel Recommendations*, compiled by the Library of Congress Congressional Research Service, for the Subcommittee on Manpower and Civil Service of the Committee on Post Office and Civil Service, House of Representatives 94th Congress, 2nd session, December 31, 1967 (Washington, DC: US Government Printing Office, 1976), 4.

189. Edward Glaeser, "Public Ownership in the American City," in *Urban Issues and Public Finance: Essays in Honor of Dick Netzer*, ed. Amy E. Schwartz (Northampton, MA: Edward Elgar, 2003), 130–62.

190. U.S. Office of Personnel Management, https://archive.opm.gov/about_opm/tr/history.asp.

191. See http://www.societyofthecincinnati.org/.

192. Stanley J. Idzerda, Roger E. Smith, and Linda J. Pike, eds., *Lafayette in the Age of the American Revolution—Selected Letters and Papers, 1776–1790: December 7, 1776–March 30, 1778* (Utica, NY: Cornell University Press, 1977), v:209. For the concerns of Matthew Ridley (who wrote to John Adams at The Hague), John Adams (who fumed about the disregard of the Articles of Confederation), and John Jay, see Adams Papers, xv, 437, 468–69; Jay Papers, iii, 557, 559–60. See "From Benjamin Franklin to Sarah Bache, 26 January 1784," Founders Online, National Archives, https://founders.archives.gov/documents/Franklin/01-41-02-0327. Original source: *The Papers of Benjamin Franklin*, ed. Ellen R. Cohn, vol. 41, *September 16, 1783, through February 29, 1784* (New Haven and London: Yale University Press, 2014), 503–11.

193. Benjamin Franklin, To Sarah Bache (unpublished), Passy, January 26, 1784, http://franklinpapers.org.

194. Ibid.
195. Ibid.
196. Ibid.
197. Ibid.
198. Ibid.
199. Ichisada Miyazaki, *China's Examination Hell*, trans. Conrad Schirokauer (New York: Weatherhill, 1976), 13–17.
200. Six Dynasties (also called *Liuchao*六朝; 220–589) is a term for six Chinese dynasties. Immediately following the fall of the powerful Han dynasty in 220 AD, this era was one of disunity, instability, and warfare.
201. The system of recruiting public employees according to examinations was based on Confucian ideas. The oldest example of a merit-based civil service system was found in 200 BC. During the time, the Han dynasty (206 BC–220 AD) established Confucianism as the basis of its political philosophy and structure. This system replaced administrative appointments based on the nobility of blood with those based solely on merit. Only an individual who passed the examination could be offered a public service position. Later, in the Sui dynasty (581–618 AD), the merit system was formally started and was fully developed during the Tang dynasty (618–907). The system continued to be used by all later dynasties throughout Chinese history until 1905, when the system was stopped by the imperial court.
202. Dave Wang, "Benjamin Franklin, George Washington, Thomas Jefferson and Chinese Civilization," *Virginia Review of Asian Studies* (2009), http://www.virginiareviewofasianstudies.com/.
203. By 1792 there were about 780 federal employees on the federal payroll. See *History of Civil Service Merit System*, 3. According to the Office of Personnel Management, as of December 2011, there were approximately 2.79 million civil servants employed by the U.S. government. As of 2014, there are 4,185,000 federal employees. *Federal Employee Reports*, https://www.opm.gov/.
204. *The Development of Bureaucracy*, http://www.ushistory.org/gov/8a.asp.
205. Ibid.
206. Kelle S. Sisung and Gerda-Ann Raffaelle, "The John Adams Administration," in *Presidential Administration Profiles for Students* (Boston: Gale Group, 1999), 1, 3.
207. Katheryn Turner, "Republican Policy and the Judiciary Act of 1801," *William and Mary Quarterly* 22 (January 1965): 5.
208. Kelle S. Sisung and Gerda-Ann Raffaelle, "The Thomas Jefferson Administration," in *Presidential Administration Profiles for Students* (Boston: Gale Group, 1999), 3.
209. The Midnight Appointments, also called the Judiciary Act of 1801, was John Adams's attempt to appoint Federalist supporters to the newly created court positions. The appointments were called the Midnight Appointments because they were completed in the last nineteen days of Adams's presidency.
210. See http://www.encyclopedia.com/history/united-states-and-canada/us-history/spoils-system.
211. Sisung and Raffaelle, "The Thomas Jefferson Administration," 3.

212. John Dickerson, "The Original Attack Dog: James Callender Spread Scurrilous Stories about Alexander Hamilton and John Adams," *Slate*, August 9, 2016 http://www.slate.com/articles/news_and_politics/history/2016/08/james_callender_the_attack_dog_who_took_aim_at_alexander_hamilton_and_thomas.html.

213. Jill Lepore, "Party Time," *The New Yorker*, September 17, 2007, p. 94.

214. Michael Durey, *Transatlantic Radicals and the Early America Republic* (Lawrence: University of Kansas Press, 1997).

215. Jefferson supported Callender financially. For example, Jefferson paid him $15.14 for Callender's series of pamphlets History of the United States for 1796. See MB 2:963, 975, 980, 1002, 1005, 1018, 1028, and 1042, which covers the years 1797 to 1801 See James A. Bear Jr. and Lucia C. Stanton, eds., *Jefferson's Memorandum Books: Accounts, with Legal Records and Miscellany, 1767–1826* (Princeton: Princeton University Press, 1997). See https://www.monticello.org/site/research-and-collections/james-callender and http://www.history.com/this-day-in-history/richmond-recorder-publishes-report-of-presidential-concubine.

216. Lepore, "Party Time."

217. Dumas Malone, *Jefferson the President, First Term, 1801–1805*, Jefferson and His Time Series, Volume IV (Boston: Little, Brown, 1970), 209, in a letter from James Callender to James Madison on April 27, 1801, after Jefferson failed to respond to a Callender letter of April 12, 1801.

218. *Dictionary of American Biography*, s.v. "Callender, James Thomson."

219. Lepore, "Party Time."

220. James Callender, "The President, Again," *The Recorder; or, Lady's and Gentleman's Miscellany*, September 1, 1802.

221. Sally Hemings was a young slave girl who served Jefferson's eldest daughter, Martha, at the Jefferson home, Monticello. When Jefferson was sent as an American diplomat to Paris in 1787, he took with him Polly, his youngest daughter, and Sally Hemings as a companion for Polly. Critics charge that while in Paris, Jefferson began a sexual relationship with Hemings. See http://www.wallbuilders.com/libissuesarticles.asp?id=124.

222. John Rorrey Morse, *Thomas Jefferson*, American Statesmen Series (Boston: Houghton Mifflin, 1898), 202.

223. James Truslow Adams, *The Living Jefferson* (New York: Charles Scribner's Sons, 1936), 315.

224. See http://www.phrases.org.uk/bulletin_board/32/messages/793.html.

225. Daniel W Howe, *What Hath God Wrought: The Transformation of America, 1815–1848*. (Oxford: Oxford University Press, 2007), 334.

226. Leonard D. White, *The Jacksonians: A Study in Administrative History, 1829–1961* (New York: ACLS History E-Book Project, 1954), 309–13. See also Murray N. Rothbard's 1995 treatise, "Bureaucracy and the Civil Service in the United States," *Journal of Libertarian Studies* 11, no. 2 (Summer 1995): 308.

227. Gordon S. Wood, *Revolutionary Characters: What Made the Founders Different* (New York: Penguin, 2006), 116.

228. See http://watchingthewatchers.org/news/1221/corruption-cronies-and-19th-century.

229. Caleb J. McNulty (1816–1946), a clerk from Pennsylvania, member of the Ohio House of Representatives, 1841–1842. He was elected clerk of the United States House of Representatives for the 28th Congress and served until his dismissal on January 18, 1845 (December 6, 1843–January 18, 1845). See http://history.house.gov/People/Detail/38442.

230. Rothbard, "Bureaucracy and the Civil Service in the United States," 3–75.

231. White, *The Jacksonians*, 309–13. See also Rothbard, "Bureaucracy and the Civil Service in the United States," 3–75.

232. See http://lincolnmemory.blogspot.com/2009/04/lincoln-and-patronage.html.

233. John G. Nicolay and John Hay, *Abraham Lincoln: A History*, vol. IV (New York: Century, 1890), 68–69.

234. Richard N. Current, ed., *Sections and Politics: Selected Essays by William B. Hesseltine* (Madison: Wisconsin Historical Society, 1968), 115.

235. Paul P. Van Riper, *History of the United States Civil Service* (Evanston, IL: Row, Peterson and Company, 1958), 43. Also see David H. Rosenbloom, *Federal Service and the Constitution: The Development of the Public Employment Relationship* (Washington, DC: Georgetown University Press, 2014), 56. Also see Rothbard, "Bureaucracy and the Civil Service in the United States," 3–75.

236. Ari Hoogenboom, "Thomas A. Jenkes and Civil Service Reform," *Mississippi Valley Historical Review* 47, no. 4 (March 1961): 637.

237. Philip H. Burch, Jr., *Elites in American History*, vol. II, *The Civil War to the New Deal* (New York: Holmes & Meier, 1981), 16, 23–24, 48, 54.

238. Ibid., 55.

239. The term *carpetbaggers* refers to Northerners who moved to the South after the Civil War, during Reconstruction. Scalawags were white Southerners who cooperated politically with black freedmen and Northern newcomers. Scalawags typically supported the Republican Party. "Carpetbaggers and Scalawags," Boundless U.S. History, November 20, 2016, https://courses.lumenlearning.com/boundless-ushistory/.

240. William Marcy Tweed was elected to the U.S. House of Representatives in 1853. Five years later, he became the head of Tammany Hall, the central organization of the Democratic Party in New York. In 1867, he was elected to the New York State Senate. The Tweed ring brought New York's budget into their own pockets by embezzlement, bribery, and kickbacks.

241. Hoogenboom, "Thomas A. Jenckes and Civil Service Reform," 643.

242. See http://592807.xobor.com/t7798f29-How-Bureaucrats-Captured-Government.html.

243. William S. McFeely and C. Vann Woodward, *Responses of the Presidents to Charges of Misconduct* (New York: Delacorte, 1974), 133–34; James McPherson, *Liberty, Equality, Power: A History of the American People* (Boston: Cengage, 2012), 593.

244. The Grant administration was marked by widespread political corruption. It was said that it established a woeful record. Major scandals included the Credit Mobilier, the Whiskey Ring, and the Indian Ring.

245. In 1871, Curtis was appointed as the chair of the commission on civil service reform by President Ulysses S. Grant. From then until his death, he led this

movement. In 1884, he refused to support James G. Blaine as candidate for the presidency and left the Republican Party to become an independent. See https://www.britannica.com/biography/George-William-Curtis.

246. Thomas Allen Jenckes was a U.S. congressional representative for the state of Rhode Island. He was an avid supporter of civil service reform.

247. Eaton was a lawyer. He played important role in American federal civil service reform. He was a member of the U.S. Civil Service Commission from 1873 to 1875. In 1877, he went to examine the experience of Great Britain's adoption of the Chinese merit system. In 1880 he published *Civil Service* in Great Britain. He drafted the Pendleton Civil Service Act of 1883, and later became a member of the new commission it established.

248. George W. Curtis, introduction to *Civil Service in Great Britain: A History of Abuse and Reforms and Their Bearing Upon American Politics*, by Dorman B. Eaton (New York: Harper & Brothers, 1880), v.

249. Ibid.

250. Ibid.

251. Ibid.

252. Mr. Andrews, late Minister to Sweden, to Mr. Fish, *Papers Related to the Foreign Relations of the United States*, https://history.state.gov/historicaldocuments/frus1877/d310.

253. Ibid.

254. Thomas A. Jenckes, *Speech of Hon. Thomas A. Jenckes of Rhode Island, The Bill to Regulate the Civil Service of the United States and Promote the Efficiency Thereof: delivered in the House of Representatives, May 14, 1868* (Washington, DC: F&J Rives & Geo. A. Bailey, Reporters and Printers of the Debates of Congress, 1868), 5.

255. Dorman B. Eaton, *Civil Service in Great Britain: A History of Abuse and Reforms and Their Bearing Upon American Politics* (New York: Harper & Brothers, 1880), 334–35.

256. "John Stuart Mill, Letter 1402 to an Unidentified Correspondent," in *Collected Works of John Stuart Mill*, ed. J. M. Roberson, vol. XVII (Toronto: University of Toronto Press), 1572, 73.

257. Ibid.

258. Rea T. Markin, "Rights of the Public Employee under the Illinois Civil Service System: A Progression of the Law," *John Marshall Law Review* 8, no. 1 (1974): 53, http://repository.jmls.edu/lawreview/vol8/iss1/3.

259. Hoogenboom, "Thomas A. Jenckes and Civil Service Reform," 641.

260. *The Nation* was a New York periodical founded by young British journalist Edwin Lawrence Godkin, a supporter of the civil service reform.

261. *Nation* IV, April 11, 1867, 286.

262. Rothbard, "Bureaucracy and the Civil Service in the United States," 3–75.

263. Jed Shugerman, *The Founding of the DOJ and the Failure of Civil Service Reform, 1865–1870*, 6, http://www.americanbarfoundation.org/uploads/cms/documents/shugerman_doj_and_civil_service.doc.

264. Hoogenboom, "Thomas A. Jenckes and Civil Service Reform," 647.

265. Shugerman, *Founding of the DOJ*, 6.
266. *A Bill to Regulate the Civil Service of the United States, and Promote the Efficiency Thereof*, Senate No. 430, 39 Cong., I Sess., forms the basis for the ensuing discussion of the Jenckes bill. This bill was introduced by Henry B. Anthony of Rhode Island, Jenckes's friend. The bill is identical with Jenckes's bill.
267. Ari Hoogenboom, "Pennsylvania in the Civil Service Reform Movement," *Pennsylvania History* 28, no. 3 (July 1961): 268.
268. Jenckes, *Speech of Hon. Thomas A. Jenckes of Rhode Island*, 8.
269. Ibid.
270. Thomas A. Jenckes, *The Civil Service: Report* (Washington, DC: U.S. Government Printing Office, 1868), 13.
271. Hoogenboom, "Thomas A. Jenkes and Civil Service Reform," 636.
272. Jenckes, *Speech of Hon. Thomas A. Jenckes of Rhode Island*, 5.
273. Cong. Globe, 39 Cong., 2 sess., 1034 (February 6, 1867).
274. Jenckes, *The Civil Service: Report*, 124.
275. The Five Classics (五经wujing) and Four Books (四书si shu) collectively create the foundation of Confucianism. The Five Classics and Four Books were the basis of the civil examination in imperial China and can be considered the Confucian canon. The Five Classics consists of the 诗经*Book of Odes*, 史记*Book of Documents*, 易经*Book of Changes*, 礼记*Book of Rites*, and 春秋 *the Spring and Autumn Annals*. The Four Books are comprised of 中庸*the Doctrine of the Mean*, 大学*the Great Learning*, 孟子*Mencius*, and 论语*the Analects*.
276. Jencks, *The Civil Service: Report*, 126.
277. Ibid., 125.
278. Ibid., 131.
279. Ibid., 134.
280. Ibid.
281. Ibid.
282. Argus Panoptes (or Argos) is a many-eyed *giant* in *Greek mythology*. It is known for having spawned the saying "the eyes of Argus," as in to be "followed by," "trailed by," "watched by," among others, the eyes; the saying is used to describe being subject to strict scrutiny in one's actions to an invasive, distressing degree.
283. The Ear of Dionysius (*Italian*: Orecchio di Dionisio) is a *limestone* cave carved out of the Temenites hill in the city of *Syracuse*, on the island of *Sicily* in *Italy*. The term *Ear of Dionysius* is used to refer to surveillance, specifically that for political gain.
284. Jencks, *The Civil Service: Report*, 131.
285. Ibid.
286. Jencks, *The Civil Service: Report*, 125.
287. Hoogenboom, "Thomas A. Jenkes and Civil Service Reform," 642.
288. Ibid.
289. Jenckes, *Speech of Hon. Thomas A. Jenckes of Rhode Island*, 11.
290. Ibid.
291. Ibid.
292. Ibid.

293. Ibid.
294. Ibid.
295. Ibid., 15.
296. Cong. Globe, 39 Cong. 2d Sess. 837-41 (January 29, 1867).
297. Ibid.
298. Jenckes had the support of forty-seven Republicans and twenty-two Democrats, but was opposed by fifty-six Republicans and eleven Democrats. See Cong. Globe, 39 Cong., 2d Sess., 1036 (February 6, 1867).
299. Cong. Globe, 39 Cong., 2d Sess., 1036 (February 6, 1867).
300. Gale to Jenckes, November 25, 1868, *Jenckes Papers*.
301. Rothbard, "Bureaucracy and the Civil Service in the United States," 3–75.
302. When the Chinese Embassy visited Boston in the summer of 1868 a banquet was given them at the St. James Hotel, on August 21. Ralph Waldo Emerson (1803–1882) made a speech at the banquet. "Speech at Banquet in Honor of Chinese Embassy Boston, 1868," in *The Complete Works of Ralph Waldo Emerson* (Boston: Houghton Mifflin, 1904), Vol. XI. Miscellanies XXVI.
303. Rothbard, "Bureaucracy and the Civil Service in the United States," 3–75.
304. Ibid.
305. Cong. Globe, 41st Cong., 3d Sess., 378 (January 9, 1871).
306. *History of Civil Service Merit System*, 4.
307. See http://www.presidency.ucsb.edu/ws/?pid=29520.
308. See http://biography.yourdictionary.com/dorman-bridgman-eaton.
309. Ibid., 4.
310. Ibid., 354–55.
311. Curtis, introduction to *Civil Service in Great Britain*, iii.
312. Charles A. Beard and Mary R. Beard, *The Rise of American Civilization* (New York: Macmillan, 1927).
313. The Pendleton Civil Service Reform Act (ch. 27, 22 Stat. 403) is a U.S. federal law, enacted in 1883, that established that positions within the federal government should be awarded on the basis of merit instead of political affiliation: http://www.digitalhistory.uh.edu/disp_textbook.cfm?smtID=3&psid=1098.
314. See http://www.saylor.org/site/wp-content/uploads/2012/08/POLSC2313.3.1.pdf.
315. In 1883, with the passage of the Pendleton Act, some 13,900 employees, about 10.5 percent of the federal civilian employees, were initially placed in the classified service and subject to the merit principles. By the mid-1970s, more than 90 percent of federal civilian employees were under the merit system. See *History of Civil Service Merit System*, 3.
316. Eaton, *Civil Service in Great Britain*, 438.
317. Ibid., vi.
318. Stephen Skowronek, *Building a New American State: The Expansion of National Administrative Capacities, 1877–1920* (New York: Cambridge University Press, 1982), 67.
319. Theodore Roosevelt, U.S. Civil Service Commissioner, in a letter dated February 8, 1895.

320. Jenckes, *The Civil Service: Report*, 124.

321. James Carpenter, "Thomas Jefferson and the Ideology of Democratic Schooling," *Democracy & Education* 21, no. 2 (2013): 1.

322. Johann Neem, "Is Jefferson a Founding Father of Democratic Education?" *Democracy & Education* 22, no. 2 (2013): 1.

323. The Spring and Autumn period (春秋时代) was from approximately 771 to 476 BC. The period's name derives from the Spring and Autumn Annals, a chronicle of Chinese history between 722 and 479 BC, which tradition associates with Confucius.

324. Friedrich Max Müller, *The Sacred Books of the East*, vol. 28, part 4 (Oxford: Clarendon Press, 1885), 82.

325. *Morals of Confucius*, 47.

326. 知者不惑，仁者不忧，勇者不惧。(Confucian *Analects*, trans. James Legge, 1893, chapter 19).

327. *Morals of Confucius*, 57.

328. Confucius taught, "This is what Confucius propos'd to the Princes, to instruct them how to rectify and polish first their own reason. . . . His person being thus perfected, his family, forming itself according to this Model, will be reform'd and amended. His Family being arriv'd at this Perfection, 'twill severs as an Example to all Subjects of the particular Kingdom, and the Members of the particular Kingdom to those that compose the Body of the Empire." *Morals of Confucius*, 36–37.

329. The Classic of Poetry, also Shijing, translated variously as the Book of Songs, Book of Odes, or simply known as the Odes or Poetry (詩) is the oldest existing collection of Chinese poetry, comprising 305 works dating from the eleventh to seventh centuries BC. It is one of the "Five Classics" compiled by Confucius.

330. The Zhou dynasty (周朝) was a Chinese dynasty that followed the Shang dynasty and preceded the Qin dynasty. The Zhou dynasty was the longest dynasty in Chinese history.

331. Marsha Elaine Covington, "Great Teachers on Teaching Adults: Comparison of Philosophy and Practice from Antiquity to the Present" (doctor of education thesis, Montana State University, 1997).

332. Colin Power, The Power of Education: Education for All, Development, Globalisation and UNESCO, Education in the Asia-Pacific Region: Issues, Concerns and Prospects Series (New York: Springer, 2014), 185.

333. Michael Kazin, Rebecca Edwards, and Adam Rothman, *The Princeton Encyclopedia of American Political History*, vol. 2 (Princeton: Princeton University Press, 2010), 142. One of the oldest examples of a merit-based civil service system existed in the imperial bureaucracy of China. Chung Tan and Yinzheng Geng, *India and China: Twenty Centuries of Civilization Interaction and Vibrations* (Ann Arbor: University of Michigan Press, 2005), 128. China produced not only the world's first "bureaucracy" but also the world's first "meritocracy." Melvin Konner, *Unsettled: Anthropology of the Jews* (New York: Viking Compass, 2003), 217. China is the world's oldest meritocracy.

334. Thomas J. Sienkewicz, *Encyclopedia of the Ancient World* (Hackensack, NJ: Salem Press, 2003), 434.

335. Jane Burbank and Frederick Cooper, *Empires in World History: Power and the Politics of Difference* (Princeton: Princeton University Press, 2010), 51.

336. Ibid.

337. Kazin, Edwards, and Rothman, *Princeton Encyclopedia of American Political History*, 142.

338. Schwarz, *Expansion of England*, 229.

339. Charlene Tan, "Confucianism and Education: Curriculum and Pedagogy, Educational Theories and Philosophies," *Oxford Research Encyclopedias*, November 2017, http://education.oxfordre.com/view/10.1093/acrefore/9780190264093.001.0001/acrefore-9780190264093-e-226.

340. "The Mather School is Marking 375 years of Public Education; NYPD's Bratton, an Alumnus, to Speak at Assembly," Dorchester Reporter, https://www.dotnews.com/2014/mather-school-marking-375-years-public-education-nypd-s-bratton-alumnu.

341. Louis B. Wright, *The Cultural Life of the American Colonies, 1607–1673*, New American Series, ed. Henry Steele Commager and Richard B. Morris (New York: Harper & Row, 1957), 100.

342. Kevin R. G. Gutzman, *Thomas Jefferson—Revolutionary: A Radical's Struggle to Remake America* (New York: St. Martin's, 2017), 198.

343. Linda L. Arthur, "A New Look at Schooling and Literacy: The Colony of Georgia," *Georgia Historical Quarterly* 84, no. 4 (2000): 563–88.

344. Wise, *History of Education*, 346.

345. Thomas Jefferson, Letter to John Adams, July 5, 1814.

346. Ibid.

347. Thomas Jefferson, Letter to Littleton Waller Tazewell, 1805.

348. Benjamin Justice, "A Window to the Past: What an Easy Contest Reveals about Early American Education," *American Educator* (Summer 2015): 33.

349. Fawn M. Brodie, *Thomas Jefferson: An Intimate History* (New York and London: W.W. Norton & Company, 1974), 151.

350. James Carpenter, "The Complexity of Thomas Jefferson: A Response to 'The Diffusion of Light': Jefferson's Philosophy of Education," *Democracy & Education* 22, no. 1 (2014).

351. Jon Meacham, *Thomas Jefferson: The Art of Power* (New York: Random House, 2012), 324.

352. Thomas Jefferson, "Notes on the State of Virginia," *The Founders' Constitution*, vol. 1, chap. 18, doc. 16, http://press-pubs.uchicago.edu/founders/documents/v1ch18s16.html, University of Chicago Press, ed. William Peden (Chapel Hill: University of North Carolina Press for the Institute of Early American History and Culture, Williamsburg, Virginia, 1954).

353. G. C. Lee, ed., *Crusade against Ignorance: Thomas Jefferson on Education*, 5th ed. (New York: Teachers College Press, 1967), 118.

354. Thomas Jefferson, copied into his Commonplace Book.

355. Thomas Jefferson to Peter Carr, September 7, 1814, http://founders.archives.gov/documents/Jefferson/03-07-02-0462.

356. Thomas Jefferson to Littleton Waller Tazewell, 1805.

357. Thomas Jefferson, to George Washington, Paris January 4, 1785, http://founders.archives.gov/documents/Jefferson/01-09-02-0135.

358. Thomas Jefferson, Notes on the State of Virginia with Related Documents, ed. David Waldstreicher (Boston and New York: Bedford/St. Martin's, 2002), 182–85.

359. Jeff Sparagana, *The Educational Theory of Thomas Jefferson*, http://www.newfoundations.com/GALLERY/Jefferson.html.

360. "Thomas Jefferson, from Thomas Jefferson to Mann Page, 30 August 1795," Founders Online, National Archives, http://founders.archives.gov/documents/Jefferson/01-28-02-0347. Original source: The Papers of Thomas Jefferson, ed. John Catanzariti, vol. 28, January 1, 1794–February 29, 1796 (Princeton: Princeton University Press, 2000), 440–41.

361. Thomas Jefferson, Notes on the State of Virginia, 182.

362. "Thomas Jefferson to John Adams, 28 Oct. 1813," *The Founders' Constitution*, vol. 1, chap. 15, doc. 61, http://press-pubs.uchicago.edu/founders/documents/v1ch15s61.html, University of Chicago Press, The Adams-Jefferson Letters: The Complete Correspondence between Thomas Jefferson and Abigail and John Adams, ed. Lester J. Cappon, 2 vols. (Chapel Hill: University of North Carolina Press for the Institute of Early American History and Culture, Williamsburg, Virginia, 1959).

363. A Bill for the More General Diffusion of Knowledge, 18 June 1779," Founders Online, National Archives, http://founders.archives.gov/documents/Jefferson/01-02-02-0132-0004-0079. Original source: The Papers of Thomas Jefferson, ed. Julian P. Boyd, vol. 2, 1777–June 18, 1779 (Princeton: Princeton University Press, 1950), 526–35.

364. "Thomas Jefferson, Autobiography," in *The Founders' Constitution*, vol. 1, chap. 15, doc. 20, http://press-pubs.uchicago.edu/founders/documents/v1ch15s20.html, University of Chicago Press, The Works of Thomas Jefferson, collected and edited by Paul Leicester Ford, Federal Edition, 12 vols. (New York and London: G. P. Putnam's Sons, 1904–1905).

365. Dustin Hornbeck, "Seeking Civic Virtue: Two Views of the Philosophy and History of Federalism in U.S. Education," Journal of Thought (Fall–Winter 2017): 62.

366. National Park Service, *Thomas Jefferson's Plan for the University of Virginia: Lessons from the Lawn*, "Reading 1: Education as the Keystone to the New Democracy," https://www.nps.gov/articles/thomas-jefferson-s-plan-for-the-university-of-virginia-lessons-from-the-lawn-teaching-with-historic-places.htm.

367. Willard Sterne Randall, Thomas Jefferson: A Life (New York: Henry Holt, 1993), 288.

368. William K. Medlin, The History of Educational Ideas in the West (New York: Center for Applied Research in Education, 1964), 108.

369. "Thomas Jefferson to John Banister, Jr., 15 October 1785," Founders Online, National Archives, http://founders.archives.gov/documents/Jefferson/01-08-02-0499. Original source: The Papers of Thomas Jefferson, ed. Julian P. Boyd, vol. 8, 25 February–31 October 1785 (Princeton: Princeton University Press, 1953), 635–38.

370. Robert A. Gross, *An Extensive Republic: Print, Culture, and Society in the New Nation, 1790–1840*, History of the Book in America Series, vol 2, ed. Mary Kelley (Chapel Hill: University of North Carolina Press, 2010), 250.

371. D. H. Myer, "The Uniqueness of the American Enlightenment," American Quarterly 28, no. 2 (Summer 1976): 23.

372. Daniel J. Boorstin, *The Americans: The Colonial Experience* (New York: Random House, 1958), 109–10.

373. From Thomas Jefferson to John Banister Jr., October 15, 1785, Founders Online, National Archives, http://founders.archives.gov/documents/Jefferson/01-08-02-0499. Original source: The Papers of Thomas Jefferson, ed. Julian P. Boyd, vol. 8, February 25–October 31, 1785 (Princeton: Princeton University Press, 1953), 635–38.

374. Ibid.

375. Myer, "The Uniqueness of the American Enlightenment," 173.

376. Jacques Barzun, From Dawn to Decadence: 500 years of Western Cultural Life, 1500 to Present (New York: HarperCollins, 2000), 408.

377. "To Thomas Jefferson from William Jarvis, 18 February 1809," Founders Online, National Archives, https://founders.archives.gov/documents/Jefferson/99-01-02-9828.

378. "Thomas Jefferson to John Adams, 28 Oct. 1813," *The Founders' Constitution*, vol. 1, chap. 15, doc.61, http://press-pubs.uchicago.edu/founders/documents/v1ch15s61.html, University of Chicago Press, The Adams-Jefferson Letters: The Complete Correspondence between Thomas Jefferson and Abigail and John Adams, ed. Lester J. Cappon, 2 vols. (Chapel Hill: University of North Carolina Press for the Institute of Early American History and Culture, Williamsburg, Virginia), 1959.

379. Herrlee Glessner Creel, Confucius: The Man and the Myth (London: Routledge & Kegan Paul, 1951), 5.

380. Ibid., 98.

381. Catalogue of the library of Thomas Jefferson, https://www.loc.gov/item/52060000/.

382. "Charles J. Ingersoll to Thomas Jefferson, 4 July 1818," Founders Online, National Archives, https://founders.archives.gov/documents/Jefferson/03-13-02-0127. Original source: *The Papers of Thomas Jefferson, Retirement Series*, ed. J. Jefferson Looney, vol. 13, *April 22, 1818 to January 31, 1819* (Princeton: Princeton University Press, 2016), 124.

383. Ibid.

384. "Thomas Jefferson to Charles J. Ingersoll, 20 July 1818," Founders Online, National Archives, https://founders.archives.gov/documents/Jefferson/03-13-02-0155. Original source: *The Papers of Thomas Jefferson, Retirement Series*, ed. J. Jefferson Looney, vol. 13, *April 22, 1818 to January 31, 1819* (Princeton: Princeton University Press, 2016), 142.

385. "Report on Books for Congress, [23 January] 1783," Founders Online, National Archives, https://founders.archives.gov/documents/Madison/01-06-02-0031. Original source: *The Papers of James Madison*, ed. William T. Hutchinson and William M. E. Rachal, vol. 6, *January 1, 1783–April 30, 1783* (Chicago: University of Chicago Press, 1969, 62–115.

386. "Thomas Jefferson to John Adams, 28 Oct. 1813," *The Founders' Constitution*, vol. 1, chap. 15, doc. 61, http://press-pubs.uchicago.edu/founders/documents/v1ch15s61.html, University of Chicago Press, The Adams-Jefferson Letters: The Complete Correspondence between Thomas Jefferson and Abigail and John Adams, ed. Lester J. Cappon, 2 vols. (Chapel Hill: University of North Carolina Press for the Institute of Early American History and Culture, Williamsburg, Virginia), 1959.

387. Ibid.

388. Derk Bodde, "Chinese Ideas in the West," in *China: A Teaching Workbook*, Asia for Educators, Columbia University, http://www.learn.columbia.edu/nanxuntu/html/state/ideas.pdf.

389. 孟子，盡心章句下（十四） 孟子曰：民為貴，社稷次之，君為輕。Mencius said, "The people are the most prized, the gods of land and cereals come next, and the sovereign is the lightest. Therefore, he who wins the heart of the people may become a king; who wins the heart of the king may become a state ruler; he who wins the heart of the state ruler may be appointed a high-ranking official. 吴国珍，孟子·大学·中庸·平解·英译，471.

390. Creel, Confucius: The Man and the Myth, 98.

391. Edward L. Shaughnessy, *Confucius and the University of Chicago: Of Myths and Men*, June 2010, http://cccp.uchicago.edu/downloads/Confucius_and_the_University_of_Chicago.pdf.

392. Douglas L. Wilson and Lucia Stanton, eds., Jefferson Abroad (New York: Modern Library, 1999), 27. Jefferson bought the 1732 French edition. The book was written in Spanish by Juan de Palafox y Mendoza (June 26, 1600–October 1, 1659), a Spanish politician, administrator, and Catholic clergyman in seventeenth-century Spain and vice regal Mexico. His Historia de la conquista de la China por el Tartaro (History of the Conquest of China by the Tartars) reported on the conquest of the Ming China by the Manchus, based on reports that reached Mexico by the way of the Philippines. The work was first published in Spanish in Paris in 1670; a French translation appeared the same year. An English translation, whose full title was *The History of the Conquest of China by the Tartars together with an Account of Several Remarkable things, Concerning the Religion, Manners, and Customs of Both Nation's, but especially the Latter*, appeared in London in 1676. Palafox's work, based on hearsay, was generally less informed than De bello tartarico, an eyewitness account by the Chinese-speaking Jesuit Martino Martini.

393. Juan de Palafox y Mendoza, *The history of the conquest of China by the Tartars together with an account of several remarkable things concerning the religion, manners, and customs of both nations, but especially the latter 1600–1659*, 482. https://quod.lib.umich.edu/e/eebo/A54677.0001.001/1:4?rgn=div1;view=fulltext.

394. Ibid, 503–4.

395. Perry L. Glanzer, "The Dissenting Tradition in American Education," American Educational History Journal 35, no. 2 (2008), 393.

396. Richard Hofstadter, *About the Anti-Intellectualism in American Life* (New York: Vintage, 1962), 27.

397. Thomas Jefferson, Autobiography, in *The Founders' Constitution*, vol. 1, chap. 15, doc. 20, http://press-pubs.uchicago.edu/founders/documents/v1ch15s20.

html, University of Chicago Press, The Works of Thomas Jefferson, collected and edited by Paul Leicester Ford, Federal Edition, 12 vols. (New York and London: G. P. Putnam's Sons, 1904–1905).

398. Hornbeck, "Seeking Civic Virtue," 62.

399. Gordon S. Wood, *Empire of Liberty: A History of the Early Republic, 1789–1815* (New York: Oxford University Press, 2009), 545.

400. Wise, History of Education, 350.

Chapter 7

The Founders' Legacy

The Founding Fathers integrated numerous positive elements of Chinese civilization, ranging from agriculture and architecture to Confucian moral and political philosophy, into the American fabric as they built the foundations of their fledgling nation. As one of the most stable and successful civilizations at the time, China offered social, economic, and cultural precedents that were distinct from the founders' European heritage. Confucian moral philosophy and the civil service system became especially influential in the development of American democracy.

The Founding Fathers and other prominent Americans leveraged Chinese agricultural and industrial practices to strengthen the nation's domestic economy. Letters and other records indicate that Franklin had obtained rhubarb seeds, and that Washington and Jefferson had experimented with Chinese flowers on their personal estates. Franklin also introduced soybeans from China into Savannah, Georgia, in 1765. In addition, Franklin expressed great interest in Chinese industrial technologies such as milling, heating, shipbuilding, and papermaking. Franklin and fellow statesman Benjamin Rush promoted silk-making, or sericulture, in North America. Similarly, Jefferson borrowed elements from Chinese designs in his efforts to create a new style of architecture. George Washington, Alexander Hamilton, and Gouverneur Morris were inspired by literature on the Grand Canal of China. These Chinese technologies would eventually aid in the construction of the Erie Canal and spur the development of New York City.

Furthermore, the Founding Fathers frequently drew from Confucian philosophies in their efforts to construct a new political framework for their young nation. Many prominent colonists, including Benjamin Franklin, Thomas Jefferson, John Adams, Thomas Paine, John Bartram, and Jedidiah Morse, demonstrated their respect for Confucian moral philosophy and attempted to incorporate its principles into American culture. For instance, Franklin published excerpts adopted from *Morals of Confucius* in his widely circulated *Pennsylvania Gazette* to promote Confucian moral thinking in the colonies, and later cited Confucius as a role model. Jefferson, who himself had drawn comparisons to Confucius, regarded the philosopher's example of the "Chinese Prince" to be an ideal ruler.

In a similar vein, Thomas Paine listed Confucius with Jesus and the Greek philosophers as the world's greatest moral teachers in his "Age of Reason, 1791–1792." In his *American Universal Geography*, Jedidiah Morse cited *The Great Learning* and *The Doctrine of the Mean*, two of the four classic Confucian works. Morse extolled these two classics as "the most excellent precepts of wisdom and virtue, expressed with the greatest eloquence, elegance and precision." John Bartram, a distinguished colonial botanist, wrote a paper, *Life and Character of the Chinese Philosopher Confucius*, to introduce Confucius to his readers, describing the philosopher as "a character so truly virtuous."

The Founding Fathers also looked to China for an alternative set of political frameworks as they sought to distance themselves from European aristocratic traditions. In his 1796, Farewell Address, President Washington advised his fellow citizens that

> Europe has a primary set of interests which to us have none or a very remote interest.... Hence, therefore, it must be unwise for us to implicate ourselves by artificial ties in the ordinary vicissitudes of her politics.... Our detached and distant situation invites and enables us to pursue a different course.

Jefferson echoed Washington in expressing "the desirability of Chinese isolation and of the need to place an ocean of fire between us and the old world."[1]

Confucian ideals played a particularly important role in the formation of the American political system. Noah Webster, regarded as the father of American scholarship and education, had once remarked that Confucian principles were one of the most influential forces in developing the U.S. Constitution. The Confucian civil service system also offered a political framework in which social advancement was based on ability and scholarship rather than genealogy. One beneficiary of this system was Alexander Hamilton, a foreign-born and illegitimate son who would come to be "something of a symbol of meritocracy, of throwing off European class distinction."[2] Hamilton's life offered an "extraordinary objective lesson in social mobility."[3]

The borrowing of positive elements from Chinese civilization helped create a pattern of integrating elements from other cultures into American culture. Today, as has been the case over the last several centuries, America is an ethnic melting pot in which citizens of all backgrounds consume intellectual concepts and technological products with various cultural roots. Americans have since embraced many Chinese cultural elements, such as the meritocratic way as the main means of selecting public employees. This cross-cultural pollination began, in large part, with the Founding Fathers in the formative days of the new nation.

NOTES

1. Robert W. Tucker and David C. Hendrickson, *Empire of Liberty: The Statecraft of Thomas Jefferson* (New York: Oxford University Press, 1990), 246.
2. Cokie Roberts, *Founding Mothers: The Women Who Raised Our Nation* (New York: HarperCollins, 2004), 190.
3. Ron Chernow, *Alexander Hamilton* (New York: Penguin, 2004), 345.

Epilogue

Visitors to the U.S. Supreme Court in Washington, DC, are often surprised to find a sculpture of Confucius along with Moses and Solon on the east pediment of the building. The sculpture serves as a reminder of Confucius's own influence on the development of American civilization. Many are surprised to learn how greatly Chinese cultural and technological thinking influenced American civilization even before the country was born.

Although significantly influenced by Europe, the American founders did not blindly follow Europe's example. The founders needed to integrate a new system of ideas beyond Europe. Positive elements from Chinese civilization bolstered a special and unique integration of elements into American culture.

The founders' focus on China was not unanimous. Alexander Hamilton "looked East, not west, saw America as a commercial empire." Jefferson looked to China because he envisioned the United States as an "agrarian republic." It widely recognized that Jefferson in his *Notes on Virginia* revealed "his conception that democracy should have an agricultural basis."

Some historians of the preindependence era of the United States point out that the notion of aristocracy—such as coastwise aristocracy and planting aristocracy—"had dominated the governmental machinery of the mainland colonies." The introduction of Confucian meritocracy changed this. The United States was more open to individuals of talent than any of the other countries in the world. In Europe, hereditary aristocracy dominated social promotion. The American founders introduced Confucian meritocratic ideas into American political thinking.

A person's social advancement was based more on merit than a fixed ancestral or class hierarchy. Alexander Hamilton, foreign-born and a well-known illegitimate, became "something of a symbol of meritocracy, of throwing off European class distinction." It would have been more difficult for Hamilton to be elevated as a national leader without such a nontraditional merit-based system. Hamilton's own life "offered an extraordinary objective lesson in social mobility." John Adams made the statement that Benjamin Franklin was "more universal than that of Leibniz or Newton, Frederic or Voltaire."[1]

The meritocratic system has become a social organism within which individuals could realize their potential and dreams based on their efforts and abilities. It has become a cornerstone of American democracy. Even in the twenty-first century, America's meritocracy-based system has become one of the indispensable elements of a democracy; equal opportunity applies to everyone regardless of national origin or social identity.

What makes the American founders who studied and admired Chinese civilization so remarkably different from their intellectual peers in Europe was that they ventured far and beyond by incorporating the positive elements of Chinese civilization. The founders applied those positive elements in their aspirations for a new, independent nation the likes of which the world had never seen. These Founding Fathers believed that their fellow citizens should adopt positive elements from Confucian philosophy and follow these moral examples to cultivate their own sense of virtue.

I have come to realize that my book is not merely about the measures taken by the American founders to inculcate Chinese cultural influences. It is much more than that. It is common knowledge that history helps us better understand our world. Never has Americans' understanding of their history mattered more and never has the work of the foundation been more relevant.[2] By looking back to the past, we can better understand the present and predict the future. Our world today has dramatically changed compared to the founding era of the United States. Do the founders' vision and efforts still have value to guide us in today's world? I hope that my book offers a scholarly explanation to the standard conventional wisdom. My desire is for an opening to a wider perspective from which to overcome our present preoccupations. It can provide readers with insights to face difficult, complex, and sometimes conflicting truths and confront how those truths reverberate in the present.

In the book, I formulated the notion of Franklin's theory of social progress. This is found in the context that the best direction for human beings is to combine the best of the West with the best of the East. The historical experiences and contemporary development have proved that Franklin's theory has as much relevance and vitality today as it did in America in the eighteenth century.

We are in the midst of the first global pandemic in more than a century. In this period of darkness, there were shining lights that emerged. All places, such as Japan, South Korea, Vietnam, and Taiwan, that have combined the tradition of Western social progress with the positive moral and social principles of Eastern Confucianism, have achieved great success in fighting against the COVID-19 virus. In fact, they are leading the way in all aspects of social development.

Singapore has adopted a Western-style political system since independence. At the same time, the republic also maintains a strong connection with Confucian tradition. Confucianism uses the family as the basis of society, and the relationships of the family members define proper social and political behavior. Lee Kuan Yew (1923–2015) was Singapore's founding father and long-term leader. In his second memoir, published in 2000, Lee wrote that Singapore is " a Confucian society which placed the interests of the community above those of individuals."[3] He recognized clearly that the city-state's success and prosperity depends on the strength and influence of Confucian value to "keep society orderly and maintain a culture of thrift, hard work, filial piety, and respect for elders and for scholarship and learning. These values make for a productive people and help economic growth."[4]

History and contemporary social development are constantly demonstrating the significance of Benjamin Franklin's theory. America's founders incorporated some positive elements from other civilizations. In today's world, no matter your background, education, and career, an understanding of how past societies has drawn strength from other cultures is a key to humanity's progress in the future.

We have reason to believe that the road pointed out by Franklin will be more and more realized by the world. The history of the founders' efforts to apply positive elements from Chinese civilization encourages a deeper understanding of differences. I am confident that as long as we draw inspiration from the great men of the past, we will overcome all obstacles and build a more beautiful world.

In his influential article, the late professor Samuel Huntington writes that in his thesis of the clash of civilizations is "to set forth descriptive hypothesis as to what the future may be like."[5]

However, if we are to be successful in the future, we must study the past. Readers will find from reading this book that mutual learning is one the themes of the progress of human civilization.

I present following quote from Dr. Wilton Dillon's book, *Smithsonian Stories: Chronicle of a Golden Age, 1964–1984*, published by Transaction Publishers, 2015. Dr. Dillon (1923–2015) says:

> I met Dave Wang at an Aspen Institute meeting of Friends of Franklin. Meeting this Chinese scholar from St. John's University in New York opened up a floodgate of new insights about Chinese influence on our founding fathers and colonial North America. Prof. Wang travels the world now to share his new findings. I have given copies of some of his papers to former US senators Larry Pressler, Republican from South Dakota, and Harris Wofford, Democrats

from Pennsylvania, when they lectured in China on "the two-party system." Celebrating one nation's cultural gifts to another—and especially, the capacity to receive—makes for good diplomacy.

How China Helped to Shape American Culture: The Founding Fathers and Chinese Civilization is the title of Wang's 2010 summary of his findings, published in Virginia Review of Asian Studies (2010). Confucian philosophy, tea, porcelain, wallpaper, rhubarb, soybeans, house heating, canal and shipbuilding, ideas about reason, rocketry, and alternative medicine were among many cultural contributions coming from China. Franklin designed a wooden wall inspired by the Great Wall to protect Philadelphia from Indians after the French and Indian War. Jefferson's architecture showed hints of Chinese design. Wang traces Chinese influence on Thomas Paine, John Bartram, Benjamin Rush, and Jedidiah Morse, among others.

His essay starts with a quote from President Barack Obama in his July 27, 2009, remarks at the U.S.-China Strategic and Economic Dialogue:

Americans know the richness of China's history because it helped to shape the world and it helped to shape America. We know the talent of the Chinese people because they have helped to create this great country.

Lines need to be drawn between pandering for political, economic, and security goals on the one hand and historical studies of cultural contact on the other. Western, particularly U.S. influence, has helped to revolutionize Greater China. The Asian idea of yin and yang would help both interdependent parties to feel more comfortable with each other.[6]

NOTES

1. Leo Lemoy, *The Life of Benjamin Franklin,* Vol. 1, Journalist, 1706–1730, (Philadelphia: University of Pennsylvania Press), 229.

2. Carly Fiorina, "History Matters—Especially Today," *Trend & Tradition* (Spring 2021), 4–5.

3. Lee Kuan Yew, "From Third World to First: The Singapore Story, 1965–2000," in *Memoirs of Lee Kuan Yew* (Singapore: Singapore Press Holdings, 2000), 542.

4. Surain Subramaniam, "The Dual Narrative of 'Good Governance': Lessons for Understanding Political and Cultural Change in Malaysia and Singapore," *Contemporary Southeast Asia* 23, no. 1 (2001): 65–80, http://www.jstor.org/stable/25798528.

5. Samuel Huntington, "The Clash of Civilizations?" *Foreign Affairs* (Summer 1993).

6. Wilton Dillon, *Smithsonian Stories: Chronicle of a Golden Age, 1964–1984* (Piscataway, NJ: Transaction Publishers, 2015).

Bibliography

吴国珍，论语：平解·英译，北京出版社，2017.
吴国珍，孟子·大学：平解·英译，北京出版社，2017.
杨伯峻，论语译注，中华书局，2017.
朱熹，论语集注，济宁市新闻出版局，1997.
Achenwall, Gottfried. "Some Observations on North America from Oral Information by Dr. Franklin." Translated from "Einige Anmerkungen über Nordamerika, und über dasige Grosbritannische Colonien. (Aus mündlichen Nachrichten des Hrn. Dr. Franklins.)." Hannoverisches Magazin, 17tes, 18tes, 19tes, 31tes, 32tes Stücke (Feb. 27, Mar. 2, 6, Apr. 17, 20, 1767), cols. 257–96, 482–508 (Princeton University Library). it is available online at http://franklinpapers.org/franklin/framedVolumes.jsp.
Adams, James Truslow. *The Living Jefferson*. New York: Charles Scribner's Sons, 1936.
The Adams-Jefferson Letters: The Complete Correspondence between Thomas Jefferson and Abigail and John Adams. Edited by Lester J. Cappon. 2 vols. Chapel Hill: University of North Carolina Press for the Institute of Early American History and Culture, Williamsburg, Virginia, 1959.
Adams Papers Digital Edition by the Massachusetts Historical Society. This digital edition includes all text of the historical documents and all editorial text. https://www.masshist.org/publications/adams-papers/.
The Adams Papers Digital Edition by University of Virginia. *The Adams Papers* collects the correspondence and other significant papers of our nation's first great political family. https://www.upress.virginia.edu/content/adams-papers-digital-edition.
Adams, Willi Paul. The First American Constitutions: Republican Ideology and the Making of the State Constitutions in the Revolutionary Era. Lanham, MD: Rowman & Littlefield, 2001.

Alden, John Richard. *The American Revolution, 1775–1783*. New American Nation Series, edited by Henry Steele Commager and Richard B. Morris. New York: Harper & Row, 1954.
Aldridge, A. Owen. *American Literature: A Comparatist Approach*. Princeton: Princeton University Press, 1982.
———. *The Dragon and the Eagle: The Presence of China in the American Enlightenment*. Detroit: Wayne State University Press, 1993.
Anderson, M. S. *Europe in the Eighteenth Century 1713–1789*. London and New York: Pearson Education, 2016.
Anderson, Paul, and Max Harold Fisch. *Philosophy in America: From the Puritan to James*. New York: Appleton Century, 1939.
Andrews, Charles M. *The Colonial Period of American History, England's Commercial and Colonial Policy, With a New Introduction by Leonard W. Labaree*. New Haven and London: Yale University Press, 1969.
Andrist, Ralph K., ed. *The Founding Fathers: George Washington—A Biography in His Own Words*, vol. 1. New York: Newsweek Book Division, 1972.
Appleby, Joyce. *Thomas Jefferson*. New York: Times Books—Henry Holt and Company, 2003.
Arthur, Linda L. "A New Look at Schooling and Literacy: The Colony of Georgia." *Georgia Historical Quarterly* 84, no. 4 (2000).
Asimov, Isaac. *The Birth of the United States, 1763–1816*. Boston: Houghton Mifflin, 1974.
Bader, John. *The Failure of America's First "Chinese Wall."* http://thepolitic.org/the-failure-of-americas-first-chinese-wall/.
Bailyn, Bernard. "Political Experience and Enlightenment Ideas in Eighteenth Century America." In *The Causes of the American Revolution*, 3rd ed., edited by John C. Wahlke. Lexington, MA: D. C. Heath, 1973.
Barck, Oscar Theodore. *New York City During the War for Independence: With Special Reference to the Period of British Occupation*. New York: Columbia University Press, 1931.
Bartram, John. *Life and Character of the Chinese Philosopher Confucius: Autograph Manuscript*. Pierpont Morgan Library Department of Literary and Historical Manuscripts, Morgan Library and Museum.
Barzun, Jacques. *From Dawn to Decadence: 500 years of Western Cultural Life, 1500 to Present*. New York: HarperCollins, 2000.
Beard, Charles A., and Mary R. Beard. *The Rise of American Civilization*, vol. II. New York: Macmillan, 1927.
Beeman, Richard R. *Perspectives on the Constitution: A Republic, If You Can Keep It*. https://constitutioncenter.org/learn/educational-resources/historical-documents/perspectives-on-the-constitution-a-republic-if-you-can-keep-it.
Bell, Daniel A., and Changyang Li, ed., *The East Asian Challenge for Democracy: Political Meritocracy in Comparative Perspective*. New York: Cambridge University Press, 2013.
Berkowitz, Peter, ed., *Never a Matter of Indifference: Sustaining Virtue in a Free Republic*. Stanford: Hoover Institution Press, 2003.

Bernstein, Richard B. *The Founding Fathers Reconsidered*. Oxford: Oxford University Press, 2009.

Beschloss, Michael. *Presidential Courage: Brave Leaders and How They Changed America 1789–1989*. New York: Simon & Schuster, 2007.

Betts, Edwin Morris, ed. *Thomas Jefferson's Garden Book, With Relevant extracts from his Writings, 1760–1824*. Philadelphia: American Philosophical Society, 1944.

Betts, Edwin Morris, and Hazlehurst Bolton Perkins. *Thomas Jefferson's Flower Garden at Monticello*. Charlottesville: University of Virginia, 1971.

Bigelow, John, ed. *The Complete Works of Benjamin Franklin*. New York: G. P. Putnam's Sons, 1888.

———. *The Works of Benjamin Franklin*. New York: G. P. Putnam's Sons, 1904.

Blodget, Samuel. *Economica: Statistical Manual for the United States of America*. Washington, DC: Kelley, 1806.

Bodde, Derk. "Chinese Ideas in the West." In *China: A Teaching Workbook*. Asia for Educators, Columbia University. http://www.learn.columbia.edu/nanxuntu/html/state/ideas.pdf.

Boorstin, Daniel J. *The Americans: The Colonial Experience*. New York: Random House, 1958.

Bowen, Catherine Drinker. *Miracle at Philadelphia: The Story of the Constitutional Convention, May to September 1787*. Boston and Toronto: Little, Brown, 1966.

Boyle, John Andrew. "The Alexander Legend in Central Asia." *Folklore* 85, no. 4 (1974): 217–28.

Bridenbaugh, Carl. "The Press and the Book in Eighteenth Century Philadelphia." *Pennsylvania Magazine of History and Biography* LXV, no. 1 (1941): 1–30.

Brinker, William J. "Commerce, Culture, and Horticulture: The Beginnings of Sino-American Cultural Relations." In *Aspects of Sino-American Relations since 1784*, edited by Thomas H. Etzold. New York and London: New Viewpoints, A Division of Franklin Watt, 1978.

Brissot de Warville, Jacques-Pierre. *New Travels in the United States of America, 1788*, translated by Mara Sconceanu Vamos and Durand Echeverria; edited by Durand Echeverria. Cambridge, MA: Belknap Press, 1964.

Brodie, Fawn M. *Thomas Jefferson: An Intimate History*. New York and London: W.W. Norton & Company, 1974.

Brown, Michael K. "Piecing Together the Past: Recent Research on the American China Manufactory, 1769–1772." *Proceedings of the American Philosophical Society* 133, no. 4 (1989).

Burbank, Jane, and Frederick Cooper. *Empires in World History: Power and the Politics of Difference*. Princeton: Princeton University Press, 2010.

Burch, Philip H. Jr. *Elites in American History*. Vol. II, *The Civil War to the New Deal*. New York: Holmes & Meier, 1981.

Burstein, Andrew. *Jefferson's Secrets: Death and Design at Monticello*. New York: Basic Books, 2005.

Callender, James. "The President, Again." *The Recorder; or, Lady's and Gentleman's Miscellany*, September 1, 1802.

Campbell, James. *Recovering Benjamin Franklin: An Exploration of a Life of Science and Service.* Chicago and La Salle, IL: Open Court, 1999.

Carpenter, James. "The Complexity of Thomas Jefferson: A Response to 'The Diffusion of Light': Jefferson's Philosophy of Education." *Democracy & Education* 22, no. 1 (2014).

———. "Thomas Jefferson and the Ideology of Democratic Schooling." *Democracy & Education* 21, no. 2 (2013).

Casey, Wilson. *Firsts: Origins of Everyday Things That Changed the World.* New York: Penguin, 2009.

Chambers, William. *Designs of Chinese Buildings, Furniture, Dresses, Machines, and Utensils, Engraved by the Best Hands, From the Originals drawn in China, Mr. Chambers, Architect, Member of the Imperial Academy of Arts at Florence. To Which is annexed, A Description of their Temples, Houses, Gardens, etc.* London, 1757.

Chernow, Ron. *Alexander Hamilton.* New York: Penguin, 2004.

Chippendale, Thomas. *The gentleman and cabinet-maker's director: being a large collection of . . . designs of household furniture in the Gothic, Chinese and modern taste . . . to which is prefixed, a short explanation of the five orders of architecture and rules of perspective, with proper directions for executing the most difficult pieces, the mouldings being exhibited at large, and the dimensions of each design specified. . . .* London: Printed for the author, and sold at his house . . . also by T. Osborne, . . . H. Piers, . . . R. Sayer, . . . J. Swan . . . [and by 2 others in 2 other places], 1754. Digitized by Smithsonian.

Christy, Arthur E., ed. *The Asian Legacy and American Life.* New York: John Day Company, 1942.

Clark, Harrison. *All Cloudless Glory: The Life of George Washington,* vol. 2: *Making a Nation.* Washington, DC: Regnery, 1996.

Clark, Ronald W. *Benjamin Franklin: A Biography.* New York: Random House, 1983.

Cohen, Warren I. "American Perception of China." In *Dragon and Eagle: United States-China Relations: Past and Future,* edited by Michael Oksenberg and Robert B. Oxnam. New York: Basic Books, 1973.

———. *America's Response to China: A History of Sino-American Relations.* New York: Columbia University Press, 1990.

Collins, Michael. "China's Confucius and Western Democracy." *Contemporary Review* 290, no. 1689 (Summer 2008).

Commager, Henry Steele. *The American Mind: An Interpretation of American Thought and Character since the 1880's.* New Haven: Yale University Press, 1950.

Coner, George W., ed. *The Autobiography of Benjamin Rush.* Princeton, NJ: American Philosophical Society, 1948.

Confucius. *Analects.* http://www.confucius.org/lunyu/.

———. *The Great Learning,* translated by James Legge, 1893. http://www.sacred-texts.com/cfu/conf2.htm.

———. *The Morals of Confucius: A Chinese Philosopher, Who Flourished above Five Hundred Years before the Coming of our LORD and Saviour JESUS CHRIST.*

Being One of the Choicest Pieces of that Nation, 2nd ed. London: Printed for T. Horne, at the South Entrance into the Royal Exchange, Cornhill, 1691.

Covington, Marsha Elaine. "Great Teachers on Teaching Adults: Comparison of Philosophy and Practice from Antiquity to the Present." Doctor of education thesis, Montana State University, 1997.

Creel, Herrlee Glessner. *Confucius: The Man and the Myth*. New York: John Day Company, 1949.

Current, Richard N., ed. *Sections and Politics: Selected Essays by William B. Hesseltine*. Madison: Wisconsin Historical Society, 1968.

Curtis, George William. Introduction to *Civil Service in Great Britain: A History of Abuse and Reforms and Their Bearing Upon American Politics*, by Dorman B. Eaton, iii. New York: Harper & Brothers, 1880.

Danton, George H. *The Culture Contacts of the United States and China: The Earliest Sino-American Cultural Contacts, 1784–1844*. New York: Columbia University Press, 1931.

Daufenbach, Claus. "Jefferson's Monticello and the Poetics of Landscape Gardening." *Soundings: An Interdisciplinary Journal* 78, no. 3/4 (Fall/Winter 1995).

Davis, David Brion. *The Problem of Slavery in the Age of Revolution, 1770–1823*. Ithaca, NY and London: Cornell University Press, 1975.

Davis, Kiesten Larsen. "Secondhand Chinoiserie and the Confucian Revolutionary: Colonial America's Decorative Arts 'after the Chinese Taste.'" Master's thesis, Brigham Young University, 2008.

Davis, Walter W. "China, the Confucian Ideal, and the European Age of Enlightenment." *Journal of the History of Ideas* 44, no. 4 (October–December 1983).

Deans, Bob. *The River Where American Began: A Journey Along the James*. Lanham, MD and New York: Rowman & Littlefield, 2007.

Debow, J. D. B. *Statistical View of the United States, Being a Compendium of the Seventh Census to which We Added the Results of Every Previous Census, Beginning with 1790*. Washington, DC: Beverly Tucker, 1854.

Denker, Ellen Paul. *After the Chinese Taste: China's Influence in America, 1730–1930*. Salem, MA: Peabody Museum, 1985.

Dennett, Tyler. *Americans in Eastern Asia; a Critical Study of the Policy of the United States with Reference to China, Japan and Korea in the 19th Century*. New York: Macmillan, 1922.

Detweiler, Susan Gray. *George Washington's Chinaware*. New York: Harry N. Abrams, Inc., 1982.

Dickerson, John. "The Original Attack Dog: James Callender Spread Scurrilous Stories about Alexander Hamilton and John Adams." *Slate*, August 9, 2016. http://www.slate.com/articles/news_and_politics/history/2016/08/james_callender_the_attack_dog_who_took_aim_at_alexander_hamilton_and_thomas.html.

Dillon, Wilton. *Smithsonian Stories: Chronicle of a Golden Age, 1964–1984*. Piscataway, NJ: Transaction Publishers, 2015.

Drinker, Elizabeth. *Extracts from the Journal of Elizabeth Drinker, Period from 1759–1807*. Edited by Henry D. Biddle. Philadelphia: J. B. Lippincott, 1889.

Du Halde, J. B. *The General History of China*. London: J. Watts, 1741.

Dulles, Foster Rhea. *The Old China Trade*. Boston and New York: Houghton Mifflin, 1930.

Durey, Michael. *Transatlantic Radicals and the Early America Republic*. Lawrence: University of Kansas Press, 1997.

Eaton, Dorman B. *Civil Service in Great Britain: A History of Abuse and Reforms and Their Bearing Upon American Politics*. New York: Harper & Brothers Publishers, 1880.

Ellis, John. "Directions for Bringing over Seeds and Plants, From the East Indies and Other Distant Countries, in A State of Vegetation: Together with a Catalogue of Such Foreign Plants as Are Worthy of Being Encouraged in Our American Colonies, For the Purposes of Medicine, Agriculture, and Commerce." (1784). In *Aphrodite's Mousetrap: A Biography of Venus's Flytrap with Facsimiles of an Original Pamphlet and the Manuscripts of John Ellis*, edited by E. Charles Nelson. Aberystwyth, Wales: published by Boethius Press, in association with Bentham-Moxon Trust and the Linnean Society, 1990.

Ellis, Joseph J. *American Creation: Triumph and Tragedies at the Founding of the Republic*. New York: Alfred A. Knopf, 2007.

———. *American Dialogue: The Founding Fathers and Us*. New York: Alfred A. Knopf, 2018.

———. *Founding Brothers: The Revolutionary Generation*. New York: Vintage, 2002.

———. *His Excellency: George Washington*. New York: Alfred A. Knopf, 2005.

Emerson, Ralph Waldo. "Speech at Banquet in Honor of Chinese Embassy Boston, 1868." In *The Complete Works of Ralph Waldo Emerson*. Boston: Houghton Mifflin, 1904. Vol. XI. Miscellanies XXVI.

Etzold, Thomas H., ed. *Aspects of Sino-American Relations since 1784*. New York and London: New Viewpoints, A Division of Franklin Watt, 1978.

Federalist Papers: Primary Documents in American History. https://guides.loc.gov/federalist-papers/full-text.

Feldman, Noah. *The Three Lives of James Madison: Genius, Partisan, President*. New York: Random House, 2017.

Ferling, John E. *John Adams: A Life*. Knoxville: University of Tennessee Press, 1992.

Fiorina, Carly. "History Matters—Especially Today." *Trend & Tradition* (Spring 2021).

Fishman, Ann. "The Greatest Naturist in the World." *Humanities: The Magazine of National Endowment of the Humanity*, January/February 1995.

Fitzpatrick, John C., ed. *The Diaries of George Washington, 1748–1799*, vol. IV, *1789–1799*. Boston and New York: Houghton Mifflin, 1925.

Fleming, Thomas. *The Perishes of Peace: America's Struggle for Survival After Yorktown*. New York: Smithsonian Books, 2007.

Foley, John, ed. *Jeffersonian Cyclopedia, A Comprehensive Collection of the Views of Thomas Jefferson*. New York and London: Funk & Wagnalls, 1900.

Fontenoy, Paul E. "Ginseng, Otter Skins, and Sandalwood: The Conundrum of the China Trade." *Northern Mariner* 7, no. 1 (January 1997).

The Founders' Constitution. vol. 1, chap. 18, doc. 16. http://press-pubs.uchicago.edu/founders/documents/v1ch18s16.html. University of Chicago Press, *Records of the Federal Convention*, article 2, section 1, clause 7, http://press-pubs.uchicago.edu/founders/documents/a2_1_7s2.html.

The Founders' Constitution. vol. 3, article 2, section 1, clause 7, doc. 2. http://press-pubs.uchicago.edu/founders/documents/a2_1_7s2.html. University of Chicago Press, *The Records of the Federal Convention of 1787*. Rev. ed., edited by Max Farrand. 4 vols. New Haven and London: Yale University Press, 1937.

The Founders Online. A cooperative project of the National Archives and Records Administration. The site collects the documents of the six Founding Fathers, including George Washington, Benjamin Franklin, Thomas Jefferson, John Jay, James Madison, and John Adams, projects at the University of Virginia, University of Chicago, Princeton University, Columbia University, the Massachusetts Historical Society, the American Philosophical Society, and Yale University. https://founders.archives.gov/.

Franklin, Benjamin. *The Autobiography of Benjamin Franklin*. Edited by Leonard W. Labaree, Ralph L. Ketcham, Helen C. Boatfield, and Hellene H. Fineman. New Haven: Yale University Press, 2003.

———. "From the *Morals of Confucius*." *Pennsylvania Gazette*, February 28 to March 7, 1738.

Fukuyama, Francis. "Confucianism and Democracy." http://www.u.arizona.edu/~zshipley/pol437/docs/fukuyama_1995.pdf.

Garrigues, Rebecca Haydock. "ALS: American Philosophical Society, Philadelphia 5th Mo 20th 1773." In *The Papers of Benjamin Franklin*. http://franklinpapers.org/franklin/framedVolumes.jsp.

Gay, Peter. *Great Ages of Man: A History of the World's Cultures—Age of Enlightenment*. New York: Time-Life Books, 1966.

George, M. Dorothy. England in Transition, rev. ed. Baltimore: Pelican, 1953.

Ginn, Roger. *New England Must Not Be Trampled On: The Tragic Death of Jonathan Cilley*. Lanham, MD: Rowman & Littlefield, 2016.

Gipson, Lawrence Henry. *The Coming of the Revolution, 1763–1775*. New American Nation Series, edited by Henry Steele Commager and Richard B. Morris. New York: Harper & Row, 1954.

Glaeser, Edward. "Public Ownership in the American City." In *Urban Issues and Public Finance: Essays in Honor of Dick Netzer*, edited by Amy E. Schwartz, 130–62. Northampton, MA: Edward Elgar, 2003.

Glanzer, Perry L. "The Dissenting Tradition in American Education." *American Educational History Journal* 35, no. 2 (2008).

Golden, James L., and Alan L. Golden. *Thomas Jefferson and the Rhetoric of Virtue*. Lanham, MD: Rowman & Littlefield, 2002.

Goldstein, Jonathan. *Philadelphia and the China Trade, 1682–1846: Commercial, Cultural, and Attitudinal Effects*. University Park: Pennsylvania State University Press, 1978.

Gowdy, J. David. *Thomas Jefferson and the Pursuit of Virtue*. http://www.liberty1.org/TJVirtue.pdf.

Grapard, Allan G. "Voltaire and East Asia—A Few Reflections on the Nature of Humanism." In *Cahiers d'Extreme-Asie*, vol. 1, 1985.

Great Britain. *The Parliamentary History of England from the Earliest Period to the Year 1803*. Vol. 18. London: T. C. Hansard, 1813.

Great Britain. *The Proceedings Before the Judicial Committee of Her Majesty Imperial Privy Council on the Special Case Respecting the Westerly Boundary of Ontario: Argued 15th, 16th, 17th, 19th, 21st and 22nd July 1884, with Notes of Explanation and Correction*. Printed by Order of the Legislative Assembly of [Ontario].

Gross, Jonathan, ed. *Thomas Jefferson's Scrapbooks: Poems of Nation, Family, and Romantic Love Collected by America's Third President*. Hanover, NH: Steerforth Press, 2006.

Gross, Robert A. *An Extensive Republic: Print, Culture, and Society in the New Nation, 1790–1840*. History of the Book in America Series, vol 2, ed. Mary Kelley. Chapel Hill: University of North Carolina Press, 2010.

Gutzman, Kevin R. G. *Thomas Jefferson—Revolutionary: A Radical's Struggle to Remake America*. New York: St. Martin's, 2017.

Hafertepe, Kenneth. "An Inquiry into Thomas Jefferson's Ideas of Beauty." *Journal of the Society of Architectural Historians* 59, no. 2 (June 2000).

Hanyan, Craig R. "China and the Erie Canal." *Business History Review* 35, no. 4 (1961): 558–66. https://www.jstor.org/stable/3111758?seq=1.

Hao, Yen-P'ing. "Chinese Teas to America—a Synopsis." In *America's China Trade in Historical Perspective: The Chinese and American Performance*, edited by Ernest R. May and John K. Fairbank. Cambridge, MA and London: Harvard University Press, 1986.

Hart, Albert Bushnell. "The Monroe Doctrine and the Doctrine of Permanent Interest." American Historical Review 7, no. 1 (October 1901).

Hatch, Peter J. "Jefferson's Retirement Garden." *Twinleaf Journal Archives*, 2009.

Haworth, Paul Leland. *George Washington: Being an Account of His Life and Agricultural Activities*. Indianapolis: Bobbs-Merrill, 1925.

Hill, Simon. "China and the American Revolution." *Journal of the American Revolution* (December 7, 2017). https://allthingsliberty.com/2017/12/china-american-revolution/.

History of Civil Service Merit System of the United States and Selected Foreign Countries, together with Executive Reorganization Studies and Personnel Recommendations. Compiled by the Library of Congress Congressional Research Service, for the Subcommittee on Manpower and Civil Service of the Committee on Post Office and Civil Service, House of Representatives 94th Congress, 2nd session, December 31, 1967. Washington, DC: US Government Printing Office, 1976.

Hochschild, Jennifer L. *Facing Up to the American Dream*. Princeton: Princeton University Press, 1995.

Hofstadter, Richard. *About the Anti-Intellectualism in American Life*. New York: Vintage, 1962.

Homans, Isaac Smith Jr. *An Historical and Statistical Account of the Foreign Commerce of the United States*. New York: Putnam, 1857.

Hoogenboom, Ari. "Pennsylvania in the Civil Service Reform Movement." *Pennsylvania History* 28, no. 3 (July 1961).

———. "Thomas A. Jenkes and Civil Service Reform." *Mississippi Valley Historical Review* 47, no. 4 (March 1961).

Hornbeck, Dustin. "Seeking Civic Virtue: Two Views of the Philosophy and History of Federalism in U.S. Education." *Journal of Thought* (Fall–Winter 2017).

Howe, Daniel W. *What Hath God Wrought: The Transformation of America, 1815–1848*. Oxford: Oxford University Press, 2007.

Huger Smith, Alice R., and D. E. Huger Smith. The Dwelling Houses of Charleston, South Carolina. Philadelphia and London: J. B. Lippincott Company, 1917.

Hunt, Michael H. *The Making of a Special Relationship: The United States and China to 1914*. New York: Columbia University Press, 1983.

Huntington, Samuel. "The Clash of Civilizations?" *Foreign Affairs* (Summer 1993).

Isaacson, Walter. *Benjamin Franklin: An American Life*. New York: Simon & Schuster, 2003.

Jack, Alex. *Thomas Jefferson's Rice Quest*. http://www.amberwaves.org/articlePages/articles/alex/thomas_jeffersons02.pdf.

Jefferson, Thomas. *Autobiography*, in *The Founders' Constitution*. Vol. 1, Chap. 15, Doc. 20. University of Chicago Press. http://press-pubs.uchicago.edu/founders/documents/v1ch15s20.html.

Jenckes, Thomas. *The Civil Service: Report*. Washington, DC: US Government Printing Office, 1868.

———. *Speech of Hon. Thomas A. Jenckes of Rhode Island, The Bill to Regulate the Civil Service of the United States and Promote the Efficiency Thereof: delivered in the House of Representatives, May 14, 1868*. Washington, DC: F&J Rives & Geo. A Bailey, Reporters and Printers of the Debates of Congress, 1868.

Johannsen, Kristin. *Ginseng Dreams: The Secret World of America's Most Valuable Plant*. Lexington: University Press of Kentucky, 2006.

Johnson, Marianne. "'More Native than French': American Physiocrats and Their Political Economy." *History of Economic Ideas* 10, no. 1 (2002).

Justice, Benjamin A. "Window to the Past: What an Easy Contest Reveals about Early American Education." *American Educator* (Summer 2015).

Kalm, Peter. "The America of 1750." In *Peter Kalm's Travels in North America*, edited and translated by Adolf B. Benson. New York: Wilson-Erickson, 1937.

Kaminski, John P., ed. *American Revolutionary Era*. Charlottesville and London: University of Virginia Press, 2019.

Kammen, Michael, ed. *The Origins of the American Constitution: A Documentary History*. New York: Penguin, 1986.

Kazin, Michael, Rebecca Edwards, and Adam Rothman. *The Princeton Encyclopedia of American Political History*. Vol. 2. Princeton: Princeton University Press, 2010.

Kennedy, David M., and Lizabeth Cohen. *The American Pageant*, vol. 1. Boston: Cengage Learning, 2012.

Kim, Young-sik. "The Ginseng 'Trade War,' Part III from A Brief History of the US-Korea relations Prior to 1945." http://www.asianresearch.org/articles/1438.html.

Kimball, Fiske. *Domestic Architecture of the American Colonies and of the Early Republic*. New York: Charles Scribner's Sons, 1927.

———. *Thomas Jefferson: Architect, Original Designs in the Coolidge Collection of the Massachusetts Historical Society with an Essay and Notes*. New York: Da Capo Press, 1968.

Kimball, Marie. *Jefferson: The Road to Glory, 1743 to 1776*. New York: Coward-McCann, Inc., 1943.

Klose, Nelson. *America's Crop Heritage: The History of Foreign Plant Introduction by the Federal Government*. Ames: Iowa State College Press, 1950.

Konner, Melvin. *Unsettled: Anthropology of the Jews*. New York: Viking Compass, 2003.

Kuo, Ping Chia. "Canton and Salem: The Impact of Chinese Culture Upon New England Life During the Post-Revolutionary Era." *New England Quarterly* III (1930).

Labaree, Leonard W., and William B. Willcox, eds. *The Papers of Benjamin Franklin*. New Haven: Yale University Press, 1959–.

Lach, Donald F. "Leibniz and China." *Journal of the History of Ideas* 6, no. 4 (1945): 436–55.

Larson, Edward J. *Franklin & Washington: The Founding Partnership*. New York: William Morrow, 2020.

Latourette, Kenneth Scott. *The History of Early Relations between the United States and China, 1784–1844*. New Haven: Yale University Press, 1917.

———. *Voyages of American Ships to China, 1784–1844*. New Haven: Connecticut Academy of Arts and Sciences, 1927.

Lea, Douglass. "Thomas Jefferson: Master Gardener." *Mother Earth News* 172 (February/March 1999).

Lee, G. C., ed. *Crusade against Ignorance: Thomas Jefferson on Education*. 5th ed. New York: Teachers College Press, 1967.

Lee Kuan Yew, *From Third World to First: The Singapore Story, 1965–2000*. Singapore: Singapore Press Holdings, 2000.

Lehmann, Karl. *Thomas Jefferson: American Humanist*. New York: Macmillan, 1947.

Leites, Edmund. "Confucianism in Eighteenth Century England: Natural Morality and Social Reform." *Philosophy East and West* 28, no. 2, Sonological Torque (April 1978).

Lepore, Jill. "Party Time." *The New Yorker*, September 17, 2007, 94.

Levine, David. "The Autobiography of Benjamin Franklin: The Puritan Experimenter in Life and Art." *Yale Review* 53, no. 2 (December 1963).

Lieberman, Benjamin. *Remaking Identities: God, Nation, and Race in World History*. Lanham, MD: Rowman & Littlefield, 2013.

Liu, James T. C. *China Turning Inward: Intellectual-Political Changes in in the Early Twelfth Century*. Cambridge, MA: Harvard University Press, 2003.

Lofgren, Lyle. *Remembering the Old Songs: Ginseng Blues*. http://www.lizlyle.lofgrens.org/RmOlSngs/RTOS-GinsengBlues.html.

Macedo, Stephen. "Meritocratic Democracy: Learning from the American Constitution." In *The East Asian Challenge for Democracy: Political Meritocracy in Comparative Perspective*, edited by Daniel A. Bell and Changyang Li. New York: Cambridge University Press, 2013.

Malone, Dumas. *Jefferson and the Rights of Man*. Jefferson and His Time Series, Volume II. Boston: Little, Brown, 1951.

———. *Jefferson the President, First Term, 1801–1805*. Jefferson and His Time Series, Volume IV. Boston: Little, Brown, 1970.

———. *Jefferson: The Virginian*. Jefferson and His Time Series, Volume I. Boston: Little Brown, 1948.

Mansfield, Harvey C. "Liberty and Virtue in the American Founding." In *Never a Matter of Indifference: Sustaining Virtue in a Free Republic*, edited by Peter Berkowitz. Stanford: Hoover Institution Press, 2003.

Markin, Rea T. "Rights of the Public Employee under the Illinois Civil Service System: A Progression of the Law." *John Marshall Law Review* 8, no. 1 (1974). http://repository.jmls.edu/lawreview/vol8/iss1/3.

Marquis de Lafayette Papers. Library of Congress. https://www.loc.gov/item/mm96083803/.

Masur, Louis P., ed. *The Autobiography of Benjamin Franklin with Related Documents*, 2nd ed. Boston and New York: Bedford/St. Martin's, 2003.

May, Ernest R., and John K. Fairbank, eds. *America' China Trade in Historical Perspective: The Chinese and American Performance*. Cambridge, MA and London: Harvard University Press, 1986.

McBride, Scott. "Building a Chinese Railing." *Taunton's Fine Homebuilding*, July 2006.

McCullough, David. *John Adams*. New York and London: Simon & Schuster, 2001.

McFeely, William S., and C. Vann Woodward, eds. *Responses of the Presidents to Charges of Misconduct*. New York: Delacorte, 1974.

McPherson, James. *Liberty, Equality, Power: A History of the American People*. Boston: Cengage, 2012.

Meacham, Jon. *Thomas Jefferson: The Art of Power*. New York: Random House, 2012.

Mendis, Patrick. *Peaceful War: How the Chinese Dream and the American Destiny Create a Pacific New World Order*. New York: United Press of America, 2013.

Medlin, William K. *The History of Educational Ideas in the West*. New York: Center for Applied Research in Education, 1964.

Mendoza, Juan de Palafox y. *The history of the conquest of China by the Tartars together with an account of several remarkable things concerning the religion, manners, and customs of both nations, but especially the latter 1600–1659*. https://quod.lib.umich.edu/e/eebo/A54677.0001.001/1:4?rgn=div1;view=fulltext.

Meyer, D. H. "The Uniqueness of the American Enlightenment." *American Quarterly* 28, no. 2 (Summer 1976).

Middleton, Richard, and Anne Lombard. *Colonial America: A History to 1763*, 4th ed. Hoboken, NJ: Wiley-Blackwell, 2011.

Milburn, William. *Oriental Commerce*. London: Black, Parry & Co., 1813.

Miller, George L. "A Revised Set of CC Index Value for Classification and Economic Scaling of English Ceramics from 1787 to 1880." *Historical Archaeology* 25 (1991).

Miller, John C. *Origins of the American Revolution: With a New Introduction and a Biography.* Stanford, CA: Stanford University Press, 1943.

Miller, Perry. "Benjamin Franklin, Jonathan Edwards." In *Major Writers of America* edited by Perry Miller. New York: Harcourt, Brace and World, 1962.

Miller, Stuart Creighton. *The Unwelcome Immigrant: The American Image of the Chinese, 1785–1882.* Berkeley and Los Angeles: University of California Press, 1969.

Mitchell, Broadus. *Alexander Hamilton: The Revolutionary Years.* Leaders of the American Revolution Series, edited by North Callahan. New York: Thomas Y. Crowell, 1970.

Miyazaki, Ichisada. *China's Examination Hell.* Translated by Conrad Schirokauer. New York: Weatherhill, 1976.

Morgan, Edmund S. *Benjamin Franklin.* New Haven and London: Yale University Press, 2002.

Morse, Hosea Ballou. *The Chronicles of the East India Company Trading to China 1635–1834.* 5 vols. Cambridge, MA: Harvard University Press, 1926–1929.

Morse, Jedidiah. *The American Universal Geography; or a View of the Present Situation of the United States and of all the Empire, Kingdoms, States, and Republics in the Known World*, 2nd ed. Vol. 2. Boston: Isaiah Thomas and Ebenezer Andrews, 1796.

Morse, John Rorrey. *Thomas Jefferson.* American Statesmen Series. Boston: Houghton Mifflin, 1898.

Müller, Friedrich Max. *The Sacred Books of the East.* Vol. 28, Part 4. Oxford: Clarendon Press, 1885.

Munford, Kenneth. *John Ledyard: An American Marco Polo.* Portland, OR: Binfords & Mort, 1939.

Myer, D. H. "The Uniqueness of the American Enlightenment." *American Quarterly* 28, no. 2 (Summer 1976).

National Park Service, *Thomas Jefferson's Plan for the University of Virginia: Lessons from the Lawn.* "Reading 1: Education as the Keystone to the New Democracy." https://www.nps.gov/articles/thomas-jefferson-s-plan-for-the-university-of-virginia-lessons-from-the-lawn-teaching-with-historic-places.htm.

Neem, Johann. "Is Jefferson a Founding Father of Democratic Education?" *Democracy & Education* 22, no. 2 (2013).

Nelson, E. Charles, and John Ellis. *Aphrodite's Mousetrap: A Biography of Venus's Flytrap with Facsimiles of an Original Pamphlet and the Manuscripts of John Ellis.* Aberystwyth, Wales: Published by Boethius Press in association with Bentham-Moxon Trust and the Linnean Society, 1990.

Nicolay, John G., and John Hay. *Abraham Lincoln: A History.* Volume IV. New York: Century, 1890.

Niemcewicz, Julian Ursyn. *Vine and Fig Tree: Travels Through America 1797–1799, 1805 with some Further Account of Life in New Jersey.* Translated and edited with an introduction and notes by Metchie J. E. Budka. Elizabeth, NJ: Grassmann Publishing Company, Inc, 1965.

Nye, Russel Blaine. *The Cultural Life of the New Nation, 1776–1830*. New York: Harper & Brothers, 1960.
Oberg, Barbara B., ed. *The Papers of Thomas Jefferson*. 38 vols. Princeton: Princeton University Press, 2005.
Oksenberg, Michael, and Robert B. Oxnam, eds. *Dragon and Eagle: United States-China Relations: Past and Future*. New York: Basic Books, 1973.
Olasky, Marvin. *Fighting for Liberty and Virtue*. Washington, DC: Regnery, 1996.
Paine, Thomas. "Age of Reason, 1794–1795." In *The Ideas that Made America: A Brief History*, edited by Jennifer Ratner-Rosenhagen. Oxford: Oxford University Press, 2019.
———. "Of the Old and New Testament." *The Prospect*, March 31, 1804.
———. *The Political Works of Thomas Paine*. 2 vols. Oxford: Oxford University, 1864.
The Papers of Alexander Hamilton Digital Edition. The University of Virginia Press. https://rotunda.upress.virginia.edu/founders/ARHN.html.
The Papers of Benjamin Franklin. Sponsored by the American Philosophical Society and Yale University. Digital Edition by the Packard Humanities Institute. https://franklinpapers.org/.
The Papers of George Washington. Founded in 1968 as a collaborative project between the Mount Vernon Ladies' Association of the Union and the University of Virginia, *The Papers of George Washington* editing project documents the life and times of this founding father and the public events in which he participated. https://www.mountvernon.org/library/research-library/washington-papers/.
The Papers of James Madison. The University of Virginia Press.
The Papers of Thomas Jefferson. Princeton University Library, Princeton, NJ 08544.
Persons, Stow. *American Minds: A History of Ideas*. New York: Henry Holt, 1958.
Peterson, Merrill D. "Thomas Jefferson and Commercial Policy, 1783–1793." *William and Mary Quarterly* 22, no. 4 (October 1965).
Petri, Anne. *George Washington and Food*. http://www.house.gov/petri/gw003.htm.
Peyrefitte, Alain. *The Immobile Empire*. New York: Knopf Doubleday, 2013.
Pitkin, Timothy. *A Statistical View of the Improvements, Together with that of the Revenues of the General Government*. New Haven: Durrie & Peck, 1835.
Powell, Jim. "The Man Who Financed the American Revolution." http://www.libertystory.net/LSACTIONROBERTMORRIS.htm.
Power, Colin. *The Power of Education: Education for All, Development, Globalization and UNESCO*. Education in the Asia Pacific Region: Issues, Concerns and Prospects Series. New York: Springer, 2014.
Ralston, Shane J. *American Enlightenment Thoughts*. https://www.iep.utm.edu/amer-enl/.
Randall, Thomas. *The Papers of Alexander Hamilton*. New York: Columbia University Press, 1961.
Randall, Willard Sterne. *Thomas Jefferson: A Life*. New York: Henry Holt, 1993.
Ratner-Rosenhagen, Jennifer, ed. *The Ideas that Made America: A Brief History*. Oxford: Oxford University Press, 2019.

Reagan, Ronald. Remarks to Chinese Community Leaders in Beijing, China, April 27, 1984. http://www.reagan.uttexas.edu/resource/speeches/1984/42784a.htm.

Reid, Gilbert. "Revolution as Taught by Confucianism." *International Journal of Ethics* 33, no. 2 (1923).

Reid, Nina. "Enlightenment and Piety in the Science of John Bartram." *Pennsylvania History: A Journal of Mid-Atlantic Studies* 58, no. 2 (April 1991).

Remini, Robert. *A Short History of the United States*. New York: Harper Perennial, 2008.

Reuter, Frank T. *Trials and Triumphs: George Washington's Foreign Policy*. Fort Worth: Texas Christian University Press, 1983.

Richter, Daniel. *Before the Revolution: America's Ancient Pasts*. Cambridge, MA: Belknap Press, 2011.

Roberts, Cokie. *Founding Mothers: The Women Who Raised Our Nation*. New York: HarperCollins, 2004.

Rogers, Lisa. "Our Man in Paris." *Humanities* 23, no. 4 (July/August 2002).

Rosenbloom, David H. *Federal Service and the Constitution: The Development of the Public Employment Relationship*. Washington, DC: Georgetown University Press, 2014.

Rothbard, Murray N. "Bureaucracy and the Civil Service in the United States." *Journal of Libertarian Studies* 11, no. 2 (Summer 1995): 3–75.

———. *Economic Thought Before Adam Smith: An Austrian Perspective on the History of Economic Thought*. Vol. I. CreateSpace Independent Publishing Platform, January 1, 2006.

Rowbotham, Arnold H. "The Impact of Confucianism on Seventeenth Century Europe." *Far Eastern Quarterly* 4, no. 3 (May 1945).

Rush, Benjamin. "Commonplace Book March 17, 1790." In *The Founders on the Founders: Word Portraits from the American Revolutionary Era*, edited by John P. Kaminski. Charlottesville and London: University of Virginia Press, 2019.

———. "Of the Mode of Education Proper in a Republic, 1798." In *The Selected Writings of Benjamin Rush*, edited by Dagobert D. Runes. New York: Philosophical Library, 1947. http://press-pubs.uchicago.edu/founders/ documents/ v1ch18s30 .html.

———. *The Selected Writings of Benjamin Rush*. Edited by Dagobert D. Runes. New York: Philosophical Library, 1947.

Saint-Méry, Mederic Louis Elie Moreau de. *Moreau de St. Méry's American Journey*. Translated and edited by Kenneth Roberts and Anna M. Roberts. Garden City, NY: Doubleday, 1947.

Sanford, Charles L., ed. *Benjamin Franklin and The American Character: Problems in American Civilization*. Boston: D. C. Heath and Company, 1955.

Santangelo, Paolo. "Confucius in the 18th Century Italy: A Case of 'Complex Cross-Cultural Reflection.'" Paper presented at the Conference held in Venice International University, September 19, 2015. https://www.academia.edu/27262975/Confucius_in_the_18th_century_Italy_a_case_of_complex_intermediate_cross_cultural_reflection_.

Schneewind, Sarah. "Thomas Jefferson's Declaration of Independence and King Wu's First Great Pronouncement." *Journal of American–East Asian Relations* 19 (2012).

Schroeder, John Frederick, ed. *Maxims of Washington: Political, Social, Moral, and Religious.* Mount Vernon, VA: Mount Vernon Ladies Association, 1942.

Schwartz, Amy E., ed. *Urban Issues and Public Finance: Essays in Honor of Dick Netzer.* Northampton, MA: Edward Elgar, 2003.

Schwarz, Bill. *The Expansion of England: Race, Ethnicity and Cultural History.* New York: Routledge, 1996.

Seely, James E. Jr., ed. *Shaping North America: From Exploration to the American Revolution.* 3 vols. Santa Barbara, CA: ABC-CLIO, 2018.

Seidel, Douglas T. *The China (Rose) Revolution.* https://www.monticello.org/house-gardens/center-for-historic-plants/twinleaf-journal-online/the-china-rose-revolution/.

The Selected Papers of John Jay. Edited by Elizabeth M. Nuxoll and Mary A. Y. Gallagher.

Sewall, Samuel. *Diary of Samuel Sewall, 1674–1729.* Reprinted in *Collections of the Massachusetts Historical Society,* 1879, ser. 5, vol. 6.

Seybert, Adam. *Statistical Annals; Embracing View of the Population, Commerce, Navigation, Fisheries, Public Lands, Post-Office Establishment, Revenue, Mint, Military and Naval Establishments, Expenditures, Public Debt, and Sinking Fund of the United States of America.* New York: Burt Franklin, 1818.

Shaughnessy, Edward L. *Confucius and the University of Chicago: Of Myths and Men.* June 2010. http://cccp.uchicago.edu/downloads/Confucius_and_the_University_of_Chicago.pdf.

Shippen, Nancy. *Nancy Shippen, Her Journal Book.* Edited by Ethel Armes. Philadelphia: Lippincott, 1935.

Shugerman, Jed. *The Founding of the DOJ and the Failure of Civil Service Reform, 1865–1870.* http://www.americanbarfoundation.org/uploads/cms/documents/shugerman_doj_and_civil_service.doc.

Sienkewicz, Thomas J. *Encyclopedia of the Ancient World.* Hackensack, NJ: Salem Press, 2003.

Sirico, Louis J. Jr. *How the Separation of Powers Doctrine Shaped the Executive.* Working Paper Series, Villanova University Charles Widger School of Law, 2008.

Silk Association of America, Annual Report, 1900.

Silk Association of America, Annual Report, 1908.

Silverman, Jason H. *American History before 1877.* New York: McGraw-Hill, 1989.

Singleton, Esther. *Furniture of Our Forefathers.* Vol. II. New York: Doubleday, Page & Company, 1901.

Skousen, Mark, ed. *The Compleated Autobiography by Benjamin Franklin.* Washington, DC: Regnery, 2006.

Skowronek, Stephen. *Building a New American State: The Expansion of National Administrative Capacities, 1877–1920.* New York: Cambridge University Press, 1982.

Smith, Gene Allen. "Thomas Jefferson: Reputation and Legacy." *Journal of American History* 94, no. 1 (June 2007).

Smyth, Albert Henry, ed. *The Writings of Benjamin Franklin.* Vol. IX, *1783–1788.* New York: MacMillan, 1906.

Sparagana, Jeff. *The Educational Theory of Thomas Jefferson.* http://www.newfoundations.com/GALLERY/Jefferson.html.

Spargo, John. *Early American Pottery and China.* Rutland, VT: Charles E. Tuttle, 1974.

Sparks, Jared. *The Life of John Ledyard: The American Traveler, Comprising Selections from His Journals and Correspondence.* Cambridge, MA: Hilliard and Brown, 1828.

Spurlin, Paul Merrill. *Montesquieu in America, 1760–1801.* Baton Rouge: Louisiana State University Press, 1940.

Staunton, George L. *An Authentic Account of an Embassy from the King of Great Britain to the Embassy of China.* London: G. Nicol, 1797.

Steele, A. T. *The American People and China.* New York, Toronto, and London: McGraw-Hill, 1966.

Stein, Susan R. *The Worlds of Thomas Jefferson at Monticello.* New York: Harry N. Abrams, Inc., 1993.

Subramaniam, Surain. "The Dual Narrative of 'Good Governance': Lessons for Understanding Political and Cultural Change in Malaysia and Singapore." *Contemporary Southeast Asia* 23, no. 1 (2001): 65–80. http://www.jstor.org/stable/25798528.

Swingle, Walter T. "Our Agricultural Debt to Asia." In *The Asian Legacy and American Life*, edited by Arthur E. Christy. New York: John Day Company, 1945.

Tan, Charlene. "Confucianism and Education: Curriculum and Pedagogy, Educational Theories and Philosophies." *Oxford Research Encyclopedias*, November 2017. http://education.oxfordre.com/view/10.1093/acrefore/9780190264093.001.0001/acrefore-9780190264093-e-226.

Tan, Chung, and Yinzheng Geng. *India and China: Twenty Centuries of Civilization Interaction and Vibrations.* Ann Arbor: University of Michigan Press, 2005.

Taylor, Alan. *American Revolutions: A Continental History, 1750–1804.* New York and London: Norton, 2016.

———. "For the Benefit of Mr. Kite." *New Republic* 224, no. 12 (March 19, 2001).

Taylor, George. *James Wilson.* Society of the Descendants of Signers of the Declaration of Independence. https://www.dsdi1776.com/signers-by-state/james-wilson/.

Temple, Sir William. "Essay on Heroic Virtue." *The Works of Sir Wm. Temple.* Vol. III. London, 1814.

Tolson, Jay. "The Many Faces of Benjamin Franklin." *U.S. News & World Reports* 134, no. 22 (June 23, 2003).

Tucker, Robert W., and David C. Hendrickson. *Empire of Liberty: The Statecraft of Thomas Jefferson.* New York: Oxford University Press, 1990.

———. "Thomas Jefferson and American Foreign Policy." *Foreign Affairs* 69, no. 2 (Spring 1990).

Turner, Frederick Jackson. *The Significance of the Frontier in American History.* http://xroads.virginia.edu/~hyper/turner.

Turner, Kathryn. "Republican Policy and the Judiciary Act of 1801." *William and Mary Quarterly* 22 (January 1965): 3–32.

Van Doren, Carl. *Benjamin Franklin.* New York: Viking, 1938 (third printing 1968).

———. "Meeting Doctor Franklin." In *Benjamin Franklin and The American Character: Problems in American Civilization,* edited by Charles L. Sanford. Boston: D. C. Heath, 1955.

Van Riper, Paul P. *History of the United States Civil Service.* Evanston, IL: Row, Peterson and Company, 1958.

Voltaire. *Essai sur les mœurs.* Tome I. Paris: Classiques Garnier, 1990.

———. *The Philosophical Dictionary.* Selected and translated by H. I. Woolf. New York: Knopf, 1924.

Waldron, Arthur. *The Great Wall of China: From History to Myth.* Cambridge and New York: Cambridge University Press, 1990.

———. "The Problem of The Great Wall of China." *Harvard Journal of Asiatic Studies* 43, no. 2 (1983): 643–63.

Wahlke, John C. ed. *The Causes of the American Revolution.* Lexington, MA: D. C. Heath and Company, 1973.

Wang, Dave. "Benjamin Franklin and China: Franklin's Efforts to Draw Positive Elements from Chinese Civilization during the Early the formative Age of the United States." *Historical Review: A Biennial Journal of History and Archaeology* XIII (2005): 1–22.

———. "Benjamin Franklin and the Great Wall of China." *Franklin Gazette* 18, no. 1 (Spring 2008).

———. "Benjamin Franklin, George Washington, Thomas Jefferson and Chinese Civilization." *Virginia Review of Asian Studies* (2009). https://virginiareviewofasianstudies.com/archived-issues/2009-2/.

———. "Benjamin Franklin's Efforts to Promote Sericulture in North America." *Franklin Gazette* 18, no. 2 (Summer 2008).

———. "Chinese Civilization and the United States: Tea, Ginseng, Porcelain Ware and Silk in Colonial America." *Virginia Review of Asian Studies* (Summer 2011).

———. "Confucius in the American Making: The Founders' Efforts to Use Confucian Moral Philosophy in Their Endeavor to Create New Virtue for the New Nation." *Virginia Review of Asian Studies* 16 (2014).

———. "Exploring Benjamin Franklin's Moral Life." *Franklin Gazette* 17, no. 1 (Spring 2007).

———. "From Confucius to the Great Wall: Chinese Cultural Influence on Colonial North America." *Asia-Japan Journal,* 10th Anniversary Special Issue (March 2011). Asia Japan Research Center, Kokushikan University.

———. "The US Founders and China: The Origins of Chinese Cultural Influence on the United States." *Education about Asia* 16, no. 2 (Fall 2011).

Wang, Yuechun, *Discover the Orient* [Faxian Dongfang]. Beijing: Beijing Library Press, 2003.

Warren, Mercy Otis. *History of the Rise, Progress, and Termination of the American Revolution*. Indianapolis: Liberty Fund, 1805.

Watanabe, Kishichi. "The Business Ideology of Benjamin Franklin and Japanese Values of the 18th Century." *Business and Economic History* 17 (1988): 79–90.

Watkin, David. *The English Vision—The Picturesque in Architecture, Landscape and Garden Design*. London: Breslich & Foss, 1982.

Watson, John Fanning, ed. *Annals of Philadelphia*. Philadelphia and New York: E. L. Carey & A. Hart, 1830.

Webster, Noah. *An examination into the leading principles of the Federal Constitution proposed by the late convention held at Philadelphia. With answers to the principal objections that have been raised against the system*. Philadelphia: Printed and sold by Prichard & Hall, in Market Street the second door above Laetitia Court. M.DCC.LXXXVII [1787].

Wees, Beth Carver. *Coffee, Tea and Chocolate in Early Colonial America*. http://www.metmuseum.org/toah/hd/coff/hd_coff.htm.

Wells, Colin. "Thomas Jefferson's Scrapbooks: Poems of Nation, Family, and Romantic Love Collected by America's Third President." *Early American Literature* 42, no. 3 (November 2007).

Whately, Thomas. Observations on Modern Gardening. London: Boydell Press, 1770.

White, Leonard D. *The Jacksonians: A Study in Administrative History, 1829–1961*. New York: ACLS History E-Book Project, 1954.

Wilbur, C. Martin. "Modern America's Cultural Debts to China." *Issues & Studies: A Journal of China Studies and International Affairs* 22, no. 1 (January 1986).

Wilson, Douglas L., and Lucia Stanton, ed. *Jefferson Abroad*. New York: Modern Library, 1999.

Wise, John E. *The History of Education: An Analysis Survey from the Age of Homer to the Present*. New York: Sheed and Ward, 1964.

Wolf, Edwin. *James Logan, 1674–1751: Bookman Extraordinary, An exhibition of books and manuscripts from the library of James Logan, supplemented by his writings and documents relating to the history of the Bibliotheca Loganiana. In honor of the visit to Philadelphia of the seventh International Congress of Bibliophiles*. Philadelphia: The Library Company of Philadelphia, 1971.

Wolf, Stephanie Grauman. *As Various as Their Land: The Everyday Lives of Eighteenth-Century Americans*. New York: HarperCollins, 1993.

Wood, Gordon S. *Empire of Liberty: A History of the Early Republic, 1789–1815*. New York: Oxford University Press, 2009.

———. *Revolutionary Characters: What Made the Founders Different*. New York: Penguin, 2006.

The Works of Thomas Jefferson. Collected and edited by Paul Leicester Ford. Federal Edition. 12 vols. New York and London: G. P. Putnam's Sons, 1904–1905.

Wright, Louis B. *The Cultural Life of the American Colonies, 1607–1673*. New American Series, edited by Henry Steele Commager and Richard B. Morris. New York: Harper & Row, 1957.

———. "'The Gentleman's Library' in Early Virginia: The Literary Interests of the First Carters." *Huntington Library Quarterly* 1, no. 1 (1937): 3–61.

Wroth, Lawrence C. *An American Bookshelf, 1755.* Philadelphia: University of Pennsylvania Press, 1934.
Wyss, Bob. *Connecticut's Mulberry Craze.* https://connecticuthistory.org/connecticuts-mulberry-craze/.
Young, Michael Dunlop. *The Rise of the Meritocracy.* New York: Thames and Hudson, 1958.
Zeitz, Joshua. "Joseph Ellis Explains Just How Revolutionary the Revolution Was." *American Heritage* 58, no. 3 (Winter 2008).
Ziff, Larzer. *Puritanism in America: New Culture in a New World.* New York: Viking, 1973.
Zukeran, Patrick. *A Brief Overview and Biblical Critique of Confucius.* https://evidenceandanswers.org/article/a-brief-overview-and-biblical-critique-of-confucius/.

Index

Adams, Abigail Smith, 90–91
Adams, John, 2, 5, 13–14, 20, 23–26, 29, 90, 105, 122–24, 127–33, 144–46, 150, 153, 157, 161, 167–68, 170–74, 176–77, 195–98, 202; "Thoughts on Government," 167
Adams, Samuel, 7, 123
Age of Enlightenment, 1, 16, 151, 156
"Age of Reason," (Paine), 20, 150, 230
agrarian republic, 233
American China Manufactory in Philadelphia, 6, 51
American civil service reform, 9, 23–24, 143, 172–75, 182–93
American expansion, 62, 133
American Philosophical Society, 26, 48, 65
American Republic, 1, 161, 173
American Revolution, 7, 9, 22, 28–29, 52, 55–61, 92–93, 103, 121, 134, 143–44, 152–53, 159, 192, 195
Andrews, Christopher Columbus, 183
Annuals of Agriculture, 93
Appalachian Mountains, 54–56, 62, 133–34
Arthur, Chester A., 190
Astor, John Jacob, 8, 125
Atlas Sinensis (Martino), 54

Babcock, Joshua, 92
Bache, Benjamin Franklin, 49
Banister, John, 196
Barlow, Joel, 29, 148
Bartram, John, 2, 6, 17, 19, 49, 58, 61, 90, 92, 97, 130, 148, 172, 229–30, 236
Bateman, Dickie, 64
Battuta, Ibn, 53
Black Friday, 182
Blackstone, 172
Book of Odes, The, 27, 151
Book of the Marvels of the World (Polo), 53
Boone, Daniel, 133
Boston Latin School, 195
Boston Tea Party, 56, 105, 107
British Parliament, 21, 54–57, 60, 107–8, 159
Burnside, Ambrose, 181

Callender, James, 177–78, 191
Campbell, James, 33
Canton, 7–8, 48–49, 107–8, 111, 121–25, 131–32
Carr, Peter, 104, 196
Cary, Robert, 110
Chambers, William, 64–66

Changbai Mountain, 129
China manufactory in Philadelphia, 6, 51
China pinks, 97
China Revolution, 96
China's system of promotion, 4, 22–25, 36, 149, 183
Chinese and Gothic Architecture Properly Ornamented (Halfpenny), 64
Chinese architectural designs, 6, 47, 51, 64–68, 77
Chinese Chatterer, 91
Chinese Chippendale patterns, 64, 104
Chinese civil service system, 174, 185
Chinese cotton, 91
Chinese designs, 6, 51, 67, 229, 236
Chinese exceptionalism, 54
Chinese export porcelain, 112
Chinese food, 49
Chinese garavances, 49, 92
Chinese gardening, 64–68
Chinese gong, 49, 104
Chinese heating technology, 2, 5, 47–48, 73–77, 229, 236
Chinese hemp, 68, 91
Chinese hogs, 104
Chinese Imperial Court, 21, 69
Chinese Ixia, 97
Chinese lattice, 6, 51, 65
Chinese legal system, 17
Chinese medical theories, 75
Chinese navigation technology, 47–50, 75–77
Chinese pagodas, 65
Chinese painted candles, 48
Chinese papermaking technology, 2, 47, 75–77, 229
Chinese pavilion, 6, 52, 66–67
Chinese pipe, 104
Chinese plants, 2, 6–7, 89–98
Chinese porcelain table, 104
Chinese rhubarb seeds, 6, 58, 90, 92, 229
Chinese roof, 64–66
Chinese rowing, 76
Chinese ship construction, 5, 48
Chinese silk, 68–70, 77
Chinese silk netting, 104
Chinese silk plant, 91
Chinese soybean seeds, 92
Chinese straw floor cloth, 104
Chinese tallow tree, 6–7, 90–92
Chinese tax system, 22
Chinese technologies, xiv, 5, 47–49, 70, 73–77
Chinese temple, 64–66
Chinese trim, 64
Chinese vinegar, 49
Chinese wallpaper, 104, 236
Chinese windmills, 48
Chinoiserie, 64
Cincinnati, Society of, 22–24, 111, 149, 161, 173
Civil Service Commission, 188–89
Civil Service in Great Britain, 183, 189
Civil Service Reform Act, 173, 190
Civil War, 181
Clegg, Edmund, 72
Cleveland, Grover, 189
Columbian Magazine, 19, 148
Common Sense (Paine), 17, 144
Confederation Congress, 160
Confucian curriculum, 194
Confucian education principles, 192
Confucian ideas, 4, 9, 16, 19, 30, 143–44, 150, 154, 171–72
Confucian merit system, 172–74, 182–90
Confucian moral philosophy, 2–3, 13, 18–20, 26, 31–36, 143–48, 152–53, 170, 175, 229
Confucian political philosophy, 154, 174, 202
Confucian principles, 144, 154–60, 167–68, 170–71, 191, 230
Confucian system of meritocracy, 4, 9, 13, 22–25, 155–56, 160–62, 169–71, 186, 192–94, 197, 202, 230–34
Congress of the United States, 14, 48, 73, 93, 122, 129, 131, 164, 173, 176, 183–90, 202

Constitutional Convention, 29, 153, 158, 162–69, 171–72
Continental Army, 22, 61, 110
Continental Congress, 48, 160
Cook's expedition, 49, 122
Coxe, Tench, 123
Creek Nation, 62
Creel, Herrlee G., 202
Cromwell, Oliver, 70
Curtis, George W., 182, 188–90

da Cruz, Gaspar, 53
Daxue, 18–19, 148
de Butré, Charles, 162
Defense of the Constitutions of the United States of America (Adams), 167
de Góis, Bento, 54
de Mendoza, Juan González, 53
Democratic-Republican Party, 176–78
Designs of Chinese Building (Chambers), 66
de Tessé, Madame (Adrienne Catherine de Noailles), 91, 97–98
de Tocqueville, Alexis, 25, 26
Dillon, Wilton, 235
Dodge, Grenville M., 181
Dolphin, 111
Dowse, Edward, 112
Drinker, Elizabeth, 148–49
Du Halde, Jean-Baptiste, 54, 202
du Pont de Nemours, Pierre-Samuel, 18, 22

East India Company, 104–7, 194
East Indies, 122, 128, 131
Eaton, Dorman B., 182–83, 189–90
Electoral College, 154, 164–66, 171, 210
Embargo Act of 1807, 8, 125
Emerson, Ralph Waldo, 188
Empress of China, 1, 7–9, 16, 105–7, 121–28, 130–34
English Protestant Tutor, 195
Erie Canal, 2, 6, 50, 229

farewell address (Washington), 10, 29, 230
Farrer, Richard, 110
Federalist Papers, 169
Federalist Party, 176
Fort Allen, 57–60
Fort Franklin, 59
Fort Norris, 59
Founding Fathers: and Chinese material culture, 103–13; and Chinese plants, 2–3, 6–7, 10, 48, 89–98; and Chinese porcelain ware, 5–6, 48, 51, 65, 103–4, 108–13, 118, 236; and Chinese technology, xiv, 5, 47–49, 70, 73–77; and Confucian classics, 13, 27–30, 156, 185, 194, 203; and Confucian moral philosophy, 1–5, 9, 13, 16–20, 25–26, 30–36, 169–70, 175, 229–30; and Confucian virtue, xiv, 2, 4, 16, 19–20, 25–28, 30–34, 36, 43, 45, 143–59, 162–63, 166–70, 173–74, 192–93, 196–98, 206, 230, 234; legacy, 10, 26, 28–30, 152, 229–31; and maritime trade with China, 7–9, 121–28, 131
Franklin, Benjamin: autobiography, 4, 30–36, 109; and Chinese heating technology, 2, 5, 47–48, 73–77, 229, 236; and Chinese medical theory, 47, 73–75; and Chinese navigation, 47–50, 75–77; and Chinese papermaking technology, 2, 47, 75–77, 229; and Chinese plants, 2–3, 6–7, 89–92, 98; and Chinese rowing, 76; Franklin stove, 5, 73–77; and management of state affairs, 21–22; and the *Pennsylvania Gazette*, 26, 30, 33, 69, 106, 147, 158, 230; and *Poor Richard's Almanack*, 4, 31; *Proposal for Promoting Useful Knowledge Among the British Plantations in America*, 91–92; and sericulture in North America, 2, 47, 68–73, 229; Theory of social progress, 3, 170, 234
Fraunces, Samuel, 110
French Academy of Science, 92

French and Indian War, 5, 55–61, 236
French Canada, 129
French royal court, 103

Gage, Thomas, 107
Gallatin, Albert, 22, 125–26
Galloway, Joseph, 21
Garden Book (Jefferson), 96
Garfield, James, 189–91
Garrigues, Rebecca Haydock, 72
General Assembly of Virginia, 196
General History of China, The (Du Halde), 202
Gilpin, Thomas, 50
ginseng, 123, 128–34; American (Flower Flag), 121, 131–34
goldenrain tree, 97–98
Grand Canal of China, 2, 50, 229
Grant, Ulysses S., 182, 188–89; administration, 182
Grayson, William, 124
Great Wall of China, 5, 47–48, 52–63, 236
Guangzhou (Canton), 7–8, 48–49, 107–8, 111, 121–25, 131–32

Halfpenny, William, 64
Hamadani, Rashid-al-Din, 53
Hamilton, Alexander, 2, 8–9, 29–30, 47, 49, 52, 123, 127, 132, 134, 154, 161–66, 176–77, 229, 230, 233–34
Hamilton, William, 91
Handbook on Good Government or *Instructions to Rulers*, 169
Han dynasty, 24, 154, 174, 194
Harrison, William Henry, 180
Harrison and Tyler administrations, 180
Haworth, Paul Leland, 95
Herder, Johann Gottfried, 54
House of Confucius at Kew, 64
House of Lords, 56
Huntington, Samuel, 235

Indian Territory, 58, 63
Ingersoll, Charles J., 202
Intorcetta, Fray, 18

Jackson, Andrew, 29, 178–80
James River, 7, 103, 123
Jartoux, Father Petrus, 129
Jarvis, William, 14, 201
Jay, John, 23, 62, 90–91, 111, 122–24, 128–30, 161, 174
Jefferson, Thomas: administration, 133; and Barboursville, 6, 51, 65; *Bill for Establishing a System of Public Education*, 196; *Bill for More General Diffusion of Knowledge*, 191, 196; and Chinese architectural and garden design, 2, 6, 47, 51, 64–68, 77, 203; and Chinese flowers, 2, 89–90, 95–98, 229, 236; and Confucian educational principles, 9, 143, 191–204; Embargo Act, 8, 125; Garden Book, 96; and management of state affairs, 21–22; and Monticello, 2, 6, 49, 51–52, 65–68, 89, 91, 95–98, 112, 130, 152, 203; *Notes on the State of Virginia* (Jefferson), 133, 169, 196, 198; Poems of the Nations, 27; *Report of the Commissioners for the University of Virginia*, 197; Rockfish Gap Report, 196
Jenckes, Thomas, 182–89
Jien pien cou fa, 94–95
Jones, Noble Wimberly, 92
Judiciary Act of 1801, 176–77

Kalm, Peter, 105–6
Kangxi (emperor), 129
Kelly, Edmond, 127
Kermorvan, Chevalier de, 61
King, Rufus, 9, 127
Knox, Henry, 22, 62, 176
Kongzi, 143

Lafayette, Marquis de (Marie-Joseph Paul Yves Roch Gilbert du Motier), 8, 23, 124, 173
Latin grammar schools, 195
Ledyard, John, 49, 122, 132

Lee, Arthur, 17
Lee, Richard Henry, 7, 9, 56, 122–23, 127
Lee Kuan Yew, 235
Leibniz, Gottfried Wilhelm, 16, 234
L'Enfant, Pierre-Charles, 23, 173
Lettsom, John Coakley, 91
Lewis, Nicolas, 130
Library Company, 19, 26
Life and Character of the Chinese Philosopher Confucius (Bartram), 19, 148, 230
Life of George Washington (Marshall), 29
Lincoln, Abraham, 181–82
Locke, John, xiii, 16, 153–54
Logan, James, 17–19, 148

Madison, James, 5, 7, 13–15, 18, 20–22, 29, 50, 67, 90–91, 122–24, 133, 144–46, 153–54, 163–69, 172, 178, 202–3; and Montpelier, 144; Virginia Plan, 164
Manchu, 61, 203, 226
Marcellinus, Ammianus, 53
Marcy, William L., 179
Marshall, John, 29
Martin, Josiah, 18
Martini, Martino, 54
Mather School, 195
Mazzei, Philip, 14
McCartney Embassy, 54
McClellan, George B., 181
McMahon, Bernard, 97
McNulty, Caleb J., 180
meritocracy, 4, 9, 13, 22–25, 155–56, 160–62, 169–71, 186, 192–94, 197, 202, 230–31, 233–34; and American civil service reform, 9, 23–24, 143, 172–75, 182–93
Midnight Appointments, 176
Miles Brewton House, 64
Mill, John Stuart, 183
Ming dynasty, 52–54
Mississippi River, 56
Monroe, James, 29, 178; administration, 133

Montesquieu, 153, 172; in *Spirit of the Laws*, 197
Monticello, 2, 6, 49, 51–52, 65–68, 89, 91, 95–98, 112, 130, 152, 203
Morals of Confucius, The, 4, 19, 30–35, 147–48, 169, 230
Morellet, André (Abbé), 23
Morris, Gouverneur, 2, 6, 47, 50, 130, 229
Morris, Robert, 3, 7, 9, 122, 127, 129, 132
Morrison, Robert, 201
Morse, Jedidiah, 2, 15, 19, 148, 229–30, 236
Mount Vernon, 7, 29, 90–95, 110–11
mulberry, 6, 69–70, 73, 89–90

Nation, The, 184
National Legislature, 164
Native Americans, 49, 54–55, 57–63, 181, 236; Creek Nation, 62; Ottawa Nation, 55
New Designs for Chinese Temples &c (Halfpenny), 64
New England Primer, 195
New Hampshire Magazine, 19, 148
New York City Hall, 182
New York Times, 184
Nicolay, John G., 181
Niemcewicz, Julian Ursyn, 65, 111
noble China vase, 108–9
North Polar Star, 152
Notes on the State of Virginia (Jefferson), 133, 169, 196, 198
Nye, Russel Blaine, 153

Obama, Barack, 236
Oglethorpe, James Edward, 89
Ohio Company, 55
Ohio Valley, 49, 62, 125
Old World, 10, 133, 144, 204, 230
Ottawa Nation, 55

Paine, Thomas, 2, 20, 25–26, 144, 150; "Age of Reason," 20, 150; *Common Sense*, 17, 144
Parker, Daniel, 110

Pendleton Civil Service Reform Act, 173, 189–90
Pennsylvania Gazette, 26, 30, 33, 69, 106, 147, 158, 230
Percival, Thomas, 21
Philadelphia Silk Filature, 70–73
physiocracy, 17
Physiocratic School, 17–18
Pickering, Thomas, 63
Poems of the Nations (Jefferson), 27
Polk, James K., 180
Polo, Marco, 53
Poor Richard's Almanack, 4, 31
post–Civil War industrialization, 9, 127
post–Civil War Reconstruction, 182
Potomac River, 7, 49, 123, 125
Pratt, Charles (Earl of Camden), 56
president of Congress, 14, 122
Pressler, Larry, 235
Pride of China, 94, 97–98
Proclamation of 1790, 62
Proposal for Promoting Useful Knowledge Among the British Plantations in America (Franklin), 91–92
Prospect, The, 4, 20, 150
Public Academy of Philadelphia (the University of Pennsylvania), 26
public virtue, 146
Punqua Wingchong, 20

Qin dynasty, 52, 54, 194
Qing dynasty, 128, 132
Qinshihuang (emperor), 52
Quebec Act of 1774, 56
Quesnay, François, 17, 156, 194

Randall, Thomas, 8, 123
Randolph, Edmund, 176
Randolph, John, 29
Reconstruction Era, 181–82
Report of the Commissioners for the University of Virginia, 197
Revere, Paul, 107

Rhoads, Samuel, 59
rhubarb, 6, 58, 90, 92, 100, 229, 236
Ricci, Matteo, 54
Riqueti, Honoré Gabriel, comte de Mirabeau, 23
Rockfish Gap Report (Jefferson), 196
Roman Empire, 53
Roosevelt, Alice, 68
Roosevelt, Theodore, 165, 189–91
Royal Botanical Gardens at Kew, 89
Royal Proclamation of 1763, 55–56
Rush, Benjamin, 2, 4–6, 20, 47, 51, 113, 144–45, 150–52, 229, 236

Second Continental Congress, 160
Shaw, Samuel, 7, 105, 122–24, 130
Shay's Rebellion, 160, 162
Shijing, 151
Shi King, 27
Shippen, Nancy, 107
shortcut to China, 3, 103
Shunzhi (emperor), 128
Silk Association of America, 68
Silk Company, 70, 72
Silk Road, 53
sloop *Dolphin*, 111
Smith, John, 103
Smith, Margaret Bayard, 49
Smithsonian Stories, 235
Society of Agriculture of Strasbourg, 162
Society of Cincinnati, 22–24, 111, 149, 161, 173
South Carolina Gazette, 64
soybeans, 6, 90, 92, 229, 236
spoils system, 176, 178–91
Spring and Autumn Period, 144, 192
Stamp Act of 1765, 55, 106–7
Stiles, Ezra, 5, 48, 70
Stuart, David, 49, 125
Stukeley, William, 54
Sui dynasty, 174
Susquehanna River, 59, 130
Swartwout, Samuel, 180

Tahio, 19
tallow tree, 6–7, 90–92
Tang dynasty, 174
Tartars, 52, 54, 61, 203, 226
Tau-fu, 49
Taunton's Fine Homebuilding Journal, 67
Taylor, Zachary, 180
Tchang seng, 75
Te, 147
tea, 6, 48, 51, 56, 90, 103–8, 111–13, 129, 134, 236; and the Boston Tea Party, 56, 105, 107; Hyson and Bohea, 107; and the Stamp Act of 1765, 55, 106–7
Temple, William, 16, 23
Tenure of Office Act of 1820, 178
thirteen colonies, 5, 55, 145
Thomson, Charles, 2, 10, 60, 169
"Thoughts on Government" (Adams), 167
Tilghman, Tench, 111
Townshend Act of 1767, 106
Treatise of China and the Adjoining Regions, 53
Tsa Hsueh, 18
Tweed Ring of New York City, 181
two-party system, 236
Two Treatises on Government (Locke), xiii, 153

Union Army, 181
Union Pacific Railroad, 181
U.S.-China relations, 125

U.S. Constitution, 3, 5, 20, 145, 154, 164, 230
U.S. Supreme Court, 233

Virginia Company, 103
Virginia Gazette, 56
Virginia legislature, 196–97
Virginia Plan, 164
Virginia Review of Asian Studies, xvi, 236
Voltaire, 16, 151, 194

Washington, George: administration, 133, 176; and Chinese flowers, 2, 7, 89–90, 92–95, 229; farewell address, 10, 29, 230; and Mount Vernon, 7, 29, 90–95, 110–11
Webster, Noah, 154, 230
Whang-ho, 121
Whitefield, George, 4, 30, 156
White House, 181
Wilson, James, 164–65
Wofford, Harris, 235
Wolfe, James, 70
Wolff, Christian, 16
Woodbridge, Frederic E., 186
Woodside House, 64
Woodward, Augustus B., 15
Wu (prince), 4, 28, 30, 151–52

Yang-ti-king, 121
Yuan dynasty, 53

Zhongyong, 19, 148
Zhou dynasty, 193

About the Author

Dr. Dave Xueliang Wang has published dozens of articles on the influence of Chinese civilization on the American Founding Fathers in academic magazines circulated in China, India, Italy, Japan, Mongolia, and the United States. His works have been referenced by well-known authors worldwide. Wang's articles have been used as teaching materials by several domestic and international universities. Most recently, *Education about Asia* recognized one of his articles as an outstanding learning reference. Dr. Wang has also delivered lectures and speeches on the Founding Fathers and Confucianism at universities in Beijing, Copenhagen, Lisbon, London, New York, Rome, Singapore, Tokyo, and elsewhere around the world. His most recent publication is "Confucian Political Ideas in the Making of American Democracy," published in the *Virginia Review of Asian Studies*, Volume 22, 2020.

www.ingramcontent.com/pod-product-compliance
Lightning Source LLC
Chambersburg PA
CBHW071404300426
44114CB00016B/2182